Platform Neutrality Rights

This book analyzes questions of platform bias, algorithmic filtering and ranking of Internet speech, and declining perceptions of online freedom.

Courts have intervened against unfair platforms in important cases, but they have deferred to private sector decisions in many others, particularly in the United States. The First Amendment, human rights law, competition law, Section 230 of the Communications Decency Act, and an array of state and foreign laws address bad faith conduct by Internet platforms or other commercial actors. Arguing that the problem of platform neutrality is similar to the net neutrality problem, the book discusses the assault on freedom of speech that emerges from public-private partnerships. The book draws parallels between U.S. constitutional and statutory doctrines relating to shared spaces and the teachings of international human rights bodies relating to the responsibilities of private actors. It also connects the dots between new rights to appeal account or post removals under the Digital Services Act of the European Union and a variety of fair treatment obligations of platforms under American and European competition laws, "public accommodations" laws, and public utilities laws. Analyzing artificial intelligence (AI) regulation from the point of view of social-media and video-platform users, the book explores overlaps between European and U.S. efforts to limit algorithmic censorship or "shadow-banning."

The book will be of interest to students and scholars in the fields of cyberlaw, the law of emerging technologies, and AI law.

Hannibal Travis has taught and practiced Internet law and the law governing authors and content creators, for nearly 25 years. His work employs economic theory, historical research, and political philosophy to articulate individual rights, especially in the context of expanding private and public power over cultural and religious expression. He has advised entrepreneurs in disputes with alleged monopolists and unfair competitors as well as content creators in the Internet search engine, video game console, and professional sports industries. His research has appeared in books from Cambridge University Press, Oxford University Press, and Routledge.

Routledge Research in Information Technology and E-Commerce Law

Titles in this series include:

International Internet Law
Joanna Kulesza

The Domain Name Registration System
Liberalisation, Consumer Protection and Growth
Jenny Ng

Law of Electronic Commercial Transactions, 2nd Edition
Contemporary Issues in the EU, US and China
Faye Fangfei Wang

Cyberthreats and the Decline of the Nation-State
Susan W. Brenner

Balancing Privacy and Free Speech
Unwanted Attention in the Age of Social Media
Mark Tunick

Social Networks as the New Frontier of Terrorism
#Terror
Laura Scaife

Global Cybersecurity and International Law
Antonio Segura Serrano

Platform Neutrality Rights
AI Censors and the Future of Freedom
Hannibal Travis

For more information about this series, please visit: www.routledge.com/Routledge-Handbooks-in-Religion/book-series

Platform Neutrality Rights

AI Censors and the Future of Freedom

Hannibal Travis

Routledge
Taylor & Francis Group
LONDON AND NEW YORK

First published 2025
by Routledge
4 Park Square, Milton Park, Abingdon, Oxon OX14 4RN

and by Routledge
605 Third Avenue, New York, NY 10158

Routledge is an imprint of the Taylor & Francis Group, an informa business

British Library Cataloguing-in-Publication Data
A catalogue record for this book is available from the British Library

Library of Congress Cataloging-in-Publication Data
Names: Travis, Hannibal, author.
Title: Platform neutrality rights : AI censors and the future of freedom / Hannibal Travis.
Description: Abingdon, Oxon [UK] ; New York, NY : Routledge, 2024. | Series: Routledge research in IT and e-Commerce law | Includes bibliographical references and index.
Identifiers: LCCN 2024006823 (print) | LCCN 2024006824 (ebook) | ISBN 9781032758190 (hardback) | ISBN 9781032802633 (paperback) | ISBN 9781003496106 (ebook)
Subjects: LCSH: Network neutrality—Law and legislation—United states. | Internet—Law and legislation—United States. | Internet—Government policy—United Statres. | Internet—Censorship—United States. | Artificial intelligence—Law and legislation—United States. | Freedom of speech—United States. | Freedom of information. | Authoritarianism. | Swartz, Aaron, 1986–2013.
Classification: LCC KF390.5.C6 T73 2024 (print) | LCC KF390.5.C6 (ebook) | DDC 343.7309/944—dc23/eng/20240214
LC record available at https://lccn.loc.gov/2024006823
LC ebook record available at https://lccn.loc.gov/2024006824

ISBN: 978-1-032-75819-0 (hbk)
ISBN: 978-1-032-80263-3 (pbk)
ISBN: 978-1-003-49610-6 (ebk)

DOI: 10.4324/9781003496106

Typeset in Times New Roman
by Apex CoVantage, LLC

Contents

Preface *vi*

Introduction 1

1 Swartz's Law: The Rise of AI Censors 13

2 Carceral Communications Law: Freedom and Censors in the Public Sphere 41

3 Coordinated Inauthentic Activity: Private Police and Political Dissent 62

4 The Freedom of Reach: Kingly Power Versus Knowledge Commons 119

5 Locking the Web "Open": Paths to a Neutral Online Environment 152

Conclusion: Authoritarianism and Freedom in Technocracy 229

Index *233*

Preface

I would like to thank Florida International University College of Law and the people of the State of Florida for a sabbatical semester and several summer research stipends that helped me complete this book. I would further like to thank my research assistants Sarah Bruno, Marianne Pazos, Riquan King, Ashley Allison, and Jessica Ciminero for all of their work. Likewise, I thank the attendees of several panels at which I presented some of the ideas that made it into this book, e.g. those at the American Bar Association Section of Business Law Annual Meeting, American University, the Association of American Law Schools Annual Meeting, Hofstra University, the University of New Hampshire, Oxford University, Nanyang Technological University in Singapore, the Society for Business Ethics, Vanderbilt Law School, and Yale Law School, for their helpful comments and feedback.

Introduction

As jurist Edward Coke once observed with some exaggeration, a monopolist who seizes someone's line of business, or professional niche, may deprive the person of a life worth living.[1] When he wrote centuries ago – and until relatively recently – a monopolist could be one of a few powerful actors in a region or a nation, and did not need to have complete control of an industry.

Should Internet users have a right to disable, alter, or appeal algorithmic rankings that threaten their livelihoods? Or is adequate disclosure of the presence or general nature of ranking algorithms sufficient for purposes of fairness and interpersonal justice? Should start-ups who lose most of their traffic from changes to an algorithm or a display on a Big Tech website or platform have any recourse? Are social media and search algorithms a challenge to fair constitutional and electoral processes, and how are people organizing to take on that threat? Does a right to be forgotten for privacy purposes have a counterpart in a right to be remembered as an autonomy or participation right? In other words, are cancellation, deplatforming, and demonetization potentially unlawful attacks on personhood?

Transparency is the lodestar of most existing proposals for blunting the impact of AI filters on expressive freedoms. The Santa Clara Principles basically adopted the preferred response of Facebook and Google to criticisms of their content filters on behalf of "civil society:" publishing regular reports concerning the amount and characteristics of speech or speakers targeted and/or removed from parts of the Internet.[2] This, it is said, will improve "trust" in what Big Tech platforms are doing to weigh expressive freedoms against "[d]emands" for "content moderation."[3]

An information-based regulatory model reflects the initial intuition of some courts and regulators confronted with problems of digital due process, algorithmic scoring, and unfair business practices. An influential decision of the Wisconsin Supreme Court urged criminal defendants to "challenge" their risk scores or other algorithmic assessments at sentencing and stated that courts should not rely on proprietary software scores alone, but it did not guarantee a defendant the ability to look under the hood of the software and ensure that it was accurate and unbiased.[4] The Federal Trade Commission's authority to regulate "unfair and deceptive" business practices was somewhat moribund on the "unfair" side for decades.[5] Only in recent years has this U.S. regulator moved beyond targeting mainly deception or collusion. The Federal Communications Commission, after a switch in its partisan

DOI: 10.4324/9781003496106-1

makeup following the 2016 election, adopted a transparency-based approach to Internet service providers blocking or slowing down lawful content or applications of subscription Internet users.[6]

Transparency might have seemed inevitable after *Citizens United v. Federal Election Commission.*[7] The Supreme Court there rebuffed an effort, fairly modest in the overall scheme of corruption in politics, to limit corporate or union spending in aid of political candidates' messaging.[8] *Citizens United* is cited for the proposition that a disclosure regime is generally a less restrictive and more constitutional alternative than to blanket bans of various kinds.[9] The Chief Justice of the Supreme Court probably intended to encourage such a reading by declaring broadly that the First Amendment does not "authorize government prohibition of political speech by a category of speakers in the name of equality – a point that most scholars acknowledge (and many celebrate)."[10] He also warned against efforts to "impede corporate speech" as being efforts "to muzzle the principal agents of the modern free economy."[11]

Transparency rules, according to *Citizens United*, aid citizens in responding to the speech of other citizens, including corporations as associations of other citizens.[12] These rules should be preferred, it is thought, over outright restrictions on independent campaign spending.[13] While the First Amendment prohibits banning political speech based on the "speaker's identity," it does not necessarily ban regulations mandating disclosure of a speaker's identity, because "disclosure is a less restrictive alternative to more comprehensive regulations of speech."[14] Identity-disclosure regulations might be unconstitutional where there is a history of threats or violence, as during the Civil Rights Movement and other cases, but not where a group has been disclosing its donor list for years with no record of threats or intimidation.[15] For example, the Court has "upheld registration and disclosure requirements for lobbyists," even though lobbying is protected speech or petitioning activity. *Citizens United* quoted one of these cases as stating that Congress "has merely provided for a modicum of information from those who for hire attempt to influence legislation or who collect or spend funds for that purpose."[16]

As Archon Fung, Mary Graham, and David Weil write in *Full Disclosure: The Perils and Promise of Transparency*, regulation by compelling warnings or other statements has a checkered history of success.[17] Their blunt assessment: transparency is often "ineffective."

This book's approach presumes that transparency will do little to improve user rights online.

Rights of access to positions, spaces, and services open to the public are obviously more powerful from a citizen's perspective than mere transparency obligations. Would it be effective if anti-discrimination laws involving race, religion, national origin, sex, or sexual orientation and gender identity were reframed as mere duties to publish reports on the incidence of bias?[18] Or if the right to work in government agencies without discrimination on the basis of one's political party – outside the highest policy-making levels – was a mere right to transparency reporting regarding how many persons had lost their jobs when the other political party took over?[19]

Transparency regulation is not particularly effective as a paradigm of campaign finance law. Most Americans, according to a poll released a couple of years after *Citizens United*, believe that Congress sells out the country for money when it comes to public policy.[20] Few people really know or care precisely which corporation or wealthy family is paying for which actual policy. Most U.S. citizens simply do not vote, other than in quadrennial presidential elections, despite the purported fairness achieved by transparency. Most of them also believe that transparency reforms fall more harshly on those challenging existing senators or representatives than on the incumbents themselves,[21] who are reelected at rates exceeding 90%; indeed, in the vast majority of states, 100% of incumbents are reelected.[22]

The idea that transparency in content-moderation practices will improve competition in social-media, e-commerce, app-store, or other markets is also questionable. The brand names, physical and human infrastructure, and market capitalizations of the dominant platforms are forbidding barriers to successful entry into these markets. Alleged manipulation of platform policies to the detriment of new entrants may also be a significant factor. The network effects relating to the number of active users and revenue-sharing accounts on a platform like Instagram or YouTube, and the number of advertisers funding new content on such platforms, may be even more difficult to overcome. New content creators find the relative lack of advertising revenue on new entrants unappealing, and new users find the resulting and relative lack of content disappointing, leading them to concentrate their use on popular incumbent platforms. Entry into oligopolistic digital markets is rare in some years or sectors, made so by the multi-billion-dollar investment needed to enter markets dominated by others. Firms are much more likely to leave the noncompetitive fringe to become major players in revenue terms if they are conglomerates like Alphabet or Bytedance, with new offerings like the Android operating system, Google Play Store or Android Store, and TikTok.

While social-media transparency is analogized to judges issuing rulings in common-law cases, the analogy does not hold. Rather than a reasoned explanation and comparison of disputed facts to relevant precedents, a report on "aggregate statistics" relating to censorship of users, categorized in very broad ways, is a bureaucratic (and boring) patina of accountability.[23] Due process involves at least the quasi-adversarial presentation of evidence and reasoned argument to an impartial body. For this reason, serving as a judge or arbiter in a case in which one has an economic or reputational interest is generally banned. The practice continues with administrative judges within agencies like the Social Security Administration, U.S. Immigration and Customs Enforcement, or the Securities and Exchange Commission, but it has come under sustained constitutional and policy-based criticism for departing from common-law principles. Even many administrative judges have civil-service and other protections, including not being employed within a direct line of supervision under a semi-permanent leader like Facebook/Meta CEO Mark Zuckerberg, and procedural obligations relating to holding hearings and the like. So-called content moderation, by contrast to common-law decisions, typically involves a bare-bones inquiry, often by contractors, as to ever-shifting rules set by the same organization running the inquiry, with little to no persuasive reasoning, internal consistency, or citation to precedent.[24]

It is said that judges and government agencies should stay far away from content moderation decisions because it would be "far too expensive" for them to be involved.[25] Yet platforms continue to host and even feature speech that they might be liable for storing or retransmitting. A website or app is not immune from criminal or civil liability for use speech in all circumstances; under Section 230 of the CDA or a similar law, it may be charged criminally or sued for facilitating speech that potentially violates criminal or intellectual property laws in the United States, and the remaining universe of speech in countries without a CDA Section 230 counterpart in their laws.[26] The benefits of hosting user speech may be too tempting to resist even in countries or in contexts where a platform is not immune from legal action as a mere host.

In any event, the way that judicial review works is that a repeat litigant changes its behavior in response to a few rulings and general trend. An employer refrains from a disputed practice like discrimination on the basis of gender identity, and an insurance company hopefully refrains from using bad-faith pretexts for denying claims. As a result, judicial review of every case that is theoretically reviewable will not and need not occur. And the slippery slope or parade of horribles for allowing some judicial review is sometimes unrealistic.

Judicial review of speech-related decisions involving the filtering or management of user speech has been implemented in diverse contexts without shutting down the Internet. Several initiatives to enhance due process for Internet users serve as my point of departure.

The European Union's Digital Services Act (DSA) and Digital Markets Act attempt to rein in the power of online gatekeepers to arbitrarily harm their own users or competitors. They grant certain forms of legal rights to users of large digital services, app stores, or e-commerce gatekeepers. Articles 16, 20–21, and 27 contain protections for users of platforms, which may result in more transparency and more successful appeals against platforms' removal of posts, account terminations, or account or post demonetizations, etc.[27] On the other hand, the DSA endorses the flagging of unlawful content, which U.S. case law has mentioned: it states that "[p]roviders of online platforms shall take the necessary technical and organizational measures to ensure that notices submitted by trusted flaggers, acting within their designated area of expertise, [relating to notifications of illegal content] are given priority and are processed and decided upon without undue delay."[28] Meanwhile, the Digital Markets Act requires gatekeepers such as Google, Meta, TikTok, or even Amazon to deal with other apps or services fairly and allow other apps or services to interoperate with them (including by providing needed data to their developers).[29]

Section 512(f) of the Digital Millennium Copyright Act (DMCA) seeks to deal with the problem of copyright owners who attempt in bad faith to get lawful uses of their works removed from websites or storage spaces.[30] Rather than setting up copyright holders or Internet platforms as lawless custodians of the Internet, the DMCA allows speakers to seek damages and attorney's fees for bad-faith conduct.[31] It does not relegate victims of wrongful copyright removals, whether automated or not, to reading transparency reports as their sole remedy. Such reports are particularly suspect when they do not identify error rates on removals, or specific types of error.[32]

The Copyright in the Digital Single Market Directive (effective in 2021) imposes "upload filters" to prevent the repetitive infringement of copyrighted works in the European Union, but it contains safeguards for websites or posts that are exempt from copyright law's prohibitions. European states and content-sharing platforms are obligated to ensure that only "manifestly" illegal content is blocked by upload filters and that users have the right to contest removals and obtain the restoration of wrongly blocked posts.[33] Consumers have a right to human review and to judicial redress for the filtering of their posts.[34] Likewise, the U.S. America Invents Act (effective 2013) empowered those upset with aggressive patent enforcement to seek lower-cost review of important issues in an administrative forum, but it preserved judicial review of the new Patent Trial and Appeals Board's decisions.[35] The General Data Protection Regulation (effective 2018) gives Internet users and other targets of data processing rights to correct or remove certain data about themselves maintained by others. Despite the interest of Internet platforms in using customer data as they see fit to improve their services or maximize advertising revenue, the regulation gives customers a right to judicial review of certain decisions by a platform, including an automated decision affecting their substantial rights.[36] States such as California and Florida have emulated the regulation in some respects, while retaining the distinctive American system of class action contingency-fee litigation for misleading privacy policies or statements.[37]

Chapter 1 focuses on platform terms of service and how they impact users' human rights to free expression. Positive liberty – the human right to access governmental institutions to remedy exclusion or censorship by other private persons or groups – is essential to ensure a democratic cultural environment. Public spheres free of domination are difficult to imagine without such legal rights, for as Chapter 4 analyzes in more detail, formal or informal alliances between public officials and economic or cultural giants result in independent voices being suppressed.

Chapter 2 explains essential concepts employed in the rest of the book. Carceral repression, communicative freedom, the liberty of expression, and the critical theory of society contain insights into how censors operate, and principles for resisting their power. Chapter 3 also describes platform users' rights from a European and U.S. perspective, and how dominant Internet companies' censorship efforts threaten user privacy and data integrity.

Chapter 4 analyzes a few recent studies about how online platforms utilize AI to reduce alleged harms, but from a very selective if not perverse standpoint on what "harm" is. A major theme of this chapter is platform neutrality as a "freedom of reach," or the ability to participate in a networked public sphere. Sometimes denied in favor of an abstract freedom of "speech," the ability to reach other people online is a part of contemporary political and economic freedom. In the law, the economic freedom to reach others has three pillars: the right to practice a lawful trade and its corollary the right to resist domination of the trade; the law's traditional condemnation of malicious or unreasonable acts; and philosophical critiques of concentrated ideological power. Bad faith action, objectification of other speakers, and efforts to construct a passive base of unfree and exploitable users erode this basic freedom.

Chapter 5 argues that there are multiple paths forward to achieving platform neutrality. As indicated already, competition law and the First Amendment may restrain private or public authorities that intrude on expressive freedoms, including by promulgating speech filters. Some paths, like those under federal communications or elections law, may require more creative lawyering than others. Subnational or supra-national laws, such as the anti-deplatforming laws of the U.S. states and certain principles of international human rights, may be less of an interpretive stretch than a challenge to existing power structures. More basic and yet potentially more revolutionary paths arise out of special-purpose digital platform laws, a "cryptocosm" of alternative platforms based on cryptocurrencies and a distributed Web, and the moral rights of online authors under copyright.

The book does not cover the field of Internet censorship or algorithmic filtering and rankings. It focuses on rights to enforce principles of Internet freedom against threats from corporate and government power. It does not rehearse stories or concepts that are readily available elsewhere, such as the histories of companies, Supreme Court cases relating to the First Amendment or the Web, the constitutionality of copyright or hate speech laws, or the economics of digital services.

Prior books and articles on this topic left much of the terrain it covers unanalyzed. First, there are books and articles that praise "content moderation" and even automated filtering without taking many problems with Internet censorship seriously, particularly when it comes to First Amendment doctrine. In their enthusiasm for private deletion of Internet speech and unappealable suspension of Internet user accounts, such books do not discuss lies and tyranny prior to social media, rather claiming that Internet speech is uniquely false and harmful. Second, there was a deluge of alarmist books painting a distorted picture of social media, the Internet, and their purported harms, while covering up or simply ignoring many of the harms inflicted by corporate media and political parties, including the Iraq and Syria wars. Third, there are books hyping the threat of copyright infringement and news aggregators to publishers, the recording industry, the movie studios, and journalism writ large. Although generally emerging prior to the waves of pro-content moderation and anti-social media studies, these books buttressed the newer sorts of studies. Each of these categories of books has its counterparts in congressional speeches and testimony. This book takes the inverse of each trend: it views online censorship skeptically and not as beneficial "content moderation," it inquires into harms inflicted by the media landscape prior to the Internet and highlights the Iraq and Syria wars, and it asks whether in their haste to protect the copyright industries policymakers have lost sight of authorship and freedom.

In order to articulate principles that may transcend contemporary debates, the book looks beyond the current state of the law to theories of society, markets, and personal autonomy. It groups these theories into three areas and attempts to map each area onto a time period. After an introduction to the early years of Internet filtering, it applies aspects of Habermasian theories of the public sphere's role in communicative reason to questions of power, exclusion, and fairness in online discourses.

The book discusses theories of postmodern or "disciplinary" power, tying them to the "coordinated inauthentic activity" that dominant websites began targeting in the second major wave of Internet censorship's consolidation. Bad faith action, objectification of other speakers, and efforts to fill in a reservoir of passive, exploitable users are relevant themes. It concludes with a look at theories of authoritarianism and resistance, as we approach a future in which competing trends shape online freedoms: AI filters and Web3, or the "cryptocosm."

Notes

1 Sir Edward Coke, *The Third Part of the Institutes of the Laws of England: Concerning High Treason, and Other Pleas of the Crown, and criminal Causes* (W. Clarke & Sons, 1809[1644]), p. 181.

2 Santa Clara principles on transparency and accountability in content moderation (May 7, 2018), www.santaclaraprinciples.org/. See also, Suzor, *Lawless: The Secret Rules That Govern our Digital Lives* (Cambridge University Press, 2019), p. 138. The Santa Clara Principles have reportedly been endorsed by nearly all the U.S. tech giants, or Big Tech, including Apple, Facebook and Instagram (Meta), Google, LinkedIn, Medium, Reddit, Snap, Tumblr, Twitter, and YouTube. E.g., The Santa Clara Principles on Transparency and Accountability in Content Moderation, www.santaclaraprinciples.org/history/.

3 Suzor, *Lawless*, p. 139. See also, Jonathan Zittrain, *The Future of the Internet – and How to Stop It* (Yale University Press, 2008), p. 222. A "platform" is definable in various ways, but for legal purposes, one definition is "an Internet website or application that is open to the public, allows a user to create an account, and enables users to communicate with other users for the primary purpose of posting information, comments, messages, or images." Tex. Bus. & Com. Code § 120.001(1) (2021). A transaction platform may be defined in a more limited way as a website, application, or program where persons or intelligent agents buy an asset, good, or service from someone on the other side of the platform. E.g., Ohio v. American Express Co., 138 S.Ct. 2274, 2286-87 (2018); US Airways v. Sabre Holdings Corp., 938 F.3d 43, 56 (2d Cir. 2019).

4 State v. Loomis, 881 N.W.2d 749, 760–62 (Wisc. 2016). Cf. also, Suzor, *Lawless*, p. 112.

5 E.g., Lina M. Khan, 'Section 5 in action: Reinvigorating the FTC Act and the rule of law,' 11 *Journal of Antitrust Enforcement* 149 (2023). But cf., Atlantic Refining Co. v. FTC, 381 U.S. 357, 369 (1965); Alterman Foods v. FTC, 497 F.2d 993 (5th Cir. 1974); Colonial Stores v. FTC, 450 F.2d 733 (5th Cir. 1971); R.H. Macy & Co. v. FTC, 326 F.2d 445 (2d Cir. 1964); American News Co. v. FTC, 300 F.2d 104 (2d Cir. 1962); Grand Union Co. v. FTC, 300 F.2d 92 (2d Cir. 1962); In re Foremost-McKesson, Inc., 109 FTC 127 (1987); but cf. also, Official Airline Guides, Inc. v. FTC, 630 F.2d 920 (2d Cir. 1980); Boise Cascade Corp. v. FTC, 637 F.2d 573 (1980).

6 ACA CONNECTS v. Bonta, 24 F.4th 1233 (9th Cir. 2022); Mozilla Corp. v. FCC, 940 F.3d 1, 46–58 (D.C Cir. 2019). Compare also, US Telecom Association v. FCC, 825 F.3d 674 (D.C. Cir. 2016) (upholding disclosure requirements imposed in connection with reclassification of broadband Internet service as telecommunications service in 2015 by FCC); Verizon v. FCC, 740 F.3d 623, 633, 659 (D.C. Cir. 2014) (striking down earlier set of no-blocking and no-throttling rules known as net neutrality, but upholding transparency rules regarding Internet service contracts); *id.* at 660–61 & n. 3 (Silberman, J., concurring in part and dissenting in part) ("The transparency rules at least have the added benefit of facilitating consumer choice by providing information, which could lead to greater competition in the broadband market.").

7 558 U.S. 310, 130 S.Ct. 876, 916 (2010).

8 As the dissent pointed out, the effort was somewhat modest in prohibiting neither stockholders' use of corporate dividends or share transactions' proceeds to spend money on

political campaigns, nor corporations' own spending on political campaigns once money was set aside in a political action committee's account. *See id* at 979 (Stevens, J., joined by Breyer, J., Ginsburg, J., and Sotomayor, J., dissenting in part and concurring in part) (citing 2 U.S.C. §§ 441b(b)(2)(C), 441b(b)(4)(A)(i)). On the other hand, the effort was immodest in limiting to some extent the freedom of speech of the corporation behind a movie quite relevant to the 2008 Democratic Party primary and November general election, with no evidence that the corporation expected or was likely to receive any "quid pro quo" or even more subtle benefits and paybacks from the Republican Party for criticizing a contender for the Democratic Party nomination for president. *Citizens United*, 130 S. Ct. at 909. See also, Lawrence Lessig, 'On what being a (small r) republican means,' 74 *Montana Law Review* 37 (2013).

9 Gaspee Project v. Mederos, 13 F.4th 79 (1st Cir. 2021); see also, Americans for Prosperity Foundation v. Bonta, 594 U.S. ___, 141 S. Ct. 2373, 2382–83 (2021) (rather than compelling state interest and least restrictive means analysis as in strict scrutiny of content bans, analysis of disclosure regimes may be justified by a sufficiently important government interest and substantial relationship to the regulation); National Association for Gun Rights, Inc. v. Mangan, 933 F.3d 1102, 1118 (9th Cir. 2019); Vermont Right to Life Committee, Inc. v. Sorrell, 758 F.3d 118, 134 (2d Cir. 2014), *cert. denied*, 135 S. Ct. 949 (2015); Worley v. Florida Secretary of State, 717 F.3d 1238, 1251 (11th Cir. 2013); Family PAC v. McKenna, 685 F.3d 800, 809 (9th Cir. 2012).

10 *Citizens United*, 130 S.Ct. at 922 (Alito, J., and Roberts, C.J., concurring).

11 *Id.* at 929.

12 See *id.* at 916 (opinion for the Court).

13 E.g., Lessig, previous n. 9, at 45 (calling this a gloss on or even a misreading of the opinion that "people" believe in).

14 *Citizens United*, 130 S. Ct. at 904–5, 915.

15 See *id.* at 915–916; NAACP v. Button, 371 U.S. 415, 433 (1963); NAACP v. Alabama ex rel. Patterson, 357 U.S. 449, 462 (1958); cf. also, Baird v. State Bar of Ariz., 401 U.S. 1, 6 (1971) (plurality opinion).

16 *Citizens United*, 558 U.S. at 915 (quoting United States v. Harriss, 347 U.S. 612, 625 (1954)).

17 Archon Fung, Mary Graham, and David Weil, *Full Disclosure: The Perils and Promise of Transparency* (Cambridge University Press, 2007).

18 E.g., Bostock v. Clayton County, Georgia, 590 U.S. 140 (2020); Davis v. Passman, 442 U.S. 228 (1979); Pittsburgh Press Co. v. Pittsburgh Commission on Human Relations, 413 U.S. 376 (1976); Heart of Atlanta Motel, Inc. v. United States, 379 U.S. 241 (1964); *Yick Wo v. Hopkins*, 118 U.S. 356, 369–74 (1886); Fair Housing Commission, San Fernando v. Roommates.com, LLC, 521 F.3d 1157, 1164, 1167 (9th Cir. 2008); Liapes v. Facebook, Inc., 95 Cal. App. 5th 910 (Cal. Ct. App., 1st Dist. 2023).

19 E.g., Elrod v. Burns, 427 U.S. 347, 353–381 (1976) (plurality opinion) (holding that state or federal employees should not be discharged or excluded from hiring on the basis of political party "or other matters of opinion") (internal citation and quotation marks omitted) (citing, inter alia, *United Public Workers v. Mitchell*, 330 U. S. 75, 100 (1947)). The rationales behind *Elrod* are somewhat relevant to Internet censorship: public employment is ever more pervasive, and loss of pay and career success are "significant penalties" for differing in opinion from party hacks. Rutan v. Republican Party of Ill., 497 US 62, 74 (1990) (citing *Elrod*, 427 U.S. at 362–63).

20 E.g., Lessig, previous n. 9, at 41.

21 Ibid., p. 49.

22 Ballotpedia's Daily Brew: 94% of incumbents won re-election on Nov. 3 – Here's the breakdown by state (2023), https://news.ballotpedia.org; Lawrence Lessig, *Republic, Lost: The Corruption of Equality and the Steps to End It* (Twelve Books, 2d ed. 2016), n. 211 and accompanying text (citing 50% say "rigged" reelection rules explain high reelection rates, Rasmussen Reports, April 28, 2009, www.rasmussenreports.com).

23 Suzor, *Lawless*, p. 138.

24 But cf., ibid., pp. 146–47 (civil society proposes that helpful appeal procedures be offered to users so they may provide further context of alleged violations of terms of service, and more fulsome explanations of which term(s) were violated and which facts about the post or account triggered the violation).

25 Suzor, Lawless, p. 146. See also, Tarleton Gillespie, *Custodians of the Internet: Platforms, Content Moderation, and the Hidden Decisions That Shape Social Media* (Yale University Press, 2018), pp. 198–99.

26 Suzor acknowledges that many countries do not have a CDA Section 230. *Lawless*, p. 146. He does not point out that these countries often have similar access to services like Facebook or YouTube that are supposedly too expensive to operate without CDA Section 230. To his credit, Gillespie does question the hyperbolic assertion that it would shut down the Internet to cut back on the Section 230 right to delete user accounts, topical speech, and entire hashtags or trending topics. *Custodians of the Internet*, pp. 43–44. This hyperbolic assertion is encapsulated in the title of the most famous book on content moderation law, Jeff Kosseff's *The Twenty-Six Words that Created the Internet* (Cornell University Press, 2019). Even though the Internet and the Web existed prior to Section 230, and survived in countries that did not have it, the book was reviewed favorably in *The Washington Post* and is featured periodically on CNN and C-SPAN.

27 Regulation on a single market for digital services and amending Directive 2000/31/EC (Digital Services Act), arts. 16, 20–21, 27, COM/2020/825, *Official Journal* L 277 (Oct. 19, 2022) [hereinafter Digital Services Act or DSA].

28 Ibid., art. 22. See also, *ibid*., arts. 11, 20–47 (creating various apparatuses of content and communications control and flows of user profiles and private data to governments and think-tanks).

29 E.g., Regulation of the European Parliament and of the Council on contestable and fair markets in the digital sector, COM/2020/842, arts. 2–3, 5–7, *Official Journal* L 335 (Oct. 12, 2022), https://eur-lex.europa.eu/legal-content/EN/TXT/?uri=CELEX%3A32022R1925; Henry Mostyn, Bianca Buzatu, and Xavier Quer Zamora, The EU Parliament approves the final text of the Digital Markets Act, *Concurrences* (July 5, 2022), https://www.concurrences.com/en/bulletin/news-issues/july-2022/the-eu-parliament-approves-the-final-text-of-the-digital-markets-act.

30 Margot Kaminski and Jennifer Urban, 'The right to contest AI,' 121 *Columbia Law Review* 1957, 2018 (2021).

31 E.g., *id.* (citing 17 U.S.C § 512(f)); *Lenz v. Universal*, 815 F.3d 1145, 1160 (9th Cir. 2016).

32 E.g., Queenie Wong, Facebook's AI is flagging more hate speech before you report it, *CNET* (November 19, 2020), https://www.cnet.com/news/facebooks-ai-is-flagging-more-hate-speech-before-you-report-it/ ("Facebook didn't share data about the accuracy of its AI systems, but [its chief technology officer] said it depends on the type of content that's being reviewed."). YouTube is now reporting how many videos are reinstated following an appeal, but it does not report how many of the vast majority of removals that are not appealed (some 7 million videos per quarter or more than 2 million per month) are removed in error or due to malicious or bad-faith flagging. E.g., Google Transparency Report (2023), https://web.archive.org/web/20231019055306/https://transparencyreport.google.com/youtube-policy/removals & https://web.archive.org/web/20231019055306/https://transparencyreport.google.com/youtube-policy/appeals, (suggesting that in second quarter of 2023, fewer than 420,000 video removal appeals were filed out of more than 7.3 million videos removed, and fewer than 10% of appeals were granted); Google Transparency Report (2021), https://web.archive.org/web/20211001032931/https://transparencyreport.google.com/youtube-policy/removals & https://web.archive.org/web/20211001032931/https://transparencyreport.google.com/youtube-policy/appeals (suggesting that in second quarter of 2021, fewer than 220,000 video removal appeals were filed out of more than 6.2 million videos removed, and fewer than 20% of appeals were granted; errors in unappealed removals not listed).

33 Directive 2019/790 on copyright in the digital single market.
34 Ibid., art. 17(9); see also, European Commission, Communication to the Parliament and the Council, Guidance on Article 17 of Directive 2019/790 on Copyright in the Digital Single Market, COM/2021/288 final (June 4, 2021), https://eur-lex.europa.eu/legal-content/EN/TXT/?qid=1625142238402&uri=CELEX%3A52021DC0288
35 Software Rights Archive, LLC v. Facebook, Inc., 640 F. App'x 995 (Fed. Cir. 2016) (affirming result on appeal from U.S. Patent and Trademark Office, Patent Trial and Appeal Board, in No. IPR2013–00478).
36 Kaminski and Urban, previous n. 30, pp. 1962, 1978–980, 1989, 2009, 2015–018; see also, *ibid.*, pp. 1963–64 & n.26 (collecting other sources); *id.*, pp. 1962–963 (discussing Council of Eur., Recommendation CM/Rec(2020)1 of the Committee of Ministers to Member States on the Human Rights Impacts of Algorithmic Systems (2020), https://rm.coe.int/CoERMPublicCommonSearchServices/DisplayDCTMContent?documentId=09000016809e1154 [https://perma.cc/YC8H-QUTX]); ibid., pp. 1977–978 & n. 115 (discussing Emily Pehrsson, The Meaning of the GDPR Article 22 (Stan.-Vienna Transatlantic Technology Law Forum, Working Paper No. 31, 2018), pp. 17–22, https://www.cdn.law.stanford.edu/wpcontent/uploads/2018/05/pehrsson_eulawwp31.pdf [https://perma.cc/T566-EZDK]).
37 Cal. Civ. Code § 1798.185(16) (2020); Fla. Stat. § 501.71(2)(d) (2024); Kaminski & Urban, previous n. 30, p. 1962.

Bibliography

2 U.S.C. § 441b(b).
17 U.S.C § 512(f).
50% say "rigged" reelection rules explain high reelection rates, *Rasmussen Reports* (April 28, 2009), https://www.rasmussenreports.com.
ACA CONNECTS v. Bonta, 24 F.4th 1233 (9th Cir. 2022).
Alterman Foods v. FTC, 497 F.2d 993 (5th Cir. 1974).
American News Co. v. FTC, 300 F.2d 104 (2d Cir. 1962).
Americans for Prosperity Foundation v. Bonta, 594 U.S. ___, 141 S. Ct. 2373, 2382–83 (2021).
Atlantic Refining Co. v. FTC, 381 U.S. 357 (1965).
Baird v. State Bar of Ariz., 401 U.S. 1 (1971) (plurality opinion).
Ballotpedia's Daily Brew: 94% of Incumbents Won Re-Election on Nov. 3 – Here's the Breakdown by State (2023), https://news.ballotpedia.org.
Boise Cascade Corp. v. FTC, 637 F.2d 573 (1980).
Bostock v. Clayton County, Georgia, 590 U.S. 140 (2020).
Cal. Civ. Code § 1798.185(16) (2020).
Citizens United v. FEC, 558 U.S. 310, 130 S.Ct. 876 (2010).
Davis v. Passman, 442 U.S. 228 (1979).
Directive (EU) 2019/790 of the European Parliament and of the Council of April 17, 2019, on copyright and related rights in the Digital Single Market and amending Directives 97/9/EC and 2001/29/EC, *Official Journal* L 130/92 (17 May 2019).
Elrod v. Burns, 427 U.S. 347 (1976) (plurality opinion).
European Commission, Communication to the Parliament and the Council, Guidance on Article 17 of Directive 2019/790 on Copyright in the Digital Single Market, COM/2021/288 final (June 4, 2021), https://eur-lex.europa.eu/legal-content/EN/TXT/?qid=1625142238402&uri=CELEX%3A52021DC0288.
Heart of Atlanta Motel, Inc. v. United States, 379 U.S. 241 (1964).
Lawrence Lessig, 'On what being a (small r) republican means,' 74 *Montana Law Review* 37 (2013).
Lawrence Lessig, *Republic, Lost: The Corruption of Equality and the Steps to End It* (Twelve Books, 2d ed. 2016).

Sir Edward Coke, *The Third Part of the Institutes of the Laws of England: Concerning High Treason, and other Pleas of the Crown, and criminal Causes* (W. Clarke & Sons, 1809 [1644]).

Colonial Stores v. FTC, 450 F.2d 733 (5th Cir. 1971).

Council of Europe, Recommendation CM/Rec(2020)1 of the committee of ministers to member states on the human rights impacts of algorithmic systems (2020), https://rm.coe.int/CoERMPublicCommonSearchServices/DisplayDCTMContent?documentId=09000016809e1154 [https://perma.cc/YC8H-QUTX].

Fair Housing Commission, San Fernando v. Roommates.com, LLC, 521 F.3d 1157 (9th Cir. 2008).

Family PAC v. McKenna, 685 F.3d 800 (9th Cir. 2012).

Fla. Stat. § 501.71(2)(d) (2024).

Archon Fung, Mary Graham, and David Weil, *Full Disclosure: The Perils and Promise of Transparency* (Cambridge University Press, 2007).

Gaspee Project v. Mederos, 13 F.4th 79 (1st Cir. 2021).

Tarleton Gillespie, *Custodians of the Internet: Platforms, Content Moderation, and the Hidden Decisions That Shape Social Media* (Yale University Press, 2018).

Google Transparency Report (2023), https://web.archive.org/web/20231019055306/https://transparencyreport.google.com/youtube-policy/removals & https://web.archive.org/web/20231019055306/https://transparencyreport.google.com/youtube-policy/appeals.

Google Transparency Report (2021), https://web.archive.org/web/20211001032931/https://transparencyreport.google.com/youtube-policy/removals & https://web.archive.org/web/20211001032931/https://transparencyreport.google.com/youtube-policy/appeals.

Grand Union Co. v. FTC, 300 F.2d 92 (2d Cir. 1962).

In re Foremost-McKesson, Inc., 109 FTC 127 (1987).

Margot Kaminski and Jennifer Urban, 'The right to contest AI,' 121 *Columbia Law Review* 1957, 2018 (2021).

Lina M. Khan, 'Section 5 in action: Reinvigorating the FTC Act and the rule of law,' 11 *Journal of Antitrust Enforcement* 149 (2023).

Jeff Kosseff, *The Twenty-Six Words that Created the Internet* (Cornell University Press, 2019).

Lenz v. Universal, 815 F.3d 1145 (9th Cir. 2016).

Liapes v. Facebook, Inc., 95 Cal. App. 5th 910 (Cal. Ct. App., 1st Dist., 2023).

Henry Mostyn, Bianca Buzatu, and Xavier Quer Zamora, The EU Parliament approves the final text of the Digital Markets Act, *Concurrences* (July 5, 2022), https://www.concurrences.com/en/bulletin/news-issues/july-2022/the-eu-parliament-approves-the-final-text-of-the-digital-markets-act.

Mozilla Corp. v. FCC, 940 F.3d 1, 46–58 (D.C Cir. 2019).

NAACP v. Alabama ex rel. Patterson, 357 U.S. 449, 462 (1958).

NAACP v. Button, 371 U.S. 415 (1963).

National Ass'n for Gun Rights, Inc. v. Mangan, 933 F.3d 1102, 1118 (9th Cir. 2019).

Emily Pehrsson, The Meaning of the GDPR Article 22, Stanford-Vienna Transatlantic Technology Law Forum, Working Paper No. 31 (May 2018), www.cdn.law.stanford.edu/wpcontent/uploads/2018/05/pehrsson_eulawwp31.pdf [https://perma.cc/T566-EZDK].

Official Airline Guides, Inc. v. FTC, 630 F.2d 920 (2d Cir. 1980).

Pittsburgh Press Co. v. Pittsburgh Commission on Human Relations, 413 U.S. 376 (1976).

R.H. Macy & Co. v. FTC, 326 F.2d 445 (2d Cir. 1964).

Regulation of the European Parliament and of the Council on contestable and fair markets in the digital sector, COM/2020/842, *Official Journal* L 335 (Oct. 12, 2022), https://eur-lex.europa.eu/legal-content/EN/TXT/?uri=CELEX%3A32022R1925.

Regulation on a single market for digital services and amending Directive 2000/31/EC (Digital Services Act), COM/2020/825, *Official Journal* L 277 (Oct. 19, 2022).

Rutan v. Republican Party of Illinois, 497 U.S. 62 (1990).

Santa Clara principles on transparency and accountability in content moderation (May 7, 2018), https://santaclaraprinciples.org/ & www.santaclaraprinciples.org/history/.
Software Rights Archive, LLC v. Facebook, Inc., 640 F. App'x 995 (Fed. Cir. 2016) (affirming result on appeal from U.S. Patent and Trademark Office, Patent Trial and Appeal Board, in No. IPR2013–00478).
State v. Loomis, 881 N.W.2d 749 (Wisc. 2016).
Nicholas Suzor, *Lawless: The Secret Rules That Govern our Digital Lives* (Cambridge University Press, 2019).
United States v. Harriss, 347 U.S. 612 (1954).
US Telecom Association v. FCC, 825 F.3d 674 (D.C. Cir. 2016).
Verizon v. FCC, 740 F. 3d 623 (D.C. Cir. 2014)
Vermont Right to Life Committee, Inc. v. Sorrell, 758 F.3d 118 (2d Cir. 2014), *cert. denied*, 135 S. Ct. 949 (2015).
Worley v. Florida Secretary of State, 717 F.3d 1238, 1251 (11th Cir. 2013).
Yick Wo v. Hopkins, 118 U.S. 356 (1886).
Queenie Wong, Facebook's AI is flagging more hate speech before you report it, *CNet* (November 19, 2020), https://www.cnet.com/news/facebooks-ai-is-flagging-more-hate-speech-before-you-report-it/.
Jonathan Zittrain, *The Future of the Internet – and How to Stop It* (Yale University Press, 2008).

1 Swartz's Law

The Rise of AI Censors

The Last Prophecy of Aaron Swartz

Aaron Swartz inspired many people with his vision of the "freedom to connect." In the early 21st century, he had learned from his friend Peter that copyright legislation could be dangerous because it meant that this freedom could be subordinated to other purposes and values.[1] One bill from 2010 had empowered the government to devise an "Internet blacklist" to reduce copyright infringement online.[2]

A system was evolving that made court actions – like those for libel, loud noise, or obscenity – moot. The government could shut down entire speakers or publications threatening to violate the law, simply by adding to a database of dangerous sources. Congress would delegate to private corporations the ability to build the database, driving an Internet censorship regime through a "blind spot" in First Amendment law, designed for copyright lawsuits.[3] Sites like Wikileaks could be shut down in a way that a bookstore could not be, even if it occasionally sold obscene publications, or a newspaper could not be, even after it published government secrets.[4]

Such a system could not be built overnight. Initial legislative efforts stalled due to Internet uprisings, citizens calling Congress, and the like. But Swartz predicted that a "different excuse" would lead to Congress successfully "clamping down on the Internet," and "some of the biggest Internet companies, frankly, would benefit from a world in which their little competitors could get censored."[5]

Swartz eventually took his own life, apparently while fighting a prosecution for downloading journal articles en masse from MIT subscription services in the cause of open access to knowledge. In 2022, a day in his memory was held, along with a hackathon. One participant remarked on Swartz's prescience as the Obama administration had given way to those of Trump and Biden. The "different excuse" advertised for censorship included the development of better "copyright filters" and the need to save the "news" media.[6] Allegations – often without evidence – that the Internet caused terrorism, fake news, hate speech, suicide, poor body image, bullying, physical inactivity, and a panoply of other harms are also used, when needed.[7]

DOI: 10.4324/9781003496106-2

The Aggregation of Power in Internet Nodes

To explore some of the concepts latent in Swartz's address, it is worth going back a little in time. The U.S. government built the early Internet as a means of decentralizing communications, so as to prevent disruption at a central node in time of war, as Iraqi and Yugoslav communications were disrupted by U.S. bombs.[8] Although the U.S. government pioneered computers as early as the 1940s and the precursor to the Internet starting in the late 1960s, members of the public only began to adopt these technologies in large numbers in the late 1980s.[9] Starting in about 1991, the World Wide Web opened up the Internet to a wider universe of readers[10] and politicians became more active in underwriting popular access to an "information superhighway" of electronic resources and federally collected information.[11] The Internet's wires and radiofrequency signals are pervasive; its antennas are studded throughout our neighborhoods and connect billions of devices with high-frequency radiation.[12]

John Perry Barlow's Declaration of the Independence of Cyberspace mocked government with the point that it lacked "any methods of enforcement we have true reason to fear." The tendencies of digital libertarianism found expression in such "cyberzines" as CNet, Wired, Slate, and Salon. The Internet's victory over the State, according to the most illustrative versions of digital libertarianism, would usher us into a free marketplace of ideas, in which the truth would prevail because there would no longer be any censors between it and "the people." As James Boyle put it, the hope was that the "state is too big, too slow, too geographically and technically limited to regulate a global citizenry's fleeting interactions over a mercurial medium."[13]

The Internet's designers envisioned an ecosystem that had more content- and application-neutral information than proprietary networks or communications systems such as AT&T's telephone network or General Electric's broadcast network, NBC. The design principle that crystallizes this commitment to neutrality is commonly referred to as the "end-to-end principle." This principle, or engineering "argument," suggests that innovation and filtering should occur at the ends or the edges of the Internet, rather than in the connections or central hub (i.e., the AT&T or GE networks). This principle was first suggested by Vinton Cerf and Robert Kahn, who explained how an "Internetwork protocol" could facilitate the sharing of information and computer resources between different networks operating on distinct protocols.[14] The principle was more fully articulated by Professor Jerome Saltzer of the computer science department at the Massachusetts Institute of Technology (MIT), who was a key player in the development of the Internet.[15] The Internet was meant to operate as a "stupid network" with "dumb pipes" just moving data along,[16] without, in the words of a federal statute, "selection of the material by the service provider" or targeting of "the recipients of the material except as an automatic response to" a request for information.[17]

A digital service is often "a series of nodes made up of videos or accounts connected by citations or links."[18] Within the broader Web, it may be "a supernode which connects and organizes the nodes for us according to citation patterns (often called Video Responses), authors or channels, relevance to keyword searches, popularity by view count or other metrics, and date of upload."[19] From an economic and cultural perspective, social media and online video sites are gift economies (from most users' perspective) in which people from around the world meet in a virtual public square and collectively paint a picture of our world and its history in still and moving images.[20] "From immigrants' rights protests in the United States to the electoral protests in Iran to the antigovernment rallies in Egypt and Libya, cellphone videos uploaded to YouTube have disseminated messages and grievances globally."[21]

Zoning the Internet

In 1997, the American Civil Liberties Union expressed concern that government-mandated industry ratings of websites could harm the freedom of speech by bringing about widespread use of Internet filters. The organization predicted that the types of Internet filtering software being rolled out in schools and school libraries would block websites for lesbian, gay, bisexual, and transgender people.[22] It started a "Don't Filter Me!" project to oppose Internet filters that restricted access to hundreds of websites of interest to lesbian, gay, bisexual, transgender, and queer (LGBTQ) youth.[23]

The net neutrality movement recognized that these kinds of filters were making their way from schools to the Internet subscription services that controlled many households' high-speed access. For example, during the U.S. invasion of Iraq, an Internet Service Provider (ISP) took down combat footage, claiming it was "adult content."[24] Most ISPs had begun imposing "acceptable use policies" with vague language allowing them to shut down websites or remove content they disagree with or that "people may find offensive."[25]

In 2003, a media scholar, a journalist, and an activist founded the activist group Free Press.[26] It became a leader of efforts to prevent ISPs like AT&T and Verizon from buying up their competitors and disfavoring unaffiliated speakers (a/k/a content providers). With the subsequent emergence of platforms like YouTube and Twitter, it is clear how the blocking or slowing-down of the more free, user-controlled sources of information and opinion could have been bad for the Internet. Slow lanes on the Internet could be created; capital-poor innovators could be crushed.[27]

From Censorship-Proof to Censorship-Prone

The government resolved to speed up and disperse censorship by privatizing it. The Communications Decency Act (CDA) privatized implementation of the regulation of Internet indecency, and the Digital Millennium Copyright Act (DMCA) privatized the implementation of copyright restrictions. The CDA asked the private sector to require credit cards and user verification for sexually indecent content, and it encouraged the filtering of indecent, excessively violent, or otherwise offensive speech by both services and end users.[28] Filtering software, or "User Empowerment

Technologies" as they were somewhat euphemistically referred to in the 1990s (including by U.S. President Bill Clinton), then came in two varieties.[29] "Listener-centered" blocking software, such as Cyber-Sitter, Net-Nanny, and their progeny, typically blocked access to a list of forbidden sites while simultaneously automatically refusing to load documents containing "forbidden strings of words."[30]

With the mid-2000s came more intelligent methods of filtration. In that era, online video and Internet user mashups of movies and television shows were evolving into a new medium of expression for Americans and people around the world. Free online video sites such as YouTube were more efficient than their licensed counterparts such as iTunes or Myspace Video because they did not prevent the online use of works that are forgotten or are without economic value, such as clips aired months or years ago on *Saturday Night Live*, the *Arsenio Hall Show*, the *Ed Sullivan Show*, or C-SPAN. YouTube became a haven for fair use of copyrighted work, shielded in part by the DMCA.[31] Access to political speeches, cultural performances, music and lyrics, and parodies of every possible description was restored. Unlike the owners of a television channel, YouTube's administrators need not monitor every host's work in detail and make close calls about the possibility of offenses or legal issues such as potential copyright infringements.

Viacom and the television and motion picture industry campaigned to mandate automated filtering of YouTube and other online video services. In *Viacom International v. YouTube, Inc.*, the media conglomerate Viacom – formed by the merger of Paramount, Viacom Media Networks (VMN), and DreamWorks SKG – sought statutory or actual damages in excess of a billion dollars under the Copyright Act.[32] In 2010, the court found that plaintiffs had the full array of remedies (including statutory damages) available to them, but Viacom was unsatisfied and sought common-law punitive damages on top of that, which were denied. Plaintiffs had won huge punitive damages in hip-hop sampling cases, no doubt inspiring a way to make YouTube less open to sampling and prone to filtering, by fear.[33] Other content owners filed a putative class action against YouTube on behalf of thousands of copyright owners.[34] Both their suit, and the one filed by Viacom, sought injunctions of the type that shut down Napster completely in 2001, because the courts' zero tolerance orders could not be obeyed.[35]

At about the same time, Viacom joined with News Corp., Microsoft, and Disney in developing the User Generated Content Principles (UGC Principles). In adopting the UGC Principles, these four conglomerates could have limited competition among themselves in the provision of user-friendly online video services. The UGC Principles outsource copyright complaints from lawyers sending letters to so-called Identification Technology, specifically in Section 3(c), which states that if YouTube or other videos match a file containing a film or television program that a copyright owner has provided for enforcement purposes, a "UGC Service" should use automated technology to block the video before it is even viewable or available. This kind of automatic preemption of copyright infringement disregards users' fair use interests and the free speech rights of people who create videos that quote from films or television shows, including the news.

Federal statutes and case law endorsed fair use evaluations of UGC on a case-by-case basis. Some copyright owners argue that responding rapidly to potential infringements is more important than evaluating or respecting fair use. Yet federal law states that copyright holders must make a fair use determination to avoid being liable for copyright misrepresentation under 17 U.S.C. § 512(f).[36] In the 2008 case of *Lenz v. Universal Music Corp.* the court stated, with respect to a demand that a homemade video with copyrighted music playing in the background be removed, that the owner should make a particularized determination not just of use, but of unfair use.[37]

For copyright purposes, an unfair use is a nebulous concept, but an absence of criticism or parody targeting the original is enough for many rightsholders, and some courts and scholars.[38] Fair use has entered the public's vocabulary as an important determinant of press freedom because courts and commentators have abandoned the original limits on copyright censorship. Prior to the 20th century, Anglo-American copyright was focused on competitive printers, rather than any use of a similar image, character, string of notes, or a subplot. The opinions of English judges in *Millar v. Taylor*, including that of Lord Mansfield, a renowned champion of common-law copyright, concluded that excerpting large parts of a book in an abridgment, translation, imitation, or adaptation into verse was a lawful form of speech and thought.[39] Courts viewed extensive quotations or "abridgements" of one work in another as an exercise of intelligence and judgment that deserved independent copyright protection for the new work, not censorship.[40] In 1985, by contrast, the Supreme Court allowed the publisher of a former President's memoirs to hold a news and opinion magazine liable for quoting and summarizing choice passages.[41] The Court, in its 1985 decision and in a follow-up decision involving Andy Warhol in 2023, permits "the statutory monopoly" of copyright to "choke off multifarious indirect uses and consequent broad dissemination of information and ideas," and to empower certain publishers to hoard revenue from citizens seeking to read former officials' statements on public affairs.[42]

The Obama administration disregarded warnings about automated take-downs. Free speech groups warned that bad-faith or groundless copyright claims have threatened the Internet accounts of ordinary citizens. In a 2013 report on copyright reform, the administration replied:

> In some contexts, licensing mechanisms have been developed as a less risky alternative to relying on fair use. Particularly promising are those that rely on commercial intermediaries to enable remixes by their individual users. One model is YouTube's Content ID system, which allows users to post remixes that may be monetized by the relevant right holders. Under this system, however, it is the right holder's decision whether to allow the posting. . . .
>
> In addition, best practices and industry-specific guidelines have been developed to help artists looking to use existing works make informed choices, including a code of best practices specifically for creating online videos.[43]

Internet copyright filtering technology such as Content ID and Audible Magic CopySense frustrated the potential of the Internet.[44] Although the Internet broadened political speech to many more participants, Internet copyright filtering squelched this development by denying to bloggers and online "channels" the same rights enjoyed by media corporations to engage in fair use quotation, commentary, parody, pastiche, and satire. Peter Yu argued that the termination of user accounts due to trade association or individual firm pressure against YouTube or similar services has "major shortcomings that will raise significant concerns among civil liberties groups, consumer advocates, and academic commentators."[45] By automatically deleting quotations of audio and video content, Internet copyright filtering made Internet versions of some episodes of network news and radio and television talk shows illegal and impossible. No one can have a show like *The Daily Show* or *The Glenn Beck Show* with strict copyright filtering, because most major news sources would ask filter providers and the filtered websites to delete clips used by the host to criticize or mock people portrayed in the clip, or other people. In 2021, ContentID was triggering around 300,000 removals, blocked uploads, or demonetization events each month that YouTube's appeal team found to be without a legal basis under copyright law due to fair use, lack of proof of ownership, or some other exception, and ContentID existed alongside two other dispute-resolution systems, the Copyright Match Tool (a re-upload filter), and manual requests for deletion or expropriation of channel revenue.[46]

As Google aggressively monetized YouTube, simply removing alleged copyright infringements when owners sent in valid complaints proved to be insufficient. The platform required comprehensive licenses from the likes of Universal Music Group, among the most aggressive copyright enforcers. As a result, YouTube tightened its algorithmic audio- and video-matching regime. The copyright monopolies of the record labels and music studios grew stronger. ContentID encouraged owners to engage in "indiscriminate flagging of legitimate uses of original content," at times seeming "blatantly hostile to users' interests because it shift[ed] the neutral presumption of fair use against them."[47]

Based on trade secret source code, algorithmic systems like ContentID have weak standards for the protection of Internet users' legitimate rights. A mere complaint or allegation, in public or private, is enough to remove speech, without much chance to defend it.[48] Despite being informed about the problem for the freedom of expression, European institutions boosted the move to algorithmic content filtering in 2016 by announcing a code of conduct for "illegal hate speech," which remained an ill-defined concept in the "code." As Orit Fischman-Aforia explained:

> Voluntary removal of content may also be classified according to the initial motivation: Some voluntary content removal is generated by commercial contractual terms originally set by the platform operator, whereas others may be initiated by public discourse and public activities that encouraged, or rather compelled, the platform to adopt a higher standard of content filtering. Moreover, some of the seemingly voluntary policies adopted by online platforms are a result of a fear or a threat of upcoming legislation. A common

> legal mechanism used to promote the adoption of further voluntary terms is a "code of conduct," which is a self-regulation tool. The most well-known example for such a code of conduct relates to the removal of illegal hate speech. The European Union Commission have crafted a recommended code of conduct, which was voluntarily adopted by major online platforms.[49]

There have been reports of independent websites and video channels having "disappeared." Jonathan Zittrain called this the "Google Death Penalty" and warned that manual intervention into Google or Amazon rankings could present complex "due process problems."[50] Competitors with Google's own website analytics and search engine advertising businesses were among the first to complain of this, only to be rebuffed on the basis that Google was exercising its First Amendment rights or engaging in generally harmless deceptive practices.[51] Then Google handed over control of its critical first page of search results in particular to organized consortia of copyright proprietors and hoarders of trademark and content licenses.[52]

In the "adpocalypse," the massive deplatforming of YouTubers occurred. The official story was that YouTube ads were found to have run on allegedly racist videos, prompting negative publicity and a threatened exodus of advertisers.[53] Demonetization on copyright grounds had been seemingly accepted prior to the adpocalypse, but the events of 2017 surprised many video creators, especially in how retroactive and arbitrary removals could be. LGBTQ creators bore some of the brunt of YouTube's demonetization campaign, as they had previously suffered from "decency" law.[54] A ban on indecency implemented by websites using credit-card verification had given way to demonetization or removal of videos featuring "sensitive topics or events" including "war."[55] Of course, graphic violence and sexual material continued to be allowed in the 2020–2022 period, as examples ranged from the George Floyd and Jacob Blake videos, to Ukraine war footage, to various types of sexually suggestive videos, music lyrics, and nudity.

In 2018, the UN Special Rapporteur on the freedom of opinion and expression issued a report finding that filtering was metastasizing in troubling ways.[56] The report warned that platforms were developing systems of "trusted" flagging by elite "users" and "government flaggers."[57] The program dated at least to the spring of 2014, a period of intense al Qaeda and ISIS offensives in Syria and Iraq; parts of Fallujah and Ramadi had already fallen to ISIS, and Mosul would follow. As Sean Buckley observed:

> The *Financial Times* reported that British security had been granted special permissions to police YouTube content. Naturally, the online community was concerned: why is a governmental body being allowed to censor online content? Well, it isn't. Google has since explained that UK officials are simply part of YouTube's Trusted Flagger program: 200 or so organizations and individuals (including "fewer than 10" government agencies according to a *Wall Street Journal* source) with access to advanced flagging tools. These so-called "super flaggers" don't have the ability to manually curate or remove videos, but they can flag up to 20 at once for internal [human] review.[58]

Deplatforming Pressures

An early example of deplatforming on a basis other than nudity or references to sexuality was political speech about or in support of Arab, Muslim, and especially Arab Palestinian causes.[59] The USA PATRIOT Act established harsh penalties for providing support to a designated foreign terrorist organization. The problem is that support or "material support" is a very broad term of art, which could extend to hosting or even hyperlinking to other people's posts or pamphlets, providing access to a telephone call or other communications tool, and providing other "advice" or "assistance."[60] Prominent on the designated organization lists, and in the media coverage of terrorist attacks especially prior to 2001, are Palestinian militant nationalist organizations, although sometimes their general aim of an independent Palestinian state is shared by various politicians and diplomats from around the world. So there is both a major incentive to avoid criminal investigations and a target-rich environment in the area of suspected terrorists' supporters or communications links. And activists like the Institute for Middle East Understanding claim that after around two decades of the USA PATRIOT Act and similar initiatives around the world, there were overreactions: "When it comes to speech advocating for Palestinians, . . . Facebook swiftly censors and removes content, often with no explanation."[61] This is despite the fact that hate speech bans are lax online when it comes to conflict, with posts calling for the death or extermination of Gaza or Palestine (as well as other states/statelets) having appeared on both Facebook and Instagram in the past.[62]

In 2016, Facebook, Twitter, and Microsoft (LinkedIn) agreed to use a shared database of images and videos calling for or depicting terrorism.[63] In the wake of al Qaeda and ISIS-related terrorism such as the assault on Charlie Hebdo editors and illustrators, the Nice attack with a truck on large crowds, and the Bataclan nightclub attack that claimed more than 100 music fans, the European Commission had threatened social media firms with large fines for failing to take such action.[64] It was predictable that a terrorism database would go wrong and sweep up innocent Arabs and Muslims. The Department of Homeland Security, Customs and Border Protection, and Transportation Security Administration have used algorithmic risk assessments for terrorism that lack validity for detecting terrorism, or so some government reports have concluded. Human evaluators of a behavioral pattern checklist resulted in "allegations that officers disproportionately targeted Black, Latino, and Muslim travelers."[65] Risk assessments use national origin, a statistic highly correlated with some religious groups, so "Muslim American travelers . . . have for years reported being singled out for questions about their religious views and national origin when traveling to or within the United States."[66]

Even if an image database worked as intended, it arguably trampled on the right of people to access the truth about the nature and global extent of terrorist organizations and their supporters.[67] It was (and probably still is) causing depictions of the human and economic toll of terrorism and war to be deleted from news sources relied upon by a substantial share of many national populations.[68] According to the same rationale underlying use of the database, should films and television programs depicting Nazi tyranny, aggression, and genocide be prohibited because neo-Nazis continue to commit crimes, and it is simply too difficult for governments to prosecute them all? Such a policy would arguably abet genocide denial by preventing such films and television shows as *Nuremberg Trial Part II* (1971), *Schindler's List*, episode 9 of *Band of Brothers*, or *Sobibor* (2018) from being streamed, as containing excessively violent images.[69] Meanwhile, it is extremely doubtful that censorship prevents interested persons from learning that terrorist groups or neo-Nazis exist, or even learning where they are and what they have said.

Many nations, religions, and races have their own examples of unjustifiable censorship on social media or the Internet, and other examples of dangerous communications that maybe should have been censored. For example, many U.S. politicians and celebrities have called for, planned, or waged wars against peoples of other nations, religions, and races over the past century or two, violating the U.N. Charter and other laws in the view of the wars' critics. The spreading of information or ideas to advance the cause of war and oppose the cause of peace – that is to say, war "propaganda" – should be excluded from the human right to exercise a freedom of expression.[70] Chapter 4 will address the perverse exemption of war propaganda from the concept of "violence" or "harm."

Instagram and Facebook are particularly notorious for shadow-banning and restricting LGBTQ speech, although YouTube, TikTok, Twitter, LinkedIn, Snapchat, and Yahoo!/Tumblr are also blamed for this practice.[71] According to one scholar's survey of journalism on this topic:

> LGBTQ persons are subjected to systemic censorship for "simply sharing images and language depicting their sexualities, bodies, and identities, for daring to publicly occupy virtual space."
>
> Facebook and Instagram, among other social media sites and dating apps, have drawn attention for their targeted deletion of queer bodies and terminology, conflating the mere expression of sexual and gender diversity with solicitation, harassment, or other "violations" of the platforms' terms of service.[72]

One blunt form of automated censorship in which platforms engage is to restrict hashtags or other links that help readers find posts, rather than scouring the posts under a hashtag for individual violations of platform rules and standards and deleting them.[73] As one journalist wrote in 2016:

> According to research compiled by Nick Drewe for his social data blog the Data Pack, the list of censored Instagram hashtags is long and slightly disturbing.
>
> Not only were #goddess and #curvy still banned, but so were tags like #woman, #women, #womencrushwednesday, #bi, #lesbian, #lesbiansofinstagram, #gays, #iamgay, and multiple other tags that represent identities.[74]

Users adding hashtags such as #lesbian to their post multiple times experienced shadow-banning on Instagram in 2018.[75] The loss of a hashtag makes it much less likely that a reader or viewer of Instagram posts will find a post on topics of interest to the LGBTQ community, other than one from a personal contact, a mainstream news source, or a celebrity. Its counterpart in the context of the operating systems for smartphones, tablets, or laptops would be the suspension or deletion of an app that appeals to LGBTQ users; the users might meet the app's other former users in another way, but it is unlikely. A report from Fight for the Future maintained that Apple has banned apps that appeal to LGBTQ users.[76] Amazon also bans searches for books or products related to LGBTQ themes where the display or purchase of them might result in criminal penalties, as in the United Arab Emirates.[77]

Like 20th-century U.S. obscenity law and its software progeny, Internet filters for families and schools, hashtags bans sweep sex education and speech related to contraception and sexual orientation or gender identity in with pornography.[78] Parental software filters (from before the age in which machine learning and deep learning algorithms were in widespread use) tended to overblock websites; in litigation regarding the constitutionality of the Child Online Protection Act under the First Amendment, a study of a sample of a week of search results subpoenaed from Google, Yahoo!, MSN, and AOL revealed that about one in four non-pornographic, non-adult sites got filtered.[79] AOL, MSN, and Verizon had already begun to deploy filters at the service provider level for their users, in a prelude to what the enormous filters of Facebook et al. would become.[80]

With the rise of AI filters, a great deal of LGBTQ imagery and text would be categorized by machine learning algorithms as "sexually explicit" and therefore worthy of a suspension, a deletion, or an account termination.[81] "Instagram, which is owned by Facebook, has also appeared to be censoring the queer community with algorithms that, intentionally or otherwise, flag queer content at a higher rate than non-queer content."[82] As a 2021 study concluded:

> While Instagram's operators are the final decision-makers around content, a number of unknown regulatory actors – humans, artificial intelligence systems and/or other entities – undertake the work of moderating content. . . . [S]ome users suggest that Instagram's executives and/or moderators censor "objectionable" images of women's bodies according to undisclosed normative values, and reports show a number of examples of potentially "censorious content moderation" on the platform. Instagram also appears to routinely censor entire hashtags.[83]

Another photographer and journalist remarked, "Twitter has treated a photo of two men being affectionate as something offensive, and the fear of that image as legitimate. The message to observers is 'this is gross,' and the message to queers is 'you are gross.'"[84]

The medical and pharmaceutical area is another one in which stiff penalties promote widespread deplatforming even of truthful speech that is beneficial to many patients and their families. In 2011, the Department of Justice imposed hundreds of millions of dollars in fines on Google and Yahoo! for allowing Canadian online pharmacies to advertise on their search engines.[85] It called Canadian pharmacies' offerings "patently unlawful" and "unsafe," but subsequent reporting and research suggested that Canadian pharmacies certified by a pharmacy association from Canada or by pharmacychecker.com were sources of authentic drugs, and much cheaper ones.[86] The Internet "gatekeepers" like Google, Facebook, and Microsoft worked with a lobbying arm of the major pharmaceutical companies on a "data sharing tool" that could result in online pharmacy directories or sites getting flagged as dangerous on search engines, leading to the loss of most visits.[87] One court found this flagging or organized boycott of online pharmacy directories to be a potentially unlawful restraint of trade.[88]

In the political domain, a traditional method of taming speech on the Internet is the proliferation of laws targeting its users and militarizing the governance of them. Criminal statutes that reach out to ban nonviolent conduct connected in some way to the violence at second or third hand help to "recruit . . . a corps of censors."[89]

Deplatforming, demonetization, and "content" muting (otherwise known as "moderation") plague Internet users in a controlled and filtered networked environment brought on by states who encourage platforms to censor. The Electronic Frontier Foundation, Lawrence Lessig, Jennifer Urban and Margot Kaminski, Julia Reda, and other advocates of open culture or a right to contest automated decisions explain how Swartz's Law works.[90] When public discourse predominantly occurs in copyright-regulated media, copyright censorship can mutate into political censorship.

The Rise of AI Censors

Search engines grew out of early work on non-hypertext document collections, which the field of information retrieval field attempted to make searchable by keyword and concept, or semantics.[91] Non-semantic search engines, including Google, use a variety of signals concerning a document and its relationship to others in a database to help rank documents for search salience. Prior to link analysis and personalization based on search history, commercial search engines were largely keyword-based.[92] The market leader in 1995 and early 1996 was Excite, which used concept-based searching and statistical concept analysis.[93] Google took over the search market in what seemed like a very short time, surpassing General Motors in market capitalization in 2004.[94] Google became the best-known brand in the world without spending much on brand advertising.[95]

Google founders Larry Page and Sergey Brin were afraid that advertisers would corrupt their search results.[96] Page also thought it was a "very serious problem" that pornographic results turned up for every search query.[97] He implemented in his algorithm a means of detecting the proximity, font, and capitalization of search terms, presumably because advertisers and spammers use collections of keywords listed at the bottom of pages in different fonts, often uncapitalized, to "rig" Google.[98]

Google's algorithm acquired layers of signals relating to spammy website detection, personal rankings recommendations, and intellectual property violation complaints.[99] By 2016, Google was using machine-learning models probably based on website engagement data gathered from Google Analytics to supplement conventional ranking signals with an AI filter, or what one expert compares to a playoffs phase or championship tournament within a league of professionals.[100] At about that time, the tidal wave of user photos, posts, and videos prompted social-media giants to automate content moderation, whether to automatically delete posts or to flag them for human review.[101] Files could be hashed for the prevention of reuploads, especially when crimes are alleged, such as child abuse or terrorist incitement.[102] Thus, by 2018 the Internet was on a path to be reined in and shaped by commercial actors, while users lost "much of our ability to set the rules of participation in social life through democratic processes and . . . to hold those responsible for enforcing the rules to account for their decisions."[103]

While causing websites or posts to disappear from the top of search results due to spamminess, irrelevance, suspected copyright issues, or content moderation decisions, the Internet giants were honing their up-ranking systems, used to recommend likable content to users. Familiar examples include the Netflix screens' rows of films and television shows related to a user's viewing history, the Instagram Explore AI-driven feed of photos and videos, swipable TikToks and dating profiles, and YouTube displays of related videos and suggestions.[104]

In 2021, the White House demanded constant updates from platforms such as Facebook and Google as to whether content was being demoted according to executive branch priorities, which included content related to the 2020 election and the safety and efficacy of COVID-19 vaccines.[105] People who criticized vaccine mandates or politicized social distancing rules or "lockdowns" saw their followers, post visibility, and feed rank suppressed on the platforms, even though aspects of those mandates and rules were eventually found to have been illegal.[106] Videos and academic documents were removed from Facebook, Twitter, and/or YouTube.[107]

The remaining chapters in this book analyze various aspects of the Internet filtering problem in the 21st century. Chapter 2 explores theories of expressive freedom and an open public sphere against the backdrop of constant pressure to arrest and isolate nonconformists. Chapter 3 takes off from the "inauthentic activity" and "fake news" debates of 2017–2019 to analyze issues of bad-faith platform behavior and respect for free participants in public debate as a philosophical and political principle. Chapter 4 questions the popular rhetorical device minimizing "freedom of reach" – or reaching audiences – as a part of freedom of speech.

Chapter 5 introduces seven theories of advancing Internet freedom, including (a) the freedom of trade under antitrust law, (b) the freedom of speech under the First Amendment, (c) the telecommunications law principle that everyone is entitled to access the content and applications of his or her choice over a nation's wires and wireless pathways, (d) a sub-national or supra-national law guaranteeing specific individual rights in cases of arbitrary or unfair intrusion into online freedoms, (e) the preservation of fair elections as a national priority, (f) the protection of the integrity of an author's or performer's online presence as an intellectual property right, and (g) principles of DWeb or distributed-web thinking as a critique of economic and power structures being recreated on an initially decentralized World Wide Web. Along with ideals associated with Web3, a fully distributed Web or

DWeb would be a resource for sharing knowledge and participating in news media and the culture industries, regardless of one's location or local assertions of control.

Notes

1 F2C2012: Aaron Swartz Keynote – "How We Stopped SOPA," *YouTube* (May 22, 2012), https://www.youtube.com/watch?v=Fgh2dFngFsg.
2 Ibid.
3 Ibid. Although Swartz does not mention the source of the "blind spot," the context of his talk was the Stop Online Piracy Act, H.R. 3261, 112th Cong. (2011), a piece of copyright legislation targeting the Internet.
4 F2C2012, previous n. 1.
5 Ibid.
6 Aaron Swartz Day 2022 Day 2 (December 2022), https://www.youtube.com/watch?v=4vHaptAhHmc (remarks of Cory Doctorow at 24:26–25:00).
7 E.g., see also, Kevin Roose, YouTube cracks down on QAnon Conspiracy Theory, citing offline violence, *The New York Times* (October 15, 2020), https://www.nytimes.com/2020/10/15/technology/youtube-bans-qanon-violence.html; Nicholas Thompson and Fred Vogelstein, Inside the two years that shook Facebook – and the world, *Wired* (February 12, 2019), https://www.wired.com/story/inside-facebook-mark-zuckerberg-2-years-of-hell/.
8 Matthew Lyon and Katie Hafner, *Where Wizards Stay Up Late: The Origins of the Internet* (Touchstone ed., 1998); Cade Metz, Paul Baran, the link between nuclear war and the internet, *Wired U.K.* (April 9, 2012), https://www.wired.co.uk/article/h-bomb-and-the-internet; Brian McWilliams, Iraq's crash course in cyberwar, *Wired* (May 22, 2003), https://www.wired.com/2003/05/iraqs-crash-course-in-cyberwar/.
9 Reno v. ACLU, 521 U.S. 844 (1997). See also, Lyons and Hafner, previous n. 8, pp. 54–62.
10 Matthew Lee, Andrew Montgomery, Steven Shapiro, Veeral Shah, and Q. Want, The World Wide Web as an engineering paradigm, MIT Technical Report No. 6.933/STS. 420, 2000, https://citeseerx.ist.psu.edu/document?repid=rep1&type=pdf&doi=8377c44fd1ce75be3cadf8498cb948c806b6ea4c; Mike Mills, Doing the speed limit on the information superhighway, *Washington Post* (August 2, 1994), p. D1; Mike Mills, A Pentagon plan became the internet, *Washington Post* (July 2, 1996), p. A6.
11 Mike Mills, Telecommunications bill passed, *Washington Post* (February 2, 1996), pp. A1, A15; Evelyn Richards, Bush to unveil high-tech initiative: $2 billion computing project would include data "superhighway," *Washington Post* (September 7, 1989), p. F1. See generally, Marina Mazzucato, *The Entrepreneurial State: Debunking Public Vs. Private Sector Myths* (Penguin, 2013).
12 European Parliamentary Research Service, Effects of 5G wireless communication on human health, (March 2020), p. 6, https://www.europarl.europa.eu/RegData/etudes/BRIE/2020/646172/EPRS_BRI(2020)646172_EN.pdf.
13 James Boyle, 'Foucault in cyberspace: Surveillance, sovereignty, and hard-wired censors,' 66 *University of Cincisnnati Law Review* 186 (1997).
14 Vinton Cerf and Robert Kahn, 'A protocol for packet network communication,' 22 *IEEE Transactions on Communications* 637 (1974).
15 J.H. Saltzer, D.P. Reed, and D.D. Clark, 'End-to-end arguments in system design,' 2 *ACM Transactions on Computer Systems* 227 (1984).
16 David S. Isenberg, 'The dawn of the stupid network,' 2 *ACM Networker* 24 (1998); David S. Isenberg, 'The rise of the stupid network,' 2 *ACM Networker* 26 (1998). These papers are available at https://www.isen.com.
17 17 U.S.C. § 512 (1998).

18 Hannibal Travis, 'YouTube from Afghanistan to Zimbabwe: Tyrannize locally, censor globally,' in *Transnational Culture in the Internet Age*, edited by Sean A. Pager and Adam Candeub (Edward Elgar, 2012), p. 78.

19 A term like *supernode* has a technical meaning in computer science and information retrieval, it may also have a connotation or symbolic meaning of a center of "clustered assemblies that concentrate" nodes, such as an Internet service provider (ISP) "that links directly to an international hub, which in turn connects to all the major cities on the planet." Peter Cochrane, Six degrees of separation and super nodes, *ZDNet* (August 26, 2004), https://www.zdnet.com/article/six-degrees-of-separation-and-super-nodes/138104.

20 Don Tapscott and Anthony Williams, *Wikinomics: How Mass Collaboration Changes Everything* (Portfolio, 2008); Jose Van Dijck and David Nieborg, 'Wikinomics and its discontents: A critical analysis of Web 2.0 business manifestos,' 11 *New Media and Soc'y*, 855 (2009); Wikinomics: How mass collaboration changes everything, talks at Google/YouTube (2008), https://www.youtube.com/watch?v=zF0k6dEm0zQ.

21 Travis, 'YouTube,' previous n. 18, pp. 78–79 (citing McClatchy Newspapers and The Washington Post), Mideast, Uprisings spur new protests in Iran, *Seattle Times* (February 14, 2011), https://www.seattletimes.com/subscribe/signup-offers/?pw=redirect&subsource=paywall&return=www.seattletimes.com/nation-world/mideast-uprisings-spur-new-protests-in-iran/; Jennifer Preston and Brian Stelter, Cellphones become the world's eyes and ears on protests, *The New York Times* (February 18, 2011), https://www.nytimes.com/2011/02/19/world/middleeast/19video.html; Richard Winton, LAPD to record its officers at incidents, *Los Angeles Times* (August 3, 2007), https://www.latimes.com/archives/la-xpm-2007-aug-03-me-lapdtv3-story.html.

22 ACLU, Censorship in a Box (1997), https://www.aclu.org/report/censorship-box-why-blocking-software-wrong-public-libraries. See also Nadine Strossen, 'Foreword, should cyberspace be a free speech zone?: Filters, "family friendliness," and the First Amendment,' 15 *New York Law School Law Journal of Human Rights* i (1998).

23 ACLU, Student Speech and Privacy (2019), https://www.aclu.org/issues/free-speech/student-speech-and-privacy.

24 *E.g.*, Tim Grieve, No dead bunnies, no dead soldiers, *Salon.com* (March 25, 2003), https://www.salon.com/2003/03/25/yellowtimes/.

25 Caron Carlson, ISPs grapple with censorship, *eWeek* (March 31, 2003), p. 1 (quoting Andrew Ulmer, an attorney with Simpson Partners LLP). *See also* Kim Gilmour and Tim Norman, Freedom vs. regulation, *Internet Magazine* (July 1, 2004), p. 25 ("ISPs and hosting companies will take down websites that contravene their conditions of service").

26 Dan Berger, 'Defining democracy: Coalition politics and the struggle for media reform,' 3 *International Journal of Communication* 3, 5–7 (2009).

27 E.g., Steven Levy, When the internet goes from free to fee, *Newsweek* (February 28, 2006), https://web.archive.org/web/20060322002225/www.freepress.net/news/14139.

28 47 U.S.C. § 223(e)(5)(B); see also id. § 223(d) (the basic prohibition, to which credit-card verification is a defense); Reno v. American Civil Liberties Union, 521 U.S. 844, 881–82 (1997).

29 Daniel J. Weitzner, 'Yelling "filter" on the crowded net: The implications of user control technologies,' in *The V-Chip Debate: Content filtering from Television to the Internet*, edited by Monroe Price (Routledge, 2013), https://books.google.com/books?hl=en&lr=&id=4yMuAgAAQBAJ&oi=fnd&pg=PT360&dq="user+empowerment+technologies"&ots=4nBHGdCXrW&sig=6ksHNS6oWI3zimzC-C5O18HqwyA#v=onepage&q="user%20empowerment%20technologies"&f=false.

30 James Boyle, 'Foucault in cyberspace: Surveillance, sovereignty, and hard-wired censors,' 66 *University of Cincinnati Law Review* 177 (1997).

31 Lawrence Lessig, Laws that choke creativity, *TED Talks* (March 2007), https://www.ted.com/talks/larry_lessig_says_the_law_is_strangling_creativity?language=en.

32 676 F.3d 19 (2d Cir. 2012).
33 *E.g.*, Bridgeport Music, Inc. v. Combs 507 F.3d 470 (6th Cir. 2007) (instructing district court to award punitive damages of closer to $369,000 to $738,000 on remand, as more proportionate to compensatory damages for unauthorized sampling of record, or to order a new trial).
34 First Amended Complaint ¶ 145, The Football Association Premier League Ltd. v. YouTube, Inc., No. 07 Civ. 3582-UA (C.D. Cal. first amended complaint filed November 6, 2007), http://tinyurl.com/6b7rk3.
35 *Ibid.*; Seth Sutel, Viacom sues YouTube for $1 billion, Associated Press/EOG.com (March 13, 2007), http://forums.eog.com/showthread.php/76795-Viacom-Sues-YouTube-for-1-Billion (Viacom sought injunction against further infringements); Napster forced to shut down, *BBC News.com* (July 3, 2001), http://tinyurl.com/5mf35o (Napster shut down by injunction against further infringements).
36 17 U.S.C. § 512(f) (2014).
37 Lenz v. Universal Music Corp., 572 F. Supp. 2d 1150 (N.D. Cal. 2008), *subsequent proceedings at* 105 U.S.P.Q.2d (BNA) 1635 (N.D. Cal. 2013) (cross-motions for summary judgment as to 512(f) liability denied).
38 Harper & Row, Publishers, Inc. v. Nation Enterprises, 471 U.S. 539, 543, 550 (1985) (finding no fair use of book in magazine article that quoted or paraphrased quantitatively small number of its words but qualitatively significant ones, while adding no independent criticism, comment, or research); *id.* at 550 ("'[A] reviewer may fairly cite largely from the original work, if his design be really and truly to use the passages for the purposes of fair and reasonable criticism. On the other hand, [a subsequent user should not] supersede the use of the original work'") (citation omitted); *id.* at 588 (Brennan, J., joined by White, J., and Marshall, J., dissenting) (no bright-line test for fair use); Lenz v. Universal Music Corp., 815 F.3d 1145, 1157 (9th Cir. 2015) ("Copyright holders cannot shirk their duty to consider – in good faith and prior to sending a takedown notification – whether allegedly infringing material constitutes fair use, a use which the DMCA plainly contemplates as authorized by the law."). See also, Campbell v. Acuff-Rose Music, Inc., 510 U.S. 569 (1994) (holding that parody may be a fair use depending on effect on market for nonparody derivative of work used and analyzing parody as a targeted criticism of the original for humorous or bowdlerizing effect); H. R. Rep. No. 94–1476, pp. 65–66 (no "generally applicable definition" or "exact rules in the statute" governing fair use).
39 E.g., Stowe v. Thomas, 23 F. Cas. 201 (C.C.E.D. Pa. 1853) ("'Certainly, bona fide imitations, translations and abridgments are different, and in respect of property, may be considered new works. . . . [The public] may improve [a work], imitate it, translate it, oppose [it]; but [has] no right to publish the identical work."') (citing Millar v. Taylor, 98 Eng. Rep. 201 (K.B. 1769) (opinions of Lord Mansfield, C.J., Aston, J., and Willes, J.) (copyright is a limited monopoly consisting in the "sole right of printing, publishing and selling" a book, not an absolute property right to prevent a new work based on an abridgement, improvement, imitation, translation, or appropriation of the conceptions thereof).
40 E.g., Story v. Holcombe, 23 F. Cas. 171, 173–74 (C.C.D. Ohio 1847) (No. 13,497) ("A fair abridgment of any book is considered a new work, as to write it requires labor and exercise of judgment. . . . All the authorities agree that to abridge requires the exercise of the mind, and that it is not copying.") (citing Strahan v. Newberry [In re Newbery], [1773] 98 Eng. Rep. 913 (Ch.), and Gyles v. Wilcox, [1740] 26 Eng. Rep. 489, 27 Eng. Rep. 682 (Ch.)); *see also*, Dodsley v. Kinnersley, [1761] 27 Eng. Rep. 270, 271 (Ch.); William F. Patry, *The Fair Use Privilege In Copyright Law* (1995), pp. 6–9 (citing these and other cases holding that republishing a "new work" that copies largely from an old one was legal in late 1700s).
41 *Harper & Row*, 471 U.S. at 557–58 (rejecting First Amendment argument of The Nation Enterprises, based on right to publish newsworthy material without a prior

restraint pursuant to *New York Times Co. v. United States*, 403 U.S. 713 (1971)). In fairness to the Court, Congress had amended the copyright statute to grant exclusive rights to reproduce a work or prepare derivative works from it, as not just a right to print, reprint, or sell it. 17 U.S.C. 106(1).

42 *Id.* at 589, 603 (Brennan, J., joined by White, J., and Marshall, J., dissenting). See also, Andy Warhol Foundation Visual Arts v. Goldsmith, 143 S. Ct. 1258, 1311 (U.S. 2023) (Kagan, J., joined by Roberts, C.J., dissenting) ("Creative progress unfolds through use and reuse, framing and reframing: One work builds on what has gone before; and later works build on that one; and . . . it is through such iterative processes that knowledge accumulates and art flourishes. But not anymore.").

43 Internet Policy Task Force, Report (July 31, 2013), p. 29, https://2010-2014.commerce.gov/blog/2013/07/31/commerces-internet-policy-task-force-releases-report-digital-copyright-policy.html (citing YouTube – Content ID, https://www.youtube.com/t/contentid; American University, Center for Social Media, Code of Best Practices for Fair Use in Online Video, http://centerforsocialmedia.org/fair-use/related-materials/codes/code-best-practices-fair-use-online-video; American University, Center for Social Media, Remix Culture, https://www.centerforsocialmedia.org/fair-use/videos/podcasts/remix-culture).

44 Audible Magic became the world's most productive copyright court, although it does not always care about fair use or some other exceptions to copyright. It "scans online files for copyrighted material, checking against a vast database of audio and video content provided by recording, movie and TV studios," and against another database of authorized uses, in order to "stop" uses that recording, movie, and TV studios do not like. Michael Liedtke, Audible magic emerging as top copyright cop in digital revolution, *Associated Press/Tuscaloosa News* (March 23, 2007), https://www.tuscaloosanews.com/story/news/2007/03/26/audible-magic-emerging-as-top-copyright-cop/27705587007/. The technology, like ContentID, could be criticized for ignoring fair use and other exceptions to copyright. *E.g.*, Br. of Amicus Curiae Computer Electronics Ass'n in Supp. of Appellees and Affirmance, at 35–37, *Viacom*, 2011 U.S. 2nd Cir. Briefs LEXIS 22, at *35–37 (2d Cir. brief filed April 4, 2011) ("Filtering technologies are overinculsive because they often filter legitimate content (such as licensed content or fair use) along with infringing content. . . . The filtering companies' amicus briefs acknowledge the false positive and false negative problems, and neither claims to be perfect."); Rebecca Tushnet, 'All of this has happened before and all of this will happen again: Innovation in copyright licensing,' 29 *Berkeley Technology Law Journal* 1447 (2014) (describing threat to fair use posed by ContentID and filters).

45 Peter K. Yu, 'Promoting Internet freedom through the copyright system,' US Embassy, July 29, 2010, http://iipdigital.usembassy.gov/st/english/publication/2010/07/20100727141034enelrahc5.498904e-02.html.

46 E.g., Paul Keller, YouTube Copyright transparency report: overblocking is real, Communia (2021), https://communia-association.org/2021/12/10/youtube-copyright-transparency-report-overblocking-is-real/; Google Support, Submit a Copyright Removal Request (2023), https://support.google.com/youtube/answer/2807622.

47 Taylor B. Bartholomew, 'Note, the death of fair use in cyberspace: YouTube and the problem with Content ID,' 13 *Duke Law and Technology Review* 66, 68 (2015).

48 E.g., Article 19, Freedom of Expression and the Private Sector in the Digital Age: Article 19's Written Comments, Office of the United Nations High Commissioner for Human Rights, https://www.ohchr.org/Documents/Issues/Expression/PrivateSector/Article19.pdf; Danielle Keats Citron, 'Technological due process,' 85 *Washington University Law Review* 1249 (2007); Danielle Keats Citron, What to do about the emerging threat of censorship creep on the Internet, CATO Institute Policy Analysis, No. 828 (2017), https://www.cato.org; Methaya Sirichit, 'Censorship by intermediary and moral rights: Strengthening authors' control over online expressions through the

right of respect and integrity,' 1 *Journal of Law, Technology, and Public Policy* 54, 119, 133–140 (2015).

49 Orit Fischman-Aforia, 'Online rulers as hybrid bodies: The case of infringing content monitoring,' 23 *University of Pennsylvania Journal of Constitutional Law* 351, 362, 364–65, 373 (2021).

50 Jonathan Zittrain, *The Future of the Internet and How to Stop It* (Yale University Press, 2008), p. 221. See also, ibid., p. 218.

51 See also, Matt McGee, Top SEOs: "We have not been banned by Google," *Search Engine Land* (October 10, 2014), https://searchengineland.com/topseos-banned-google-205622.

52 E.g., Natasha Tusikov, *Chokepoints: Global Private Regulation of the Internet* (University of California Press, 2017), pp. 127–38; Jennifer Urban and Laura Quilter, Efficient process or "chilling effects"? Takedown notices under Section 512 of the Digital Millennium Copyright Act (2005), http://mylaw.usc.edu/documents/512Rep-ExecSum_out.pdf. This occurred even though Google was aware and complained publicly about the absence of due process when websites are censored by search engines for intellectual property violates, rather than by regularly established courts. E.g., Matt McGee, Google's Schmidt: Hollywood should take content pirates to court, Search Engine Land (July 12, 2013), https://searchengineland.com/googles-schmidt-hollywood-should-take-content-pirates-to-court-166694. Many years ago, as this process was just getting underway in the wake of the Napster and Grokster disputes, one online intellectual property protection company boasted of sending out one million "automated" demands for deletion of allegedly infringing content *every month. See* BayTSP Corp., Fighting Online Software Piracy – What Works in 2005 (2005), https://www.baytsp.com/downloads2/SW_white_2005.pdf; *Trends Relating to Use of P2P File-Sharing Systems* (2006), https://www.ftc.gov/bcp/workshops/filesharing/presentations/ishikawa.pdf. Another firm offers to "automatically create a Take-Down Campaign" for "thousands of files" of content identified in advance by a copyright owner, which it says will result in demands for deletion being automatically sent to thousands of websites, p2p software providers, etc. Global File Registry, Technical White Paper (2006), www.globalfileregistry.com/assets/Global_File_Registry_White_Paper.pdf.

53 Sangeet Kumar, 'The algorithmic dance: YouTube's Adpocalypse and the gatekeeping of cultural content on digital platforms,' 8 *Internet Policy Review* 1 (2019).

54 As one analysis put it:

> [A] Nerd City video deployed an assortment of data borrowed from other YouTubers, also interested in the new social logic underpinning the YouTube algorithms and found that YouTube titles with words such as *gay* or *homosexual* were being fed into the algorithm and demonetized for no other reason than the fact that these words indicated some sort of 'sensitive social issue.' From YouTube's perspective, the war against vulnerable political minorities had evidently begun.

Yonathan Tesfai, YouTube and the LGBT+ Community: Demonitizing Pride, Masters of Media, University of Amsterdam, October 24, 2019, https://mastersofmedia.hum.uva.nl/blog/2019/10/24/youtube-and-the-lgbt-community-demonitizing-pride/ (citing Nerd City, YouTube's Biggest Lie, YouTube (2019), https://www.youtube.com/watch?v=ll8zGaWhofU).

55 Quoted in Weland Bourne, Surviving YouTube's "adpocalypse", *Creator Handbook* (September 1, 2017), https://www.creatorhandbook.net/surviving-youtubes-adpocalypse-97a0f0e0df19/. On removal, see Google, Nudity & Sexual Content Policies (2023), https://support.google.com/youtube/answer/2802008; Google, Violent or Graphic Content Policies, (2023), https://support.google.com/youtube/answer/2802008.

56 Report of the Special Rapporteur on the Promotion and Protection of the Right to Freedom of Opinion and Expression, U.N. Doc. A/HRC/38/35, paras. 13, 16, 32 (July 6, 2018).

57 Ibid., para. 34; see also, Fischman-Aforia, previous n. 49, at 362.

58 Sean Buckley, YouTube's "trusted flagger" users have an inside track to get videos removed, *Engadget* (March 17, 2014), https://www.engadget.com/2014-03-17-youtube-s-trusted-flagger-program-lets-police-call-attention-to.html.

59 For example, a significant case on the enforceability of forum selection and arbitration clauses in deplatforming disputes involved a Muslim plaintiff, Mustafa Fteja of New York. Fteja v. Facebook, 841 F. Supp. 2d 829 (S.D.N.Y. 2012). He alleged that his account had been disabled in 2010, and that Facebook "discriminated" against him "based on [his] religion and ethnicity," i.e. Islam and (presumably) Arab. Ibid., 831.

60 18 U.S.C. §§ 2339A, 2339B; Seth Kreimer, 'Censorship by proxy: The First Amendment, intermediaries, and the problem of the weakest link,' 155 *University of Pennsylvania Law Review* 11, 92–95 (2006).

61 Julia Conley, Advocates demand Facebook #StopCensoringPalestine after platform blocks livestream featuring Palestinian rights defenders, Common Dreams News Center (September 24, 2020), https://commons.commondreams.org/t/advocates-demand-facebook-stopcensoringpalestine-after-platform-blocks-livestream-featuring-palestinian-rights-defenders/82559.

62 Ibid.

63 E.g., Faiza Patel and Meghan Koushik, Countering violent extremism 32, Brennan Center for Justice/JStor (2017), https://www.jstor.org/stable/resrep28416. See also, Danielle Keats Citron, What to do about the emerging threat of censorship creep on the Internet, CATO Institute Policy Analysis, No. 828 (2017), https://www.cato.org.

64 Citron, What to do, previous n. 63, at 2, citing Lizzie Plaugic, France wants to make Google and Facebook accountable for hate speech, *The Verge* (January 27, 2015), https://www.theverge.com/2015/1/27/7921463/google-facebookaccountable-for-hate-speech-france.

65 Faiza Patel, Rachel Levinson-Waldman, and Harsha Panduranga, A course correction for homeland security 11–15, Brennan Center for Justice (2022), https://www.jstor.org/stable/resrep44688.6.

66 Ibid., 16.

67 E.g., International Covenant on Civil and Political Rights, art. 26, 99 U.N.T.S. 171, entered into force 23 March 1976 ("All persons are equal before the law and are entitled without any discrimination to the equal protection of the law. In this respect, the law shall prohibit any discrimination and guarantee to all persons equal and effective protection against discrimination on any ground such as race, colour, sex, language, *religion, political or other opinion, national or social origin*, property, birth or other status.") (emphasis added); ibid., art. 19 (right to receive information "of all kinds . . . regardless of frontiers" using media of one's choice, with exceptions for information threatening to national security, public morals or order, or rights of others etc.).

68 According to a 2019 survey, about half of adults aged 18–49 say that social media is the most common way they access politics and elections news. Pew Research Center, Those Who Get Most Political News from Social Media Most Likely to Be Under 30 (2019), https://www.pewresearch.org.

69 This actually occurred to YouTube videos posted by a history teacher, although there is no indication in my source that the aforementioned database was used. One report stated that "YouTube, likely on accident, demonetized or banned a number of channels that were not . . . Nazis, but actually ones that document them," such as the one of "history teacher Mr. Allsop, who uses World War II – era Nazi footage as a teaching tool." Justin Anderson, YouTube continues to selectively enforce its terms of service, Fairness and Accuracy in Reporting, June 10, 2019, https://fair.org/home/youtube-continues-to-selectively-enforce-its-terms-of-service/.

70 See also, International Covenant on Civil and Political Rights, art. 20(1); General Comment No. 11: Prohibition of propaganda for war and inciting national, racial or religious hatred (Art. 20), U.N. Doc. No. CCPR/C/GC/11 (July 29, 1983) ("The

prohibition under paragraph 1 extends to all forms of propaganda threatening or resulting in . . . breach of the peace contrary to the Charter of the United Nations.").

71 On TikTok, Tumblr, Twitter, and Snapchat, see Clare Southerton, Daniel Marshall, and Rob Cover, 'Restricted modes: Social media, content classification and LGBTQ sexual citizenship,' 23 *New Media and Society* 920 (2020), https://journals.sagepub.com/doi/pdf/10.1177/1461444820904362.

72 Emily Yost, 'Queering the landscape: Decriminalizing consent and remapping the permissible geographies of intimacy,' 19 *University of Maryland Law Journal of Race, Religion, Gender and Class* 201, 226–27 (2019), citing Alexander Cheves, The dangerous trend of LGBTQ censorship on the internet, *Out* (December 6, 2018), https://www.out.com/out-exclusives/2018/12/06/dangerous-trend-lgbtq-censorship-internet; Jesselyn Cook, Instagram's shadow ban on vaguely "inappropriate" content is plainly sexist, *Huffington Post* (April 29, 2019), https://www.huffpost.com/entry/instagram-shadow-ban-sex-ist_n_5cc72935e4b0537911491a4f; Dottie Lux and Lil Miss Hot Mess, Facebook's hate speech policies censor marginalized users, *Wired* (August 4, 2017), https://www.wired.com/story/facebooks-hate-speech-policies-censor-marginalized-users/; Megan Farokmanesh, YouTube is still restricting and demonetizing LGBT videos–and adding anti-LGBT ads to some, *The Verge* (June 4, 2018), https://www.theverge.com/2018/6/4/17424472/youtube-lgbt-demonetization-ads-algorithm.

73 E.g., Nerd City, previous n. 54.

74 Mary Emily O'Hara, Why is Instagram censoring so many hashtags used by women and LGBT people?, *The Daily Dot* (May 11, 2016), https://www.dailydot.com/irl/instagram-list-of-banned-tags-weird/.

75 Eli Erlick, How Instagram may be unwittingly censoring the queer community, *Them* (January 30, 2018), https://www.them.us/story/instagram-may-be-unwittingly-censoring-the-queer-community.

76 Jillian C. York, How LGBTQ+ content is censored under the guise of "sexually explicit," *Electronic Frontier Foundation Deeplinks* (August 18, 2021), https://www.eff.org/deeplinks/2021/08/how-lgbtq-content-censored-under-guise-sexually-explicit, citing Kendra Albert and Afsaneh Rigot, Apple and Google still have an LGBTQ problem, *Wired UK* (August 16, 2021), https://www.wired.co.uk/contributor/kendra-albert.

77 Julia Kollewe, Amazon bows to UAE pressure to restrict LGBTQ+ search results, *The Guardian (U.K.)* (June 30, 2022), https://www.theguardian.com/technology/2022/jun/30/amazon-bows-to-uae-pressure-to-restrict-lgbt-search-results.

78 Cheves, previous n. 72.

79 Phillip B. Stark, 'The effectiveness of Internet content filters,' 4 *I/S: A Journal of Law and Policy for the Information Society* 411, 415–18, 422–23 (2008) (citing American Civil Liberties Union v. Gonzales, 478 F. Supp. 2d 775 (E.D. Pa. 2007)).

80 Ibid., p. 419.

81 York, previous n. 76.

82 Cheves, previous n. 72.

83 Alice Witt, Nicholas Suzor, and Anna Higgins, 'The rule of law on Instagram: An evaluation of the moderation of images depicting women's bodies,' 42 *University of New South Wales Law Journal* 557, 574, 590 (2019).

84 Daniel Villareal, Two web-lebrities accuse Instagram and Twitter of censoring gay and male sexual content, *Hornet* (November 2, 2017), https://hornet.com/stories/twitter-instagram-censorship-gay/.

85 U.S. Department of Justice, Google forfeits $500 million generated by online ads and prescription drug sales by Canadian pharmacies (August 24, 2011), https://www.justice.gov/opa/google-forfeits-500-million-generated-online-ads-prescription-drug-sales-canadian-online.

86 E.g., Roger Bate, Ginger Zhe Jin, and Aparna Mathur, In whom we trust: The role of certification agencies in online drug markets, NBER Working Paper No. 17955 (2012), https://www.nber.org/papers/w17955.

87 PharmacyChecker.com, LLC v. National Association of Boards of Pharmacy, 530 F. Supp. 3d 301, 301–9 (S.D.N.Y. 2021).

88 See *id.* at 301–350. A collusive refusal to compete on the merits with online pharmacies might also be an unreasonable restraint of trade. E.g., Initial Decision of Chief Administrative Law Judge D. Michael Chappell, *FTC v. 1–800 Contacts, Inc.*, FTC Dkt. No. 9373 (FTC Aug. 8, 2016), https://www.ftc.gov/system/files/documents/cases/160808_1800contactspt3cmpt.pdf, *aff'd*, 166 F.T.C. 250 (2018), *vacated and remanded*, 1–800 Contacts, Inc. v. FTC, 1 F.4th 102, 111–12, 119–22 (2d Cir. 2021); Realcomp II, Ltd. v. FTC, 635 F.3d 815 (6th Cir. 2011); United States v. National Association of Realtors, 73 Fed. Reg. 36,104 (DOJ June 25, 2008); FTC Charges Real Estate Groups with Anticompetitive Conduct Limiting Consumers' Choice in Real Estate Services, FTC (Oct. 12, 2006), https://www.ftc.gov/news/press-releases/2006/10/ftc-charges-real-estate-groups-with-anticompetitive-conduct-limiting-consumers-choice-real-estate.

89 Kreimer, previous n. 60, at 93.

90 E.g., Lawrence Lessig, The internet under siege, *Foreign Policy* (November 1, 2001), https://www.foreignpolicy.com ("copyright laws were crafted in an era long before the Internet. And their effect on the Internet has been to transfer control over innovation in [speech] distribution from many innovators to a concentrated few."); Lessig, Laws that choke creativity, previous n. 31; Julia Reda, Extra copyright for news sites ("Link tax"), *juliareda.eu* (July 2017), https://www.juliareda.eu (collecting statements in opposition to proposal for a new European Union copyright directive that would limit republication and circulation of "snippets" from the news, on the grounds that it would stifle independent publishers and investigative reports); Margot Kaminski and Jennifer Urban, 'The right to contest AI,' 121 *Columbia Law Review*, 1957, 1969, 2019–020 (2021) (noting that influx of millions of takedown requests accelerated development of automated filters and takedown demands taking advantage of them); Katharine Trendacosta, Unfiltered: How YouTube's content id discourages fair use and dictates what we see online, *Electronic Frontier Foundation* (December 2020), pp. 4, 20–23, www.eff.org/unfiltered (observing that ContentID is used to silence criticism, and that video creators live in fear of it, rarely challenging corporations' moves to seize their channel income or block their videos).

91 E.g., Software Rights Archive, LLC v. Facebook, Inc., 640 F. App'x 995 (Fed. Cir. Sept. 2016); Lawrence Page, Sergey Brin, Rajeev Motwani, and Terry Winograd, The PageRank citation ranking: Bringing order to the web (January 1998), http://ilpubs.stanford.edu:8090/422/, Web version at 2, 11–12, original link: http://google.stanford.edu/~backrub/pageranksub.ps; Marti Hearst, 'The changing relationship between information technology and society,' 14 *IEEE Intelligent Systems and Their Applications* 8, 17 (1999) ("Companies such as AskJeeves, Direct Hit, Google, and IBM have developed a variety of approaches, including natural- language processing, link-relevancy ranking techniques (or link popularity), and combinations of human- and machine-[analysis]"); Zhanzi Qiu, Matthias Hemmje, and Erich Neuhold, 'ConSearch: Using hypertext contexts as search boundaries,' in *IEEE Advances In Digital Libraries 2000*, edited by Jeroen Hoppenbrouwers (2000), p. 48; Danny Sullivan, Google PageRank, meet Yahoo Web Rank!, *Search Engine Watch* (April 2, 2004), http://searchenginewatch.com/3334891; Danny Sullivan, Google: Can the Marcia Brady of search stay sweet?, *Search Engine Watch* (September 3, 2000), http://searchenginewatch.com/2164991; Danny Sullivan, More evil than Dr. evil?, *Search Engine Watch (SEW)* (November 1, 1999), http://searchenginewatch.com/2167621; see also, Laura B. Cohen, 'The Web as a Research Tool,' in *Choice Volume 36 Supplement* (American Library Association, 1999), p. 38.

92 John Battelle, *The Search: How Google and Its Rivals Rewrote the Rules of Business and Transformed Our Culture* (National Geographic Books, 2005), ch. 3; Dale Vidmar and Connie Anderson, 'History of Internet search tools,' in *Encyclopedia of Library and Information Science*, Volume 71, edited by Allen Kent (Marcel Dekker, 2002), pp. 154–55.

93 Battelle, *The Search*, previous n. 92, ch. 3.
94 David Vise and Mark Malseed, *The Google Story* (Penguin, 2008), pp. 1–10; Steven Pealstein, A gaggle of google critics, *Washington Post* (August 20, 2004), https://www.washingtonpost.com/archive/business/2004/08/20/a-gaggle-of-google-critics/9b163f11-5a7a-4627-965a-3851b1e7bb52/.
95 Vise and Malseed, previous n. 94, pp. 11–12.
96 Ibid., p. 47.
97 Ibid., p. 55.
98 E.g., U.S. Patent No. 8,078,629 (filed Oct. 13, 2009) ("Detecting spam documents in a phrase based information retrieval system").
99 E.g., Frank Pasquale, *The Black Box Society: The Secret Algorithms that Control Money and Information* (Harvard University Press, 2015), pp. 59–66.
100 Larry Kim, Has machine learning created a new model for SEO ranking?, *Search Engine Land* (February 22, 2017), https://searchengineland.com/new-model-seo-ranking-269419.
101 UN Special Rapporteur on the Freedom of Expression, previous n. 56.
102 Ibid.
103 Suzor, *Lawless*, p. 112.
104 E.g., Twitter, Inc. v. Taamneh, 143 S. Ct. 1206, 1210 (2023); Anderson v. TikTok, Inc., Civ. No. 22–1849, 2022 WL 14742788 (E.D. Pa. motion to dismiss granted Oct. 25, 2022); OpenTV, Inc. v. Netflix, Inc., 76 F. Supp. 3d 886, 892–95 (N.D. Cal. 2014); see also, Force v. Facebook, Inc., 934 F.3d 53, 66 (2d Cir. 2019), *cert. denied*, 140 S. Ct. 2761 (2020); Collarity, Inc. v. Google, Inc., No. CV11–1103-MPT, 2015 WL 7597413, at *4–8 (D. Del. November 25, 2015); Ivan Medvedyev, Powered by AI: Instagram's explore recommender system, *Medium* (November 26, 2019), https://instagram-engineering.com/powered-by-ai-instagrams-explore-recommender-system-7ca901d2a882; Netflix Technology Blog, Netflix recommendations, beyond the 5 stars (June 12, 2012), https://netflixtechblog.com/netflix-recommendations-beyond-the-5-stars-part-2-d9b96aa399f5?gi=6a7b0ac4ea71; Scaling machine learning at Netflix, *Netflix Technology Blog* (February 13, 2023), https://netflixtechblog.com/scaling- media-machine-learning-at-netflix-f19b400243?source=collection_archive—0–.
105 E.g., Missouri v. Biden, 83 F.4th 350 (5th Cir. 2023), *cert. pending sub nom.* Murthy v. Missouri, 144 S. Ct. 7 (2023) (No. 23A243).
106 National Federation of Independent Business v. Department of Labor, Occupational Safety and Health Administration, 595 U.S. ___, 142 S. Ct. 661 (2022) (per curiam) (workplace vaccine mandate unlawful); Calvary Chapel Dayton Valley v. Sisolak, 591 U.S. ___, 140 S. Ct. 2603 (2020) (selective lockdown of churches as opposed to casinos and marijuana dispensaries etc. unlawful); Louisiana v. Biden, 55 F.4th 1017 (5th Cir. 2022) (federal government contractor vaccine mandate unlawful); Brnovich v. Biden, 562 F. Supp. 3d 123 (D. Ariz. 2022) (federal government contractor vaccine mandate unlawful), *rev'd sub nom.* Mayes v. Biden, 67 F.4th 921 (9th Cir. 2023).
107 Missouri v. Biden, 83 F.4th at 366–67, 371–72; see also, Divino Group LLC v. Google LLC, No. 19-cv-04749-VKD, 2022 WL 4625076 (N.D. Cal. Sept. 30, 2022) (discussing "LGBTQ+" users of YouTube and their belief that their videos had been algorithmically filtered or flagged as gay, shocking, or expressive of an LGBTQ+ viewpoint, but dismissing claim [without any production of evidence] as being speculative as to "intent," under detainee abuse case law involving Arab Muslim men in New York detention centers, known as *Ashcroft v. Iqbal*, 556 U.S. 662 (2009)).

Bibliography

17 U.S.C. § 512 (1998).
18 U.S.C. §§ 2339A, 2339B.
Aaron Swartz Day 2022 Day 2 (December 2022), https://www.youtube.com/watch?v=4vHaptAhHmc (remarks of Cory Doctorow at 24:26–25:00).

ACLU, Censorship in a Box (1997), https://www.aclu.org/report/censorship-box-why-blocking-software-wrong-public-libraries.
ACLU, Student Speech and Privacy (2019), https://www.aclu.org/issues/free-speech/student-speech-and-privacy.
Kendra Albert and Afsaneh Rigot, Apple and Google still have an LGBTQ problem, *Wired UK* (August 16, 2021), https://www.wired.co.uk/contributor/kendra-albert.
American Civil Liberties Union v. Gonzales, 478 F. Supp. 2d 775 (E.D. Pa. 2007)).
American University, Center for Social Media, Code of Best Practices for Fair Use in Online Video, http://centerforsocialmedia.org/fair-use/related-materials/codes/code-best-practices-fair-use-online-video.
American University, Center for Social Media, Remix Culture, https://www.centerforsocial-media.org/fair-use/videos/podcasts/remix-culture.
Americans for Prosperity Foundation v. Bonta, 594 U.S. ___, 141 S. Ct. 2373 (2021).
Anderson v. TikTok, Inc., Civ. No. 22–1849, 2022 WL 14742788 (E.D. Pa. motion to dismiss granted Oct. 25, 2022).
Andy Warhol Foundation Visual Arts v. Goldsmith, 598 U.S. ___, 143 S. Ct. 1258 (U.S. 2023).
Article 19, Freedom of Expression and the Private Sector in the Digital Age: Article 19's Written Comments, Office of the United Nations High Commissioner for Human Rights, https://www.ohchr.org/Documents/Issues/Expression/PrivateSector/Article19.pdf.
Baird v. State Bar of Ariz., 401 U.S. 1 (1971) (plurality opinion).
Taylor B. Bartholomew, 'Note, The death of fair use in cyberspace: YouTube and the problem with Content ID,' 13 *Duke Law & Technology Review* 66 (2015).
Roger Bate, Ginger Zhe Jin, and Aparna Mathur, In whom we trust: The role of certification agencies in online drug markets, NBER Working Paper No. 17955 (2012), https://www.nber.org/papers/w17955.
John Battelle, *The Search: How Google and Its Rivals Rewrote the Rules of Business and Transformed Our Culture* (National Geographic Books, 2005).
BayTSP Corp., Fighting Online Software Piracy – What Works in 2005 (2005), https://web.archive.org/web/20230000000000*/www.baytsp.com/downloads2/SW_white_2005.pdf.
Dan Berger, 'Defining democracy: Coalition politics and the struggle for media reform,' 3 *International Journal of Communication* 3 (2009).
Weland Bourne, Surviving YouTube's "adpocalypse", *Creator Handbook* (September 1, 2017), https://www.creatorhandbook.net/surviving-youtubes-adpocalypse-97a0f0e0df19/.
James Boyle, 'Foucault in cyberspace: Surveillance, sovereignty, and hard-wired censors,' 66 *University of Cincinnati Law Review* 186 (1997).
Bridgeport Music, Inc. v. Combs, 507 F.3d 470 (6th Cir. 2007).
Brief of Amicus Curiae Computer Electronics Association in Support of Appellees and Affirmance, Viacom International v. YouTube, Inc., 2011 U.S. 2nd Cir. Briefs LEXIS 22 (2d Cir. brief filed Apr. 4, 2011).
Brnovich v. Biden, 562 F. Supp. 3d 123 (D. Ariz. 2022), *rev'd sub nom. Mayes v. Biden*, 67 F.4th 921 (9th Cir. 2023).
Sean Buckley, YouTube's "trusted flagger" users have an inside track to get videos removed, *Engadget* (March 17, 2014), https://www.engadget.com/2014-03-17-youtube-s-trusted-flagger-program-lets-police-call-attention-to.html.
Calvary Chapel Dayton Valley v. Sisolak, 591 U.S. ___, 140 S. Ct. 2603 (2020).
Campbell v. Acuff-Rose Music, Inc., 510 U.S. 569 (1994).
Caron Carlson, ISPs grapple with censorship, *eWeek* (March 31, 2003), p. 1.
Vinton Cerf and Robert Kahn, 'A protocol for packet network communication', 22 *IEEE Transactions on Communications* 637 (1974).
Alexander Cheves, The dangerous trend of LGBTQ censorship on the internet, *Out* (December 6, 2018), https://www.out.com/out-exclusives/2018/12/06/dangerous-trend-lgbtq-censorship-internet.

Citizens United v. FEC, 558 U.S. 310, 130 S.Ct. 876 (2010).

Danielle Keats Citron, 'Technological due process,' 85 *Washington University Law Review* 1249 (2007).

Danielle Keats Citron, What to do about the emerging threat of censorship creep on the internet, CATO Institute Policy Analysis, No. 828 (2017), https://www.cato.org.

Laura B. Cohen, 'The web as a research tool,' in *Choice Volume 36 Supplement* (American Library Association, 1999), pp. 19–44.

Collarity, Inc. v. Google Inc., No. CV11–1103-MPT, 2015 WL 7597413 (D. Del. November 25, 2015).

Jesselyn Cook, Instagram's shadow ban on vaguely inappropriate content is plainly sexist, *Huffington Post* (April 29, 2019), https://www.huffpost.com/entry/instagram-shadow-ban-sex-ist_n_5cc72935e4b0537911491a4f.

Directive 2000/31/EC (Digital Services Act), art. 19, COM/2020/825, *Official Journal* L 277 (Oct. 19, 2022).

Directive 2019/790 on copyright in the digital single market.

Divino Group LLC v. Google LLC, No. 19-cv-04749-VKD, 2022 WL 4625076 (N.D. Cal. September 30, 2022).

Dodsley v. Kinnersley, [1761] 27 Eng. Rep. 270, 271 (Ch.).

Eli Erlick, How Instagram may be unwittingly censoring the queer community, *Them* (January 30, 2018), https://www.them.us/story/instagram-may-be-unwittingly-censoring-the-queer-community.

European Commission, Communication to the Parliament and the Council, Guidance on Article 17 of Directive 2019/790 on Copyright in the Digital Single Market, COM/2021/288 Final June 4, 2021, https://eur-lex.europa.eu/legal-content/EN/TXT/?qid=1625142238402&uri=CELEX%3A52021DC0288.

European Parliamentary Research Service, Effects of 5G wireless communication on human health (March 2020), https://www.europarl.europa.eu/RegData/etudes/BRIE/2020/646172/EPRS_BRI(2020)646172_EN.pdf.

F2C2012: Aaron Swartz Keynote – "How we stopped SOPA", *YouTube* (May 22, 2012), https://www.youtube.com/watch?v=Fgh2dFngFsg.

Megan Farokmanesh, YouTube is still restricting and demonetizing LGBT videos – and adding anti-LGBT ads to some, *The Verge* (June 4, 2018), https://www.theverge.com/2018/6/4/17424472/youtube-lgbt-demonetization-ads-algorithm.

First Amended Complaint, *The Football Ass'n Premier League Ltd. v. YouTube, Inc.*, No. 07 Civ. 3582-UA (C.D. Cal. first amended complaint filed November 6, 2007), http://tinyurl.com/6b7rk3.

Orit Fischman-Aforia, 'Online rulers as hybrid bodies: The case of infringing content monitoring,' 23 *University of Pennsylvania Journal of Constitutional Law* 351 (2021).

Force v. Facebook, Inc., 934 F.3d 53 (2d Cir. 2019), *cert. denied*, 140 S. Ct. 2761 (2020).

FTC charges real estate groups with anticompetitive conduct limiting consumers' choice in real estate services, *FTC* (October 12, 2006), https://www.ftc.gov/news/press-releases/2006/10/ftc-charges-real-estate-groups-with-anticompetitive-conduct-limiting-consumers-choice-real-estate.

Fteja v. Facebook, 841 F. Supp. 2d 829 (S.D.N.Y. 2012).

General Comment No. 11: Prohibition of propaganda for war and inciting national, racial or religious hatred (Art. 20), U.N. Doc. No. CCPR/C/GC/11 (July 29, 1983).

Tarleton Gillespie, *Custodians of the Internet: Platforms, Content Moderation, and the Hidden Decisions That Shape Social Media* (Yale University Press, 2018).

Kim Gilmour and Tim Norman, Freedom vs. regulation, *Internet Magazine* (July 1, 2004), p. 25.

Global File Registry, Technical White Paper (2006), https://web.archive.org/web/20140101000000*/www.globalfileregistry.com/assets/Global_File_Registry_White_Paper.pdf.

Google, Nudity & Sexual Content Policies (2023), https://support.google.com/youtube/answer/2802008.

Google, Submit a Copyright Removal Request (2023), https://support.google.com/youtube/answer/2807622.

Google, Violent or Graphic Content Policies, (2023), https://support.google.com/youtube/answer/2802008.

Tim Grieve, No dead bunnies, no dead soldiers, *Salon.com* (March 25, 2003), https://www.salon.com/2003/03/25/yellowtimes/.

Gyles v. Wilcox, [1740] 26 Eng. Rep. 489, 27 Eng. Rep. 682 (Ch.).

Harper & Row, Publishers, Inc. v. Nation Enterprises, 471 U.S. 539 (1985).

Marti Hearst, 'The changing relationship between information technology and society,' 14 *IEEE Intelligent Systems & Their Applications* 8 (1999).

H. R. Rep. No. 94–1476, pp. 65–66.

Internet Policy Task Force, Report (July 31, 2013), https://2010-2014.commerce.gov/blog/2013/07/31/commerces-internet-policy-task-force-releases-report-digital-copyright-policy.html.

David S. Isenberg, 'The dawn of the stupid network,' 2 *ACM Networker* 24 (1998), https://www.isen.com.

David S. Isenberg, 'The rise of the stupid network,' 2 *ACM Networker* 26 (1998), https://www.isen.com.

Initial Decision of Chief Administrative Law Judge D. Michael Chappell, *FTC v. 1–800 Contacts, Inc.*, FTC Dkt. No. 9373 (FTC August 8, 2016), https://www.ftc.gov/system/files/documents/cases/160808_1800contactspt3cmpt.pdf, *aff'd*, 166 F.T.C. 250 (2018), *vacated and remanded*, 1–800 Contacts, Inc. v. FTC, 1 F.4th 102 (2d Cir. 2021).

International Covenant on Civil and Political Rights, 99 U.N.T.S. 171, entered into force 23 March 1976.

Ishikawa, FTC, Trends Relating to Use of P2P File-Sharing Systems (2006), https://web.archive.org/web/20130609204145/www.ftc.gov/bcp/workshops/filesharing/presentations/ishikawa.pdf.

Margot Kaminski and Jennifer Urban, 'The right to contest AI,' 121 *Columbia Law Review*, 1957 (2021).

Paul Keller, YouTube Copyright Transparency Report: Overblocking is real, *Communia* (2021), https://communia-association.org/2021/12/10/youtube-copyright-transparency-report-overblocking-is-real/.

Lina M. Khan, 'Section 5 in action: Reinvigorating the FTC Act and the rule of law,' 11 *Journal of Antitrust Enforcement* 149 (2023).

Julia Kollewe, 'Amazon Bows to UAE Pressure to Restrict LGBTQ+ Search Results,' The Guardian (U.K.), June 30, 2022, www.theguardian.com/technology/2022/jun/30/amazon-bows-to-uae-pressure-to-restrict-lgbt-search-results.

Jeff Kosseff, *The Twenty-Six Words that Created the Internet* (Cornell University Press, 2019).

Seth Kreimer, 'Censorship by proxy: The First Amendment, intermediaries, and the problem of the weakest link,' 155 *University of Pennsylvania Law Review* 11 (2006).

Sangeet Kumar, 'The algorithmic dance: YouTube's Adpocalypse and the gatekeeping of cultural content on digital platforms,' 8 *Internet Policy Review* 1 (2019).

Matthew Lee et al., The World Wide Web as an Engineering Paradigm, MIT Technical Report No. 6.933/STS. 420, 2000, https://citeseerx.ist.psu.edu/document?repid=rep1&type=pdf&doi=8377c44fd1ce75be3cadf8498cb948c806b6ea4c.

Lenz v. Universal Music Corp., 815 F.3d 1145 (9th Cir. 2015).

Dottie Lux and Lil Miss Hot Mess, Facebook's hate speech policies censor marginalized users, *Wired* (August 4, 2017), https://www.wired.com/story/facebooks-hate-speech-policies-censor-marginalized-users/.

Lawrence Lessig, The internet under siege, *Foreign Policy* (November 1, 2001), https://www.foreignpolicy.com.

Michael Liedtke, Audible magic emerging as top copyright cop in digital revolution, Associated Press/*Tuscaloosa News* (March 23, 2007), https://www.tuscaloosanews.com/story/news/2007/03/26/audible-magic-emerging-as-top-copyright-cop/27705587007/.
Louisiana v. Biden, 55 F.4th 1017 (5th Cir. 2022).
James Madison, 'Letter to Thomas Jefferson,' January 18, 1800, in *The Writings of James Madison, Vol. 6: 1790–1802*, edited by Gaillard Hunt (G.P Putnam's Sons, 1906), pp. 347, 387.
James Madison, 'Report on the Virginia resolutions,' in *The Writings of James Madison, Vol. IV: 1829–1836* (J.P. Lippincott Co., 1865), p. 544.
Matthew Lyon and Katie Hafner, *Where Wizards Stay Up Late: The Origins of the Internet* (Touchstone ed., 1998).
Marina Mazzucato, *The Entrepreneurial State: Debunking Public Vs. Private Sector Myths* (Penguin, 2013).
Matt McGee, Google's Schmidt: Hollywood should take content pirates to court, *Search Engine Land* (July 12, 2013), https://searchengineland.com/googles-schmidt-hollywood-should-take-content-pirates-to-court-166694.
Matt McGee, TopSEOs: "We have not been banned by Google," *Search Engine Land* (October 10, 2014), https://searchengineland.com/topseos-banned-google-205622
Ivan Medvedyev, Powered by AI: Instagram's explore recommender system, *Medium* (November 26, 2019), https://instagram-engineering.com/powered-by-ai-instagrams-explore-recommender-system-7ca901d2a882.
Cade Metz, Paul Baran, the link between nuclear war and the internet, *Wired U.K.* (April 9, 2012), https://www.wired.co.uk/article/h-bomb-and-the-internet.
Millar v. Taylor, 98 Eng. Rep. 201 (K.B. 1769) (opinions of Lord Mansfield, C.J., Aston, J., and Willes, J.).
Henry Mostyn, Bianca Buzatu, and Xavier Quer Zamora, The EU Parliament approves the final text of the Digital Markets Act, *Concurrences* (July 5, 2022), https://www.concurrences.com/en/bulletin/news-issues/july-2022/the-eu-parliament-approves-the-final-text-of-the-digital-markets-act.
Brian McWilliams, Iraq's crash course in cyberwar, *Wired* (May 22, 2003), https://www.wired.com/2003/05/iraqs-crash-course-in-cyberwar/.
Mike Mills, Doing the speed limit on the information superhighway, *Washington Post* (August 2, 1994), p. D1.
Mike Mills, A Pentagon plan became the internet, *Washington Post* (July 2, 1996), p. A6.
Mike Mills, Telecommunications bill passed, *Washington Post* (February 2, 1996), pp. A1, A15.
Missouri v. Biden, 83 F.4th 350. (5th Cir. Sept. 8, 2023), *stayed and cert. granted sub nom.* Murthy v. Missouri, 144 S. Ct. 7 (U.S. Oct. 20, 2023) (No. 23A243).
Mozilla Corp. v. FCC, 940 F.3d 1 (D.C Cir. 2019).
NAACP v. Alabama ex rel. Patterson, 357 U.S. 449 (1958).
NAACP v. Button, 371 U.S. 415 (1963).
Napster forced to shut down, *BBC News.com* (July 3, 2001), http://tinyurl.com/5mf35o.
National Ass'n for Gun Rights, Inc. v. Mangan, 933 F.3d 1102 (9th Cir. 2019).
National Federation of Independent Business v. Department of Labor, Occupational Safety & Health Administration, 595 U.S. ___, 142 S. Ct. 661 (2022) (per curiam).
Netflix Technology Blog, Netflix recommendations, beyond the 5 stars (June 12, 2012), https://netflixtechblog.com/netflix-recommendations-beyond-the-5-stars-part-2-d9b96aa399f5?gi=6a7b0ac4ea71.
New York Times Co. v. United States, 403 U.S. 713 (1971).
Mary Emily O'Hara, Why is Instagram censoring so many hashtags used by women and LGBT people?, *The Daily Dot* (May 11, 2016), https://www.dailydot.com/irl/instagram-list-of-banned-tags-weird/.
OpenTV, Inc. v. Netflix, Inc., 76 F. Supp. 3d 886 (N.D. Cal. 2014).

Lawrence Page, Sergey Brin, Rajeev Motwani, & Terry Winograd, The PageRank citation ranking: Bringing order to the web (January 1998), http://ilpubs.stanford.edu:8090/422/, original link: http://google.stanford.edu/~backrub/pageranksub.ps.
Faiza Patel, Rachel Levinson-Waldman, and Harsha Panduranga, A Course Correction for Homeland Security, Brennan Center for Justice (2022), https://www.jstor.org/stable/resrep44688.6.
Faiza Patel and Meghan Koushik, Countering violent extremism, Brennan Center for Justice/*JStor* (2017), https://www.jstor.org/stable/resrep28416.
William F. Patry, *The Fair Use Privilege In Copyright Law* (1995).
Emily Pehrsson, The Meaning of the GDPR Article 22 (Stanford-Vienna Transatlantic Tech. Law F., Working Paper No. 31, 2018, https://www.cdn.law.stanford.edu/wpcontent/uploads/2018/05/pehrsson_eulawwp31.pdf [https://perma.cc/T566-EZDK].
Lizzie Plaugic, France wants to make Google and Facebook accountable for hate speech, *The Verge* (January 27, 2015), https://www.theverge.com/2015/1/27/7921463/google-facebookaccountable-for-hate-speech-france.
Pew Research Center, Those who get most political news from social media most likely to be under 30 (2019), https://www.pewresearch.org.
PharmacyChecker.com, LLC v. National Association of Boards of Pharmacy, 530 F. Supp. 3d 301 (S.D.N.Y. 2021).
Zhanzi Qiu, Matthias Hemmje, and Erich Neuhold, 'ConSearch: Using hypertext contexts as search boundaries,' in *IEEE Advances in Digital Libraries 2000*, edited by Jeroen Hop-penbrouwers (IEEE Computer Society, 2000), p. 48.
Realcomp II, Ltd. v. FTC, 635 F.3d 815 (6th Cir. 2011).
Julia Reda, Extra copyright for news sites ("Link tax"), *juliareda.eu* (July 2017), https://www.juliareda.eu.
Regulation of the European Parliament and of the Council on contestable and fair markets in the digital sector, COM/2020/842, 23, *Official Journal* L 335 (Oct. 12, 2022), https://eur-lex.europa.eu/legal-content/EN/TXT/?uri=CELEX%3A32022R1925.
Reno v. ACLU, 521 U.S. 844 (1997).
Report of the Special Rapporteur on the Promotion and Protection of the Right to Freedom of Opinion and Expression, U.N. Doc. A/HRC/38/35 (July 6, 2018).
Evelyn Richards, 'Bush to unveil high-tech initiative: $2 billion computing project would include data "superhighway,'" *Washington Post* (September 7, 1989), p. F1.
Kevin Roose, YouTube cracks down on QAnon conspiracy theory, citing offline violence, *The New York Times* (October 15, 2020), https://www.nytimes.com/2020/10/15/technology/youtube-bans-qanon-violence.html.
J.H. Saltzer, D.P. Reed, and D.D. Clark, 'End-to-end arguments in system design,' 2 *ACM Transactions on Computer Systems* 227 (1984).
Santa Clara principles on transparency and accountability in content moderation (May 7, 2018), https://santaclaraprinciples.org/ and www.santaclaraprinciples.org/history/.
Scaling machine learning at Netflix, *Netflix Technology Blog* (February 13, 2023), https://netflixtechblog.com/scaling-media-machine-learning-at-netflix-f19b400243?source=collection_archive – 0.
Methaya Sirichit, 'Censorship by intermediary and moral rights: Strengthening authors' control over online expressions through the right of respect and integrity,' 1 *Journal of Law, Technology, and Public Policy* 54 (2015).
Software Rights Archive, LLC v. Facebook, Inc., 640 F. App'x 995 (Fed. Cir. September 2016).
Clare Southerton, Daniel Marshall, and Rob Cover, 'Restricted modes: Social media, content classification and LGBTQ sexual citizenship,' 23 *New Media & Society* 920 (2020), https://journals.sagepub.com/doi/pdf/10.1177/1461444820904362.
Phillip B. Stark, 'The effectiveness of Internet content filters,' 4 *I/S: A Journal of Law and Policy for the Information Society* 411 (2008).
Story v. Holcombe, 23 F. Cas. 171 (C.C.D. Ohio 1847) (No. 13,497).
Stowe v. Thomas, 23 F. Cas. 201 (C.C.E.D. Pa. 1853).

Strahan v. Newberry [In re Newbery], [1773] 98 Eng. Rep. 913 (Ch.),

Nadine Strossen, 'Foreword, Should cyberspace be a free speech zone?: Filters, "family friendliness," and the First Amendment,' 15 *New York Law School Law Journal of Human Rights* i (1998).

Danny Sullivan, Google PageRank, meet Yahoo Web Rank!, *Search Engine Watch* (April 2, 2004), http://searchenginewatch.com/3334891.

Danny Sullivan, Google: Can the Marcia Brady of search stay sweet?, *Search Engine Watch* (September 3, 2000), http://searchenginewatch.com/2164991.

Danny Sullivan, More evil than Dr. Evil?, *Search Engine Watch (SEW)* (November 1, 1999), http://searchenginewatch.com/2167621.

Seth Sutel, Viacom sues YouTube for $1 billion, *Associated Press* (March 13, 2007), http://forums.eog.com/showthread.php/76795-Viacom-Sues-YouTube-for-1-Billion.

Nicholas Suzor, *Lawless: The Secret Rules That Govern our Digital Lives* (Cambridge University Press, 2019).

Nicholas Thompson and Fred Vogelstein, Inside the two years that shook Facebook – and the world, *Wired* (February 12, 2018), https://www.wired.com/story/inside-facebook-mark-zuckerberg-2-years-of-hell.

Katharine Trendacosta, Unfiltered: How YouTube's content id discourages fair use and dictates what we see online, *Electronic Frontier Foundation* (December 2020), https://www.eff.org/unfiltered.

Rebecca Tushnet, 'All of this has happened before and all of this will happen again: Innovation in copyright licensing,' 29 *Berkeley Technology Law Journal* 1447 (2014).

Natasha Tusikov, *Chokepoints: Global Private Regulation of the Internet* (University of California Press, 2017).

Twitter, Inc. v. Taamneh, 143 S. Ct. 1206 (2023).

United States v. Harriss, 347 U.S. 612 (1954).

United States v. National Association of Realtors, 73 Fed. Reg. 36,104 (DOJ June 25, 2008).

U.S. Department of Justice, Google forfeits $500 million generated by online ads & prescription drug sales by Canadian pharmacies (August 24, 2011), https://www.justice.gov/opa/google-forfeits-500-million-generated-online-ads-prescription-drug-sales-canadian-online.

Jennifer Urban and Laura Quilter, Efficient Process or "Chilling Effects"? Takedown Notices under Section 512 of the Digital Millennium Copyright Act (2005), http://mylaw.usc.edu/documents/512Rep-ExecSum_out.pdf.

US Telecom Association v. FCC, 825 F.3d 674 (D.C. Cir. 2016).

Verizon v. FCC, 740 F.3d 623 (D.C. Cir. 2014).

Vermont Right to Life Committee, Inc. v. Sorrell, 758 F.3d 118 (2d Cir. 2014), *cert. denied*, 135 S. Ct. 949 (2015).

Viacom v. YouTube, 676 F.3d 19 (2d Cir. 2012).

Vidmar and Anderson, 'History of Internet search tools,' in *Encyclopedia of Library and Information Science*, Vol. 71, edited by Allen Kent (Marcel Dekker, 2002), pp. 154–55.

Daniel Villareal, Two web-lebrities accuse Instagram and Twitter of censoring gay and male sexual content, *Hornet* (November 2, 2017), https://hornet.com/stories/twitter-instagram-censorship-gay/.

David Vise and Mark Malseed, *The Google Story* (Penguin, 2008).

Daniel J. Weitzner, 'Yelling "filter" on the crowded net: The implications of user control technologies,' in *The V-Chip Debate: Content Filtering from Television to the Internet*, edited by Monroe Price (Routledge, 2013), https://books.google.com/books?hl=en&lr=&id=4yMuAgAAQBAJ&oi=fnd&pg=PT360&dq="user+empowerment+technologies"&ots=4nBHGdCXrW&sig=6ksHNS6oWI3zimzC-C5O18HqwyA#v=onepage&q="user%20empowerment%20technologies"&f=false.

Alice Witt, Nicholas Suzor, and Anna Higgins, 'The rule of law on Instagram: An evaluation of the moderation of images depicting women's bodies,' 42 *University of New South Wales Law Journal* 557 (2019).

Worley v. Florida Secretary of State, 717 F.3d 1238 (11th Cir. 2013).
Jillian C. York, How LGBTQ+ content is censored under the guise of "sexually explicit," *Electronic Frontier Foundation Deeplinks* (August 18, 2021), https://www.eff.org/deeplinks/2021/08/how-lgbtq-content-censored-under-guise-sexually-explicit.
Emily Yost, 'Queering the landscape: Decriminalizing consent and remapping the permissible geographies of intimacy,' 19 *University of Maryland Law Journal of Race, Religion, Gender and Class* 201, 226–27 (2019).
YouTube – Content ID (2014), https://www.youtube.com/t/contentid.
Peter K. Yu, Promoting internet freedom through the copyright system, *US Embassy* (July 29, 2010), http://iipdigital.usembassy.gov/st/english/publication/2010/07/20100727141034enelrahc5.498904e-02.html.
Jonathan Zittrain, *The Future of the Internet – and How to Stop It* (Yale University Press, 2008).

2 Carceral Communications Law

Freedom and Censors in the Public Sphere

Communications Law as a Subset of Carceral Public Law[1]

For most of Western history, and much of world history, communications law was a minor part of a broader system of political domination. Without receding into the mists of the first millennium B.C. or the history of the Roman Republic, the religious roots of Anglo-American law deserve some attention. Both English and United States common law were once said to be grounded in biblical law, including the ancient offenses of blasphemy, sodomy, adultery, fornication, lewdness or lustfulness, bearing false witness or libel, and sloth or vagrancy.[2]

One penalty for common-law crimes was incarceration. Originally this was not the limit in English law for punishment of some of the offenses just mentioned. Mutilation, suspension from stocks, whipping, hard labor as in *Les Misérables*, stretching on the rack, and beheading were on the menu of the king, the sheriff, and the mob.[3] Solitary confinement was also available in most cases of felony and some of misdemeanor.[4] This practice still occurs frequently in the United States, with an estimated 100,000 persons undergoing it on any given day in 2017. The psychological consequences are severe and rivaled mainly by those associated with rape in prison, which affects many prisoners who are not in solitary confinement.[5] Reports related to the U.S. war on (some) drugs have discussed how prisoners are often exposed to new diseases, and may spread them to the rest of society, as a result of their confinement and/or abuse.[6]

In the *Book of Matthew*, the Apostle Peter is granted a commission from Jesus Christ that served to justify extensive secular power against heresy on the part of the church, for Peter was told he had "the keys of the kingdom of heaven: and whatsoever thou shalt bind on earth shall be bound in heaven: and whatsoever thou shalt loose on earth shall be loosed in heaven."[7] In Paul's Letter to the Romans, every person is committed to the authority of "the higher powers," who like Peter (but with much wider implications, because local lords and chiefs and not simply the Church would be included) are called "ordained of God." "Whosoever therefore resisteth [a government's] power, resisteth the ordinance of God: and they that resist shall receive to themselves damnation. . . . For [the lord or chief] is the minister of God to thee for good" and "beareth not the sword in vain: for he is the minister of God, a revenger to execute wrath upon him that doeth evil."[8]

DOI: 10.4324/9781003496106-3

As the early modern university began to take shape in Paris and elsewhere, St. Thomas Aquinas and others melded biblical principles with Aristotelian metaphysics and politics to shape centuries of political theory and jurisprudence. For Aquinas, reason and faith counsel each of us to play our part in a predestined and regimented cosmological order. With Aristotle, he declares that "just as in virtue of the divinely established natural order the lower natural things need to be subject to the movement of the higher, so too in human affairs, in virtue of the order of natural and divine law, inferior are bound to obey their superiors."[9] Veering from that order is thus sedition, and not only a crime but a sin connected to damnation.[10] With the Bible generally ("By me kings reign, and princes decree justice," Proverbs 8:15) and with Paul in particular (whom Aquinas calls "the Apostle"), theology connects rebellion of any sort with divine justice. Aquinas remarks that "even an unjust law . . . is derived from the eternal law, since all power is from the Lord God, according to Romans."[11]

A different theory of society that became known as liberal made several opposing points. First, its proponents such as John Locke and William Blackstone argued that society was instituted by human beings for their mutual benefit, rather than being preplanned in heaven.[12] Second, the theory was that natural rights preceded governments, and while they could be surrendered in large part by entering into governed societies, these rights should be codified in common-law judgments and the provisions of statutes or writs like the Magna Carta.[13] Third, it suggested that the people had the right to resist governors who violate the terms of the original social compact – its "constitution" – by attempting "to take away, and destroy the property [broadly, life, liberty, and estate] of the people, or to reduce them to slavery under arbitrary power."[14]

In continental European thought, aspects of liberalism appear as freedom of the will, political community, radical evil, objectification or reification of Spirit or The Other, and construction of a standing-reserve or reserve army of dominated persons. Liberalism grew out of the thought of David Hume and Immanuel Kant in two directions: a progressive one commencing with the constitutional liberalism of G.W.F. Hegel and continuing with the socialism of Karl Marx and so on, and an individualist one commencing with the quietism of Arthur Schopenhauer and continuing in the existentialism of Friedrich Nietzsche; the two threads reconverged with Jean-Paul Sartre, Michel Foucault, Emmanuel Levinas, and other late existentialist and post-structuralist/post-modernist thinkers.[15]

Before the modern First Amendment established tests like the chilling effect, malice, content-neutrality, and the like, continental legal thought had embodied concepts of expressive and literary freedoms in the author's and artist's "moral right" of integrity.[16] I will return to these in the last chapter.

Digital media revolutionize communications and publishing infrastructure.[17] Digital media supplant traditional media's communications model of "one to many" with the Internet's model of "many to many," which allows every reader to become an author, direct distribution to replace intermediary censorship and editorial control, and public-interested publication to displace some commercial dictates.[18] They advance First Amendment aims of ensuring that ordinary citizens may exercise their liberties of speech and the press to express themselves individually and criticize and poke fun at others in a shared culture.[19] Copyright and trademark case law and theory reflect this First Amendment principle that citizens are not destined to remain passive consumers but are entitled to talk back to cultural and political imagery and arguments.[20]

The First Amendment states that "Congress shall make no law abridging the freedom of speech, or of the press."[21] A diligent inquiry into this question of what this means reveals that the persons who drafted and ratified this amendment intended Congress to pass only those laws that did not "abridge[e]" press freedom any further than the common law of Britain and the American colonies did in 1791. Madison, for example, justified the Copyright Clause of the Constitution, notwithstanding its restrictions on the trade in ideas, on the basis that copyright was acknowledged at common law in Britain.[22] Jefferson, who pleaded for an explicit Bill of Rights protecting basic freedoms when other founders such as Alexander Hamilton dismissed the idea,[23] similarly admitted that the common-law offense of libel could continue to be heard in the courts, which would restrict the right of the press to publish "false facts" injurious to the lives, property, or reputation of others.[24] Finally, when Hamilton contended that the Constitution granted Congress "no power by which restrictions [on the liberty of the press] may be imposed," surely he meant none beyond those applicable as common law.[25]

Communicative Freedom as a Filter of Filters, a Censor of the Censors

The "freedom of the press" under the First Amendment was supposed to be wide. Even before the American Revolution, in the 13 British colonies, this freedom "has not been confined to the strict limits of the common law" but extended to "*freely examining* public conduct and measures," for in a republic "the censorial power is in the people over the Government, and not in the Government over the people."[26] Its key framer, James Madison, affirmed that the First Amendment would not leave the press to the whim of Congress:

> The people shall not be deprived or abridged of their right to speak, to write, or to publish their sentiments; and the freedom of the press, as one of the great bulwarks of liberty, shall be *inviolable*. . ..
>
> The right of freedom of speech is secured; the liberty of the press is expressly declared to be *beyond the reach of this Government*.[27]

Madison clearly stated that "the freedom of the press" means the right to be "exempt . . . not only from previous restraint of the executive, as in Great Britain, but from legislative restraint also; [and] . . . from the subsequent penalty of laws."[28]

The nature of an experiment in self-government prompted broader formulations of freedom of the press than had prevailed in England, where from John Milton to William Blackstone this freedom was mainly about press licensing. Under British law, writers might suffer all manner of civil and criminal liability, particularly when it came to the monarchy or the Empire's wars.[29]

The "premise" of a more democratic order in 1776 or 1791 was that "absolute sovereignty" resided in the people to change their legislators, not in the legislators to change the people.[30] Popular sovereignty required an even greater, not lesser, "degree of freedom in the use of the press" than in England.[31] The colonists who favored a new U.S. Constitution advanced a near-absolute prohibition on Congress regulating speech and the press.[32] Madison noted with concern "the parochial, self-interested popular majorities whom [legislators] represented."[33] Thomas Jefferson advocated to Madison that the Bill of Rights be amended to include an provision that: "The people shall not be deprived or abridged of their right to speak, to write, or *otherwise* to publish anything but false facts affecting injuriously the life, liberty, property or reputation of others, or affecting the peace of the confederacy with foreign nations."[34] Thus, Jefferson "den[ied] the power of Congress 'to controul the freedom of the press.'"[35] For these reasons, the author of one of the earliest authoritative treatises on the Constitution and American law, St. George Tucker, believed that the First Amendment conferred an "*unlimited* right to [comment on public issues], either by speaking, writing, printing, or by any other mode of publishing" and that "the smallest infringement of the rights guaranteed by this article, must threaten the total subversion of the government."[36]

One might suggest that the First Amendment fades into the background when private law concerns such as copyright, contracts, or competition law arise, rather than treason or sedition. Yet First Amendment review should not disappear when new frameworks or modalities of speech control are adopted by Congress or state legislatures.[37] The First Amendment, being supreme federal law and later-adopted than the Copyright Act of 1790, should govern a nation.[38] Even as laws emerge that were adopted in quasi-democratic fashion and are generally applicable, there must be judicial review to measure each law's necessity and cut back its overreach.

A Human Right to Maximize Internet Access for Human Development

In 2018, a few lines posted as a comment on a Swiss article about Hungarian politician Victor Orbán gave rise to a decision by a Berlin court, with potentially far-reaching implications. The Hungarian prime minister had told a German daily that the interest in creating "parallel societies" allegedly shown by Muslim migrants to Europe meant they were "invaders" rather than "refugees."[39] The Facebook case was not about this offensive and potentially discriminatory report, however. It involved a user comment that the "Germans are becoming ever more stupid" on this topic because "they are every day bombarded with fake news from the left-wing media system about 'skilled workers,' declining unemployment rates or Trump."[40]

Even though the user was banned for only a month from Facebook, he retained an attorney, who persuaded a court to rule that Facebook had no right to censor him.[41] In such disputes, websites like Facebook typically emphasize the complexities of "content moderation," a task that manages to sound simultaneously technical and innocuous or beneficial. The phrase itself is a euphemism for effectively erasing the moment in which the freedom of speech is being censored as one that might spark resistance, solidarity, and demands for equal treatment. It emerged under the twin pressures of congressional efforts to impose speech (aka content) filters on the Internet via machine-readable ratings for websites, and surveillance and deterrence of expression insufficiently supportive of the Global War on Terror and its "You're with us or with the terrorists" credo.[42] Websites and apps (referred to together using the intimidating label "platforms") summarize their efforts to ban nudity, LGBT content, pornography, graphic violence, support for terrorism, news about war or terrorism, and other "hate" or "offensive" speech as Community Standards, Terms of Service, or Trust and Safety guidelines. Some courts, inside Germany and outside of it, deem the standards of Facebook and other websites and apps to be deserving of deference, and/or to appropriately balance freedom and security.[43]

One way to read the German judgment is that the user's fundamental right of freedom of expression should override Facebook's desire to impose its own will to shape public discourse. Taken at is most literal, the basic norm involved was the freedom to have a mind, or to speak one's own mind and not another person's.[44] In systems recognizing the state's obligation not to interfere with or encroach upon the freedom of expression, every person has a right to live in a free society, a right that binds private as well as public officials.

A lot of lip service is paid in the United States, especially by public officials, to the importance of freedom of speech and religion. Often other values are thrown into the mix, such as due process, the rule of law, the sovereignty of the people, fair play, and the accountability of public figures to voters and, in the case of media and telecommunications firms, their audiences.

All too often, however, freedom and the rule of law are shunted to one side when the efficient operation of large institutions is concerned. Government broadcasters exclude third party and insurgent major-party candidates from debate stages, a practice condemned by Supreme Court justices as encouraging "government [to] effectively wield the power to eliminate a political candidate from all consideration by the voters."[45] Private broadcasters leverage valuable government licenses into carefully managed news coverage that denies unpopular views of significant access to the public.[46] Recently, courts have concluded that even if the arguments of independent and third-party candidates are cleansed from public view, resulting in the rigging of presidential and other elections, that is not a "cognizable legal injury."[47] Senior civil servants in policy jobs might take solace by working within the system, blowing the whistle on corruption and mismanagement internally, but their First Amendment rights have been gutted as well – in the interests of managerial efficiency.[48] Lest too many criminal subjects exercise their right to confront their accusers and demand a unanimous jury verdict of guilty, prosecutors and legislators threaten those merely accused with such long sentences of imprisonment that the vast majority of criminal charges end with guilty pleas, sending the jury system into a decline.[49]

Common and Public Spaces

For personal freedom to flourish, even the freedom of thought, the political opposition and the means of communication must be kept free. The German Basic Law, like much of the rest of contemporary European and international law, could only exist as a result of the liberation of Europe by the United States of America, the British Empire, and the Soviet Union in 1944–1945.[50] It origins go back to 1948, along with the passage of the Universal Declaration of Human Rights, work on the binding provisions on the International Covenant on Civil and Political Rights, the signing of the Genocide Convention, and the initial adoption of draft conventions on war crimes.[51] The Judgment of the International Military Tribunal at Nuremberg had, the previous year, described the absence of civil rights in Europe prior to the liberation as follows:

> Through the effective control of the radio and the press, the German people, during the years which followed 1933, were subjected to the most intensive propaganda in furtherance of the regime. Hostile criticism, indeed criticism of any kind, was forbidden, and the severest penalties were imposed on those who indulged in it.
>
> Independent judgment, based on freedom of thought, was rendered quite impossible. . . .
>
> Even persons who were only suspected of opposing any of the policies of the German occupation authorities were arrested, and on arrest were interrogated by the Gestapo [the Nazi state police] and the SD [Nazi intelligence] in the most shameful manner. . . .
>
> The brutal suppression of all opposition to the German occupation was not confined to severe measures against suspected members of resistance movements themselves, but [it] was also extended to their families.[52]

The Basic Law and the International Covenant on Civil and Political Rights (ICCPR) share a significant aspect. The former states, in part: "Every person shall have the right freely to express and disseminate his opinions in speech, writing and pictures, and to inform himself without hindrance from generally accessible sources."[53] The ICCPR, elegantly, goes a bit further: "Everyone shall have the right to freedom of expression; this right shall include freedom to seek, receive and impart information and ideas of all kinds, regardless of frontiers, either orally, in writing or in print, in the form of art, or through any other media of his choice."[54] The right to receive information is freed to some extent from being in "generally accessible sources," and expression of facts not amounting to an opinion is covered, as are art and auditory media. The right to be informed about the world is also expressly made transnational in scope. The right to "hold opinions without interference" is also separately specified, which may have implications for times when an individual has *some* alternative means to express an opinion or ideas, but the state has attempted – with or without corporate or non-state support – to intervene.[55] Finally, these rights are subject to limitations, but these must be set forth in advance by laws and be "necessary" to protect one of six human interests: the rights of others, the reputation of others, national security, public order, public health, or public morals.[56]

There is no statement in the Basic Law or the ICCPR that the expression or receipt of information should be subject to any ideological or partisan litmus test. It is understandable, placing oneself in the shoes of those deliberating on new basic laws in the early decades after Nazi terror and aggression ended, why criticism of a political regime would not be made an exception to the freedom to speak and develop one's mind, and why propaganda aiding the state (or the current occupants of its offices) would not be granted a privileged position.

The Frankfurt School or Institute for Social Research attempted to theorize aspects of Europe's descent into homicidal manias and the prospects for a more peaceful and legitimate world order after Nazism. Its participants – notably Theodor Adorno, Max Horkheimer, Herbert Marcuse, and Franz Neumann – published some of the more influential attempts to diagnose the ills of emerging totalitarianism by studying qualitative data from the mass culture and the economy.[57]

Most relevant for my purposes, Jürgen Habermas studied aspects of modern culture and economics as a post-doctoral student advised by Adorno[58] and turned his attention decades later to the Basic Law and to the freedom of expression in general. Habermas analyzes freedom of expression as a precondition of a non-totalitarian system of governance, arguing that a "system of rights states the conditions under which the forms of communication necessary for the genesis of legitimate law can be legally institutionalized."[59] He claims that without procedurally just enactment, preceded and achieved by rational agreement rather than mere force, law lacks legitimacy.[60] Rational legislation issues from "communicative power" rather than mere police or military power, or brainwashing of some kind.[61]

Drawing on the ideas of John Stuart Mill, Immanuel Kant, and John Dewey, Habermas conceives of an autonomous human being as governing himself or herself by participating in an active public sphere that informs each individual about current affairs – and through public opinion formation, that informs and disciplines the legislator.[62] The freedom to inform oneself, to seek out the ideas of one's fellow subjects, and to express what one learns and generates alone or in association with a group of more or less like-minded persons is a prerequisite of rational laws. As one German court stated in addressing the deletion of a Facebook comment and a 30-day ban of its author, a private actor must respect the "essence of freedom of expression" in order to ensure the survival of constitutional and "democratic opinion-forming."[63]

The First Amendment, as articulated by James Madison, might seem to be a good vehicle with which to deliver the personal autonomy and open debate that Habermas sees as important in a non-totalitarian society. Unfortunately, the Supreme Court and lower federal courts did not apply either an originalist theory or a freedom-of-information theory of the First Amendment for most of U.S. history. Indeed, they still do not do so in many cases. Rather, they employ "ad hoc" interest balancing, with government interests weighed against the suppression of speech, the press, or assemblies.

Prominent jurists and scholars objected to ad hoc balancing. They opined that originalist applications of the Constitution and Bill of Rights would be frequently more protective of liberty and democracy than such subjective balancing or judicial findings of "reasonableness."[64] Justice William J. Brennan in particular proved the advantage of a careful attention to the intent and historical context of the First Amendment over either ad hoc or "definitional" balancing. He introduced the analysis of legislation for overbreadth and vagueness, which chill protected speech, rather than simply asking whether the First Amendment allowed regulation of the category of speech affected because there is a significant government interest like decency, efficiency of public or private projects, regulation of noise or traffic, promotion of safety, etc.[65]

Bringing the Carceral Police State to Cyberlaw

The rejection of broad First Amendment rights leads to the subjective balancing of speech interests with government interests and to narrower the domains of personal autonomy and political freedom. By 2023, nearly three in four Americans told a pollster that their country was "becoming a police state."[66] One might chalk up this high number to people associating a police state not so much with a totalitarian or carceral state as a country that has police, jails, and penal laws, which the United States certainly does. However, those surveyed were told that a *police state* means a "tyrannical government that engages in mass surveillance, censorship, ideological indoctrination, and targeting of political opponents."[67]

The next two chapters describe the operation of some forms of the censorship, indoctrination, surveillance, and political targeting that Americans are debating. The final chapter identifies the pillars of a free and open Internet for everyone to use for self-expression and public debate.

Notes

1 Parts of this chapter were previously published as 'Of blogs, ebooks, and broadband: access to digital media as a First Amendment right,' 35 *Hofstra Law Review* 1519 (2007).

2 E.g., Bowers v. Hardwick, 478 U.S. 186 (1986) (discussing "sodomy"); Loving v. Virginia, 388 U.S. 1 (1977) (discussing adultery, fornication, and so-called anti-miscegenation laws); Manual Enterprises, Inc. v. Day, 370 U.S. 478 (1962) (discussing indecency, lewdness, filth, vulgarity, etc., as well as sedition and inciting unrest). Cf. New York v. Ferber, 458 U.S. 747, 754 (1982) ("The original States provided for the prosecution of libel, blasphemy, and profanity"); Adderly v. Florida, 385 U.S. 39, 56 (1966) ("Today a trespass law is used to penalize people for exercising a constitutional right. Tomorrow a disorderly conduct statute, a breach-of-the-peace statute, a vagrancy statute will be put to the same end. . . . [S]uch arrests are usually sought to be justified by some legitimate function of government.") (Douglas, J., joined by Warren, the Chief Justice, Brennan J., and Fortas, J., dissenting); State v. Harlowe, 174 Wash. 227, 24 P. 2d 601, 603 (1933) (where statute made it a crime to be vagrants or "lewd, disorderly or dissolute persons," court overrode objection to ban on "a state of being," stating: "Society recognizes that vagrancy is a parasitic disease, which, if allowed to spread, will sap the life of that upon which it feeds.").

3 Sir William Blackstone, *Commentaries on the Laws of England . . . The Twentieth Edition, Incorporating the Alterations Down to the Present Time. By James Stewart*, Vol. 4 (John Murray, 1862), pp. 439–42.
4 Ibid.
5 Charlie Eastaugh, *Unconstitutional Solitude: Solitary Confinement and the US Constitution's Evolving Standards of Decency* (Springer, 2017), p. xlii–liv. The Department of Justice estimated that more than 200,000 inmates were sexually abused on an annual basis in 2008. E.g., Human Rights Watch, US: Comments submitted to Department of Justice on proposed standards to end prison rape (April 3, 2011), https://www.hrw.org/news/2011/04/04/us-comments-submitted-department-justice-proposed-standards-end-prison-rape. Nearly 100,000 may be suffering solitary confinement, which can devastate the psyche of a person. Eastaugh, previous, pp. xlii–iii; Sridevi Nambiar, UN Committee on torture says U.S. must reform its use of solitary confinement, *Solitary Watch* (December 5, 2014), http://solitarywatch.com/2014/12/05/un-committee-against-torture-says-u-s-must-reform-its-use-of-solitary-confinement/. See also, Brian O. Hogan, et al., 'History of solitary confinement is associated with post-traumatic stress disorder symptoms among individuals recently released from prison,' 95 *Journal of Urban Health* (2017), https://www.researchgate.net/publication/314484304_History_of_Solitary_Confinement_Is_Associated_with_Post-Traumatic_Stress_Disorder_Symptoms_among_Individuals_Recently_Released_from_Prison.
6 The Global Commission on Drug Policy, The Negative Impact of the War on Drugs on Public Health: The Hidden Hepatitis C Epidemic (2013), pp. 11–16; Human Rights Watch, Averting an imminent catastrophe: Recommendations to US local, state and federal officials to address COVID-19 in jails and prisons (April 29, 2020), https://www.hrw.org/news/2020/04/29/averting-imminent-catastrophe-recommendations-us-local-state-and-federal-officials (noting that COVID-19 spread exponentially in jails, as it did elsewhere in the United States, and that release of some infected prisoners might present "a specific and known risk of harm to others that cannot be managed through measures other than detention," with some prosecutors specifically raising this prospect early on).
7 Matthew 16:18–19.
8 Romans 13:1–2, 4.
9 Thomas Aquinas, *On Law, Morality, and Politics*, edited by Richard Regan and William Baumgarth (Hackett, 1988), p. 234.
10 Ibid, 231.
11 Ibid., 38.
12 John Locke, *Second Treatise of Government*, edited by C.B. MacPherson (Hackett, 1980) [1690] p. 8. See also, *ibid.*, p. 51 ("government has no other end but the preservation of property"); ibid., at 9 (to resist destruction); ibid., p. 68 (common good); William Blackstone, *Commentaries on the Laws of England*, Vol. 1 (University of Chicago Press, 1979 [1765]), p. *47 ("wants and fears of individuals" the "true" basis of society); ibid., pp. *121–22 (to "the general advantage of the publick" and the "common utility").
13 E.g., Smothers v. Gresham Transfer, Inc., 23 P. 2d 333, 342–44 (Or. 2001) (citing Julius Goebel, Jr., *Constitutional History and Law*, 38 Columbia Law Review 555, 565 (1938); Kermit L. Hall, *The Magic Mirror: Law in American History* (Oxford University Press, 1998), pp. 57–58; 1 F.N. Thorpe, *Constitutional History of the American People, 1776–1850* (1898), p. 38; 1 Blackstone, previous n. 12, pp. *56, *123).
14 Locke, previous n. 12, p. 111.
15 Michael Allen Gillespie, *Nietzsche's Final Teaching* (University of Chicago Press, 2019), pp. 34–38, 162, 190.
16 E.g., Immanuel Kant, *Of the Injustice of Counterfeiting Books* (Illustrated) (Delphi Classics, 2017 [1785]).
17 Reno v. ACLU, 521 U.S. 844, 868–70 (1997); compare, Turner Broadcasting System, Inc. v. FCC, 512 U.S. 622, 626 (1994); Lorain Journal v. United States, 342 U.S. 143, 146, 149 (1951); Byars v. Bluff City News Co., 609 F.2d 843, 845–47, 856–58 (6th Cir. 1979).

18 E.g., Niva Elkin-Koren, 'Cyberlaw and social change: A democratic approach to copyright law in cyberspace,' 14 *Cardozo Arts and Entertainment Law Journal* 215, 259 (1996); Mike Godwin, *Cyber Rights: Defending Free Speech in the Digital Age* (1998); Margaret Chon, 'Erasing race?: A critical race feminist view of Internet identity-shifting,' 3 *Journal of Gender Race and Justice* 439, 446 (2000).

19 E.g., Zacchini v. Scripps-Howard Broad. Co., 433 U.S. 562, 576–82 (1977) (Powell, J., joined by Brennan, J., and Marshall, J., dissenting); *Harper & Row*, 471 U.S. at 590–98 (Brennan, J., joined by White, J., and Marshall, J., dissenting); San Francisco Arts & Athletics v. United States Olympic Cmte., 483 U.S. 522, 569 (1987) (Brennan, J., dissenting); L.L. Bean, Inc. v. Drake Publishers, Inc., 811 F.2d 26, 29 (1st Cir. 1987); White v. Samsung Elec. Am., Inc., 989 F.2d 1512, 1513–14 (9th Cir. 1993) (Kozinski, J., dissenting) (collecting cases); Wendt v. Host Int'l, Inc., 197 F.3d 1284, 1288–89 (9th Cir. 1999) (Kozinski, J., dissenting) (collecting cases); Suntrust Bank v. Houghton Mifflin Co., 252 F.3d 1165, *substituted opinion at* 268 F.3d 1257, 1277 (11th Cir. 2001); Mattel, Inc. v. MCA Records, 296 F.3d 894, 901 (9th Cir. 2002); Nissan Motor Co. v. Nissan Computer Corp., 378 F.3d 1002, 1017 (9th Cir. 2004); Lamparello v. Falwell, 420 F.3d 309 (4th Cir. 2005); Floyd Abrams, 'First Amendment and copyright,' 35 *Journal of the Copyright Society* 1, 11 (1987); C. Edwin Baker, 'First Amendment limits on Copyright,' 55 Vand. Law Review 891, 893, 900, 908 (2002); Julie Cohen, 'A right to read anonymously: A closer look at "Copyright Management" in cyberspace,' 28 *Connecticut Law Review* 981 (1996); Stephen Fraser, 'The conflict between the First Amendment and copyright law and its impact on the Internet,' 16 *Cardozo Arts and Entertainment Law Journal* 1 (1998); Arlen W. Langvardt, 'Trademark rights and First Amendment wrongs: Protecting the former without committing the latter,' 83 *Trademark Reporter* 633, 651–52 (1993); David Lange, 'Copyright and the Constitution in the age of intellectual property,' 1 *Journal of Intellectual Property Law* 119, 133–34 (1994); Dorean M. Koenig, 'Joe Camel and the First Amendment: The dark side of copyrighted and trademark-protected icons,' 11 *Thomas M. Cooley Law Review* 803 (1994); Pamela Samuelson, 'Mapping the digital public domain: Threats and opportunities,' 66 *Law and Contemporary Problems* 147, 169–70 (2003); Alfred C. Yen, 'A First Amendment perspective on the idea/expression dichotomy and copyright in a work's "total concept and feel,"' 38 *Emory Law Journal* 393, 432–33 (1989); Diane Leenheer Zimmerman, 'Information as speech, information as goods: Some thoughts in marketplaces and the Bill of Rights,' 33 *William and Mary Law Review* 665, 681 (1992); Diane Leenheer Zimmerman, 'Is there a right to have something to say? One view of the public domain,' 73 *Fordham Law Review* 297, 348–49 (2004).

20 E.g., *Suntrust Bank*, 252 F.3d 1165 (First Amendment rights of an author to use existing characters to express new message would be violated by injunction based on copyright in the characters); Abrams, previous n. 19, at 11 (First Amendment may be offended by injunctions in copyright cases); Baker, 'First Amendment Limits,' previous n. 19, at 893, 900, 908 (First Amendment should condemn as unconstitutional any effort by "one private party to limit another's speech"); Lange, previous n. 19, pp. 133–34 (urging a revival of First Amendment's role in curtailing ability of intellectual property laws to censor creativity); Koenig, previous n. 19 (arguing that overbroad trademark rights threaten free speech); Cohen, 'Right to Read,' previous n. 19 (copyright owners' efforts to monitor readers of their work and prevent them from copying or printing it out for incorporation into new works are objectionable from the standpoint of First Amendment); Yen, previous n. 19, pp. 432–33 (maintaining that First Amendment values have vital role to play in preserving "basic rights of expression" against chilling effect of overbroad copyrights); Zimmerman, 'Information as Speech,' previous n. 19, p. 681 (expansion of intellectual property doctrines has threatened First Amendment values by encroaching upon public domain or linguistic "common"); Zimmerman, 'Is there a right,' previous n. 19, at 348–349 (judges should use First Amendment to prevent copyrights from censoring thought and communication among citizens and friends).

Cf. Zacchini, 433 U.S. at 576–82 (Powell, J., joined by Brennan, J., and Marshall, J., dissenting) (declaring that First Amendment should protect news broadcasts from certain state law intellectual property claims); *Wendt*, 197 F.3d at 1288–9 (Kozinski, J., dissenting) (criticizing use of intellectual property laws to "snuff out creativity" in form of "literary work," which is "worthy of the highest First Amendment protection from intrusive state laws"); *White*, 989 F.2d at 1513–14 (Kozinski, J., dissenting) (overprotecting intellectual property amounts to unconstitutional interference with freedom of speech); *L.L. Bean*, 811 F.2d at 29 (First Amendment forbids use of trademarks to "quash an unauthorized use of the mark by another who is communicating ideas or expressing points of view") (citation omitted).

21 U.S. Const., Am. I.

22 James Madison, 'Federalist 43 (Madison),' in *The Federalist Papers*, edited by Clinton Rossiter (1961), pp. 271–72. *See also* Wheaton v. Peters, 33 U.S. 591, 602 (1834) (argument for appellants).

23 'Letter from Thomas Jefferson to James Madison (December 20, 1787),' The Founders' Constitution, 2005, http://press-pubs.uchicago.edu/founders/documents/v1ch14s30.html; 'Letter from Thomas Jefferson to President George Washington (September 9, 1792),' in Jared Sparks, *The Writings of George Washington, Being His Correspondence, Addresses, Messages and Other Papers, Official and Private* (1838), pp. 517, 521.

24 'Letter from Thomas Jefferson to James Madison (August 28, 1789),' in *Papers of Thomas Jefferson*, Vol. 15 (1903), p. 367, http://press-pubs.uchicago.edu/founders/documents/amendI_speechs15.html. *See also* Thomas Jefferson, *Notes on the State of Virginia* (1784), http://press-pubs.uchicago.edu/founders/documents/amendI_religions40.html.

25 Alexander Hamilton, 'Federalist 84 (Hamilton),' in *The Federalist Papers*, http://press-pubs.uchicago.edu/founders/documents/bill_of_rightss7.html ("[A bill of rights] would contain various exceptions to powers which are not granted. . . . Why for instance, should it be said, that the liberty of the press shall not be restrained, when no power is given by which restrictions may be imposed?").

26 New York Times Co. v. Sullivan, 376 U.S. 254, 274–75 (1964) (quoting James Madison, 'Report on the Virginia Resolutions,' in James Madison and Jonathan Elliott, *The Debates in the Several State Conventions on the Adoption of the Federal Constitution* (Elliot's Debates) (1799–1800), Vol. 4 (J.P. Lippincott & Co., 1836), p. 570, and James Madison, 'The President's Speech (House Debate), November 27, 1794,' 3 *Annals of Congress* 934 (1794), https://memory.loc.gov/ll/llac/004/0400/04650933.gif).

27 James Madison, 'Amendments to Constitution (House Debate), June 8, 1789,' 1 *Annals of Congress* 434, 738, http://press-pubs.uchicago.edu/founders/documents/amendI_speechs14.html (emphasis added). He also stated that: "'In every state, probably, in the Union, the press has exerted a freedom in canvassing the merits and measures of public men, of every description, which has not been confined to the strict limits of the common law. On this footing the freedom of the press has stood; on this foundation it yet stands.'" *Sullivan*, 376 U.S. at 275 (quoting *The Debates in the Several State Conventions on the Adoption of the Federal Constitution (Elliot's Debates)* (1799–1800), Vol. 4 (1876), p. 570).

28 Thus, the "standard of [press] freedom in the United States" was intended to go at least as far as the common law's protection of the press, as supplemented by the actual practice of press freedom in Britain, where "public opinion" and fear of "impeachment" persuaded legislators to give much more leeway. *Ibid*, p. 569–70. Jefferson also rejected the notion that freedom of the press simply meant the absence of pre-publication censorship. Madison and Jefferson roundly condemned the Sedition Act of 1798, even though it was a subsequent punishment arguably within the enumerated powers of Congress over national security, and even though it still contained protections from truthful or unintentionally false speech or publications from subsequent punishment. *E.g.*, Leonard W. Levy, *Emergence of a Free Press* (1985), pp. xi, 13, 128–29, 201–03, 297, 303. Leonard Levy famously argued that Madison and Jefferson endorsed the Blackstonian definition of "freedom of the press" as a freedom against prior restraint, not subsequent

punishment. Leonard Levy, *Legacy of Suppression: Freedom of Speech and Press in Early American History* (1960); Leonard Levy, Jefferson And Civil Liberties (1963); Leonard Levy, 'Liberty and the First Amendment: 1790–1800,' 68 *American Historical Review* 22 (1962). This account, however, cannot explain Madison's express references to "subsequent penalty" as prohibited by the First Amendment. James Madison, 'Letter to Thomas Jefferson,' January 18, 1800, in *The Writings of James Madison, Vol. 6: 1790–1802*, edited by Gaillard Hunt (G.P Putnam's Sons, 1906), pp. 347, 387. Nor can it explain or to the legislative discretion of the British Parliament to regulate post-publication speech as being inconsistent with popular sovereignty in the United States, or to the importance of "unrestrained" speech that is not subject to "strict limits." James Madison, 'Report on the Virginia Resolutions,' in *The Writings of James Madison, Vol. IV: 1829–1836* (J.P. Lippincott Co., 1865), p. 544. Levy's account is also internally inconsistent in that he concedes that the Framers intended that Congress be prohibited from making any law establishing penalties for speech after it has been published, but in doing so used the very phrase "freedom of the press" that he claims means only freedom from prior restraint of the press. David A. Anderson, 'The Origins of the Press Clause,' 30 *UCLA Law Review* 455, 501–06 (1983).

29 In re Fries, 9 F. Cas. 826, 839–41 (C.C.D. Pa. 1799) (quoting William Blackstone, *Commentaries on the Laws of England*, Vol. 4 (The Clarendon Press, 1765), p. *151).

30 *Sullivan*, 376 U.S. at 274.

31 *Id.* at 275 (quoting *Elliot's Debates*, Vol. 4, pp. 569–70).

32 *E.g.*, Thomas Jefferson, 'Letter to James Madison,' November 17, 1798, in *The Works of Thomas Jefferson*, Vol. 8, edited by Paul Leicester Ford (G.P. Putnam's Sons, 1904), pp. 464–65 ("libels, falsehood, and defamation, equally with heresy and false religion, are withheld from the cognizance of federal tribunals"), *quoted in* Alan J. Koshner, 'The Founding Fathers and political speech: The First Amendment, the Press and the Sedition Act of 1798,' 6 *St. Louis University Public Law Review* 395, 398 (1987).

33 Jack N. Rakove, *Declaring Rights: A Brief History with Documents* (St. Martin's, 1998), p. 108.

34 Thomas Jefferson, 'Letter to James Madison, 1789,' in *Writings of Thomas Jefferson*, Vol. 7, edited by Paul Leicester Ford (G.P. Putnam's Sons, 1903), p. 450 (emphasis in original).

35 *Sullivan*, 323 U.S. at 276 (quoting Thomas Jefferson, 'Letter to Abigail Adams,' 1804, *quoted in* Dennis v. United States, 341 U.S. 494, 522, n. 4 (1951) (Frankfurter, J., concurring)). Thus, both he and Madison opposed the Alien and Sedition Acts of 1798, 1 Stat. 566, 570, 596, which prohibited intentionally making false statements as part of a combination to impede execution of U.S. law. *E.g.*, *Sullivan*, 376 U.S. at 274 ("The [Sedition] Act allowed the defendant the defense of truth, and provided that the jury were to be judges both of the law and the facts. Despite these qualifications, the Act was vigorously condemned as unconstitutional in an attack joined in by Jefferson and Madison."). Madison led an effort in the Virginia legislature to condemn the Sedition Act as claiming " 'a power . . . expressly and positively forbidden by [the First Amendment] – a power which, more than any other, ought to produce universal alarm, because it is levelled against the right of freely examining public characters and measures, and of free communication among the people thereon, which has ever been justly deemed the only effectual guardian of every other right.' " *Id.* at 276 (quoting *Elliot's Debates*, vol. 4, previous n. 31, at 553–54). "Jefferson, as President, pardoned those who had been convicted and sentenced under the Act and remitted their fines" *Id.* See also, Columbia Broadcasting System, Inc. v. Democratic National Committee, 412 U.S. 94, 156–57 (1973) (Douglas, J., concurring) (Jefferson believed Sedition Act to be "plainly unconstitutional"). Although Jefferson goes on in the passage from his letter to Abigail Adams quoted in *Sullivan* to concede the right of states to "controul" the press as at common law, it is not clear to what extent Madison agreed with that interpretation. As one scholar

puts it, Congress "was the Framers' primary target" but not necessarily "their sole target." Anderson, previous n. 28, p. 502. Most courts and commentators have agreed that the First Amendment was also "intended to limit the federal executive and judiciary," even though the purposeful use of the word "Congress" by the First Amendment and by Jefferson would permit federal executive censorship as much as state censorship. *Ibid.* See also, *New York Times v. United States*, 403 U.S. at 718–19. In any event, the adoption of the Fourteenth Amendment and the incorporation of First Amendment rights as fundamental rights protected against intrusion by the states extended the freedom of speech and the press before Congress to the states. *Cf. Thomas v. Review Bd. of the Indiana Employment Sec. Div.*, 450 U.S. 707, 721–22 (1981) (Rehnquist, J., dissenting) ("[T]he decision by this Court that the First Amendment was 'incorporated' into the Fourteenth Amendment and thereby made applicable against the States, Stromberg v. California, 283 U.S. 359 (1931); Cantwell v. Connecticut, 310 U.S. 296 (1940), . . . greatly expanded the number of statutes which would be subject to challenge under the First Amendment.").

36 St. George Tucker, *Blackstone's Commentaries*, vol. 1, at Appendix, Note D, § 12 (Birch and Carr, 1803) (emphasis added).

37 Lawrence Lessig, 'Creative economies,' 2006 *Michigan State Law Review* 33, 41 (2006).

38 See previous n. 35.

39 The Bridge Initiative, Victor Orban, https://bridge.georgetown.edu/wp-content/uploads/2019/11/Viktor-Orban-November-2019-factsheet.pdf (updated November 10, 2019).

40 David Meyer, Court tells Facebook: Stop deleting 'offensive' comment, *Vox* (April 13, 2018), https://www.zdnet.com/article/court-tells-facebook-stop-deleting-offensive-comment/. Vox's translation says "littered" rather than "bombarded," which does not sound quite right in English.

41 Ibid.; Landgericht Berlin, decision of March 23, 2018, Az. 31 O 21/18, https://www.gerichtsentscheidungen.berlin-brandenburg.de/jportal/portal/t/279b/bs/10/page/sammlung.psml?pid=Dokumentanzeige&showdoccase=1&js_peid=Trefferliste&documentnumber=1&numberofresults=1&fromdoctodoc=yes&doc.id=JURE180006250&doc.part=L&doc.price=0.0#focuspoint; Arno Lampman, Was Geht Vor: Die Meinungsfreiheit Oder Das Hausrecht Facebooks?, LHR Rechtsanwlte, September 19, 2018, https://www-lhr-law-de/magazin/social-media-recht/was-geht-vor-meinungsfreiheit-oder-das-hausrecht-facebooks/.

42 E.g., Lawrence Lessig, *Code and Other Laws of Cyberspace* (Basic Books, 1999), pp. 164–81; Paul Schiff Berman, 'Cyberspace and the state action debate: The cultural value of applying constitutional norms to private regulation,' 71 *University of Colorado Law Review* 1263, 1273–74 (2000); Seth Kreimer, 'Censorship by proxy: The First Amendment, intermediaries, and the problem of the weakest link,' 155 *University of Pennsylvania Law Review* 11, 22–26, 91–93 (2006).

43 E.g., Lampman, previous n. 41 (citing Landgericht Frankfurt, decision of September 10, 2018, Az. 2–03 O 310/18; Landgericht Heidelberg, decision of August 28, 2018–1 O 71/18; Oberlandesgericht Karlsruhe, decision of June 25, 2018, Az. 15 W 86/18).

44 Ibid. (citing Landgericht Berlin, previous n. 41; Oberlandesgericht Munich, decision of August 24, 2018, Az. 18 W 1294/18). The freedom of expression, in German, reads "*Meinungsfreiheit*," where "*freiheit*" is freedom and "*Meinung*" connotes both mind and "what's mine" (*mein*). A fundamental right, in German, is a "*Grundrecht*," where "*grund*" is both a ground and a foundation/fundamental, and "*recht*" connotes both right and justice.

45 Arkansas Educational Television Commission v. Forbes, 523 U.S. 666, 690 (1998) (Stevens, J., joined by Ginsburg, J., and Souter, J., dissenting). See also, Perot v. FEC, 97 F.3d 553, 559 (D.C.Cir. 1996) (refusing to limit discretion of Commission on Presidential Debates to exclude third-party candidate who led in the three-way polls at one point

in 1992, because "staging the debates" and "choosing debate participants" was part of the Commission's "First Amendment rights."); Becker v. Federal Election Commission, 112 F. Supp. 2d 172, 184–5 (D. Mass. 2000) (allowing Commission on Presidential Debates to exclude third party candidates in the interest of major parties whose allies staff the commission and negotiate with parties regarding terms of debates).

46 E.g., Ralph Nader and Theresa Amato, 'So you want to run for president? Ha! barriers to third-party entry,' 90 *National Civic Review* 163 (2001); Plaintiff's Complaint, Johnson v. Commission on Presidential Debates, No. 15–1580 (RMC) (D.D.C. complaint filed January 8, 2016).

47 Johnson v. Commission on Presidential Debates. 869 F.3d 976, 983–84 (D.C. Cir. 2017). See also, FCC v. League of Women Voters of California, 468 U.S. 364 (1984); Columbia Broadcasting System, Inc. v. Democratic National Committee, 412 U.S. 94 (1973)

48 E.g., Garcetti v. Ceballos, 547 U.S. 410 (2006); Michael P. Scharf and Colin T. McLaughlin, On terrorism and whistle-blowing, Case Western Reserve School of Law Paper Series in Legal Studies No. 07–5 (February 2007), https://www.ssrn.com. But cf., Turner v. US Agency for Global Media, 502 F. Supp. 3d 333, 375–84 (D.D.C. 2020) (exclusion of administrators' on-job speech from First Amendment does not apply to university faculty's teaching and writing and perhaps U.S.-funded international-facing journalists as well); Pernell v. Florida Board of Governors of the State University System, 641 F.Supp.3d 1218. (N.D. Fla. 2022) (professors retain First Amendment rights as public employees including as regards in-classroom speech).

49 E.g., National Association of Criminal Defense Lawyers, 'The trial penalty: The sixth amendment right to trial on the verge of extinction and how to save it,' 13 *Federal Sentencing Reporter* 331 (2018); Sophia Waldstein, 'Open-file discovery: A plea for transparent plea-bargaining,' 92 *Temple Law Review* 517 (2019).

50 Federal President Frank-Walter Steinmeier, 75th Anniversary of the End of the 2nd World War, https://www.bundespraesident.de/SharedDocs/Reden/EN/Frank-Walter-Steinmeier/Reden/2020/05/200508-75th-anniversary-World-War-II.html (last updated May 8, 2020); U.S. Holocaust Memorial Museum, Liberation of Nazi Camps, Holocaust Encyclopedia, https://encyclopedia.ushmm.org/content/en/article/liberation-of-nazi-camps (last updated February 12, 2021).

51 Germany's most important book, *Deutschland.de* (April 17, 2019), https://www.deutschland.de/en/topic/politics/german-basic-law-the-key-facts.

52 International Military Tribunal at Nuremberg, Judgment on the Major War Criminals, 1947, https://avalon.law.yale.edu/imt/judnazi.asp#consol & https://avalon.law.yale.edu/imt/judwarcr.asp#civilian. The opinion does set forth a somewhat exaggerated sense of German mental helplessness, ignoring the ability of some Germans to exercise independent judgment in various ways, including by flight, resistance, and righteousness.

53 Grundgesetz für die Bundesrepublik Deutschland [GG] [Constitution] July 11, 2012, art. 5, § 1 (Ger.).

54 G.A. Res. 2200A(XXI), art. 19(2), adopted December 16, 1966, entered into force March 23, 1976, 999 U.N.T.S. 171.

55 *Id.*, art. 19(1).

56 See *id.*, art. 19(3).

57 Joel Anderson, 'The "third generation" of the Frankfurt School,' 22 *Intellectual History Newsletter* 49 (2000), https://dspace.library.uu.nl/handle/1874/20315.

58 Ibid.

59 Jürgen Habermas, *Between Facts and Norms: Contributions to a Discourse Theory of Law and Democracy*, translated by William Rehg (Wiley, 2018), p. 104.

60 Jürgen Habermas, *The Theory of Communicative Action: Reason and the Rationalization of Society*, translated by Thomas McCarthy (Policy Press, 2015), p. 236.

61 Habermas, *Between Facts and Norms*, previous n. 59, p. 147.

62 Ibid., p. xii, 32–33, 83, 127, 171, 368, 447, 469, 474.

63 Lampman, previous n. 41.

64 E.g., Barenblatt v. United States, 360 U.S. 109, 142–44 (1959) (Black, J., dissenting) ("[I reject] the notion that . . . laws directly abridging First Amendment freedoms can be justified by a congressional or judicial balancing process . . . [or that] neither the First Amendment nor any other provision of the Bill of Rights should be enforced unless the Court believes it is reasonable to do so. Not only does this violate the genius of our written Constitution, but it runs expressly counter to the injunction to Court and Congress made by Madison when he introduced the Bill of Rights. [¶] 'If [the Bill of Rights is] incorporated into the Constitution, independent tribunals of justice will consider themselves in a peculiar manner the guardians of those rights; they will be an impenetrable bulwark against every assumption of power in the Legislative or Executive; they will be naturally led to resist every encroachment upon rights expressly stipulated for in the Constitution by the declaration of rights.'") (quoting 1 *Annals of Congress* 434–36, 439–57 (1789)); Roger K Newman, *Hugo Black: A Biography* 130–31 (Pantheon Books, 1997) (reasonableness tests and balancing are inconsistent with the "philosophy of Thomas Jefferson," who opposed "those who believe in restricting and shackling the human intellect."); Eugene Volokh, 'Crime-facilitating speech,' 57 *Stanford Law Review* 1095, 1137 (2005) (criticizing ad hoc balancing in First Amendment context as an "unexamined, un-self-conscious intuitive inquiry [that] can easily be influenced by factors that judges ought not consider, such as the ideology of the speaker or the perceived merits of the political movement to which he belongs"); Melville B. Nimmer, 'The right to speak From *Times* to *Time*: First Amendment theory applied to libel and misapplied to privacy,' 56 *California Law Review* 935, 939–41 (1968) (similar). I find the following books and articles to be exemplary of the fruitfulness of criticizing existing constitutional doctrine and engaging in originalist expositions of the Bill of Rights. See, e.g., Akhil Reed Amar, *The Bill of Rights: Creation and Reconstruction* (Yale University Press, 1998); Akhil Reed Amar, 'The Bill of Rights and the Fourteenth Amendment,' 101 *Yale Law Journal* 1193 (1992); Akhil Reed Amar, 'The Bill of Rights as a Constitution,' 100 *Yale Law Journal* 1131 (1991); Akhil Reed Amar, 'The Case of the Missing Amendments: *R.A.V. v. City of St. Paul*,' 106 *Harvard Law Review* 124 (1992); Akhil Reed Amar, 'Did the Fourteenth Amendment incorporate the Bill of Rights against states?', 19 *Harvard Journal of Law and Public Policy* 443 (1996); Akhil Reed Amar, 'The Fifteenth Amendment and political rights,' 17 *Cardozo Law Review* 2225 (1996); Akhil Reed Amar, 'Fourth Amendment first principles,' 107 *Harvard Law Review* 757 (1994); Akhil Reed Amar, 'Hugo Black and the hall of fame,' 53 *Alabama Law Review* 1221 (2002); Akhil Reed Amar, Original intent for liberals (and for conservatives and moderates, too), *Slate* (2005), https://www.slate.com/id/2126680/; Akhil Reed Amar, 'The Supreme Court, 1999 term – foreword: The document and the doctrine,' 114 *Harvard Law Review* 26 (2000); Akhil Reed Amar, 'On impeaching presidents,' 28 *Hofstra Law Review* 291 (1999); Robert M. Bloom and William J. Dunn, The Constitutional Infirmity of Warrantless NSA Surveillance: The Abuse of Presidential Power and the Injury to the Fourth Amendment, Boston College Law School Faculty Papers – Paper 163, at pp. 44–45 (2006), http://lsr.nellco.org/bc/bclsfp/papers/163; Richard Delgado, 'Inequality "from the top": Applying an ancient prohibition to an emerging problem of distributive justice,' 32 *UCLA Law Review* 100 (1984); John Nichols, *The Genius of Impeachment: The Founders' Cure for Royalism* (The New Press, 2006); Scott v. Sanford, 60 U.S. 393, 564–633 (1857) (Curtis, J., dissenting); Daniel J. Solove, 'The First Amendment as Criminal Procedure,' 82 *The New York University School of Law Review* 112 (2007); Charles Sumner, *The Barbarism of Slavery* (Buell & Blanchard, 1860); Scott Turow, Scalia the civil libertarian?, *The New York Times* (November 26, 2006), pp. 6-22–6-23.

65 E.g., Speiser v. Randall, 357 U.S. 513 (1958) (invalidating a loyalty oath aimed at violent sedition whose overbreadth and vagueness would deter legitimate speech as well); Smith v. California, 361 U.S. 147 (1959) (overturning law criminalizing the possession of obscene books that might deter booksellers from carrying lawful books); NAACP v. Button, 371 U.S. 415, 433 (1963) (although a law might be addressed to a form of

speech or conduct subject to reasonable regulation, the law's overbreadth and vagueness may be "objectionable" because the "threat of sanctions may deter the exercise" of the freedom of speech, which is "delicate and vulnerable, as well as supremely precious in our society," and needs "breathing space" to "survive"); New York Times v. Sullivan, 376 U.S. 254 (1964) (although libel and defamation may be legitimate subjects of state regulation, such regulation needs to be limited in cases involving public officials to false statements made with "actual malice," so that " 'the field of free debate' " will have "breathing space" and remain "uninhibited, robust, and wide-open."); Freedman v. Maryland, 380 U.S. 51 (1965) (invalidating law prohibiting exhibition of films not approved by state licensing boards, which might deter exhibitors from showing films containing protected expression); Brandenburg v. Ohio, 395 U.S. 444 (1969) (although inciting violent acts may not be worthy of protection in itself, regulation of such incitement needs to be restricted by First Amendment to cases involving advocacy intended to and likely to cause "imminent lawless action," or it might "sweep within its condemnation speech which our Constitution has immunized from governmental control."); see also, Morton J. Horwitz, *The Warren Court and the Pursuit of Justice* (Farrar, Straus and Giroux, 1999), pp. 34–37, 68–73 (Justice Brennan recognized broad First Amendment protections in areas that other justices regarded as being beyond the reach of the First Amendment by definition or as a result of a balancing of state and individual interests, including treason and sedition, unlawful associations, obscenity, and defamation); Robert D. Richards, *Uninhibited, Robust, and Wide Open: Mr. Justice Brennan's Legacy to the First Amendment* (Parkway Publishers, 1994), pp. 19–25, 47–68, 98–99, 110–12 (Justice Brennan defended against government censorship previously unprotected acts such as publishing classified information, exhibiting motion pictures without a license, inciting violence, lewd and obscene speech, and defamation); Memorial Resolution Adopted by the Bar of the Supreme Court of the United States to Record Our Deep Respect and Affection for Justice William J. Brennan, Jr., https://www.brennancenter.org/programs/programs_cele_memorial.html (visited June 2, 2006) (Justice Brennan vindicated free speech rights against traditional restrictions on publishing classified information, engaging in indecent speech, defamation, and broadcasting in violation of licensing requirements).

66 Paul Bedard, Voters: Biden's America becoming a "Police State," MSN, September 21, 2023, https://msn.com/en-us/news/politics/voters-biden-s-america-becoming-a-police-state/ar-AA1h43Kj.

67 Rasmussen Reports, Questions – Police State – September 14 and 17–18, 2023, https://www.rasmussenreports.com/public_content/politics/questions/questions/september_2023/questions_police_state_septembe'r_14_and_17_18_2023. Others might question the pollster's reliability, but it was the third most accurate poll of presidential voting intentions in 2020, and less likely to overestimate support for then-candidate Joe Biden than polls by NBC/*The Wall Street Journal*, Harvard/Harris, or Reuters/Ipsos. E.g., Costas Panagopoulos and Kyle Endres, Which 2020 election polls were most – and least – accurate?, *Thewashingtonpost.com* (November 25, 2020), https://www.washingtonpost.com/politics/2020/11/25/which-2020-election-polls-were-most-least-accurate/.

Bibliography

Floyd Abrams, 'The first amendment and copyright,' 35 *Journal of the Copyright Society* 1 (1987).

1 *Annals of Congress* 434 (1789), http://press-pubs.uchicago.edu/founders/documents/amendI_speechs14.html.

3 *Annals of Congress*, 934 (1794).

Adderly v. Florida, 385 U.S. 39 (1966) (Douglas, J., joined by Warren, the Chief Justice, Brennan J., and Fortas, J., dissenting).

Akhil Reed Amar, *The Bill of Rights: Creation and Reconstruction* (Yale University Press, 1998).
Akhil Reed Amar, 'Did the Fourteenth Amendment incorporate the Bill of Rights against states?,' 19 *Harvard Journal of Law & Public Policy* 443 (1996).
Akhil Reed Amar, 'Fourth Amendment first principles,' 107 *Harvard Law Review* 757 (1994).
Akhil Reed Amar, 'Hugo Black and the Hall of Fame,' 53 *Alabama Law Review* 1221 (2002).
Akhil Reed Amar, 'On impeaching Presidents,' 28 *Hofstra Law Review* 291 (1999).
Akhil Reed Amar, Original intent for liberals (and for conservatives and moderates, too), *Slate* (2005), https://www.slate.com/id/2126680/.
Akhil Reed Amar, 'The Bill of Rights and the Fourteenth Amendment,' 101 *Yale Law Journal 1193* (1992).
Akhil Reed Amar, 'The Bill of Rights as a Constitution,' 100 *Yale Law Journal* 1131 (1991).
Akhil Reed Amar, 'The case of the missing amendments: *R.A.V. v. City of St. Paul*,' 106 *Harvard Law Review* 124 (1992).
Akhil Reed Amar, 'The Fifteenth Amendment and political rights,' 17 *Cardozo Law Review* 2225 (1996).
Akhil Reed Amar, 'The Supreme Court, 1999 term – Foreword: The document and the doctrine,' 114 *Harvard Law Review* 26 (2000).
Alien and Sedition Acts of 1798, 1 Stat. 566.
David A. Anderson, 'The origins of the press clause,' 30 *UCLA Law Review* 455 (1983).
Joel Anderson, 'The "Third generation" of the Frankfurt school,' 22 *Intellectual History Newsletter* 49 (2000), https://dspace.library.uu.nl/handle/1874/20315.
Thomas Aquinas, *On Law, Morality, and Politics*, edited by Richard J. Regan and William Baumgarth (Hackett, 1988).
Arkansas Educational Television Commission v. Forbes, 523 U.S. 666 (1998) (Stevens, J., joined by Ginsburg, J., and Souter, J., dissenting).
C. Edwin Baker, 'First Amendment limits on copyright,' 55 *Vanderbilt Law Review* 891 (2002).
Barenblatt v. United States, 360 U.S. 109, 142–44 (1959) (Black, J., dissenting).
Becker v. Federal Election Commission, 112 F. Supp. 2d 172 (D. Mass, 2000).
Paul Bedard, 'Voters: Biden's America becoming a "police state,"' MSN (September 21, 2023), https://msn.com/en-us/news/politics/voters-biden-s-america-becoming-a-police-state/ar-AA1h43Kj.
Paul Schiff Berman, 'Cyberspace and the state action debate: The cultural value of applying constitutional norms to private regulation,' 71 *University of Colorado Law Review* 1263 (2000).
Sir William Blackstone, *Commentaries on the Laws of England*, Vol. 1 (University of Chicago Press, 1979 [1765]).
Sir William Blackstone, *Commentaries on the Laws of England . . . The Twentieth Edition, Incorporating the Alterations Down to the Present Time. By James Stewart*, Vol. 4 (John Murray, 1862 [1770]).
Robert M. Bloom and William J. Dunn, The Constitutional Infirmity of Warrantless NSA Surveillance: The Abuse of Presidential Power and the Injury to the Fourth Amendment, Boston College Law School Faculty Papers – Paper 163 (2006), http://lsr.nellco.org/bc/bclsfp/papers/163.
Bowers v. Hardwick, 478 U.S. 186 (1986).
Brandenburg v. Ohio, 395 U.S. 444 (1969).
The Bridge Initiative, Victor Orban, https://bridge.georgetown.edu/wp-content/uploads/2019/11/Viktor-Orban-November-2019-factsheet.pdf.
Byars v. Bluff City News Co., 609 F.2d 843 (6th Cir. 1979).
Cantwell v. Connecticut, 310 U.S. 296 (1940).
Columbia Broadcasting System, Inc. v. Democratic National Committee, 412 U.S. 94, 156–57 (1973) (Douglas, J., concurring)

Margaret Chon, 'Erasing race?: A critical race feminist view of Internet identity-shifting,' 3 *Journal of Gender Race & Justice* 439 (2000).
Julie Cohen, 'A right to read anonymously: A closer look at "copyright management" in cyberspace,' 28 *Connecticut Law Review* 981 (1996).
Columbia Broadcasting System, Inc. v. Democratic National Committee, 412 U.S. 94 (1973).
The Debates in the Several State Conventions on the Adoption of the Federal Constitution (Elliot's Debates) (1799–1800), Vol. 4 (1876), p. 570).
Richard Delgado, 'Inequality "from the top": Applying an ancient prohibition to an emerging problem of distributive justice,' 32 *UCLA Law Review* 100 (1984).
Niva Elkin-Koren, 'Cyberlaw and social change: A democratic approach to copyright law in cyberspace,' 14 *Cardozo Arts & Entertainment Law Journal* 215 (1996).
Charlie Eastaugh, *Unconstitutional Solitude: Solitary Confinement and the US Constitution's Evolving Standards of Decency* (Springer, 2017).
FCC v. League of Women Voters of California, 468 U.S. 364 (1984).
Federal President Frank-Walter Steinmeier, 75th Anniversary of the End of the 2nd World War (2020), https://www.bundespraesident.de/SharedDocs/Reden/EN/Frank-Walter-Steinmeier/Reden/2020/05/200508-75th-anniversary-World-War-II.html.
James Madison, 'Federalist 43 (Madison),' in *The Federalist Papers*, edited by Clinton Rossiter (Mentor Books, 1961), pp. 271–72.
Alexander Hamilton, 'Federalist 84 (Hamilton),' in *The Federalist Papers*, http://press-pubs.uchicago.edu/founders/documents/bill_of_rightss7.html.
Stephen Fraser, 'The conflict between the first amendment and copyright law and its impact on the Internet,' 16 *Cardozo Arts & Entertainment Law Journal* 1 (1998).
Freedman v. Maryland, 380 U.S. 51 (1965).
G.A. Res. 2200A(XXI), adopted December 16, 1966, entered into force March 23, 1976, 999 U.N.T.S. 171.
Garcetti v. Ceballos, 547 U.S. 410 (2006).
Germany's most important book, *Deutschland.de* (April 17, 2019), https://www.deutschland.de/en/topic/politics/german-basic-law-the-key-facts.
Michael Allen Gillespie, *Nietzsche's Final Teaching* (University of Chicago Press, 2019).
The Global Commission on Drug Policy, The Negative Impact of the War on Drugs on Public Health: The Hidden Hepatitis C Epidemic (2013).
Mike Godwin, *Cyber Rights: Defending Free Speech in the Digital Age* (Times Books, 1998).
Julius Goebel, Jr., 'Constitutional history and law,' 38 *Columbia Law Review* 555 (1938).
Grundgesetz für die Bundesrepublik Deutschland [GG] [Constitution] July 11, 2012, art. 5, § 1 (Ger.).
Jürgen Habermas, *Between Facts and Norms: Contributions to a Discourse Theory of Law and Democracy*, translated by William Rehg (Wiley, 2018).
Jürgen Habermas, *The Theory of Communicative Action: Reason and the Rationalization of Society*, translated by Thomas McCarthy (Policy Press, 2015).
Morton J. Horwitz, *The Warren Court and the Pursuit of Justice* (Farrar, Straus and Giroux, 1999).
International Military Tribunal at Nuremberg, Judgment on the Major War Criminals (1947), https://avalon.law.yale.edu/imt/judnazi.asp#consol; https://avalon.law.yale.edu/imt/judwarcr.asp#civilian.
Kermit L. Hall, *The Magic Mirror: Law in American History* (Oxford University Press, 1998), pp. 57–58.
Harper & Row Publishers v. Nation Enterprises, Inc., 471 U.S. 539, 579 (1985) (Brennan, J., joined by White, J., and Marshall, J., dissenting).
Human Rights Watch, Averting an imminent catastrophe: Recommendations to US local, state and federal officials to COVID-19 in jails and prisons (April 29, 2020), https://www.hrw.org/news/2020/04/29/averting-imminent-catastrophe-recommendations-us-local-state-and-federal-officials.
Human Rights Watch, US: Comments submitted to Department of Justice on proposed standards to end prison rape (April 3, 2011), https://www.hrw.org/news/2011/04/04/us-comments-submitted-department-justice-proposed-standards-end-prison-rape.

In re Fries, 9 F. Cas. 826 (C.C.D. Pa. 1799) (quoting William Blackstone, *Commentaries on the Laws of England*, Vol. 4 (The Clarendon Press, 1765)).
Thomas Jefferson, 'Letter to James Madison, 1789,' in *Writings of Thomas Jefferson*, Vol. 7, edited by Paul Leicester Ford (G.P. Putnam's Sons, 1903), p. 450.
Thomas Jefferson, 'Letter to James Madison (August 28, 1789),' in *Papers of Thomas Jefferson*, Vol. 15 (1903), p. 367, http://press-pubs.uchicago.edu/founders/documents/amendI_speechs15.html.
Thomas Jefferson, 'Letter to James Madison (December 20, 1787),' *The Founders' Constitution* (2005), http://press-pubs.uchicago.edu/founders/documents/v1ch14s30.html.
Thomas Jefferson, 'Letter to James Madison,' November 17, 1798, in *The Works of Thomas Jefferson*, Vol. 8, edited by Paul Leicester Ford (G.P. Putnam's Sons, 1904), pp. 464–65.
Thomas Jefferson, 'Letter to President George Washington (September 9, 1792),' in *The Writings of George Washington, Being His Correspondence, Addresses, Messages and Other Papers, Official and Private*, edited by Jared Sparks (Little, Brown and company, 1st ed. 1838), pp. 517, 521.
Thomas Jefferson, *Notes on the State of Virginia*, 1784, http://press-pubs.uchicago.edu/founders/documents/amendI_religions40.html.
Johnson v. Commission on Presidential Debates, 869 F.3d 976 (D.C. Cir. 2017).
Immanuel Kant, *Of the Injustice of Counterfeiting Books* (Illustrated) (Delphi Classics, 2017 [1785]).
Dorean M. Koenig, 'Joe Camel and the First Amendment: The dark side of copyrighted and trademark-protected icons,' 11 *Thomas M. Cooley Law Review* 803 (1994).
Alan J. Koshner, 'The Founding Fathers and political speech: The First Amendment, the Press and the Sedition Act of 1798,' 6 *St. Louis University Public Law Review* 395 (1987).
Seth Kreimer, 'Censorship by proxy: The first amendment, intermediaries, and the problem of the weakest link,' 155 *University of Pennsylvania Law Review* 11 (2006).
L.L. Bean, Inc. v. Drake Publishers, Inc., 811 F.2d 26 (1st Cir. 1987).
Lamparello v. Falwell, 420 F.3d 309 (4th Cir. 2005);
Arno Lampman, Was geht vor: Die Meinungsfreiheit oder das Hausrecht Facebooks?, *LHR Rechtsanwlte* (September 19, 2018), https://www-lhr-law-de/magazin/social-media-recht/was-geht-vor-meinungsfreiheit-oder-das-hausrecht-facebooks/.
Landgericht Berlin, Decision of March 23, 2018, Az. 31 O 21/18, https://www.gerichtsentscheidungen.berlin-brandenburg.de/jportal/portal/t/279b/bs/10/page/sammlung.psml?pid=Dokumentanzeige&showdoccase=1&js_peid=Trefferliste&documentnumber=1&numberofresults=1&fromdoctodoc=yes&doc.id=JURE180006250&doc.part=L&doc.price=0.0#focuspoint.
Landgericht Frankfurt, decision of September 10, 2018, Az. 2–03 O 310/18.
Landgericht Heidelberg, decision of August 28, 2018–1 O 71/18.
David Lange, 'Copyright and the Constitution in the age of intellectual property,' 1 *Journal of Intellectual Property Law* 119, 133–34 (1994).
Arlen W. Langvardt, 'Trademark rights and first Amendment wrongs: Protecting the former without committing the latter,' 83 *Trademark Reporter* 633 (1993).
Lawrence Lessig, 'Creative economies,' 2006 *Michigan State Law Review* 33 (2006).
Leonard W. Levy, *Emergence of a Free Press* (Oxford University Press, 1985).
Leonard W. Levy, *Legacy of Suppression: Freedom of Speech and Press in Early American History* (The Belknap Press, 1960).
Leonard W. Levy, 'Liberty and the first Amendment: 1790–1800,' 68 *American Historical Review* 22 (1962).
Leonard W. Levy, *Jefferson and Civil Liberties: The Darker Side* (The Belknap Press, 1963).
Lawrence Lessig, *Code and Other Laws of Cyberspace* (Basic Books, 1999).
Lawrence Lessig, *The Future of Ideas: The Fate of the Commons in a Connected World* (Random House, 2001).
John Locke, *Second Treatise of Government*, edited by C.B. MacPherson (Hackett, 1980[1690]).
Lorain Journal v. United States, 342 U.S. 143 (1951).

Loving v. Virginia, 388 U.S. 1 (1977).

James Madison, 'House debate, June 8, 1789,' 1 *Annals of Congress* 440–57 (1794), http://press-pubs.uchicago.edu/founders/documents/amendI_speechs14.html.

James Madison, 'Letter to Thomas Jefferson, January 18, 1800,' in *The Writings of James Madison, Vol. 6: 1790–1802*, edited by Gaillard Hunt (G.P Putnam's Sons, 1906), pp. 347, 387.

James Madison, 'Report on the Virginia Resolutions,' in *The Writings of James Madison, Vol. IV: 1829–1836* (J.P. Lippincott Co., 1865), p. 544.

James Madison, *Report on the Virginia Resolutions* (1798), quoted in *Elliot's Debates*, Vol. 4 (1876), pp. 546–80, 553–54, 569–71, and *Annals of Congress*, Vol. 4 (1794), p. 934, http://press-pubs.uchicago.edu/founders/documents/amendI_speechs14.html.

Manual Enterprises, Inc. v. Day, 370 U.S. 478 (1962).

Mattel, Inc. v. MCA Records, 296 F.3d 894 (9th Cir. 2002).

Matthew 16:18–19.

Memorial Resolution Adopted by the Bar of the Supreme Court of the United States to Record Our Deep Respect and Affection for Justice William J. Brennan, Jr., https://www.brennancenter.org/programs/programs_cele_memorial.html.

David Meyer, Court tells Facebook: Stop deleting 'offensive' comment, *Vox* (April 13, 2018), https://www.zdnet.com/article/court-tells-facebook-stop-deleting-offensive-comment/.

NAACP v. Button, 371 U.S. 415 (1963).

National Association of Criminal Defense Lawyers, 'The trial penalty: The Sixth Amendment right to trial on the verge of extinction and how to save it,' 13 *Federal Sentencing Reporter* 331 (2018).

New York v. Ferber, 458 U.S. 747 (1982).

New York Times Co. v. Sullivan, 376 U.S. 254 (1964).

Nissan Motor Co. v. Nissan Computer Corp., 378 F.3d 1002 (9th Cir. 2004).

Ralph Nader and Theresa Amato, 'So you want to run for president? Ha! barriers to third-party entry,' 90 *National Civic Review* 163 (2001).

Sridevi Nambiar, UN Committee on torture says U.S. must reform its use of solitary confinement, *Solitary Watch* (December 5, 2014), http://solitarywatch.com/2014/12/05/un-committee-against-torture-says-u-s-must-reform-its-use-of-solitary-confinement/.

Roger K. Newman, *Hugo A. Black: A Biography* (Pantheon Books, Paperback ed. 1997).

John Nichols, *The Genius of Impeachment: The Founders' Cure for Royalism* (The New Press, 2006).

Melville B. Nimmer, 'The right to speak from *Times* to *Time*: First Amendment theory applied to libel and misapplied to privacy,' 56 *California Law Review* 935 (1968).

Oberlandesgericht Karlsruhe, decision of June 25, 2018, Az. 15 W 86/18.

Oberlandesgericht Munich, decision of August 24, 2018, Az. 18 W 1294/18.

Brian O. Hogan, et al., 'History of solitary confinement is associated with Post-Traumatic Stress Disorder symptoms among individuals recently released from prison,' 95 *Journal of Urban Health* (2017), https://www.researchgate.net/publication/314484304_History_of_Solitary_Confinement_Is_Associated_with_Post-Traumatic_Stress_Disorder_Symptoms_among_Individuals_Recently_Released_from_Prison.

Costas Panagopoulos and Kyle Endres, Which 2020 election polls were most – and least – Accurate?, *Thewashingtonpost.com* (November 25, 2020), https://www.washingtonpost.com/politics/2020/11/25/which-2020-election-polls-were-most-least-accurate/.

Plaintiff's Complaint, Johnson v. Commission on Presidential Debates, No. 15–1580 (RMC) (D.D.C. complaint filed January 8, 2016).

Pernell v. Florida Board of Governors of the State University System, No. 4: 22cv304-MW, slip op. (N.D. Fla. preliminary injunction granted in part November 17, 2022).

Perot v. FEC, 97 F.3d 553 (D.C.Cir. 1996).

Jack N. Rakove, *Declaring Rights: A Brief History with Documents* (Bedford/St. Martin's, 1998).

Rasmussen Reports, Questions – Police State – September 14 and 17–18, 2023, https://www.rasmussenreports.com/public_content/politics/questions/questions/september_2023/questions_police_state_september_14_and_17_18_2023.

Robert D. Richards, *Uninhibited, Robust, and Wide Open: Mr. Justice Brennan's Legacy to the First Amendment* (Parkway Publishers, 1994).

Reno v. ACLU, 521 U.S. 844 (1997).

Romans 13:1–2, 4.

San Francisco Arts & Athl. v. United States Olympic Cmte., 483 U.S. 522, 528 (1987) (Brennan, J., dissenting).

Pamela Samuelson, 'Mapping the digital public domain: Threats and opportunities,' 66 *Law & Contemporary Problems* 147 (2003).

Michael P. Scharf and Colin T. McLaughlin, On terrorism and whistle-blowing, Case Western Reserve School of Law Paper Series in Legal Studies No. 07–5 (February 2007), https://www.ssrn.com.

Scott v. Sanford, 60 U.S. 393 (1857) (Curtis, J., dissenting).

Smith v. California, 361 U.S. 147 (1959).

Smothers v. Gresham Transfer, Inc., 23 P. 2d 333 (Or. 2001).

Daniel J. Solove, 'The First Amendment as criminal procedure', 82 *N.Y.U. Law Review* 112 (2007).

Speiser v. Randall, 357 U.S. 513 (1958).

St. George Tucker, *Blackstone's Commentaries*, Vol. 1 (Birch and Carr, 1803).

Stromberg v. California, 283 U.S. 359 (1931).

Charles Sumner, *The Barbarism of Slavery* (Buell & Blanchard, 1860).

Suntrust Bank v. Houghton Mifflin Co., 252 F.3d 1165, *substituted opinion at* 268 F.3d 1257 (11th Cir. 2001).

Thomas v. Review Bd. of the Indiana Employment Sec. Div., 450 U.S. 707 (1981) (Rehnquist, J., dissenting).

F.N. Thorpe, *Constitutional History of the American People, 1776–1850*, Vol. 1 (Harper and Brothers, 1898).

Hannibal Travis, 'Of blogs, ebooks, and broadband: Access to digital media as a First Amendment right,' 35 *Hofstra Law Review* 1519 (2007).

Turner Broadcasting System, Inc. v. FCC, 512 U.S. 622 (1994).

Turner v. US Agency for Global Media, 502 F. Supp. 3d 333 (D.D.C. 2020).

U.S. Const., am. I.

Scott Turow, Scalia the civil libertarian?, *The New York Times* (November 26, 2006), pp. 6-22–6-23.

U.S. Holocaust Memorial Museum, Liberation of Nazi Camps, Holocaust Encyclopedia, https://encyclopedia.ushmm.org/content/en/article/liberation-of-nazi-camps (accessed February 12, 2023).

Sophia Waldstein, 'Open-file discovery: A plea for transparent plea-bargaining,' 92 *Temple Law Review* 517 (2019).

Wheaton v. Peters, 33 U.S. 591 (1834) (argument for appellants).

White v. Samsung Elec. Am., Inc., 989 F.2d 1512 (9th Cir. 1993) (Kozinski, J., dissenting).

Wendt v. Host Int'l, Inc., 197 F.3d 1284 (9th Cir. 1999) (Kozinski, J., dissenting).

Alfred C. Yen, 'A First Amendment perspective on the idea/expression dichotomy and copyright in a work's "total concept and feel," ' 38 *Emory Law Journal* 393, 432–33 (1989).

Zacchini v. Scripps-Howard Broad. Co., 433 U.S. 562, 576–82 (1977) (Powell, J., joined by Brennan, J., and Marshall, J., dissenting).

Diane Leenheer Zimmerman, 'Information as speech, information as goods: Some thoughts on marketplace and the Bill of Rights,' 33 *William and Mary Law Review* 665 (1992).

Diane Leenheer Zimmerman, 'Is there a right to have something to say? One view of the public domain,' 73 *Fordham Law Review* 297 (2004).

3 Coordinated Inauthentic Activity

Private Police and Political Dissent

The Internet as a Structural Authenticator of Public Discourse

Digital media accessible over the Internet are more free than traditional print and broadcast media, for several mutually reinforcing and interrelated reasons. First, like the pamphleteering and epistolary discourse of the 18th century, they avoid the strategic bottleneck power exercised by owners of printing presses or television infrastructure.[1] Second, they are more often open to ownership and control by women, young people, the politically unpopular, members of minority ethnic or religious groups, and those lacking official credentials or renowned expertise in a specific subject area.[2] Third, they disseminate more diverse and truthful speech faster than the traditional media, which frequently operate primarily as a private ministry of propaganda and sounding board for government officials.[3] Finally, at their best they evade the bureaucratic permission and clearance culture of the traditional media, which stifle creativity by censoring and raising the cost of speech.[4]

Despite their superior capacity to fulfill First Amendment values, digital media experienced widespread censorship as the 21st century Supreme Court increasingly construed the First Amendment as a privilege of large corporations to bribe politicians and advertise dangerous products, rather than a right of unpopular citizens to criticize public officials.[5]

Prior to the deplatforming debate, this issue tended to be discussed as search or social traffic neutrality, or remedies for user account termination. As Frank Pasquale and Oren Bracha wrote, the problem of website demotion in search results, or the "Google Death Penalty," created a need to modify the U.S. law governing "common carriers" (infrastructure) to cover some search engines.[6] According to other studies, user account terminations could degrade both political dissent and the integrity of individuals' expressions of their identities and creative ideas.[7]

The following section analyzes how social media sites help make public discourse useful to political parties by shaping it in favor of allied politicians, monetizing it in ways that generate taxable income and opening up user activity for spies to use. To surveil and control public discourse may be the hidden agenda motivating a regulatory straitjacket tightening around the free and public examination of issues ranging from sexuality to nation, war, science, and empire.

DOI: 10.4324/9781003496106-4

Theories of Networked Class Power

Artificial intelligence (AI) and public-private partnerships have coalesced into protocols for regularizing Internet discourses, to a degree that may surprise many of us. The deployment of AI by such partnerships to rewire formerly free networks of discourse is addressed in other chapters.

Theories of liberalism part ways on the meaning and operationalization of the freedom and legality, when proclaimed as liberal ideals. Liberalism's advocates portray the movement as bringing about ordered lives governed by individual choice constrained only by settled, known laws in the general interest. Its critics, notably Michel Foucault, question whether the apparent freedoms of liberalism conceal and enable the rise of modern authoritarian and totalitarian practices, especially those involving carcerality.[8] Indeed, Foucault suggests that any ideology or political vocabulary will serve as an instrument of interpersonal domination.[9] From a U.S. perspective, his work presaged critiques of (neo-)liberalism for open abuse of power and enslavement of inmates in prisons, the abetting of and reliance upon dictatorial regimes and war criminals abroad, and encouragement of the worst kind of economic exploitation in developing countries.

Internet platform docility shares certain characteristics of Foucault's theory of docile bodies in liberal societies. Foucault wrote that disciplines and disciplinary power transformed French society because they helped produce "subjected and practiced bodies, 'docile' bodies."[10] In other words, bodies were calculatingly engineered to suit the structural needs of a changing political and economic system. Accordingly, Foucault's most explicit definition of discipline calls it a "unitary technique by which the body is reduced as a 'political' force at the least cost and maximized as a useful force."[11] Discipline, then, is "a recoding of existence" so as to extract productivity and to sterilize sites of resistance.[12]

Networked disciplinary power may bring about platform docility by several pathways. Content moderation shapes the Internet into the image of 1980s broadcast television, a medium of normalized conformity in which official propaganda and political parties dominate public debate.

Government officials are looking to AI to augment their control over public discourse both online and in other media. They seek to compel private platforms to remove thousands or millions of accounts for a variety of offenses, ranging from copying text or multimedia to imitating product names or designs to failing "fact checks" or "offensiveness" filters of various kinds. These tactics were described in Chapter 2, and they feature in the next chapter as well.

Alexander Galloway calls the postmodern deployment of decentralized mechanisms of implementing central government rhetoric *protocol power*, or "ultrarapid forms of apparently free-floating control," foremost among them algorithmic filters.[13] Social credit scores and environmental and social governance-based employee compensation and asset pricing also carve up the social body by algorithmically identifying and suppressing its "uglier" features.[14] Unlike modern methods of wielding power by ensuring the fearful ubiquity of the center's face throughout civil society, postmodern protocol-type power would optimally act invisibly, ensuing loyalty, security, and regularity by automation.

Protocol Power in the Identification of "Offline Harm"

Theories of liberalism may be useful to analyze how online content controls have a dialectical relationship with political and social movements to reduce ethnonational, intercultural, and socioeconomic inequalities. Platform docility seems to be a relatively decentered network of modulations to diverse power relationships: buyer and seller, educated and the less so, the rich and the poor or middle class, manager and employee, etc. Yet structuralist and post-structuralist thought directs our attention to how states deploy ideology, which protects politicians, parties, jurists, religious institutions, and nations from certain critiques, insults, privacy violations, and offensive symbols to which the ordinary citizen is often exposed. A study of how power operates in decentralized network environments that connects ideology to control for docility is needed.

YouTube's ContentID upload filter, which enables the initial monetization of user-generated content that may contain copyrighted material, has its counterparts in other filters for detecting, flagging, downranking, and suspending the authors or fans of speech that threatens a variety of state and nonstate interests. These systems securitize platforms or ensure the "security" of sites against "threat actors." A signal or indicator is often linked to nations that are rivalrous with or targeted by the United States.[15] Google's desire is to automate as much as possible with machine learning, but with human review for "novel" or "grey area" questions.[16] It is said to be an ethical mandate and crucial to the Internet consumer to delete automated fake news.[17]

Prior to 2018, complaints surrounding arbitrary takedowns on social media were voiced in our courts, legislatures, and online forums, only to be generally ignored or dismissed with little thought to the speakers' situation. Deletions of user accounts, videos, posts, memes, and other social and political speech were typically excused as a merely private decision by one company among many.[18] Users were told to find another service if they did not like the terms of use on a platform. This trend continued, citing the same early cases into the 2019–2023 period.[19]

Public hearings in the U.S. Congress started to blow up this cozy story. The heads of Google, Facebook, and Apple have testified that they work hand in glove with public officials to identify and remove user speech.[20] This undermined their own arguments in court against users trying to hold them to the First Amendment standards applicable to state actors. It also destroyed one argument against reforming platform law to regulate arbitrary or discriminatory takedowns, namely that these are private actions developed altruistically or in a nonpartisan environment.

Thus, at least four developments have emerged to disrupt the dominant narrative pre-2018 that content moderation by websites is generally neutral, beneficial, and private. First, government officials have openly pressured social media giants to toe various party lines, and evidence is coming forth that the giants, being no fools, have complied. Second, efforts against "fake news" and "foreign interference" have accelerated violations of privacy by the PRISM companies, or those that began funneling user content to intelligence agencies during the Bush II years. Third, it is argued that trends in news, visibility, and viewability on search engines and social media are no longer organic, but they are heavily manipulated for partisan reasons. Fourth, a combination of platform leaks and litigation brought by users and state governments have exposed the breadth and extreme partisan bias of censorship online since 2019.

Whistleblowers have claimed that tech platforms wage the government's war on various viewpoints and topics of speech. At a 2016 hearing, members of the Senate openly demanded that speech they dislike be removed from Facebook, Twitter, and YouTube, even as a member of the subcommittee holding the hearing pointed out that these censorial powers destroyed a public forum and ended up harming Americans who were simply politically unpopular.[21] According to an internal account, that of a former Facebook employee who contacted a Republican member of the Senate Judiciary Committee in 2020, Google, Facebook, and Twitter began coordinating which content to ban or restrict online.[22] Facebook CEO Mark Zuckerberg testified that the three companies share "signals" about "security-related" issues with online speech, using the examples of terrorism, child exploitation, or foreign influences.[23] In 2019–2022, the Trump and Biden administrations pressured online platforms to suspend or terminate the accounts of specific individuals, who often lost their account access as a result.[24]

Digital platforms openly discriminate against foreign speakers, which they describe as Chinese, Russian, and Iranian "influence" efforts or more broadly as Chinese/Russian/Iranian/fill-in-the-blank "malice" or "misinformation tactics" or "[s]tate-sponsored influence and misinformation operations."[25] At the outset, most of this framing is misleading in the extreme because it falsely equates military operations with social media posts, and because both attribution to a foreign government and imputation of the mental state of malice or intentional lying are extremely complex questions that often require a trial to resolve after voluminous document discovery, if due process is in any way sought. Much of the needed evidence may be classified, and withheld from public view or even judicial review, just as some evidence tying Osama bin Laden to the 9/11 hijackers was often withheld from U.S. military commissions, precluding a timely judgment.

Often the evidence that a given bit of (mis)information is actually emanating from a specific country – let alone its government – is shaky. For example, in the Twitter Files, documents released by X Corp. (then Twitter) CEO Elon Musk to journalists including Matt Taibbi, it was revealed that a group co-founded by Clint Watts was falsely flagging Americans or other non-Russians as Russians and strongly implying that they be censored on account of their national origin. Watts was a former FBI agent in the post-9/11 era, when agency leaders were criticized for their tactics resonant of entrapment, false claims about foreign threats, and mass surveillance challenged as illegal searches and seizures under the U.S. Constitution.[26] The former acting director of the CIA served on this group's board. Along with scholars from the Brookings Institution, the leading source of propaganda in favor of U.S. wars with and bombing of Iraq and Syria, Watts wrote an infamous article in *Foreign Policy* defending U.S. efforts to befriend jihadist terrorists in Syria, such as Ahrar al-Sham.[27] With respect to Twitter, his group targeted journalists skeptical of endless wars and mountains of civilian casualties, such as Joe Lauria, as well as U.S. lawyers and scholars, calling them Russian agents or worse.[28]

Although correlation is not always causation, Twitter had placed one in five of the accounts tracked by Hamilton 68 and Watts on a "trends blacklist" as early as late 2016 or 2017. Some of those accounts or other ones tracked were on search blacklists or had been issued an abuse "strike." Taibbi and others saw such reports as confirming accounts of algorithmic shadow-banning, which throttles visibility of flagged or targeted speakers (and lowers their follower counts). It is no wonder that Twitter took Hamilton 68's "fabulist" and "bullsh-t" assertions seriously, because powerful Senators Richard Blumenthal, Mark Warner, and Dianne Feinstein urged it to do so.[29]

Meanwhile, propagandists advocating war or embargos against Iraqis, Syrians, Libyans, Iranians, Russians, or Chinese – up to and including nuclear war or threats of it, at times – operate completely unhindered. Advocates of the invasion and devastation of Iraq, Iran, Libya, Serbia, Syria, and Yemen – and the bombing of Pakistan and Somalia, as well as the bombing, invasion, occupation, and reconstruction of Bosnia, Kosovo, and Afghanistan – also enjoy wide followings and are boosted in visibility by digital platforms. Watts himself, far from being censored or shamed as an apologist for violent groups in Syria, became a CNN contributor, testified before a credulous Congress, and led efforts to censor Americans and Europeans and to alter algorithms.[30] This large wave of algorithmic censorship targeted "Russian bots," but people who examined the alleged evidence said that many people listed were neither Russian nor bots. Still, the project seemingly gave a major push to Internet censorship efforts, with Big Tech CEOs repeatedly referring to inauthentic activity and similar synonyms for Russian bots as an excuse.[31] For example, Facebook CEO Mark Zuckerberg testified that due to the threat posed by "foreign actors," the company had to step up its use of AI to "identify malicious fake accounts."[32]

The "malice" and "offline harms" of most U.S.-led wars are completely ignored as a reason for filtering Internet expression, even as the harms of some disfavored wars and groups are magnified for public consumption, sometimes out of proportion to the underlying events.

Both Turkish and U.S diplomats are allowed unfettered access to social-media platforms, even though, with the express aim of destroying the political independence and territorial integrity of its neighbor, Turkey set up bases for thousands of former Syrian soldiers, Syrian civilians, and their foreign supporters, who were fighting alongside al Qaeda, in part.[33] The Obama administration strongly backed Turkey's role, "conducting covert operations along the Turkish–Syrian border to . . . develop supply routes and distribute guns, anti-tank missiles and other ammunition to the militant groups," even though members of the administration would acknowledge both publicly and privately that Turkey's policy was aiding al Qaeda in Syria.[34] By 2015, former Iraqi Prime Minister Nouri al-Maliki told the United

States that the Turkish government, the Saudi royal family, and others had brought about the "disintegration" of Iraq, with Kurdish forces retreating from positions around Mosul, and Saudi Arabia fomenting Sunni killings of the Shi'a, vividly illustrated when hundreds of Shi'a Iraqi recruits were slain.[35]

Second, platforms feed unprecedented reams of the most sensitive user data to governments, in "fora" veiled by secrecy and brigaded by legal immunities. As the platforms' lobbying group recently explained:

> Major U.S. technology companies and online platforms work with U.S. law enforcement, military, and intelligence agencies to combat a variety of national security and criminal threats. The head of U.S. Cyber Command in 2020 discussed the importance of the U.S. government's engagement with the tech industry. . . .
>
> The nature and scale of these platforms gives them a broad and deep view of the threat landscape. This allows those companies to secure U.S. data and infrastructure against foreign threats with an agility, speed and thoroughness that is not feasible for smaller, fragmented companies that have limited apertures. The critical missions of national security and law enforcement agencies, of course, also benefit from this security proficiency. Not only are the threats more rapidly detected and mitigated, but trend and threat analysis can be quickly shared with these agencies in multiple matured fora that have evolved over the last 10 years.[36]

One of the mass surveillance (or PRISM program) partners of the National Security Agency, Facebook, experienced serious pressure to violate the privacy of its users who stored communications with the platform relating to their purchase of advertisements relating to 2020 U.S. politics.[37] Watts, the former FBI agent, argued that Russian trolls and news stories may have driven politicians hostile to Russia out of contention for the presidency in 2016: first Marco Rubio, then Hillary Clinton.[38] This created pressure on Facebook to threaten its users' privacy by disclosing private user data relating to political ads to law enforcement and/or Congress.[39]

The rhetoric of the docile platforms therefore increasingly emphasizes the advantages of their size and reach in implementing central government aims. Over time, it may contribute to bogging down efforts to create more level playing fields for smaller competitors, end users, and independent journalists and activists. The "smaller, fragmented companies that have limited" windows into Internet users' private messages will not be as useful. Therefore they should be permitted to slowly wither away in the shadows of giant platforms' growth.

Third, whistleblowers have alleged that trends are manipulated not to reflect objective public interest but subtle political aims of a platform and their political allies. Former editors of Facebook's trending posts section alleged this kind of manipulation occurred in May 2016, in the lead-up to the 2016 congressional and presidential elections in the United States.[40] In November 2016 and into 2017, Google News joined the movement, banning ads on or massively downranking both U.S. conservative/Republican and international leftist/socialist websites as "fake news."[41]

Even before these changes had been made, Google recommended the majority of news readers read a mere handful out of all the thousands of online sources of news and opinion.[42] Three of these sources had been caught up in the rise of fake news and propaganda concerning Iraq (and formerly Serbia): CNN, *The New York Times*, and *The Washington Post*.[43] By late 2018 and 2019, in the lead-up to the 2020 elections, Fox News had joined these three outlets in the top five news sources recommended on Google's search pages (distinct from Google News), displacing *The Huffington Post*.[44] Yet the top eight news publishers accounted for one-third of articles recommended by Google, a proportion extremely disproportionate to their share of writing.[45] The bottom third of news sources is heavily disfavored and extremely unlikely to be recommended on Google.[46] Similarly, coverage of leading British politicians on Google News is heavily skewed toward three outlets – the BBC, *The Guardian*, and *The Daily Mail* – with those three accounting for nearly half of referral traffic from Google News in one study. Even within the top 25 websites indexed on Google News that cover British politics, the bottom tier of them receive 1/100th as many referrals as the BBC or *The Guardian*.[47]

In 2021, the CEO of YouTube announced that the company was downranking "borderline content" to feature "authoritative sources."[48] The news came days after the Center for Countering Digital Hate had alleged that a "Disinformation Dozen" of social-media users existed, a project apparently picked up with gusto by the White House "Digital Media" directorate in 2021, which demanded that Facebook "help" it with "vaccine hesitancy."[49] The downranking gambit came a few months before the White House began insisting that online platforms censor criticism of vaccines and vaccine mandates related to COVID-19, including the so-called Disinformation Dozen.[50] The first half of April 2021 was a very active time for encouraging and demanding online censorship, even according to public reports as of July 2023.[51] The White House had urged YouTube to become more like Facebook, a sanitized and heavily controlled version of the global public square which was working actively with the White House to curate reality for a credulous American and global population. Its Digital Media director thanked YouTube for downranking borderline content, just as Facebook had done.[52]

A lawsuit by several state attorneys general has given a major boost to the anti-complicity theme in Internet censorship disputes. The White House Digital Media directorate demanded that Facebook issue strikes for criticizing vaccines, vaccine mandates, or the Biden family, just like YouTube issues copyright strikes.[53] The courts have begun to declare such cooperation between government and private platforms in limiting public debate to be unlawful censorship.[54] A finding that federal officials or other government officials had pressured Internet platforms to limit the reach of user speech would not necessarily be the end of the matter. Courts would still hear evidence that the restraint was necessary to prevent imminent death or destruction, for example, or that the speech constituted a true threat that was removed in accordance with due process.[55]

By judicial consensus, the First Amendment only applies to "state actors," while some federal and state statutes such as the Civil Rights Act of 1871 may also protect lawful advocacy in favor of the election of members of Congress or of electors of the president. Chapter 5 will return to the First Amendment and civil-rights law approaches to reining in complicit private censorship that carries out the partisan or ideological preferences of government officials.

Deplatforming and Philosophical Theories of Authenticity[56]

Prior to the Internet, and even in its early decades, there was very little ability to authenticate – to assess the sincerity and accuracy of – public discourse. We were at the mercy of oligopolies.

Falsehoods, whether intentional or accidental, were the norm. Like the evil counterparts to Steven Covey's *7 Habits of Highly Effective People* (1989), print and broadcast media had six ineffective habits from the standpoint of pursuing the truth:

1. Racial Lumping
2. Double Standards
3. Selective Quotation
4. Poor Sourcing
5. Ignoring the Elephant in the Room
6. Advertiser Influence

Racial Lumping. Newspapers justified racist enslavement and segregation in the United States that especially victimized African-Americans, although Native Americans were also enslaved on occasion, when they were not massacred.[57] The press later shifted its coverage to selective reporting on crime in a manner that buttressed mass incarceration disproportionately affecting African-Americans and Native Americans.[58] Racial lumping carefully cultivated destructive stereotypes of African-Americans and other minorities.[59] Prime-time television programming avoided nuanced coverage of political ideology and public policy; instead, it was and is saturated with violence.[60] In terms of European newspapers and radio, the calumnies spread by Nazis and allied European fascists against Jews and "Asiatic" peoples such as Russian or Polish Slavs and Roma/Sinti people were among the worst in history, judged from their consequences.[61]

Double Standards. Basic concepts are not used properly or consistently in television or newspaper coverage of important events. *Aggression, genocide, terrorism, torture, authoritarianism, coup d'état,* and *malicious* or *malign influence operations* are terms employed in a biased manner. Double standards in the media came to the fore once again with the war in Ukraine and observers wondering how wars by U.S. allies or trading partners of the United States or Britain evade similar coverage.[62] Graphic photos of Ukrainian war victims were prominent in newspaper and television coverage after having been censored from coverage of Iraq, Afghanistan, Libya, Syria, Yemen, Nigeria, Ethiopia, and other conflicts in which the United States, Britain, or their allies and arms exports markets play major roles. The media widely echoed the White House, calling Ukraine a genocide and violation of territorial integrity after many years in which outlets downplayed the deaths of 600,000 or more persons in each of many different countries due to bombardment, refugee flight, economic blockades, and violations of internationally recognized borders and the independence of U.N. members.[63] An estimated 1.3 million war deaths will occur in Yemen by 2030, after 1.5 million excess deaths in Iraq, 600,000 in Ethiopia, and untold numbers elsewhere.[64] Multiple invasions of Syria's territory and dispatches of armed groups committing political violence against public officials and essential infrastructure, including airports, somehow evade classification as aggression, invasions, occupations, violations of territorial integrity, or international terrorist attacks.

Selective Quotation.[65] Prior to the Internet, it was easy to distort news coverage of important events simply by strategically quoting from sources of news, such as public officials or experts. For example, U.S. corporate media selectively quoted intelligence reports and U.N. weapons inspectors in a misleading manner in the lead-up to the U.S. invasions of Iraq, Libya, and Syria. CNN repeatedly quoted the chief of the International Atomic Energy Agency as saying Iraq had been six months away from developing a nuclear weapon in 1991 and that the country had to cooperate with inspections to show that it had no banned nuclear materials,[66] but it did not quote the agency as saying that Iraq had *no* "physical capability for the production of amounts of weapons-usable nuclear material of any practical significance."[67] CNN quoted the agency as characterizing Iraq's compliance with inspections "evasive," but it did not quote it as stating that there was no evidence of a nuclear-weapons program and that U.S. claims that Iraq was developing nuclear bombs were "misleading."[68] CNN quoted the chief U.N. non-nuclear weapons inspector as being "not satisfied" with Iraq's compliance with relevant resolutions,[69] but it did not quote his statement that the United Nations had no evidence to show that Iraq had any nuclear, biological, or chemical weapons, or that any such weapons had been designed, bought, produced, or stored in Iraq since 1998.[70] It quoted another weapons inspector as saying Iraq had the will to build a nuclear weapon,[71] but it did not quote him as admitting in the year 2000 – long before the crucial 2002–2003 period – that U.N. inspectors "felt that in all areas we have eliminated Iraq's [WMD] capabilities fundamentally."[72] CNN quoted U.S. Secretary of State Colin Powell several times, stating that Iraq had multiple mobile biological weapons factories, but it never quoted him,[73] during the lead-up to the war in late 2002 and early 2003, as saying Iraq "has not developed any significant capability with respect to weapons of mass destruction."[74]

Poor Sourcing. War correspondent Robert Fisk made the classic statement of this fundamental problem with U.S. and to some extent British or other media: "You listen to the news coming out of Washington, it's like Americans are living in this kind of fantasy world that bears no relation to planet Earth." Journalists "wish to rely upon these utterly bankrupt comments from various unnamed anonymous intelligence sources." One might as well call parts of the press "Officials say" as a brand name, he notes.[75] Why not just call newspapers "American officials said," he wondered.[76] There is a parasitism and improper dependency at work, he argues. People "are going to the Internet because they believe they're being lied to by the American press."[77]

Ignoring the Elephant in the Room. Silence regarding the misdeeds of party leaders and allied governments is a prime source of inauthenticity and ineffectiveness in media companies. For example, Noam Chomsky focuses in many of his works on how the media and commentators ignore atrocities such as the killing of Southeast Asian or Iraqi children with bombs, bomblets, or economic sanctions.[78] Denial of imperial famines by the British, Soviets, and other great powers was nearly as atrocious, because it forestalled efforts to alleviate the plight of starving peoples, notably the Bengalis and Ukrainians.[79] In the late Cold War and New World Order (1991–) periods, cover-ups and misdirection regarding the Bangladesh, Cambodia, Sudan, and Iraq famines were nearly as destructive.[80]

Advertiser Influence. In the critical period leading up to the Iraq and Syria wars, more balanced or antiwar radio and television channels like Air America, Newsworld International, and Current TV suffered from explicit or implicit boycotts by advertisers.[81] Even more highly rated shows like Phil Donahue's MSNBC show or *Politically Incorrect with Bill Maher* were cancelled because they allowed antiwar voices on, and advertisers preferred less-balanced hosts like Joe Scarborough or Tucker Carlson.[82]

The Internet disrupted the dominance of advertisers on dominant local television networks and one-newspaper cities. By 2000, more than 90% of American cities had only one local newspaper to read, as well as those like *USA Today* that were distributed more widely.[83] The American film and broadcast industries, unlike print, have been very concentrated almost from the beginning. Six or seven large movie studios have produced most films since the 1930s, including films claiming 90% of the U.S. box office as of the late 1990s.[84] Meanwhile, beginning with the Radio Act of 1927, the federal government has repeatedly "given away radio and TV licenses . . . exclusively and preferentially to too few people."[85] In the 1990s, three companies controlled 60% of the stations in the top 100 U.S. radio markets,[86] while four companies determined what two-thirds of listeners to radio news got to hear.[87] Initially, there were only three major television companies (NBC, ABC, and CBS).[88] For decades, the three television networks "exclusively" exercised the "power to determine form and content" of the images and words broadcast to the public.[89] The three networks had a combined 70% market share in 1986.[90] Cable television, lauded as a 500-channel alternative, took away only 20% of the three networks' market share by 2001.[91] The vast majority of television markets, about 70%, had four or fewer networks producing original news, as of 2003.[92] One-half of broadcast television networks were "tight oligopolies," while most of the rest were either local monopolies or duopolies.[93] Despite the rise of streaming services, most news was produced by five conglomerates in 2023, and a great deal of entertainment (it's hard to say how much) is produced by one of them or by Netflix, a sports league, or a Meta, TikTok, Twitter/X, or YouTube channel.[94]

The Internet empowers end users to communicate with one another directly. Further, it helps them leverage open protocols and technologically neutral network architecture to build new and distinctive methods of communication, such as peer-to-peer file sharing, cryptocurrencies, and the like. The regulatory dilemma is how to compel the Internet to recapitulate the ineffective performance of more traditional media and telecommunications technologies, including the one-to-many communications paradigm of television and the closed character of proprietary networks. The Web and social media enable the peoples of the world to do many inconvenient things from the standpoint of those in power, such as broadcast themselves and their own stories, avoid editors and gatekeepers, criticize powerful economic and political actors, defend unpopular foreign governments and local social movements, expose wrongdoing and blow the whistle using leaks, and shatter propaganda with a commitment to excavating the modern memory hole.

Cyberlaw is coming to resemble National Security Law. Its themes include whether the public will ever obtain accurate information about the policies of their government amidst official secrecy and threats against leakers and speakers.[95] Insincere and mendacious public discourse is destructive of aspirations to democracy. When the mass media pollutes public opinion, and wealthy families or intelligence agencies pollute the mass media, the result is distorted or missing governance of powerful institutions. These beliefs are part of what unify First Amendment theory with philosophies of personal and electoral authenticity.[96]

By the 2020s, the existence of digital platforms that promote open cultures was at a crossroads. More people seemed to be aware of the online environment as a threat to basic freedoms, as well as a place to exercise them. The scale of interference with speakers' rights, and the sweeping announcements that even broader enforcement of new rules against "bad" speakers would be imminent, seemed to be causing serious concern. Arbitrary and (one might add) inauthentic sanctions against users of various gatekeeper platforms seemed to be quite common.

The Rise of "Deplatforming"

"Deplatforming" and "demonetization" of social media and e-commerce accounts are recurring targets of free speech advocates, fans of "remix culture," critics of military occupation and imperialism, and those on the political right who complain of Big Tech's political biases. Lexico.com, powered by the *Oxford English Dictionary*, defines deplatforming as: "The action or practice of preventing someone holding views regarded as unacceptable or offensive from contributing to a forum or debate, especially by blocking them on a particular website."[97] The term seemingly entered the archives of news and opinion websites with the GamerGate controversy of 2016 and the disinvitation of a number of speakers to platforms such as public radio stations and college campuses in 2017.[98] It gained more visibility in legal journals, newspapers, and other publications with the banning or restriction by Twitter, Facebook, YouTube, and others of accounts linked to supporters of former President Donald Trump, and eventually the ban of Trump's own accounts as well as of posts that might evade that ban.[99]

Chapter 2 described how speech related to foreign policy, gender and sexual relations, and commentary on or reframings of copyrighted work came to be suppressed online. A further blow to independent websites occurred when Google released and repeatedly tightened rules relating to low-quality, unreliable, untrustworthy content,[100] rules which notably seem to have exempted government and journalistic websites involved in false or misleading narratives that Iraq threatened the United States, that the White House was inactive and passive during the Turkish-backed campaign of terror and subversion in Syria, that Russia rigged the outcome of the 2016 presidential election, and the COVID-19 vaccines prevent transmission of the virus and ensure that vaccinated persons will not contract it. Notably, a June 2019 update to Google's algorithms penalized independent news websites that Google "raters" (frequently outsourced subcontractors) deemed "low-quality content."[101] As one report on Google's seemingly growing bias and incompleteness argued in posts that went viral in 2022, independent blogs and social media posts had been purged in favor of corporate websites, with his conclusion being "Google Search Is Dying," as authenticity is overridden by algorithms.[102]

As the sensitivity and usability of website (later app) filters advanced, the Internet became more vulnerable to censorship due to the rise of powerful Internet companies flush with cash and staffed by legions of middle managers. The decentralized Web and email systems of the 1980s and 1990s had fewer users as a share of the entire Internet, and fewer highly specialized markets prone to monopolization or collusion across a few major companies. In the early 1990s, fewer than roughly one in ten North American Internet users subscribed to services like Prodigy or America Online that could control their Web or email access.[103] There were also a wide variety of low-cost options for basic Web and email service. This state of affairs, however, was destined to change.

In the decade since the early decisions, ever greater centralization has come to portions of the World Wide Web and the Internet-connected software applications economy. As the U.S. House of Representatives concluded, in "social networking, general online search, and online advertising," Facebook and Google seem to have won "control over key channels of distribution and . . . to function as gatekeepers."[104] The result was the same for mobile operating systems, mobile app stores, and e-commerce, although the data in these areas was somewhat more consistent with oligopolies or mere "market power."[105] The House made these findings after holding public hearings with Big Tech CEOs, interviewing users and competitors of Facebook-Apple-Amazon-Google, and reviewing thousands of documents under subpoena or provided by competitors, the press, market research firms. Acquisitions of hundreds of smaller companies, often data- or technology-rich but cash-flow-poor ones, served as a stealth tactic to protect large market shares from erosion. In contrast, IBM and Microsoft had attracted swifter federal investigations and major-competitor lawsuits for strong-arming smaller rivals with contractual clauses, threats, and strategic pricing or designs.[106] Other regulators, such as the U.K. Competition and Markets Authority, the European Commission, India's authorities, and Russia's authorities have made similar findings about the mobile operating system and app store markets.

Starting with among the most level playing fields ever created in an industry, the computer and communications industry has developed oligopolies and submarkets where dominance is exercised. In 2013, the Federal Trade Commission staff drafted a report on Google's alleged monopolization of search and advertising markets. The staff recommended filing a monopolization and/or unfair competition complaint against Google.[107] The FTC accepted Google's commitments to reform its exclusive advertising syndication agreements and some of its data scraping practices in the local search market, instead of going to court.[108]

In 2020, the U.S. Department of Justice and most U.S. state governments sued Google for monopolizing and restraining trade in search and online advertising.[109] They alleged that Google had a market share of 88% in *general* Internet search (as opposed to finance, travel, law, medicine, or other specialties), 70% of Internet search advertising, and more than 70% of *general* Internet search text (as opposed to display) advertising. They pointed out that YouTube had become a mandatory app on mobile devices accounting for 70% of all such device usage worldwide. They emphasized Google's mobile device strategy (centered around the Android operating system, the Google Play Store, the Chrome browser app, the Google mobile app, the YouTube app, and the Google Maps app), was helping maintain Google's search advertising and search engine usage market shares. Google acquired more than 200 companies for more than $25 billion in cash and equity. Additionally, it paid Apple reportedly as much as $12 billion per year to be the default search engine on the Safari browser, shipped with hundreds of millions of iPhones and iPads, contributing about 20% of Apple's $64 billion or so in annual income.

Google's power continued to grow in 2020–2022. Net income grew from $7 billion in the first quarter of 2020 to $16 billion in the same period in 2022. Annual revenue rose from $162 billion in 2019 to more than $275 billion in 2022.[110] Advertising revenues rose from $33.9 billion in the third quarter of 2019 to nearly $60 billion in the third quarter of 2022. YouTube's revenue rose by 50% in a few years' time, from an estimated $16 billion in 2019 to $25 billion or so by 2021.

In 2021, 36 U.S. states and the European Commission sued Google for monopolizing the Android operating system for smartphones (basically the entire market for licensable mobile device operating systems), and 14 U.S. states and the District of Columbia challenged an alleged scheme devised by Google along with Facebook to rig online ad markets.[111] The Eleventh Circuit U.S. Court of Appeals found in 2022 that an online publisher and advertising network stated a claim against Google for monopolizing search advertising, online video advertising, all online advertising, Internet search, and ad servers; the lower court had already upheld a claim against Google for using its power to interfere with the company's revenue growth in violation of state law.[112] The states similarly allege that Google's control of the Android App Store squelches the development of new ways for publishers to be paid more for their work on entertaining or informative apps, for example with compensation for time spent from Amazon, or with bonuses from Samsung.[113] The app market was worth $32 billion in 2020, and smart device users spent the vast majority of their time on apps rather than on websites via browsers.[114]

An agency of the United States government filed suit against Facebook in 2020 for building a monopoly in what the government called "personal social networking services," as opposed to professional networking like LinkedIn, messengers like WhatsApp or iMessage, one-to-many video or photo sharing services like YouTube or Flickr, or entertainment or news sites like Yahoo![115] By 2017, Facebook was the "third largest web property in the world . . . and accounted for approximately 3 in every 4 minutes spent on social networking sites and 1 in every 7 minutes spent online around the world."[116] In terms of all Web properties, Facebook apps were also the most-downloaded in a five-year stretch leading up to 2019, although Apple and Google/Alphabet preinstalled apps like Apple Music or YouTube, which made downloading such bundled apps unnecessary.[117] YouTube probably accounted for an even larger share of minutes spent online in 2021, and its subscription option was the highest grossing in app stores in 2021, far ahead of Spotify or Disney+.[118] There is a question, however, concerning whether its "reach the masses" business model differs from Facebook's "friends and family" emphasis; if not, the two services will appeal to the same users and be economically interchangeable.[119]

When it comes to devices, Apple iOS helped run about half of Americans' smartphones and tablets by 2020.[120] In Western Europe and the United States, courts and regulators have found that Apple has market power in niche markets such as premium smartphones, mobile wallets, app distribution, and mobile gaming transactions.[121] As the European Commission explains: "For app developers, the App Store is the sole gateway to consumers using Apple's smart mobile devices running on Apple's smart mobile operating system iOS. Apple's devices and software form a 'closed ecosystem.'"[122] Although it connects users to more than 1.5 million independent apps, Apple's App Store typically ranks Apple's own apps above competitors' apps in the App Store search engine.[123] Apple's control over the app ecosystem, particularly for iPhones, results in extraordinary profit margins on App Store transactions, well over a 50% margin where most retailers and distributors earn less than a 10% margin.[124] In Central, Eastern, and Southern Europe, however, as in Asia outside of Japan and much of Africa and South Asia, Android is by far the dominant OS, running on Samsung and other devices.[125]

A U.S. House majority report on Big Tech practices found that business users had been at the mercy of Amazon.com's reach and power. Amazon allegedly used the power of its size to threaten sellers with destocking, loss of certain buy or pre-order buttons, or lower appearance in user search results.[126] Moreover, the report focused on how Amazon's product search algorithm downranks sellers with low sales, resulting in an arms race or an effective tie of seller account services to advertising services.[127] A Center for American Progress investigation found that Amazon's online retail search algorithm appears to favor goods sold by third-party sellers who use Amazon warehousing services or who purchase ads on Amazon.[128] Appearance in Amazon's "Buy Box" on its platform appears to be the result of an algorithm structured to favor companies that use other Amazon services.[129] In the future, as more searches come in by Alexa, smart appliance, Ring drone, or other new technologies, the chances for Amazon to favor goods that it makes will multiply. Amazon might especially dominate household staples, which it finds easier to duplicate than a complex good like an iPhone, and utilizes its website, mobile app, and smart home assistant Alexa to grab the most attention.[130]

Being the default item on a product page may result in a considerable boost to sales, although it is far from impossible or even that difficult to make sales as the non-default, e.g., with lower prices. A key metric that Amazon uses to determine who fills the buy box is shipping and delivery estimates, for which Amazon views its own fulfillment and logistics as the best.[131] Online marketing experts xcellco and cpcstrategy argue that stock levels, shipping performance, feedback, and other data help dictate the lucrative default position in Amazon's "buy box."[132]

The House Judiciary Committee's subcommittee report from 2018 accused Amazon of doing something similar to what Google, Apple, and Facebook did to certain competitive apps by deciding to discriminate against retail users of its website who fulfill, or perform and deliver, their own sales. The evidence, the committee stated, was that Amazon treated "FBA" or "fulfilled by Amazon" customers differently in assessing Buy Box eligibility.[133] As discussed in Chapter 5, the European Commission and Italian antitrust commission have found Amazon in violation of competition law for this practice. The Attorney General of the District of Columbia has filed similar charges, but the D.C. Superior Court found that Amazon had not monopolized online marketplaces or suppressed price competition between its own sellers' Amazon storefronts and the same sellers' offerings on their own websites or other platforms, because sellers remained able to switch platforms at will; Walmart, Target, and eBay were large competitors; and Amazon had a legitimate interest in demanding that its sellers feature their best available pricing on Amazon.[134] As of this writing, the U.S. Federal Trade Commission (FTC) seems poised to challenge Amazon's Buy Box control and self-dealing, the agency having "amassed evidence that the company disadvantages sellers that don't use [Amazon's fulfillment and logistics] services, and . . . investigating an algorithm that selects merchants for the web store's coveted 'Buy Box,' where consumers can add products to their cart with one click."[135]

With market power often comes commercialization and market discipline. Spam is a major target of social networks and streaming sites, as it was for email services and auction sites before them. If the user was just going to delete spam anyway, why waste bandwidth and storage space on the backend delivering it to them? This was the question raised by email and Internet access services early on in Internet history. Filtering email or other malicious or unwanted content based on its subject line, sender address, or signatures of scams or malware in the message text ran contrary to the "end-to-end principle" that empowers the Internet user to access content and applications of their choice but promised to save energy, hardware and human time, and money (from scams).[136] Dominant Web portals and search engines, followed by social networks, invented complex ways of filtering the Internet, often using collaborative filtering and AI methods.[137]

Collaborative filtering bootstraps recommendations or counter-recommendations based on user similarity. Users are correlated using statistical techniques, and then search engine rankings for hyperlinked social media posts, movies (as on

Netflix or Amazon), or websites may be modified to bootstrap one user's recommendations with another's.[138]

Bad-Faith Deplatforming and the Immunities of Platforms

The Communications Decency Act is an important liability shield for websites and smart device apps, and an inducement to delete Internet users' speech that is obscene, adult-oriented, "excessively violent," harassing, or "otherwise objectionable."[139] The CDA, "enacted in large part in response to the prevalence of obscene and pornographic materials on websites that children might access, provides for immunity to information providers on the internet."[140] Its effect spans several areas of law: first, it blocks many State and local laws from having their ordinary effect; second, it says that a website or app provider shall not be regulated like the speaker or publisher of speech it did not create or commission; and third, it immunizes from civil lawsuits "any action taken in good faith to restrict access to or availability of material that the provider or user considers to be obscene, lewd, lascivious, filthy, excessively violent, harassing, or otherwise objectionable, whether or not such material is constitutionally protected."[141]

According to general principles of U.S. law, a person filing a lawsuit is not required to allege that the defendant is not entitled to certain defenses that might apply. Rather, the person being sued should file an answer placing those defenses into the case and should develop proof supporting these defenses using affidavits, documents, experts, and trial witnesses. As one court explained, this means that the defendant in a case supposedly subject to CDA Section 230 should have to state in its answer and prove at trial that it acted in good faith:

> The CDA statutory immunity is an affirmative defense which plaintiff is not required to negate in its Complaint. The plain language of the CDA only provides immunity for actions "voluntarily taken in good faith." 47 U.S.C. § 230(c)(2)(A). While the CDA defense may properly be considered if it is apparent from the face of the complaint, that is not the situation in this case. Here, plaintiff has included allegations within its Second Amended Complaint that Google failed to act in good faith when removing its websites from Google's search results.[142]

The court also addressed the First Amendment right of an Internet service to withhold its services from speakers identified with unsolicited commercial promotion, or "spam." It rejected the position of Google that it could de-list websites from the most popular search engine, ban all future websites from the same entity, ignore the entity's changes to its speech to satisfy the search engine's rules, and falsely suggest to the public that the search engine is uncensored:

> While publishers are entitled to discretion for editorial judgment decisions, plaintiff has alleged that Google's reason for banning its websites was not

> based upon "editorial judgments," but instead based upon anti-competitive motives. . . . *Pittsburgh Press Co. v. Pittsburgh Comm'n on Human Relations*, 413 U.S. 376, 386, 93 S.Ct. 2553, 37 L.Ed.2d 669 (1973); . . . *Levitch v. Columbia Broad. Sys., Inc.*, 495 F.Supp. 649, 662 (S.D.N.Y.1980) ("[A]bsent . . . purely editorial conduct, plaintiffs' claims must be tested against the normal pleading requirements applicable in federal court."). Further, a fact published maliciously with knowledge of its falsity or serious doubts as to its truth is sufficient to overcome the editorial judgment protection afforded by the Constitution. *Pittsburgh Press Co.*, 413 U.S. at 386, 93 S.Ct. 2553. Plaintiff has adequately alleged that it did not violate any of Google's policies and that the representations made by Google that e-ventures' pages violate Google's policies are false.[143]

The court noted in passing that the plaintiff had alleged that Google targeted alternative services that would improve businesses' chances of connecting with members of the public, branding them as "spam" for anti-competitive purposes.[144] This would not be an editorial decision so much as an anti-competitive scheme, or course of conduct. The Supreme Court had found non-editorial decisions to be unprotected by statute decades prior.

Although courts are divided on the question, some others have adopted the same approach.[145] As one study of nearly two decades of decisions leading up to 2015 concluded, either complicity in the wrongful publication of charges, or a persistent failure to explain sanctions against a user, may violate the "good faith" condition and cause a website or app to lose Section 230 immunity.

> In theory, an ISP may lose its Section 230 safe harbor should its editorial activities go beyond "Good Samaritan" blocking and screening to provide or generate content to serve its own interests. Some courts have reacted to this seemingly uncapped power by reading "good faith" restriction into [sic] the Good Samaritan safe harbor. A Massachusetts District Court recently developed a theory that the CDA's Section 230 (c)(2) does not mandate a dismissal of a claim arising from the fact that the defendant interactive service provider engages in unscrupulous or bad faith manipulation of customer reviews that constitutes a misrepresentation of plaintiff's business.[146]

One year after invoking the malicious or reckless exception to the First Amendment's protections, the court in *e-ventures* concluded that Google's exclusion of the plaintiff's sites was an editorial judgment, and that the plaintiff failed to rebut Google's showing that policies had been violated. Accordingly, the court dismissed the action as being precluded by the First Amendment protection of decisions regarding which sites to include in a search engine, finding such a decision to be analogous to a newspaper selecting articles for its front page or opinion page. While an "unfair" decision by Google would not trigger a First Amendment defense, reckless editorializing by Google might be part of that platform's own freedom.[147]

Where deplatforming occurs in bad faith and for anticompetitive purposes, Section 230 is much less likely to apply. The Ninth Circuit has held that even if Section 230 immunity applies to malware or other objectionable content or applications that do not contain sexually indecent or excessively violent materials, a bad-faith intent to harm competition defeats the immunity.[148] There is a basis to argue, for this reason, that inauthentic, inconsistent, and duplicitous use of platform standards to deplatform or demonetize others is not immunized.

The First Amendment and Unnecessary Deplatforming

There are four main reasons to doubt whether a search engine has an absolute First Amendment right to hide or ban websites, and to deny that a social network or marketplace must be free to "speak" by arbitrarily suspending or terminating user accounts. First, services open to the public are common carriers with a First Amendment status distinct from newspapers. Second, by serving the public, platforms may incur the nondiscrimination duties of a place of accommodation, under state law but also federal and foreign law as well. Third, tech platforms often bind themselves to terms of service limiting their discretion and advertise themselves in ways that should have consequences in tort law. Fourth, federal and state governments' significant encouragement and assistance to deplatforming campaigns trigger the constitutional right of the Internet user not to be victim of a conspiracy involving a deprivation of civil rights. There is a fifth reason as well, but it is more difficult to justify and may be even more of a minority view. It involves the theory or assertion that tech platforms do not have a free speech interest in the editing, curation, algorithmic arrangement, community standards, and "feel" of their services.

One Ohio decision indicates that Big Tech firms are potentially common carriers, depending on whether one holders itself out to the public as (neutrally?) carrying information, as other firms like airlines, railroads, ferries, taxis, elevators, and escalators carry people and as doctors serve the public.[149] As Ohio's attorney general, the attorneys general of Texas and Florida, and scholars like Philip Hamburger and Clare Morell point out, large digital services like Facebook/Instagram, Google/YouTube/Android, and Twitter/X serve the public and enjoy special "conduit" privileges like Section 230, Section 512 of the DMCA, and the law of the cloud.[150] "They serve a public function, providing the public square or conduit for the information age. We meet and communicate on their services or platforms much more than on the grass of the village green."[151] There are precedents and sound policy reasons for treating firms that are hired to carry communications by wire or wireless means and that are not radio stations as common carriers.[152] Special duties rightly accrue to a business that holds itself out to carry the goods (or more recently the communications) of all comers, thereby heightening the public concern with the business, and public vulnerability to its arbitrariness.[153] The growing role of Big Tech as storage, communications, and commerce utilities helps justify fairness regulation.[154]

Other common carriers and places of public accommodation have political beliefs and corporate standards without being exempt from public-interest or civil-rights must-carry regulation. For example, Supreme Court case law on shopping malls and cable networks indicates that editorial discretion is essential to be exempted from the obligation to carry the speech of others, while Congress has declared that Internet intermediaries are more like warehouses for or distributors of books and newspapers than the publishers thereof, let alone the editors.[155] When Verizon Communications argued that it had a First Amendment right and a property right not to be regulated as a neutral communications carrier, its argument was at first set aside,[156] and then rejected in a case involving a related trade association's challenge to net neutrality.[157]

A First Amendment right to be free from economic regulation of one's conduct should be based on a danger that one's own message will be suppressed, chilled, or distorted.[158] No reasonable person would believe that a job fair agrees ideologically with every employer represented there, for example.[159] The fair is not the booth. Therefore, law schools do not have a First Amendment right to deny employers with whom they disagree access to their recruiting events. Similarly, it is unreasonable to blame a shopping mall for the speech of protesters or signature gatherers at the mall or blame a cable network for broadcast television shows retransmitted by cable.[160]

In upholding the FCC's cable television mandates against First Amendment challenges, the Supreme Court concluded that it is permissible to force an economic actor who is already open to other members of the public to carry additional channels or speech. It declared that such a mandate is appropriately viewed as a content-neutral regulation, which may be upheld if the underlying government interest is "substantial," and if the form of regulation chosen is not substantially more burdensome than it needs to be to achieve that interest.[161] It further reasoned that even if cable systems' channel line-up is editorial speech, the duty to carry more channels is a content-neutral speech regulation, and it regulates speech without regard to its viewpoint or subject matter (as opposed to content-based speech regulations, which target particular viewpoints or subject matter).[162] Content-based speech regulations are subject to the most exacting First Amendment scrutiny and rarely pass First Amendment muster.

In addressing a challenge to a form of net neutrality regulation that it issued in 2005, the FCC concluded that it is the interest of Internet users that must prevail over the interests of Internet infrastructure owners.[163] The FCC's 2008 decision has substantial roots in public utilities law as applied to telecommunications media.[164] The Supreme Court has held that broadcast television stations may be regulated as to their content in order to protect the public interest in uninhibited and fair debate.[165] Silencing Internet apps or user accounts that are not themselves committing crimes or torts violates the same principle that underlines the Interstate Commerce Act: the obligation of essential infrastructure to serve the public on fair and nondiscriminatory terms.[166]

Ashutosh Baghwat argues that platforms cannot be common carriers, for then they will lack any editorial rights at all, including the right not to be compelled to host speech that they abhor.[167] This is not necessarily true, however. Consider the application of anti-discrimination law to newspapers and television networks. Whether or not a newspaper or website that engages in racial or sex-based discrimination is itself expressive, "speech proposing an illegal transaction is excluded from First Amendment protection."[168] Just as a newspaper may be regulated as to advertising narcotics, it may be regulated as to employment discrimination or fraud.[169] Even the choice of who represents a broadcast network as its mouthpiece, for example as anchor of the local news, is subject to regulation as to age, gender, race, or national-origin discrimination.[170]

Second, services open to the public become public accommodations and should be subject to basic antidiscrimination norms. Corporations that exercise editorial or other personal discretion are not immune from antidiscrimination laws, whether those concerning employment or customer service. As the Supreme Court explained in 2018, while business owners may have rights of conscience, their freedom of belief does not extend to "deny[ing] protected persons equal access to goods and services under a neutral and generally applicable public accommodations law."[171] In 2018–2023, the Supreme Court articulated a freedom of religious or personal conscience as a limit on being forced to speak in ways with which one disagrees in order to serve a customer, and a further right to refrain from paying for employee benefits that one objects to on limited protected grounds.[172] Even in these decisions, however, it reaffirmed that the state and federal governments have the power to "protect gay persons, just as . . . other classes of individuals, in acquiring whatever products and services they choose on the same terms and conditions as are offered to other members of the public."[173]

Next, consider the enforcement of antitrust law against the media. If major newspapers were to engage in a group boycott of an upstart newspaper seeking to participate in the Associated Press news-sharing system or other wire service, in a bid to crush this upstart, they could not claim a right of editorial discretion that would override their duty of fair conduct under antitrust law. Similarly, when Microsoft claimed a right as a private operating system provider to exclude icons for Netscape or other programs while including icons for Internet Explorer, the courts disagreed, stating among other things that a property right does not override antitrust duties.

There are many other legal exceptions to editorial freedom or, to be more precise, the freedom of shareholders to select executives who dictate how a platform or media outlet will be operated. A book author, for example, might seek specific performance of a publishing contract, or in any event money damages for its breach, even though book publishers and editors have First Amendment editorial rights.[174]

There is no compelling reason to permit bad-faith conduct by Big Tech or other large corporations. Traditionally, bad faith was known in common law as "malice" and made subject to punitive damages.[175] A party to an ordinary contract should be compensated for the other side's lack of good faith in interpreting or applying it.[176] In many countries, the law of unfair dismissal from employment allows those terminated in bad faith to gain their jobs back. In the United States, bad faith termination on a ground that is not regulated by employment law may be legal, but persons with tenure or members of a protected group may be compensated for a bad-faith pretextual firing, e.g. where someone not in the group was not or would not be fired. A lack of good faith in accommodating workers or customers having disabilities, or in ensuring that workers or customers are not harassed on racial or gender grounds, can result in liability for employment discrimination, disability discrimination, and/or sex or race harassment.[177] Bad-faith statements to investors may amount to securities fraud[178]; bad-faith statements to consumers may violate advertising laws.[179] Professional licensing laws may be designed, in part, to ensure that bad-faith overbilling of Medicare or bad-faith handling of legal matters does not harm the public interest.

Lobbyists for platforms, and some scholars and politicians, argue that the cost of litigating bad faith by platforms will be too high. The idea that this will prevent any speech from being carried on large platforms seems to be undermined by the operation of the same platforms in countries or regions where such litigation may be possible, as it sometimes is in California and the Ninth Circuit, or countries other than the United States that do not have a Section 230. In addition, platforms continue to carry vast amounts of material that might be subject to a criminal statute or an intellectual property right somewhere in the world, even though CDA Section 230 exempts such laws from its extension of immunity from liability for publishing or depublishing material.

One court addressed the analogous situation of sharing economy platforms that wish to avoid state or local regulation of their listings under the First Amendment:

> [E]ven accepting that the Platforms will need to engage in efforts to validate transactions before completing them, incidental burdens like these are not always sufficient to trigger First Amendment scrutiny. . . . "[S]ubjecting every incidental impact on speech to First Amendment scrutiny 'would lead to the absurd result that any government action that had some conceivable speech inhibiting consequences . . . would require analysis under the First Amendment.'" . . . Furthermore, to the extent that the speech chilled advertises unlawful rentals, "[a]ny First Amendment interest . . . is altogether absent when the commercial activity itself is illegal and the restriction on advertising is incidental to a valid limitation on economic activity." See *Pittsburgh Press Co. v. Pittsburgh Comm'n on Human Relations*, 413 U.S. 376, 389, 93 S.Ct. 2553, 37 L.Ed.2d 669 (1973).[180]

As the Supreme Court explained in one of the cases that the Ninth Circuit cited, denying access to the public sphere through means such as employment discrimination is an illegal economic practice, not shielded by the use of a newspaper column or other eloquent form adjacent to it:

> Any First Amendment interest which might be served by advertising an ordinary commercial proposal and which might arguably outweigh the governmental interest supporting the regulation is altogether absent when the

commercial activity itself is illegal and the restriction on advertising is incidental to a valid limitation on economic activity.[181]

Third, digital services often promise the public that they will respect free expression or only deplatform users in certain narrow cases or after some number of prior warnings.[182] The First Amendment often does not excuse noncompliance with written or implied contractual obligations.[183] Thus, in one case involving Twitter before Elon Musk's purchase, a deplatformed user could invoke Twitter's commitments to him, if nothing else or no other legal theory.[184]

Digital services and sympathetic courts often state that any broad and nonspecific guarantees of free speech or openness are not enforceable because terms of use or community standards pages are more detailed and present numerous important caveats to these bromides.[185] These decisions are very brief and do not seriously engage about what platforms actually hold themselves out to users as being or doing. They also provide little insight into what users reasonably believe their relationship with platforms is, or what commitments they think platforms have made to them. One hopes that in future decisions this theory will be explored in more depth and seriousness.

Fourth, state action in enlisting, goading, or threatening platforms to censor more in order to promote various public policies turns private censorship into a conspiracy with the state. This body of law will be the subject of the next section of this chapter.

Finally, the largest digital services lack any consistent theme in their messaging that would support a First Amendment right to be free of their conduct with regard to content creators. In a case some scholars find analogous, a First Amendment right to engage in sex discrimination was rejected where same-sex fellowship was not important to the defendant, which was a Rotary Club chapter, part of a large social group in the United States that has lectures and events, and publishes newsletters and other material.[186] There is a "general rule" that political beliefs "do not allow business owners and other actors in the economy and in society to deny protected persons equal access to goods and services under a neutral and generally applicable public accommodations law."[187] By contrast, persons and groups motivated by deeply personal or conscientious motives, such as religious scruples, are sometimes exempted from generally applicable antidiscrimination laws, in a state of affairs often decried by justices and scholars.[188]

Advocates of the view that dominant websites or apps cannot be treated as in any way like common carriers sometimes contradict themselves. They suggest, like Judge Newsom writing for a panel of the Eleventh Circuit, that common carriers must serve all members of the public "indiscriminately," and that social media do not qualify because their platforms have community standards.[189] However, they also point out that even common carriers could refuse service to obnoxious persons, and that telephone services for example could refuse to carry indecency or blasphemy.[190] This means that common carriers did not – and did not have to – serve the public indiscriminately. Yet they were prohibited by law from unnecessarily or unfairly denying service to a member of the public. As a near-majority of the Supreme Court once stated:

> If Congress finds that cable operators are leaving some channels empty – perhaps for ease of future expansion – it can compel the operators to make the free channels available to programmers who otherwise would not get carriage. See *PruneYard Shopping Center v. Robins*, 447 U.S. 74, 88 (1980) (upholding a compelled access scheme because it did not burden others' speech). Congress might also conceivably obligate cable operators to act as common carriers for some of their channels, with those channels being open to all through some sort of lottery system or time-sharing arrangement. Setting aside any possible Takings Clause issues, it stands to reason that if Congress may demand that telephone companies operate as common carriers, it can ask the same of cable companies; such an approach would not suffer from the defect of preferring one speaker to another.[191]

Though a common carrier, like a railroad, may deny service to elephants, or passengers who do not pay the fare, this does not mean that it may discriminate among qualified customers.[192]

First Amendment advocates should not be fans of unnecessary deplatforming. Forcing broadband providers that own HBO or NBC not to discriminate against Netflix or YouTube does not violate the First Amendment. Forcing cable networks to carry NBC to save local news or local employment does not violate the First Amendment, properly understood. Perhaps it would violate the First Amendment to force an anti-gay parade organizer to allow gay or lesbian participation in the parade, or to require the Russian Orthodox Church to ordain a non-Christian or non-Russian-speaking minister.[193] And perhaps forcing an anti-LGBT baker or website designer to bake certain cakes or design certain websites raises First Amendment issues. But an anti-deplatforming law regulates bad-faith or discriminatory conduct, or a mixture of such conduct and low-input speech mostly involving the ordering of others' speech, just as in many areas of the economy clothed with expressive significance, like university policy or carrying ads.

The Unconstitutionality of the CDA's Deplatforming Function

Exceptions to Internet user rights that are intended to incentivize action against indecency, lewdness, war footage, etc. threaten speech and press freedoms. As four justices explained decades ago, "the First Amendment does more than just bar government from intentionally suppressing speech of which it disapproves. It also generally prohibits the government from excepting certain kinds of speech from regulation because it thinks the speech is especially valuable."[194] Another important principle goes back even further: the government should not be able to conscript private actors so as to censor indirectly what it may not censor directly.[195]

There is case law that should have reined in "censorship by proxy," or the conscription of Internet sites into a censorship project by threatening everyone with crushing civil liability but exempting sites that take down lewd, lascivious, offensive, or excessively violent content.[196] With some notable exceptions, however, U.S. courts generally refrained from applying this case law to the benefit of Internet speakers. First Amendment jurisprudence from before the Internet age, as well as during it, seeks to provide a remedy for persons with unorthodox viewpoints who might be the victim of governmental pressure on private actors to silence or intimidate them, as Chapter 5 will explore in more detail. As one case explains with some precision:

> In *Bantam Books [Inc. v. Sullivan]* the Rhode Island Commission sent notices to book distributors stating that it was charged by the legislature with "prevent[ing] the sale, distribution or display of indecent and obscene publications" and that lists of "objectionable" publications were being circulated to Chiefs of Police with the order that "they are not to be sold, distributed or displayed to youths under the eighteen years of age." 372 U.S. [58,] 63 n. 5 [1963]. The notices also informed the distributors that "[t]he Attorney General will act for us in case of non-compliance," and were followed by a police visit to the distributors. *Id.* The Supreme Court found that the notices were "phrased virtually as orders," and that the distributors faced a genuine threat of prosecution. *Id.* at 68. . . . The Court therefore held that the Commission's notices and related enforcement scheme amount to an impermissible prior restraint on publication that "provide[d] no safeguards whatever against the suppression of . . . constitutionally protected matter." 372 U.S. at 70. . . . The Supreme Court has also made clear, however, that government officials "may cajole and exhort" without violating the First Amendment. *Gravel v. United States*, 408 U.S. 606, 625 . . . (1972). . . . "[W]here a public official, without engaging in *any* threat, coercion, or intimidation, 'exhorted' private entities not to distribute a board game whose ideas the official viewed as pernicious, the official's speech [may] violate any constitutional right of the game's authors." . . .
>
> The question to be answered . . . is whether "the [evidentiary] record, taken in the light most favorable to [plaintiffs], reveals statements by [defendants] that a reasonable factfinder could find, . . . '[i]ntimat[e] that some form of punishment or adverse regulatory action w[ould] follow' if the [plaintiffs] continued to air [unpopular speakers'] views."[197]

In another relevant case, the Supreme Court found that American Bar Association standards censoring advertising by attorney members of the bar, which had been adopted by the State of Arizona, were immune from antitrust attack as state laws, but not from citizens' rights under the First Amendment.[198] The Chief Justice and two other dissenters would have allowed the "organized bar" to control attorney advertising of the price of legal services, but their view did not prevail.[199] This case is relevant to efforts to threaten websites for hosting offensive, adult, or misleading advertisements because the resulting liability risk may far outweigh their advertising rates, but the advertisers may be unable to challenge the threats despite bearing the brunt of the harm.[200] The government should not be conscripting low-cost private police in this way.[201]

Coordinated Inauthentic (Intelligence) Activity

There is a danger that the public's access to tools for uninhibited political and cultural discourse will be restricted in collusive ways, under the influence of entities that bring together companies which should be competing, prompting the companies to act similarly. These entitles prominently include the so-called "intelligence community," or the FBI, the Department of Homeland Security, the Central Intelligence Agency, the Directorate of National Intelligence, the intelligence agents of the Department of State, the political appointees of the Department of Justice, the Defense Intelligence Agency, and the National Security Agency. There are other government agencies that may be exceeding their statutory or constitutional authority to censor online dissent, like the White House's Digital (Strategy) Directors, the European Commission's online safety experts, and the Cybersecurity and Infrastructure Security Agency working group.[202]

A wave of deplatforming began in March or April 2018 and continued through January 2019 and even later. It allegedly involved law enforcement in the United States complaining to Facebook and other Big Tech giants about "coordinated inauthentic activity." These are supposed to be networks of social media accounts, bots, and perhaps botnets that do a variety of scary-sounding things like "influenc[ing] . . . elections," "inflaming social and political tensions," and engaging in "information operations" and even the peddling of "disinformation."[203]

Nonprofits can be the architects of "public-private partnerships" that allow regulatory regimes to be implemented by governments without the benefit of traditional procedures for adopting legislation or federal agency rules (in the United States). As Twitter Files journalist Michael Schellenberger observes:

> [Renee DiResta once stated that] "public-private partnerships I think, are absolutely key. . . . I know that triggers some people who get worried about privacy and such, but I don't think that there's any way to do it other than to treat it as an information war." . . .
>
> The censorship complex employs various tactics. One is the relentless demand for censorship, as we saw with the Twitter Files and the Facebook Files, released by the Attorneys General of Missouri and Louisiana. Another is directing government and philanthropic money toward research and advocacy for greater censorship of social media platforms, the specific task of at least two organizations, News Guard and the Disinformation Index.
>
> These two tactics go hand in hand. The new censors seek legislation that would give increasing control over the content moderation of social media platforms to establishment experts and elites, while others in their network seek to direct advertiser revenue away from disfavored news media corporations, mostly conservative and libertarian but also some radical Leftwing

> ones, and toward favored news organizations, mostly liberal and establishment-friendly progressive ones.
>
> What's more, government and nongovernmental censors work together to threaten to revoke the Section 230 protections of social media, on the one hand, and demand censorship on the other. Sometimes they boast that the tech firms only caved thanks to the "huge regulatory stakes" for not censoring.
>
> Censors work together to deplatform disfavored individuals. This starts with labeling them "superspreaders" of disinformation.[204]

This is a long-ago predicted misuse of private power over online speech due to "censorship creep" and inauthentic behavior by platforms that would like to be free but need *money*.[205]

The intelligence or national security "blob" extends beyond currently serving public officials, however. Many former officials continue to have security clearances while working in Big Tech, the media, defense contractors, or think tanks. The "blob" may also include former intelligence or policy officials ensconced in multinational corporations or civil society organizations. An estimate likely out of date long ago was that nearly a million Americans had a "top secret" security clearance after a $2 trillion post-9/11 federal binge on programs to track new threats.[206]

Buttressing all this is another trend that affects Internet freedom negatively: the rhetoric of Internet "content." The use of the term *content* for cultural and political speech is a pernicious trend that threatens the freedoms of speech and of the press, and religious liberty. As technology law practitioner Andrew P. Bridges explains, it is an insidious rhetorical device. He represented companies that are sued for technological innovations and thus got caught up in the "copyright wars." He noticed that copyright lobbyists were shifting the terminology from the "knowledge economy" to the "consumption of content." He realized that this rhetoric reduced speech, knowledge, and narrative to a thing plopped into a container, like cans or units of merchandise. These things are "consumed," like a burning home, or an emptied gas can. The user depletes, incinerates, and exhausts. The viewer of content is a buyer, not a scholar or a spiritual being:

> [Y]ou never heard anybody say, "The content you posted on Facebook last night really got me thinking." . . . I go to a Springsteen show. . . . "He delivered some great content." You don't say that. . . . Or "next week, our book club will consume Anne Lamott's latest content." . . . When you go to a concert, you're experiencing something. When you read a book that moves you, you're experiencing something. . . . It's about interacting with other people's education. . . . You are connected with people . . . and are engaging in community. . . . You're gaining something, and you are growing as a person. . . .
>
> And it's not "moderation," what people refer to by content moderation. A moderator moderating a panel says, "Jim, that's a great idea. Sally, what do you think about what Jim said?" . . . A moderator does not say, "Sally, I don't like what you're saying, shut up."[207]

The Internet came to be inauthentically regulated, according to politicians and commentators to both the left and the right of the U.S. Democratic Party, when former Obama administration officials influenced large websites and apps in 2020 to remove or downrank speech that criticized Democratic presidential candidate Joe Biden, U.S. allies or U.S. policy towards Russia and China, or other U.S. policies other than those favored by the Green Party, the Libertarian Party, the Democratic Socialists, or the Republicans.[208] Then, some of these officials reentered government as part of the Biden administration and urged platforms to censor various topics.[209] The topics typically censored included criticism of U.S. and Chinese biological toxin research and biolabs (the "lab leak"), the suppression of off-label drugs for treating COVID-19 (that showed promise in some studies but not others and that the Food and Drug Administration or Centers for Disease Control discouraged taking at the time), the effectiveness or safety of mRNA vaccines for COVID-19, or U.S. policy toward eastern Ukraine and the Russian invasion to forestall a Ukrainian offensive against rebellious provinces in 2022.[210] All this was despite the fact that criticism of U.S. vaccine policy, biolab insecurity, or foreign policy was not only allowed but amplified on major platforms prior to 2021.[211] By September 2020, half of U.S. adults reported to surveys that they probably or definitely would not receive a COVID-19 vaccine, even though the Trump administration touted its "warp speed" vaccine program as a cure-all and an end to lockdowns.[212]

Another development related to declining Internet freedom was discussed in Chapter 2. Tech giants looked to government agencies for middle management and departmental staff trained in national security, law enforcement, and political influence operations. As journalist Glenn Greenwald tallied, drawing on LinkedIn pages and other data, dozens of ex-CIA officials occupy such staff positions, including posts tasked with policing online speech for "misinformation," alongside former FBI, Department of Homeland Security, and National Security Agency employees.[213] The revolving door between government and online gatekeepers facilitates the routine submission of account names or page links by government to platforms for prompt deletion.[214] Scholars write of "revolving door corruption," which they identify as one way, along with campaign contributions, lobbying, and regulatory capture, that oligarchy sustains itself.[215]

In 2020–2021, secretive account removals accelerated, and many speakers blamed platforms for acting in collusion with governments. Activists alleged that Facebook had sought out former government officials with experience in banning lots of websites or accounts to serve on its staff.[216] Greenwald asks whether all this is a mere continuation of the Internet surveillance and interference revealed by Edward Snowden in 2013, leading to official inquiries into illegality.[217]

As a result of these trends, laws relating to how digital platforms to promote open culture and consumer choice is an urgent task. As noted in prior chapters, the European Commission and Parliament and some U.S. states propose to restrict unfair treatment particularly of small and medium-sized enterprises (SMEs) that were assured of open access to subscribers only to have that access degraded. A considerable barrier to these efforts is a body of case law and statutes that persuade online platforms that they are free of "must-carry" obligations in the style of cable or telephone network regulation. Some foreign countries have already fined U.S.-based platforms for mistreating local SMEs, but the platforms continue to challenge such fines.[218]

The next two chapters survey recent developments in these areas and propose solutions to the problems of bans from essential facilities, degraded access, and trampling on consumer choice. Among other original contributions, they draw connections between U.S. constitutional and statutory doctrines relating to shared spaces and the teachings of international human rights bodies relating to the responsibilities of private actors. The concepts of infrastructure, "public accommodations," and public utilities loom large. Doctrines generated using these concepts exist in competition law, antidiscrimination law, and even copyright law. Such doctrines may limit deplatforming and bring about a degree of convergence between U.S. and European law on Internet bans, account suspensions, and chilling effects.

Notes

1 Reno v. ACLU, 521 U.S. 844, 868–70 (1997); *Turner Broadcasting*, 512 U.S. at 626; Lorain Journal v. United States, 342 U.S. 143, 146, 149 (1951); Byars v. Bluff City News Co., 609 F.2d 843, 845–47, 856–58 (6th Cir. 1979). Digital media supplant traditional media's communications model of "one to many" with the Internet's model of "many to many," which allows every reader to become an author, direct distribution to replace intermediary censorship and editorial control, and public-interested publication to displace commercial dictates. Niva Elkin-Koren, 'Cyberlaw and social change: A democratic approach to Copyright law in cyberspace,' 14 *Cardozo Arts and Entertainment Law Journal* 215, 259 (1996); Mike Godwin, *Cyber Rights: Defending Free Speech in the Digital Age* (1998); Margaret Chon, 'Erasing race?: A critical race feminist view of Internet identity-shifting,' 3 *Journal of Gender, Race and Justice* 439, 446 (2000).

2 E.g., Pew Internet and American Life Project (PIALP), How Women and Men Use the Internet, 2005, pp. 2, 20, 47, https://www.pewinternet.org/pdfs/PIP_Women_and_Men_online.pdf (66% of American women are online, 8% have their own blogs, and 11% have their own websites); PIALP, Bloggers a Portrait of the Internet's New Storytellers, 2006, https://www.pewinternet.org/pdfs/PIP%20Bloggers%20Report%20July%2019%202006.pdf ("The blogging population is young, evenly split between women and men, and racially diverse. . . . 11% [of bloggers] are African-American, 19% are "English-speaking Hispanic and 10% identify as some other race."). Assuming that there are 12 million American blogs, that means about 6 million American women, 1.3 million African-Americans, 2.3 million Latinos/Latinas, and 1.2 million Asian-Americans, Native Americans, and others had a voice in digital media. Television news sources, talk show hosts and guests, as well as newspaper editors, by contrast, were overwhelmingly male, European-American, and (for television but not newspapers) Republican. *See* Kay Semion, Who we are and what we do: an internet-researched update, The Masthead, Autumn 2006, https://www.findarticles.com/p/articles/mi_qa3771/is_200610/ai_n16756010; Media Matters for America, If It's Sunday, It's Conservative: An Analysis of the Sunday Talk Show Guests on ABC, CBS, and NBC, 1997–2005 (2006), http://mediamatters.org/static/pdf/MMFA_Sunday_Show_Report.pdf; Carole Ashkinaze, A Matter of Opinion: Female Pundits Are Still Missing From The Media, Ms. Mag., Summer 2005, http://msmagazine.com/summer2005/opinion.asp; Steve Rendall and Tara Broughel, Amplifying Officials, Squelching Dissent, Extra! (2003), https://www.fair.org/index.php?page=1145; Fairness and Accuracy in Reporting, Who's On the News? Study Shows Network News Sources Skew

White, Male & Elite (2002), https://www.fair.org/index.php?page=1865. The ideal of cyberspace, utopian and overly romantic though it may be, is of "a world that all may enter without privilege or prejudice accorded by race, economic power, military force, or station of birth . . . a world where anyone, anywhere may express his or her beliefs, no matter how singular, without fear of being coerced into silence or conformity." John Perry Barlow, A Declaration of the Independence of Cyberspace (1995), https://www.eff.org/Publications/John_Perry_Barlow/barlow_0296.declaration. Notably, over 40% of relatively low-income Americans posted information to the Internet by 2004 or 2005, surely many more than had been published in the traditional media by that time. Molly Shaffer Van Houweling, 'Distributive values in Copyright,' 83 *Texas Law Review* 1535, 1563 (2005).

3 In the 20th century, American newspapers, broadcast networks, and movie studios apparently reached an understanding with politicians in Washington to the effect that the government's perspective on important issues would be amplified in the public press, while dissenters would be denied effective access to it. James Q. Wilson, Press at war, *Wall Street Journal Online* (November 6, 2006), https://www.wsj.com ("television accounts between 1962 and 1968 were not critical of the American effort in Vietnam," only shifting after the Tet offensive in January 1968 indicated a "stalemate"); Angela Woodall, Survey: U.S. media censors Iraq reporting, *UPI* (April 5, 2005), https://www.upi.com/Defense-News/2005/04/05/Survey-US-media-censors-Iraq-reporting/12121112720885/ ("The news media are self-censoring reports about Iraq because of concern for public reaction to graphic images and details about death and torture, according to a survey of 210 U.S. and international journalists. . . . There is an 'unspoken rule' against publishing images of what would be horrifying, [such as dead bodies]."); Jon Whiten, If news from Iraq Is Bad, it's coming from U.S. Officials, Extra! Update, February 2004, https://www.fair.org/index.php?page=1167 (76 percent of "on-camera sources appearing in stories about Iraq on the nightly network newscasts–ABC World News Tonight, CBS Evening News and NBC Nightly News–in the month of October 2003 . . . were current or former government or military officials."; ibid. ("By allowing U.S. officials and appointees to make up 73 percent of total sources, the networks clearly promoted the official line on the war and minimized dissenting views. . . . Seventy-nine percent of the [sources who were] current U.S. civilian officials were Republicans."); Steve Rendall and Tara Broughel, Amplifying Officials, Squelching Dissent, Extra!, May/June 2003, https://www.fair.org ("Since the invasion of Iraq began in March, official voices have dominated U.S. network newscasts, while opponents of the war have been notably underrepresented, according to a study. . . . [V]iewers were more than six times as likely to see a pro-war source as one who was anti-war; with U.S. guests alone, the ratio increases to 25 to 1.").

4 Yochai Benkler, 'Free As the Air to Common Use: First Amendment Constraints on Enclosure of the Public Domain,' 74 *The New York University Law Review* 354, 388, 401, 406, 408–11 (1999) (describing how companies that own many copyrights exercise bureaucratic control over creation of books and their distribution to the public); Center for Social Medial Untold Stories: Creative Consequences of the Rights Clearance Culture for Documentary Filmmakers (November 2004), https://www.centerforsocialmedia.org/rock/backgrounddocs/printablerightsreport.pdf (similar, focusing on documentary films); Kembrew McLeod, *Freedom of Expression®* (Doubleday, 2005), pp. 62–113, 133–58 (similar, focusing on how music sampling clearances censor and raise costs of musicians' artistry); Jason Mazzone, 'Copyfraud,' 81 *The New York University Law Review* 1026, 1058–71 (2006) (similar, focusing on films and classroom teaching).

5 Compare, *e.g.*, Randall v. Sorrell, 126 S. Ct. 2479, 2485–86 (2006) (statute limiting corporate payments to public officials that could influence their positions and public acts was unconstitutional under First Amendment); Lorillard Tobacco Co. v. Reilly,

533 U.S. 525, 533, 554–71, 586–90, 599 (2001) (extending First Amendment protections to corporate advertising of tobacco that threatened to cause children to become addicted), Central Hudson Gas & Elec. Corp. v. Public Service Commission, 447 U.S. 557 (1980) (extending First Amendment protections to corporate advertising that threatened to increase consumers' electricity bills), Eastern R.R. Presidents Conference v. Noerr Motor Freight, Inc., 365 U.S. 127, 137–40 (1961) (First Amendment protects "corporate aggrandizement" via lobbying for monopolies), and Meredith Corp. v. FCC, 809 F.2d 863 (D.C. Cir. 1987) (remanding for determination by FCC whether limits on corporate broadcasters' ability to censor political speech violated corporations' First Amendment rights), *with* Beard v. Banks, 126 S. Ct. 2572 (2006) (First Amendment did not prohibit prison officials from censoring individual prisoners' access to newspapers and magazines), Garcetti v. Ceballos, 126 S. Ct. 1951 (2006) (First Amendment did not prohibit firing public employee for exposing unconstitutional government action), Milkovich v. Lorain Journal Co., 497 U.S. 1 (1990) (First Amendment did not necessarily protect individual author against defamation suit brought by public official and premised upon author's expressions of opinion about a local controversy in a newspaper), *id.* at 34–36 (Brennan, J., joined by Marshall, J., dissenting) (criticizing majority for striking at "heart" of First Amendment's protections for political debate by individuals), Hazelwood Sch. Dist. v. Kulmeier, 484 U.S. 260 (1988) (upholding school's censorship of articles dealing with pregnancy and divorce), Harper & Row, Publishers, Inc. v. Nation Enters., 471 U.S. 539 (1984) (censoring political magazine's exposé of President Gerald Ford's bombing of Cambodia and pardon of Richard Nixon); Members of City Council Taxpayers v. Vincent, 466 U.S. 789 (1984) (upholding ordinance prohibiting posting of political signs on utility poles), Perry Educ. Ass'n v. Perry Local Educ. Ass'n, 469 U.S. 37 (1983) (upholding censorship of public school teachers' communications with one another on union matters), Connick v. Myers, 461 U.S. 138 (1983) (upholding termination of assistant D.A. for "insubordination" in the form of questioning politicization of legal obligations), Greer v. Spock, 424 U.S. 828 (1976) (upholding censorship of political speeches, demonstrations, and literature), and United States v. O'Brien, 391 U.S. 367 (1968) (upholding prosecution of individual for expressing opposition to Vietnam War by burning a draft card).

6 E.g., Frank Pasquale and Oren Bracha, 'Internet nondiscrimination principles: Commercial ethics for carriers and search engines,' 2008 *University of Chicago Legal Forum* 263, 276–77, 285–89, 296–90.

7 E.g., Rebecca MacKinnon, *Consent of the Networked: The Worldwide Struggle for Internet Freedom* (Basic Books, 2012); Sirichit, previous n. 48, pp. 54–58, 62.

8 Michel Foucault, *The Birth of Biopolitics: Lectures at the Collège de France, 1978–1979* (Picador, 1988), p. 67; Michel Foucault, *Psychiatric Power: Lectures at the Collège de France, 1973–1974* (Picador, 2008), p. 174; Keith Douglas Smith, *Liberalism, Surveillance, and Resistance: Indigenous Communities in Western Canada, 1877–1927* (Athabasca University Press, 2009), pp. 15–16. *See also*, Michel Foucault, *Society Must Be Defended: Lectures at the Collège de France, 1975–1976* (Picador, 2003), pp. 236, 242–62 (liberalism or modern revolutionary aspirations claim to abolish unjust inequalities and make everyone part of a self-governing society, but republics allegedly founded on such aspirations have greater power than ever over bodies, processes of life, and the daily liberties of the citizen).

9 Michel Foucault, 'Confinement, psychiatry, prison,' in *Politics, Philosophy, Culture: Interviews and Other Writings of Michel Foucault*, edited by Lawrence D. Katzman (Routledge, 1988), p. 197.

10 Foucault, *Discipline*, previous n. 8, p. 138.

11 Ibid., p. 221.

12 Ibid., p. 236.

13 Alexander Galloway, *Protocol: How Control Exists After Decentralization* (The MIT Press, 2004), p. 81.
14 E.g., Larry Catá Backer and Matthew B. McQuilla, 'The algorithmic law of business and human rights: Constructing private transnational law of ratings, social credit and accountability measures,' 19 *International Journal of Law in Context* 32 (2023); Stefan J. Padfield, 'An introduction to anti-ESG legislation,' 24 *Transactions: The Tennessee Journal of Business Law* 6 (2023); cf. also, Robert G. Eccles and Eli Lehrer, It's time to call a truce in the red state/blue state ESG culture war, Harvard Law School Forum on Corporate Governance (2023), https://corpgov.law.harvard.edu/2023/05/29/its-time-to-call-a-truce-in-the-red-state-blue-state-esg-culture-war/.
15 Statement of Colin Stretch, Facebook Vice President and General Counsel, Before the Senate Committee on the Judiciary, Subcommittee on Crime and Terrorism, 2018, https://www.c-span.org/video/?436454-1/facebook-google-twitter-executives-russian-disinformation.
16 Statement of Richard Salgado, Google Law Enforcement and Information Security Director, in ibid.
17 Ibid. See also, Sean Egbert, Acting General Counsel, Twitter Inc., in ibid.; Nerd City, YouTube's biggest lie, *YouTube* (2019), https://www.youtube.com/watch?v=ll8zGaWhofU.
18 E.g., Prager Univ. v. Google LLC, No. 17-CV-06064-LHK, 2018 WL 1471939 (N.D. Cal. March 26, 2018), *aff'd*, 951 F.3d 991 (9th Cir. 2020); Nyabwa v. Facebook, No. 2:17-CV-24, 2018 WL 585467 (N.D. Cal. January 26, 2018); Taylor v. Twitter, Inc., No. CGC-18–564460 (Cal. Super. Ct., San Francisco County, transcript of ruling granting motion to dismiss in part, and denying it in part, June 14, 2018), *aff'd in part, rev'd in part sub nom.* Twitter, Inc. v. The Superior Court for the City and County of San Francisco, No. A154973 (Cal. Ct. App., 1st Dist., August 17, 2018); Shulman v. Facebook.com, No. CV 17–764 (JMV), 2017 WL. 5129885 (D.N.J. 2017); Doe v. Cuomo, No. 10-CV-1534 TJM/CFH, 2013 WL 1213174 (N.D.N.Y. February 25, 2013).
19 E.g., Prager University v. Google LLC, 951 F.3d 991, 999 (9th Cir. 2020) (no state action by YouTube in censoring videos because: "YouTube's representation that it is committed to freedom of expression, or a single statement made by its executive before a congressional committee that she considers YouTube to be a 'neutral public fora,' cannot somehow convert private property into a public forum."); Daniels v. Alphabet Inc., No. 20-CV-04687-VKD, 2021 WL 1222166, at *6 (N.D. Cal. March 31, 2021) (ECF No. 31) (no state action because plaintiff failed to allege that "the federal government directed a particular result with respect to his [YouTube] videos," and even if it were true that officials "wanted certain kinds of videos removed and [plaintiff's] videos fell within that category," that was not enough to infer state action in plaintiff's case); Divino Group LLC v. Google LLC, No. 19-cv-04749-VKD, 2021 WL 51715, at *6–12 (N.D. Cal. January 6, 2021) (ECF No. 65) (no state action under *Prager University*, 951 F.3d at 997–98, where YouTube allegedly removed LGBTQ+ accounts or made their videos less visible than others in discriminatory ways, after adult-oriented, or indecent content was targeted for deletion by Congress and White House via CDA); Federal Agency of News LLC v. Facebook, Inc., 432 F. Supp. 3d 1107, 1125–26 (N.D. Cal. 2020) (no state action based on statements indicating that Facebook "partner[ed]" with government actors because those statements did not "mention [plaintiff] at all," much less suggest that Facebook's specific decision to "delete [plaintiff's] Facebook page" was a result of "joint action"); Doe v. Cuomo, No. 10-CV-1534 TJM/CFH, 2013 WL 1213174, at *9 (N.D.N.Y. February 25, 2013) (because Facebook "retain[ed] the independent ability and power to choose whether and how to impose limitations [on the use of Facebook], irrespective of state procedures, no state action . . . occurred"); see also, Huber v. Biden, No. 21-CV-06580-EMC, 2022 WL 827248 (N.D. Cal.

March 18, 2022), *aff'd*, No. 22–15443, 2022 WL 17818543 (9th Cir. December 20, 2022); Berenson v. Twitter, Inc., No. C 21–09818 WHA, 2022 WL 1289049 (N.D. Cal. April 29, 2022); Children's Health Defense v. Facebook Inc., No. 20-CV-05787-SI, 2021 WL 2662064 (N.D. Cal. June 29, 2021), *appeal pending* (9th Cir. oral argument held May 17, 2022); Rutenburg v. Twitter, Inc., No. 4:21-CV-00548-YGR, 2021 WL 1338958 (N.D. Cal. April 9, 2021), *appeal docketed*, No. 21–16074 (9th Cir. June 25, 2021); Tulsi Now, Inc. v. Google, LLC, No. 2:19-cv-06444-SVW-RAO, 2020 WL 4353686, at *2 (C.D. Cal. March 3, 2020); Twitter, Inc.'s and Jack Dorsey's Notice of Motion and Motion to Dismiss First Amended Complaint; Memorandum of Points and Authorities in Support Thereof, pp. 4–16, Huber v. Biden, No. 3:21-cv-0680-EMC, 2021 WL 8267976 (N.D. Cal. memorandum in support of motion to dismiss filed November 8 2021).

20 Tim Cook, A message to our customers, *Apple* (February 16, 2016), https://www.apple.com/customer-letter/ [https://perma.cc/7BY4-4TCU].

21 S. Hrg., 115–316, 115th Cong., 2d Sess., January 17, 2018, https://www.govinfo.gov/content/pkg/CHRG-115shrg31316/html/CHRG-115shrg31316.htm. See also, Written Testimony of Richard Salgado, Hearing on "Extremist Content and Russian Information Online: Working with Tech to Find Solutions," Senate Judiciary Subcommittee on Crime and Terrorism, October 31, 2017, http://judiciary.senate.gov/imo/media/doc/10-31-17%20Salgado%20Testimony.pdf; David Newhoff, Senate hearings: A sea change for social media companies & users, *Illusion of More* (November 1, 2017), https://illusionofmore.com/senate-hearings-a-sea-change-for-social-media-companies-users/.

22 Facebook and Twitter CEOs testify on regulating social media content [Senate Judiciary Committee], *C-Span* (November 17, 2020), https://www.c-span.org/video/?478048-1/facebook-twitter-ceos-testify-regulating-social-media-content.

23 *Ibid.*

24 E.g., Federal Agency of News LLC v. Facebook, Inc., 432 F. Supp. 3d 1107, 1125 (N.D. Cal. 2020) (independent Web publisher argued that Facebook had admitted to being "actively engaged with the Department of Homeland Security, the FBI, including their Foreign Influence Task Force, Secretaries of State across the US . . . on our efforts to detect and stop information operations" and using "tip[s]" from US law enforcement to remove 100 or more Facebook Pages, Groups, and accounts, and dozens of Instagram accounts in a single month); Newsweek, Psaki: "We're flagging problematic posts on Facebook that spread disinformation," *YouTube* (July 15, 2021), https://www.youtube.com/watch?v=zqEvQKO5_gM (White House Press Secretary announced that the Biden Administration is in "regular touch with the social media platforms" and is "flagging problematic posts for Facebook").

25 CCIA, previous n. 31, p. 3.

26 Matt Taibbi, Move over Jayson Blair: Meet Hamilton 68, the king of media fraud, Racket News (January 27, 2023), https://t.co/vxnKAoI9T7. See also, Clint Watts, Wikipedia (2023), https://en.wikipedia.org/wiki/Clint_Watts; ACLU, Dimming the beacon of freedom: U.S. violations of the International Covenant on Civil and Political Rights (June 2006), https://www.aclu.org/documents/dimming-beacon-freedom-us-violations-international-covenant-civil-political-rights-table; ACLU, FBI audit exposes widespread abuse of Patriot Act powers, https://www.aclu.org/press-releases/fbi-audit-exposes-widespread-abuse-patriot-act-powers; ACLU, "The FBI's Terror Machine, Tonight on HBO" (2014), https://www.aclu.org/news/national-security/fbis-terror-machine-tonight-hbo; ACLU, Top ten abuses of power since 9/11, https://www.aclu.org/documents/top-ten-abuses-power-911; Full text: Words of C.I.A. and F.B.I. chiefs, *The New York Times* (February 11, 2003), https://www.nytimes.com/2003/02/11/politics/full-text-words-of-cia-and-fbi-chiefs.html.

27 E.g., Michael Doran, William McCants, and Clint Watts, 'The good and bad of Ahrar al-Sham: An Al-Qaeda linked group worth defending,' *Foreign Policy* (January 23,

2014), https://www.foreignaffairs.com/articles/syria/2014-01-23/good-and-bad-ahrar-al-sham. See also, Ahrar al-Sham, Mapping Militant Organizations, Stanford University, https://web.stanford.edu/group/mappingmilitants/cgi-bin/groups/view/523; International Crisis Group, Tentative jihad: Syria's fundamentalist opposition (October 12, 2012), https://www.crisisgroup.org/middle-east-north-africa/eastern-mediterranean/syria/tentative-jihad-syria-s-fundamentalist-opposition; Joshua Landis, The Raqqa Story: Rebel Structure, Planning, and Possible War Crimes, Syria Comment, (April 4, 2013), https://www.joshualandis.com/blog/the-raqqa-story-rebel-structure-planning-and-possible-war-crimes/; Tom Miles and John Irish, Syrian terrorist list produces 163 names and no agreement, *Reuters* (February 17, 2016), https://www.reuters.com/article/us-mideast-crisis-syria-terrorist/syrian-terrorist-list-produces-163-names-and-no-agreement-idUSKCN0VQ25E; 'US "kills Osama Bin Laden ally in Syria,"' BBC/The Star, Kenya (February 9, 2017), https://www.the-star.co.ke/news/2017/02/09/us-kills-osama-bin-laden-ally-in-syria_c1503759. Cf. The Brookings Institution, Syrian Islamists reach out to the U.S., but serious issues remain, (July 2015), https://www.brookings.edu/blogs/markaz/posts/2015/07/14-syrian-islamists-us-issues-lister.

28 Taibbi, Move over Jayson Blair, previous n. 26; see also, Joe Lauria, CN editor named on secret 'disinfo' list, *Consortium news* (January 27, 2023), https://consortiumnews.com/2023/01/27/cn-editor-named-on-secret-disinfo-list/.

29 Taibbi, Move over Jayson Blair, previous n. 26; see also, David McCabe, Senate-commissioned reports show scale of Russian misinformation campaign, *Axios* (December 17, 2018), https://www.axios.com/senate-reports-russian-interference-2016-election-9d0daca6-1e2d-4617-9295-f8eec61c1719.html.

30 Taibbi, Move over Jayson Blair, previous n. 26; David McCabe, Big Tech goes back to Congress, *Axios* (January 17, 2018), https://www.axios.com/2018/01/17/big-tech-goes-back-to-congress-1516167391; David McCabe, Former FBI agent says Russian interference began in 2014, *Axios* (February 2017), https://www.axios.com/2017/12/15/former-fbi-agent-says-russia-interference-began-in-2014-1513306576; David McCabe and Sara Fischer, U.K. leapfrogs U.S. on regulating bad content, *Axios* (October 11, 2017), https://www.axios.com/2017/12/15/uk-leapfrogs-us-on-regulating-bad-content-1513306105. See also, below n. 39. Cf., Clint Watts: Social media freedom leads to the wrong politicians rising up in polls, *Rumble* (September 19, 2023), https://rumble.com/v281vw0-clint-watts-social-media-freedom-leads-the-wrong-politicians-rising-up-in-p.html.

31 E.g., Alyssa Newcomb, Facebook says it will hand Russia-linked ads over to Congress, *NBC News* (September 21, 2017), https://www.nbcnews.com/storyline/hacking-of-america/zuckerberg-shares-facebook-s-next-steps-russian-election-meddling-probe-n803581.

32 Mark Zuckerberg testimony as it happened: Facebook CEO grilled by Senators, *NBC News* (April 10, 2018), https://www.nbcnews.com/tech/tech-news/blog/mark-zuckerberg-testimony-live-blog-facebook-ceo-testify-congress-n863926.

33 CNN Wire Staff, Syrian rebels plan "huge operations," *CNN* (January 4, 2012), https://www.cnn.com/2012/01/04/world/meast/syria-unrest/index.html; Jackson Diehl, Turkey's government is the new normal in the middle east, *The Washington Post Post-Partisan Blog* (January 19, 2012), https://www.washingtonpost.com; David Ignatius, Endgame in Syria, *The Washington Post Post-Partisan Blog* (January 31, 2012); John Rosenthal, Al Qaeda in rebel Syria, *The National Review* (2012), https://www.nationalreview.com/articles/292904/al-qaeda-rebel-syria-john-rosenthal?pg=2; Jonathan Steele, 'Diary: In Syria,' 34 *The London Review of Books* (March 22, 2012), https://www.lrb.co.uk/v34/n06/jonathan-steele/diary; Reuters, Russia says 15,000 foreign terrorists in Syria, *The Chicago Tribune* (March 8, 2012), https://www.chicagotribune.com. This may have made it easier for al Qaeda or ISIS recruiters near Istanbul to send Turkish nationals to Syria to attack its government. International Crisis Group, previous n. 27; Alev Scott and Alexander Christie-Miller, Exclusive: ISIS starts recruiting in Istanbul's

vulnerable suburbs, *Newsweek* (September 12, 2014), https://www.newsweek.com/authors/alexander-christie-miller.

34 Paul Antonopoulos, Turkey's interests in the Syrian war: From neo-ottomanism to counterinsurgency, *Global Affairs* (March 15, 2018), p. 5, https://doi.org/10.1080/23340460.2018.1455061. See also, Agence France-Presse, Two-thirds of Christians have left Syria: Aleppo Bishop (March 16, 2016), https://www.i24news.tv/en/news/middle-east/106479-160317-two-thirds-of-christians-have-left-syria-aleppo-bishop; Nour Samaha, Syria's Assyrians: "No one helped us," *Al Jazeera (English)* (March 1, 2015), https://www.aljazeera.net; Dominique Soguel, 'In Northeast Syria, a Christian Community Fights for Survival,' *The Christian Science Monitor* (April 10, 2019); Hannibal Travis, 'Exile or Extinction: The Assyrian Genocide from 1915 to 2015,' in *The Assyrian Genocide: Cultural and Political Legacies*, edited by Hannibal Travis (Routledge, 2018), pp. 269–75; Raf Sanchez and Richard Spencer, Turkish government co-operated with Al Qaeda in Syria, says former Ambassador, *The Telegraph (U.K.)* (September 12, 2014), https://www.telegraph.co.uk/news/worldnews/europe/turkey/11093478/Turkish-government-co-operated-with-al-Qaeda-in-Syria-says-former-US-ambassador.html; Hannibal Travis, 'Why Was Benghazi "Saved," While Sinjar Was Allowed to Be Lost? New Failures of Genocide Prevention, 2007–2015,' 10 *Genocide Studies International* 139, 176–77 (2017). On the military aid, see also, Neta Crawford, United States Budgetary Costs of Post-9/11 Wars Through FY2018, November 2017, p. 8 ($28 billion spent on Defense Department, State Department, and USAID emergency or contingency activities in Syria, 2001–2017); Ben Norton, US Ambassador confirms billions spent on regime change in Syria, debunking "Obama did nothing" myth, *The Grayzone* (February 9, 2018), https://thegrayzone.com/author/ben-norton/. See also, Tara McElvey, Arming Syrian rebels: Where the US went wrong, *BBC News* (October 10, 2015), https://www.bbc.com.

35 Edward Yaraman, Former Iraqi PM blames fall of Mosul on Turkey's Erdogan, *Voice of America* (August 15, 2015), https://www.voanews.com/content/maliki-blames-fall-mosul-on-turkeys-erdogan. See also, Reuters, Survivors demand justice after Iraq massacre, *Reuters Gulf Financial News* (October 2, 2014). On incitement in or connected with Saudi Arabia, see Iraq Shi'i Leader Al-Hakim Calls for Banning Anti-Shi'I Fatwas, BBC International Reports (Middle East)/WestlawNext (March 21, 2007), https://1.next.westlaw.com (subscription required); Hannibal Travis, *Genocide in the Middle East: The Ottoman Empire, Iraq, and Sudan* (Carolina Academic Press, 2010), pp. 523–27.

36 CCIA, National Security Issues, previous n. 31, p. 3.

37 E.g., Schuchardt v. President of the United States, 839 F.3d 336 (3d Cir. 2016), *on remand*, No. 2–14-cv-00705 (W.D. Pa. order dismissing case granted Feb. 2019), *aff'd*, No. 19–1366 slip op. (3d Cir. March 2, 2020). PRISM was the alleged name of a U.S. intelligence program begun under the "U.S.A. PATRIOT Act" that persuaded email, search engine, social media, video call, and online video sharing providers to allow the National Security Agency to collect, process, and exploit "all" user data stored by these providers. 839 F.3d at 340. Edward Snowden released documentation of PRISM to *The Washington Post* and *The Guardian (U.K.)*. *Id.*

38 U.S. Senate, User clip: Clinton Watts testimony to Senate Intelligence Committee hearing (March 30, 2017), https://www.c-span.org/video/?c4673195/user-clip-clinton-watts-testimony-senate-intelligence-committee-hearing-march-30–2017.

39 E.g., Ryan Goodman, Can Facebook legally disclose Russian ads – What does the Stored Communications Act say?, *Just Security* (October 27, 2017), https://www.justsecurity.org/46347/expert-views-facebook-legally-disclose-russian-ads-stored-communications-act-1986/. While Jennifer Daskal and Jennifer Granick opined that disclosing the content of election-related communications to Congress, at least without a subpoena, would violate the Stored Communications Act, other experts disagreed.

Ibid. For the testimony of Mr. Watts with recommendations relating to political ads and privacy (around the time that Facebook agreed to disclose "Russian" purchasers – or recipients? – consistent with its obligations if any to preserve the privacy of user data, see U.S. Senate, User Clip, previous n. 38; Clinton Watts, Written statement prepared for the U.S. Senate Committee on the Judiciary Subcommittee on Crime and Terrorism "Extremist Content and Russian Disinformation Online: Working with Tech to Find Solutions" (October 31, 2017), p. 4, https://nsarchive.gwu.edu/document/16020-united-states-congress-clint-watts-statement.

40 Cf. Seung Lee, Ex-editors claim employees blacklisted conservative news from Facebook "trending" section, *Newsweek* (May 9, 2016), https://www.newsweek.com/ex-editors-claim-employees-blacklisted-conservative-news-facebook-trending-457596.

41 Romain Dillet, Google and Facebook ban fake news sites from their advertising networks, *TechCrunch* (November 15, 2016), https://techcrunch.com/2016/11/15/google-and-facebook-ban-fake-news-sites-from-their-advertising-networks/; Andre Damon, Google escalates blacklisting of left-wing web sites and journalists, *World Socialist Website* (October 20, 2017), https://www.wsws.org/en/articles/2017/10/20/goog-o20.html.

42 Seth Lewis and Efrat Nechushtai, Google News serves conservatives and liberals similar results, but favors mainstream media, *The Conversation* (August 31, 2018), https://theconversation.com/google-news-serves-conservatives-and-liberals-similar-results-but-favors-mainstream-media-102389.

43 Ibid.

44 Anna Kawakami, Khonzodakhon Umarova, and Eni Mustafaraj, 'The media coverage of the 2020 US presidential election candidates through the lens of Google's Top Stories,' in *Proceedings of the Fourteenth International AAAI Conference on Web and Social Media*, edited by Munmun De Choudhury et al. (ICWSM, 2020), p. 868–69, https://ojs.aaai.org/index.php/ICWSM/article/view/7352.

45 Ibid., p. 869.

46 Ibid., p. 871.

47 Rasmus Kleis Nielsen and Richard Fletcher, 'Concentration of online news traffic and publishers' reliance on platform referrals: Evidence from passive tracking data in the UK,' 2 *Journal of Quantitative Description: Digital Media* 1 (2022), https://ora.ox.ac.uk/objects/uuid:7c74d76d-d74d-4ba2-a340-ea2116158ca0.

48 World Economic Forum, An insight, an idea with Susan Wojcicki | Global Technology Governance Summit 2021, *YouTube* (April 8, 2021), https://www.youtube.com/watch?v=cF50hjiwRoM&t=878s. See also, Caitlin Johnstone, Silicon Valley Algorithm manipulation is the only thing keeping mainstream media alive (May 3, 2021), https://caitlinjohnstone.com/2021/05/03/silicon-valley-algorithm-manipulation-is-the-only-thing-keeping-mainstream-media-alive/.

49 Plaintiffs' Complaint 140–46, Dressen v. Flaherty, No. 3:23-cv-00155-JVB (S.D. Tex. May, 22, 2023) (ECF No. 1).

50 Plaintiffs' Memorandum in Support of Motion for Preliminary Injunction, pp. 15–17, Missouri v. Biden, No. 3:22-cv-01213-TAD (W.D. La. memorandum filed June 14, 2022) (ECF No. 11–1).

51 Missouri v. Biden, No. 3:22-CV-01213-TAD, 2023 WL 4335270 (W.D. La. July 4 memorandum ruling on request for preliminary injunction entered July 4, 2023); Plaintiffs' Complaint, 140–59, *Dressen*.

52 Plaintiffs' Proposed Findings of Fact, pp. 13–16, 37–39, *Missouri v. Biden*, No. 3:22-CV-01213-TAD (ECF No. 212–13). For example, in February 2021, Facebook had emailed the White House Digital Media directorate to assure it that vaccine "false claims" defined as those "debunked by public health experts," were being banned. *Ibid.*, pp. 13–16; see also, *Missouri v. Biden*, 83 F.4th 350. On April 23, 2021, Facebook removed a large group of user threads where adverse reactions to vaccines could be discussed, including blood clots and impacts related to DNA. E.g., Tom Parker, Facebook deletes

120,000-member group where people posted stories of alleged adverse vaccine reactions, *Reclaim the Net* (April 23, 2021), https://web.archive.org/web/20210428104733/https://reclaimthenet.org/facebook-removes-covid-19-vaccine-victims-group/.

53 Plaintiffs' Complaint, 140–159, *Dressen* (citing Plaintiffs' Proposed Findings of Fact, pp. 13–16, 37–39, Missouri v. Biden, No. 3:22-CV-01213 (W.D. La. 2023) (ECF No. 212–3)).

54 *Missouri v. Biden*, 83 F.4th at 377–82 (following *Bantam Books*, 372 U.S. 58; *Backpage.com, LLC v. Dart*, 807 F.3d 229), *aff'd in part and modified*, No. 23–30445, 2023 WL 5821788 (5th Cir. September 8, 2023), *stayed*, No. 23–30445 (5th Cir. September 26, 2023), *withdrawn on rehearing and modified*, No. 23–30445, slip op. (5th Cir. October 3, 2023), https://cases.justia.com/federal/appellate-courts/ca5/23-30445/23-30445-2023-10-03.pdf?ts=1696375826.

55 Counterman v. Colorado, 600 U.S.___, 143 S. Ct. 2106, 2114 (2023); Elonis v. United States, 575 U.S. 723 (2015); Watts v. United States, 394 U.S. 705 (1969) (per curiam).

56 Parts of this section were previously published as 'Free speech institutions and fair use: A new agenda for Copyright reform,' 33 *Cardozo Arts and Entertainment Law Journal* 673 (2016).

57 Brian Gabrial, *The Press and Slavery in America, 1791–1859: The Melancholy Effects of Popular Excitement* (University of South Carolina Press, 2016); USA Today Network, Southern newspapers were vocal supporters of the confederacy. It lasted for generations, *The Tennessean* (July 30, 2020), https://www.tennessean.com/in-depth/news/2020/07/30/southern-newspapers-were-vocal-supporters-confederacy-lasted-generations/5486399002/. See also Andrés Reséndez, *The Other Slavery: The Uncovered Story of Indian Enslavement in America* (Houghton Mifflin Harcourt, 2016); Andrés Reséndez, The Other Slavery, Smithsonian Institution National Museum of the American Indian (2021), https://americanindian.si.edu/sites/1/files/pdf/seminars-symposia/the-other-slavery-perspective.pdf.

58 Dennis Rome, *Black Demons: The Media's Depiction of the African American Male Criminal Stereotype* (Praeger, 2004); Scott Tighe, 'Of course we are crazy': Discrimination of Native American Indians through criminal justice, 11 *Justice Policy Journal* 1 (2014), https://www.cjcj.org/media/import/documents/tighe_discrimination_final_formatted.pdf; cf. Ediberto Roman, 'Who exactly is living *La Vida Loca*?: The legal and political consequences of Latino-Latina ethnic and racial stereotypes in film and other media,' 4 *Journal of Gender, Race and Justice* 37 (2000); Mari Matsuda, 'Public response to racist speech: Considering the victim's story,' 87 *Michigan Law Review* 2320, 2357 (1989).

59 Marissa Lee, Study: 'Television news often perpetuates racial stereotypes,' *Chicago Defender* (August 20, 2008); Tighe, previous n. 58.

60 Robert W. McChesney, *Rich Media, Poor Democracy* (University of Illinois Press, 1999), pp. 15–77; Newton Minow and Craig LaMay, *Abandoned in the Wasteland* (Macmillan 1995), pp. 21–46, 129–53, 163–88, 210–37; Parents Television Council, TV Bloodbath: Violence on Prime Time Broadcast TV (2003), https://www.parentstv.org. See also, Brennan Center for Justice, Fact Sheets on Media Democracy (2006), pp. 1–3, https://www.fepproject.org/factsheets/mediademocracy.html ("Six corporations own or have controlling interests in most of the American mass media today," which have turned away from "public affairs and local programming"); John Dunbar, 'Lawyer Says FCC Ordered Study Destroyed,' *Houston Chronicle*, September 15, 2006; Jennifer Harper, Study finds "near blackout" of local public issues on TV, *Wash. Times* (October 28, 2003), https://www.highbeam.com/doc/1G1-109357225.html; James F. Hoge, Jr., 'Foreign News: Who Gives a Damn?,' *Columbia Journalism Review*, November-December 1997, pp. 48, 49–51.

61 E.g., Anti-Eastern European and anti-slavic racism, *illiberalism.org* (2022), https://www.illiberalism.org/between-marginalization-and-instrumentalization-anti-eastern-european-and-anti-slavic-racism/; John Connelly, 'Nazis and Slavs: From racial theory

to racist practice,' 32 *Central European History* 1 (1999); Targeting the Sinti and Roma, Facing History and Ourselves (2022), https://www.facinghistory.org/resource-library/targeting-sinti-roma.

62 E.g., Zeeshan Aleem, Why the U.S.'s double standards on Russia-Ukraine matter, *MSNBC* (March 28, 2022), https://www.msnbc.com/opinion/msnbc-opinion/why-u-s-s-double-standards-russia-ukraine-war-matter-n1293171.

63 E.g., Eugene Finkel, What's happening in Ukraine is genocide. Period, *Washington Post* (April 5, 2022), https://www.washingtonpost.com/opinions/2022/04/05/russia-is-committing-genocide-in-ukraine/; Google News (2023), https://news.google.com/search?q="genocide%20in%20ukraine"%20"cnn"&hl=en-US&gl=US&ceid=US%3Aen; Eric McDaniel, Biden accuses Russia of committing a "genocide" in Ukraine, *NPR* (April 12, 2022), https://www.npr.org/2022/04/12/1092460473/biden-appeared-to-accuse-putin-of-committing-a-genocide-in-ukraine. Since 1980, some countries meeting the 600,000 threshold would include Iraq, Sudan, Syria, Yemen, Angola, Ethiopia, and the Democratic Republic of the Congo. In Yemen the 600,000 would mean than at least half of the 1.3 million excess deaths estimated to occur by 2030 due to the war that intensified in 2014 would need to have already occurred by 2023.

64 Stephanie Savell, How death outlives war, Costs of War Project of the Watson Institute at Brown University (May 15, 2023), p. 10, https://watson.brown.edu/costsofwar/files/cow/imce/papers/2023/Indirect%20Deaths.pdf (460,000 excess deaths in Iraq in 2003–2011, before western Mosul and at least 70 other cities and towns were destroyed and 2 million more people were displaced in the fighting between a U.S.-led coalition and ISIS); Mark Siegal, Former UN official says sanctions against Iraq amount to "genocide," *Cornell Chronicle* (September 30, 1999), https://news.cornell.edu/stories/1999/09/former-un-official-says-sanctions-against-iraq-amount-genocide (1 to 1.5 million Iraqis died from sanctions-related malnutrition or health problems in 1991–1999, according to former U.N. Iraq coordinator); Tigray War Project (Ghent University) and Every Casualty Counts, Call for Input to inform the High Commissioner's report to the Human Rights Council on the impact of casualty recording (February 20, 2023), https://www.ohchr.org/sites/default/files/documents/issues/casualtyrecording/cfis/hrc-res-50-11/subm-casualty-recording-academia-ghent-university-51.docx (300,000 to 800,000 in Ethiopia as of 2022); U.N. News, Yemen recovery possible if war stops now: UNDP report, *United Nations* (November 23, 2021), https://news.un.org/en/story/2021/11/1106362 (1.3 million by 2030 in Yemen). It was possible that fewer than 1.3 million excess deaths would occur in Yemen if the conflict ended in 2021, but the Red Cross has called it "worsening" and "unrelenting." ICRC, Health crisis in Yemen (2023), https://www.icrc.org/en/where-we-work/middle-east/yemen/health-crisis-yemen. Syria and Libya suffer from many of the same factors that cause excess deaths in Iraq and Yemen: displacement, sanctions, destruction of buildings and cities, terrorist attacks, bombing of roads, and damage to health care and clean water infrastructure. Savell, previous, pp. 2, 22–23, 26–33.

65 Parts of this section were previously published as 'Postmodern censorship of pacifist content on television and the Internet,' 25 *Notre Dame Journal of Law, Ethics and Public Policy* 47 (2011).

66 Iraq promises U.N. it is clear of weapons of mass destruction; Bush asks Congress for the green light to head for Iraq, *CNN/CNN Transcripts on Lexis* (September 19, 2002), https://advance.lexis.com (subscription required); Blix, El-Baradei brief press, *CNN/CNN Transcripts on Lexis* (November 17, 2002), https://advance.lexis.com.

67 Gunning for Saddam: Saddam Hussein's weapons of mass destruction, *PBS Frontline* (February 4, 2011), https://www.pbs.org/wgbh/pages/frontline/shows/gunning/etc/arsenal.html; Letter, Iraq: No obstacles to inspections, *CNN.com* (October 12, 2002), http://articles.cnn.com/2002-10-12/world/Iraq.letters_1_al – saadiweapons-inspectors-unmovic?s=PM:WORLD; Blix urges US and UK to hand over Iraq evidence,

The Guardian (U.K.) (December 20, 2002), http://www.guardian.co.uk/world/2002/dec/20/iraq.foreignpolicy.

68 Joseph Curl, Nuclear agency disavows report on Iraq nuclear weapons arms, *Washington Times* (September 27, 2002), https://www.rense.com/general29/chagen.htm; Roger D. Hodge, Weekly review, *Harper's Magazine* (October 1, 2002), https://web.archive.org/web/20120315060839/www.harpers.org/archive/2002/10/WeeklyReview2002-10-01.

69 CNN Live Event/Special: Blix speaks with reporters, *CNN Transcripts* (January 23, 2003), https://transcripts.cnn.com/show/se/date/2003-01-23/segment/05; see also, Blix 'not satisfied' with Iraq's weapons accounting, *CNN.com* (January 9, 2003), http://articles.cnn.com/2003-01-09/world/iraq.tracker.update_1_chief-un-weapons–inspector–aluminum–tubes-hansblix?s=PM:WORLD.

70 Blix urges US and UK to hand over Iraq evidence, *The Guardian (U.K.)* (December 20, 2002), https://www.guardian.co.uk/world/2002/dec/20/iraq.foreignpolicy.

71 Q&A with Zain Verjee, *CNN Transcripts* (October 1, 2002), http://edition.cnn.com/TRANSCRIPTS/0210/01/i_qaa.01.html.

72 Quoted in Fairness and Accuracy in Reporting, The Great WMD Hunt, (July 1, 2003), https://fair.org/extra/the-great-wmd-hunt/.

73 E.g., Senate Foreign Relations Committee holds hearing on Iraq, *CNN/CNN Transcripts on Lexis* (July 31, 2002), https://advance.lexis.com.

74 The network did quote him as saying this after the invasion was complete. E.g., Interview, by Judy Woodruff, with Colin Powell, U.S. Secretary of State, *CNN Transcripts* (September 28, 2003), http://archives.cnn.com/TRANSCRIPTS/0309/28/le.00.html.

75 Robert Fisk: We might as well name our newspapers 'officials say', Democracy Now!/YouTube (2013), https://www.youtube.com/watch?v=puioIJJsQWA. Robert McChesney makes the same judgment. E.g., McChesney, previous n. 60.

76 State of Denial: Western Journalism and the Middle East | Robert Fisk, Center for International and Regional Studies/YouTube (2013), https://www.youtube.com/watch?v=l6ASJA7fbcE.

77 Ibid. Media scholar Robert McChesney observes this as well. E.g., Urbana Public Television, Digital Disconnect: How Capitalism is Turning the Internet Against Democracy (2014), https://archive.org/details/Digital_Disconnect_-_How_Capitalism_is_Turning_the_Internet_Against_Democracy (comments of Robert McChesney at minutes 1:02:00–1:03:00 and 1:09:00–1:10:00).

78 E.g., Noam Chomsky, *Failed States: The Abuse of Power and the Assault on Democracy* (Metropolitan Books, 2006), pp. 52–54 (Iraq and Indochina); Noam Chomsky, *Rogue States: The Rule of Force in World Affairs* (Haymarket Books, 2015), p. 54 (Cambodia and Laos bombing).

79 The British Empire reportedly banned media coverage of the Bengal "famine" as such. Janam Mukherjee, *Hungry Bengal: War, Famine and the End of Empire* (Oxford University Press, 2015), p. 125. The Soviet secret police arrested persons suspected of discussing the famine in Ukraine, even after it was over. See James E. Mace, 'Man-Made Famine in Ukraine,' in *Century of Genocide: Critical Essays and Eyewitness Accounts* (Samuel Totten, William Parsons and Israel Charny eds., Transaction Publishers, 2000), pp. 93, 118–19. Even the 1937 census results were reportedly withheld. Ibid., p. 102. See also Marco Carynnyk, 'Starvation deliberate, diabolical; Malcolm Muggeridge on Stalin's Famine in 1933,' in *Collectivization and Its Impact on the Ukrainian Population* (Government Printing Office, 1984), pp. 43–44.

80 E.g., J. Millard Burr, *Requiem for The Sudan: War, Drought, and Disaster Relief on the Nile* (Routledge, 2018); Indo-Asian News Service, US, China suppressed genocide reports during Bangladesh Liberation War, *Zee News* (March 25, 2015), https://web.archive.org/web/20210224235443/https://zeenews.india.com/news/north-east/us-china-suppressed-genocide-reports-during-bangladesh-liberation-war_1567599.html; Ilona Ross, 'Cambodia Plan,' *Associated Press*, December 18, 1979, https://books.google.com/books?id=LOb40W5m5rEC&pg=PA181. On the famine in Iraq, kept under

some control by a government rations system in the mid-1990s, which was undermined in some ways by war and insurgency from 2003 to 2017, see Peter Pellett, 'Sanctions, food, nutrition, and health in Iraq,' in *Iraq Under Siege: The Deadly Impact of Sanctions and War*, edited by Anthony Arnove (Pluto Press, 2003), pp. 170, 190; Barbara Nimri Aziz, 'Targets – Not Victims,' in *ibid.*, pp. 161, 170. A study of media coverage of Iraq discovered that both sanctions-related hunger and victims of US- and UN-led bombing campaigns were ignored. *See* Ali Abunimah and Rania Masri, 'The media's deadly spin on Iraq,' in *ibid.*, pp. 101–120.

81 Air America on Ad Blacklist? ABC document: Sponsors Shun Liberal Network, Fairness and Accuracy in Reporting (FAIR) (October 31, 2006), https://fair.org/take-action/media-advisories/air-america-on-ad-blacklist/; Jim Naureckas, Why progressive TV is DOA, *FAIR* (November 1, 2003), https://fair.org/extra/why-progressive-tv-is-doa/.

82 E.g., Bill Maher on Larry King Live after "Politically Incorrect" is cancelled by ABC (2002), CNN/Frank West/YouTube (2015), https://www.youtube.com/watch?v=Ksezhy1n1ZQ (denying Maher's ratings were bad); David Gurney, 'Everything changes forever (temporarily),' in A *Decade of Dark Humor: How Comedy, Irony, and Satire Shaped Post-9/11 America*, edited by David Gurney (University Press of Mississippi, 2011), https://www.google.com/books/edition/A_Decade_of_Dark_Humor/YwSiDwAAQBAJ?hl=en&gbpv=1&dq="maher"+advertisers+abc+2002&pg=PT54&printsec=frontcover (ratings improved after Maher questioned courage involved in air wars, but sponsors like Sears and FedEx boycotted the show); Phil Donahue on his 2003 firing from MSNBC, when liberal network couldn't tolerate antiwar voices, Democracy Now!/YouTube (2013), https://www.youtube.com/watch?v=ozxzNjRqCiE (Donahue thought he was fired as he wasn't "good for business"); Spencer Snyder, After 25 years, there's a reason MSNBC can't look back, *FAIR* (August 28, 2011), https://fair.org/home/after-25-years-theres-a-reason-msnbc-cant-look-back/ (highest ratings).

83 Eli M. Noam, Testimony before the Commerce Committee of the United States Senate (July 17, 2001), https://www.gpo.gov/fdsys/pkg/CHRG-107shrg89019.html.

84 Robert W. McChesney, Oligopoly: The big media game has fewer and fewer players, *The Progressive* (1999), https://www.lehigh.edu/~jl0d/J246-02/oligopoly.html. As of 2004, the top five companies appear to have accounted for over 80% of the domestic box office, by themselves or through subsidiaries. Studio Market Share: 2004, *Box Office Mojo* (January 17, 2005), https://www.boxofficemojo.com/studio.

85 Rev. Jesse L. Jackson, Sr., The challenge of our time (May 23, 1998), https://www.rainbowpush.org/speeches/1998/speechtxt/05-23-97/05.23.97.html. For details on how the government excluded all but a minority of potential broadcasters from the airwaves, see the Radio Act of 1927, 47 U. S. C. §§ 81–119 (1928), the Communications Act of 1934, 47 U.S.C. § 309(a) (1958), Nat'l Broad. Co. v. United States, 319 U.S. 190 (1943), and the Telecommunications Act of 1996, 47 U.S.C. § 1302 (1996).

86 Eric Boehlert, Pay for play, *Salon.com* (March 14, 2001), https://www.salon.com/2001/03/14/payola_2/.

87 Alexandra Marks, Media future: Risk of monopoly, *Christian Science Monitor* (September 19, 2002), https://www.csmonitor.com/.

88 Noam, previous n. 83.

89 Ted Turner, My beef with Big Media, *The Washington Monthly* (July/August 2004), https://www.washingtonmonthly.com (quoting decision of Federal Communications Commission).

90 Noam, previous n. 83.

91 Ibid.

92 149 *Congressional Record* H4179–07 (daily ed. May 15, 2003) (Statement of Congressman Bernie Sanders on "The Growing Concentration of Media Ownership").

93 Christa Corrine McLintock, 'Comment, The destruction of media diversity, or: How the FCC learned to stop regulating and love corporate dominated media,' 22 *John*

Marshall Journal of Computer and Information Law 569, 582 (2004) (citing Rachel Coen, Media giants cast aside regulatory "chains": FCC should resist attempt to gut ownership restrictions, Fairness and Accuracy in Reporting, https://www.fair.org/activism/fcc-giants.html.

94 E.g., Adam Levy, The big 6 largest media conglomerates, *The Motley Fool* (April 21, 2023), https://www.fool.com/investing/stock-market/market-sectors/communication/media-stocks/big-6 ("Most media you consume – everything from news to Internet to TV – is owned by these six companies: Time Warner, Disney, News Corporation, Comcast, Viacom and Sony."); but cf. Manish Singh, Netflix's biggest competition isn't sleep – It's YouTube Web, *VentureBeat* (December 10, 2018), https://venturebeat.com/media/netflixs-biggest-competition-isnt-sleep-its-youtube (average American spent 90 minutes a day with digital video in 2018, especially Netflix or YouTube); Emily A. Vogels et al., Teens, social media and technology 2022, *Pew Research Center* (August 10, 2022), https://www.pewresearch.org/internet/2022/08/10/teens-social-media-and-technology-2022/ ("A majority of teens (58%) visit TikTok daily, while about half say the same for Snapchat (51%) and Instagram (50%). After those platforms come Facebook with 32% and smaller shares who use Twitter [23%], Twitch [20%], WhatsApp, Reddit and Tumblr."); *but cf. also* Matt Binder, Tucker Carlson's Trump interview doesn't have 230 million video views on Twitter, *Mashable* (August 24, 2023), https://mashable.com/article/tucker-carlson-x-trump-interview-twitter-video-view-count.

95 E.g., Stephen Dycus, William C. Banks, Peter Raven Hansen, and Stephen I. Vladeck, *National Security Law* (Aspen Publishing, 2022), pp. 32–34, 158–59, 435, 553, 588, 1121, 1217–118, 1250–1299.

96 Alexander Meiklejohn, *Political Freedom* (New York: Oxford University Press, 1965). Personal and social authenticity are linked in the eighteenth and nineteenth century ideal that we can be free as people to think and to write and publish, and use this freedom to shape the society around us, up to and including our government. Cf., also, Jürgen Habermas, *The Philosophical Discourse of Modernity: Twelve Lectures*, translated by Frederick G. Lawrence (The MIT Press, paperback ed. 1995), pp. 20–68; John Durham Peters, *Speaking into the Air: A History of the Idea of Communication* (University of Chicago Press, paperback ed. 2000), pp. 109–226. Election authenticity depends on legal structures that ensure the opinions of the public have a path to be reflected in election results. Inter-American Commission on Human Rights, Report on the Situation of Human Rights in Haiti, OAS No. OEA/ser.L/V/II.77, doc.18, rev.1 (1990). As such, it could be called an outgrowth of the philosophical ideal of an authentic or at least an autonomous public sphere that is not "bred" by the powerful for their own benefit. Habermas, *Philosophical Discourse*, pp. 364–66.

97 Deplatforming, Lexico, www.lexico.com/definition/deplatforming (last visited August 20, 2022). Similarly, demonetizing refers to allowing a video or post to remain on a platform that shares ad revenue with video or other content creators, but to deny the creators' their former or ordinary share of ad revenue. Demonetized, *Urban Dictionary*, https://www.urbandictionary.com/define.php?term=demonetized (last visited August 20, 2022).

98 WestlawNext, https://m.next.westlaw.com (last visited August 2, 2021) (searches for "GamerGate" and "deplatforming").

99 Elijah O'Kelley, 'State constitutions as a check on the New Governors: Using state Free Speech clauses to protect social media users from arbitrary political censorship by social media platforms,' 68 *Emory Law Journal* 111 (2019); Deplatforming, Wikipedia, https://en.wikipedia.org/wiki/Deplatforming (last visited August 20, 2022).

100 Matt McGee, An interview with a search quality rater, *Search Engine Land* (January 20, 2012), https://searchengineland.com/interview-google-search-quality-rater-108702; Matt McGee, Google search quality raters instructions gain new "page quality" guidelines, *Search Engine Land* (September 7, 2012), https://searchengineland.com/google-search-quality-raters-instructions-gain-new-page-quality-guidelines-132436.

101 Damian Ryan, *Understanding Digital Marketing* (Kogan Page Ltd., 5th ed. 2021), p. 271. One website targeted was the U.K. tabloid *The Daily Mail*, which had covered the Wikileaks revelations about falsehoods by the U.S. government during the wars in Iraq and Afghanistan, corruption in the Democratic Party, and U.N. investigators' findings that Syrian rebels may have manufactured and used chemical weapons in an incident the Trump administration blamed on Syria's government. E.g., Media Lens, Nearly every war has been the result of media lies. *Popular Resistance* (December 27, 2022), https://popularresistance.org/nearly-every-war-has-been-the-result-of-media-lies-julian-assange-state-corporate-media-and-ukraine/.

102 Kyle Chayka, What Google search isn't showing you, *The New Yorker* (March 10, 2022), https://www.newyorker.com/culture/infinite-scroll/what-google-search-isnt-showing-you.

103 George McCurdo, 'The net by numbers,' 22 *Journal of Information Science* 381, 386 (1995); Steven S. Ross, 'Public relations in cyberspace,' 51 *The Public Relations Journal* 36 (1995). This figure may have grown to one-sixth of email users controlled by AOL, and half of the "online population"; this is presumably referring to those simultaneously online as one-fifth of *all* email and Web users. Cyber Promotions, Inc. v. American Online, Inc., 948 F. Supp. 436, 455 (E.D. Pa. 1996) ("AOL currently has approximately seven million members who constitute no more than one-sixth to one-seventh of the current total e-mail population of 40 to 50 million and approximately one-half of the current total online population of 12 million.").

104 U.S. House of Representatives, Committee on the Judiciary, Subcommittee on Antitrust, Commercial and Administrative Law, Investigation of Competition in Digital Markets: Majority Staff Report and Recommendations (2020), p. 11, https://bit.ly/32JPE1r [hereinafter House Subcommittee Report].

105 Ibid., pp. 15–19, 254–55, 334–35.

106 Ibid.; see also, United States v. Microsoft Corp., 253 F.3d 34, 58 (D.C. Cir. 2001); Transamerica Computer Co., Inc. v. IBM Corp., 698 F.2d 1377 (9th Cir. 1983); In re IBM, 302 F. Supp. 796 (J.P.M.L. 1969); United States v. IBM, No. 69 Civ. 200 (D.D.C. filed 1969); Joseph P. Bauer, 'Reflections on the Manifold Means of Enforcing the Antitrust Laws: Too Much, Too Little, or Just Right,' 16 *Loyola Consumer Law Review* 303 (2003).

107 FTC, Memorandum, Google, Inc., File No. 111–0163 (2013).

108 Craig Timberg, FTC: Google did not break Antitrust Law with search practices, *Washington Post* (January 3, 2013).

109 Plaintiff's Complaint, United States of America v. Google, LLC, No.1:20-CV-03010 (D.D.C. compl. filed Oct. 20, 2020 and amended compl. filed January 15, 2021), https://storage.courtlistener.com/recap/gov.uscourts.dcd.223205/gov.uscourts.dcd.223205.94.0.pdf; Joint Status Rep., *Google*, No. 1:20-CV-03010 (D.D.C. report filed March 18, 2021) (listing 49 states as plaintiffs in 2021, along with the District of Columbia, Commonwealth of Puerto Rico, and Territory of Guam); see also, Richard J. Gilbert, "The U.S. Federal Trade Commission Investigation of Google Search," in *The Antitrust Revolution: Economics, Competition, and Policy*, edited by John E. Kwoka Jr. and Lawrence J. White (Oxford University Press, 7th ed. 2020); Inform, Inc. Inc. v. Google, Inc. No. 1:19-cv-05362-JPB (N.D. Ga. first amended complaint filed Oct. 9, 2020) (citing, inter alia, Search Engine Market Share, *Statcounter* (2020), https://gs.statcounter.com/search-engine-market-share/all/worldwide/2020); Press Release, U.S. Department of Justice, Justice Department sues monopolist Google for violating Antitrust Laws (October 20, 2020), https://www.justice.gov/opa/pr/justice-department-sues-monopolist-google-violating-antitrust-laws.

110 For these figures and other data, see Google's annual reports, or tables of time series data on Yahoo! Finance or Gurufocus. Yahoo! Finance (2022), finance.yahoo.com; Gurufocus (2022), https://www.gurufocus.com.

111 *See, e.g.*, Plaintiffs' Complaint, at 10–11, 19–67, State of Utah v. Google, LLC, No. 3:21-CV-005227 (N.D. Cal. July 7, 2021); In Re Digital Advertising Antitrust Litigation, 555 F. Supp. 3d 1372 (J.P.M.L. 2021); Plaintiffs' First Amended Complaint, State of Texas v. Google LLC, No. 4:20–00957 (E.D. Tex. amended compl. filed March 15, 2021); Complaint, State of Texas v. Google LLC, C.A. No. 4:20–00957 (E.D. Tex. compl. filed 2000).

112 Inform Inc. v. Google, LLC, No. 21–13289, 2022 WL 3703958 (11th Cir. August 26, 2022).

113 Plaintiffs' Complaint, at 52, *Utah*, No. 3:21-CV-005227. See also, *ibid.*, pp. 41–53.

114 *See ibid.*, pp. 10.

115 FTC v. Facebook, 560 F. Supp. 3d 1 (D.D.C. 2021), *further proceedings at* 581 F. Supp. 3d 34 (D.D.C. 2022); Press Release, Fed. Trade Comm'n, FTC sues Facebook for illegal monopolization (December 9, 2020), https://www.ftc.gov/news-events/news/press-releases/2020/12/ftc-sues-facebook-illegal-monopolization.

116 House Subcommittee Report, previous n. 104, pp. 91, 155; see also, Klein v. Facebook, Inc., 20-CV-08570-LHK, slip op. (N.D. Cal. motion to dismiss denied in part January 14, 2022).

117 SensorTower, Q4 and Full Year 2018 (2019), http://sensortower.com/blog/top-apps-games-publishers-2018; see also, Indo-Asian News Service, Google tops Facebook for first time in 5 years in Q4 2019: Sensor tower, *Gadgets360* (January 17, 2020), https://www.gadgets360.com/apps/news/google-facebook-tiktok-disney-plus-sensor-tower-q4-2019-figures-2165151.

118 E.g., YouTube average visit length per user worldwide 2020–2021, *Statista* (2021), https://www.statista.com/statistics/1257254/youtubecom-time-spent-per-visit.

119 E.g., *Facebook*, 581 F. Supp. 3d at 15, 17 ("Whether due to network effects or the norms around what sort of content is generally posted on different platforms, it is not a stretch to imagine that users are reluctant to share a highly personal milestone on LinkedIn or post a video of their child's first steps to YouTube."). But see, Lenz v. Universal Music Corp., 815 F. 3d 1145, 1149 (9th Cir. 2015) ("On February 7, 2007, Lenz uploaded to YouTube a 29-second home video of her two young children in the family kitchen dancing to the song *Let's Go Crazy* by Prince. . . . About four seconds into the video, Lenz asks her thirteen month-old son, 'What do you think of the music?' after which he bobs up and down.").

120 House Subcommittee Report, previous n. 104, p. 333.

121 On smart devices and mobile wallets, see European Commission, Antitrust: Commission Sends Statement of Objections to Apple on App Store Rules for Music Streaming Providers (2023), https://ec.europa.eu/commission/presscorner/detail/en/ip_21_2061; European Commission, Antitrust: Commission sends statement of objections to Apple over practices regarding Apple Pay (May 2, 2022), https://ec.europa.eu/commission/presscorner/detail/en/ip_22_2764; Press Release, European Commission, Statement by Executive Vice-President Margrethe Vestager on the Statement of Objections Sent to Apple on App Store Rules for Music Streaming Providers (2021), https://ec.europa.eu/commission/presscorner/detail/en/speech_21_2093. On mobile gaming transactions and app stores, see *Epic Games, Inc. v. Apple Inc.*, 67 F.4th 946, 984–85, 996–97 (9th Cir. 2023), *affirming in part* 559 F. Supp. 3d 898, 989–990 (N.D. Cal. 2021).

122 European Commission, Statement of Objections (Music Streaming Providers), previous n. 121.

123 House Subcommittee Report, previous n. 104, pp. 358–59.

124 *Epic Games*, 67 F.4th 946.

125 Apple or Android Nation?, Statista (July 2020), https://cdn.statcdn.com/infographic/images/normal/22702.jpeg.

126 House Subcommittee Report, previous n. 104, pp. 268–292.

127 Ibid., pp. 291–93.

128 Julia Cusick, Release: CAP brief finds evidence of anti-competitive behavior by Amazon, Apple, Facebook, and Google, *AmericanProgress.org* (July 28, 2020), https://www.americanprogress.org/press/release/2020/07/28/488194/release-cap-brief-finds-evidence-anti-competitive-behavior-amazon-apple-facebook-google/.

129 Marc Jarsulic, Using antitrust law to address the market power of platform monopolies, *AmericanProgress.org* (July 28, 2020), https://www.americanprogress.org/issues/economy/reports/2020/07/28/488201/using-antitrust-law-address-market-power-platform-monopolies/.

130 House Subcommittee Report, previous n. 104 ("This demonstrates the problem, however, given that voice shopping is most useful for products in which consumers do not have to do much research or engage in price comparison. Alexa's algorithm, in conjunction with the AmazonBasics business model, provides a convenient avenue for Amazon to favor first-party products.").

131 E.g., XSellco, cpcstrategy, and Tinuity, Debunking the 2018 Amazon Buy Box Algorithm, *Slideshare.net* (March 29, 2018), https://www.slideshare.net/CPCStrategy-ConvertRetailIntent/debunking-the-2018-amazon-buy-box-algorithm.

132 E.g., ibid.; Lisa Byrne, How to win the Amazon Buy Box webinar, *XSellco* (2020), https://www.xsellco.com/resources/how-to-win-the-buy-box-webinar/; XSellco, Why winning the Amazon buy box is essential in 2023 (March 5, 2022), https://www.repricer.com/blog/amazon-buy-box-ultimate-guide/.

133 House Subcommittee Report, previous n. 104, p. 277.

134 District of Columbia [DC] v. Amazon.com, Inc., No. 2021 CA 001775 B, slip op. at 9, 15 (D.C. Super. Ct. motion for reconsideration denied August 1, 2022); *Amazon.com*, No. 2021 CA 001775 B, transcript (D.C. Super. Ct. transcript of hearing on motion to dismiss, March 18, 2022).

135 Anne Edgerton and Leah Nylen, 'Lina Khan is coming for Amazon, armed with an Antitrust Lawsuit,' *Bloomberg/Portland Press Herald* (June 29, 2023), https://www.pressherald.com/2023/06/29/lina-khan-is-coming-for-amazon-armed-with-an-ftc-antitrust-suit/.

136 David D. Clark, 'Rethinking the design of the internet: The end to end arguments vs. the brave new world,' Paper Submitted to TPRC Conference (August 10, 2000), https://www.mit.edu.

137 E.g., U.S. Patent No. 7,668,861 (issued 2010) [System and method to determine the validity of an interaction on a network]; U.S. Patent No. 8,793,255 (issued 2014) [Generating a reputation score based on user interactions]; U.S. Patent No. 10, 216,803 (issued 2019) [Ranking and filtering comments based on author and content]; U.S. Patent No. 11,216,746 (issued 2022) [Utilizing machine learning and composite utility scores from multiple event categories to improve digital content distribution].

138 E.g., U.S. Patent No. 10,033,685 [issued 2018] (Social network site recommender system and method) (citing U.S. Patent No. 7,716,225 [issued 2010] (Ranking documents based on user behavior and/or feature data)); U.S. Patent No. 11,551,280 [issued 2023] (Techniques for recommending items to users); U.S. Patent No. 11,540,017 [issued 2022] (System and method for generating models representing users of a media providing service).

139 47 U.S.C. § 230.

140 e-ventures Worldwide, LLC v. Google, Inc., No. 2:14-cv-646-PAM, 2017 WL 2210029, at *2 (M.D. Fla. February 8, 2017).

141 47 U.S.C. § 230(c)-(e).

142 e-ventures Worldwide, LLC v. Google, Inc., 188 F.Supp.3d 1265, 1273 (M.D. Fla. 2016).

143 *Id.* at 1274–75.

144 *Id.* at 1275–76.

145 E.g., Enhanced Athlete Inc. v. Google LLC, 479 F. Supp. 3d 824, 831 (N.D. Cal. 2020).

146 Methaya Sirichit, 'Censorship by intermediary and moral rights: Strengthening authors' control over online expressions through the right of respect and integrity,' 1 *Journal of Law, Technology, and Public Policy* 54, 79 (2015) (citing Moving and

Storage, Inc., v. Panayotov, No. 12–12262-GAO, 2014 WL 949830 at *2 (D. Mass. March 12, 2014); Smith v. Trusted Universal Standards in Electronic Transactions Inc., No. 09–4567 (RBK), 2011 WL 900096 at *9 (D.N.J. March 15, 2011)).

147 The court explained:

> e-ventures' websites were in violation of Google's Guidelines, and thus the removal of those websites was true speech, if it was speech at all. But there is a more fundamental reason why the First Amendment bars e-ventures' claims. Google's actions in formulating rankings for its search engine and in determining whether certain websites are contrary to Google's guidelines and thereby subject to removal are the same as decisions by a newspaper editor regarding which content to publish, which article belongs on the front page, and which article is unworthy of publication. The First Amendment protects these decisions, whether they are fair or unfair, or motivated by profit or altruism.

e-ventures Worldwide, LLC v. Google, Inc., No. 2:14-cv-646-PAM, 2017 WL 2210029, at *4 (M.D. Fla. February 8, 2017).

148 Enigma Software Group USA, LLC v. Malwarebytes, 946 F.3d 1040, 1045–52 (9th Cir. 2019), *cert. denied*, 141 S. Ct. 13 (2020).

149 Ohio v. Google LLC, No. 21-CV-H-06–0274 (Ohio Ct. Common Pleas, Delaware County, June 2022), https://www.scribd.com/document/575713086/Judge-grants-and-denies-Google-s-motion-to-dismiss-Ohio-lawsuit?irclickid=0oiRksWRnxyIUpj1wW34mUdNUkDxukTduQcC1A0&irpid=27795&utm_source=impact&utm_medium=cpc&utm_campaign=affiliate_pdm_acquisition_Sovrn%20Commerce%20%28formerly%20Viglink%29&sharedid=&irgwc=1#from_embed; J. Wyatt Fore, Court green lights Ohio AG's case to declare Google a "common carrier," Constantine Cannon/*Lexology* (June 2, 2022), https://www.lexology.com/library/detail.aspx?g=c32009e6-5691-4320-86f8-91ab94ebca76.

150 The law of the cloud includes a privilege from liability for hosting copies of copyrighted works as a result of automated satisfaction of user requests to back up or transmit data. Parker v. Google, Inc., 242 F. App'x 833, 836 (3d Cir. 2007); Monica Horten, 'The *Aereo* dilemma and copyright in the cloud,' 3 *Internet Policy Review* No. 4 (2014) (citing Cartoon Network LP v. CSC Holdings, Inc., 536 F.3d 121 (2d Cir.2008)); Robyn L. Rothman, 'Beyond the cloud: Why the narrow decision in *American Broadcasting Cos. v. Aereo, Inc.* may have broader implications for cloud-computing,' 32 *Touro Law Review* 275 (2016). See generally, CoStar Group, Inc. v. LoopNet, Inc., 373 F.3d 544, 551 (4th Cir. 2004) ("There are thousands of owners, contractors, servers, and users involved in the Internet whose role involves the storage and transmission of data in the establishment and maintenance of an Internet facility. Yet their conduct is not truly 'copying' as understood by the [Copyright] Act; rather, they are conduits from or to would-be copiers and have no interest in the copy itself."). YouTube data and Android data from smartphones appear to be commingled at a repository whose gateway is www.googleapis.com, see Douglas J. Leith, Mobile handset privacy: Measuring the data iOS and Android send to Apple and Google, Paper Presented to Security and Privacy in Communication Networks: 17th EAI International Conference, SecureComm 2021, Virtual Event, September 6–9, 2021 (2021), draft at pp. 7–9, http://la.buvette.org/vrac/apple_google.pdf. Instagram and WhatsApp apparently consolidate much of their user data with Facebook's data repositories. E.g., Kate O'Flaherty, All the data WhatsApp and Instagram send to Facebook, *Wired UK* (July 24, 2021), https://www.wired.co.uk/article/whatsapp-instagram-facebook-data.

151 Philip Hamburger and Clare Morell, The First Amendment doesn't protect Big Tech censorship, *The Wall Street Journal* (July 31, 2021), https://www.wsj.com.

152 Adam Candeub, 'Bargaining for free speech: Common carriage, network neutrality, and Section 230,' 22 *Yale Journal of Law and Technology* 391 (2020) (arguing that common carrier law defends free speech by ensuring that "a dominant network [that] furnishes public goods that flow from a universal communications platform" has a

duty not to "control online behavior and censor speech," in exchange for liability protection for carrying the speech); Richard Epstein and The Federalist Society, Is common carrier the solution to social-media censorship?, YouTube (2021), https://fedsoc.org/events/is-common-carrier-the-solution-to-social-media-censorship (noting that Google, Facebook, and Twitter capture such a large share of their respective markets that under principles of antitrust, utility, and First Amendment law, their private discretion to deny service should be limited in the public interest); Eugene Volokh, 'Treating social media like common carriers?', 1 *Journal of Free Speech Law*, 377, 379, 382–83 (2021) (similar, citing 47 U.S.C. §§ 13101(a), 14101(a); Primrose v. W. Union Tel. Co., 154 U.S. 1, 14 (1894); Nat'l Assn' of Reg. Util. Comm'rs v. FCC, 525 F.2d 630, 641 (D.C. Cir. 1976)); see also, Tunku Varadarajan, The "common carrier" solution to social-media censorship, *The Wall Street Journal* (January 15, 2021), https://www.wsj.com (relating views of Richard Epstein on the matter)

153 E.g., Biden v. Knight First Amendment Institute at Columbia University, 141 S. Ct. 1220, 1223 (2021) (Thomas, J., concurring) (citing *Primrose*, 154 U.S. at 14; German Alliance Ins. Co. v. Lewis, 233 U.S. 389, 411 (1914); Ingate v. Christie, 3 Car. & K. 61, 63, 175 Eng. Rep. 463, 464 (N. P. 1850)); NetChoice, LLC v. Paxton, 49 F.4th 439, 476 (5th Cir. 2022) ("Here, the Texas legislature found that 'social media platforms with the largest number of users are common carriers by virtue of their market dominance,' and this finding is reasonable."); *id.* at 478–79 (holding that common carriers like telegraph services have historically been required to act impartially and in good faith, and that this principle applies to Meta and Alphabet as it does to bakeries, ferries, mills, steamboats, stagecoaches, railroads, water lines, telegraph services, and telephone companies, all of which "government may . . . regulate . . . to prevent invidious discrimination.") (citing *Western Union*, 162 U.S. at 651); NetChoice, LLC v. Paxton, 573 F. Supp. 3d 1092, 1107 (W.D. Tex. 2021) ("Equal access obligations . . . have long been imposed on telephone companies, railroads, and postal services, without raising any First Amendment issue.") (quoting United States Telecom Ass'n v. FCC, 825 F.3d 674, 740 (D.C. Cir. 2016)), *rev'd*, 49 F.4th 439; *id.* ("Little First Amendment concern exists because common carriers 'merely facilitate the transmission of speech of others.' In *United States Telecom*, the Court added broadband providers to its list of common carriers.") (internal citations omitted).

154 E.g., Dipayan Ghosh, 'Don't break up Facebook – Treat it like a utility,' *Harvard Business Review* (May 30, 2019); Lina Khan, 'Amazon – An infrastructure service and its challenge to current antitrust law', in *Digital Dominance: The Power of Google, Amazon, Facebook, and Apple*, edited by Martin Moore and Damien Tambini (Oxford University Press, 2018), pp. 98, 120–22; K. Sabeel Rahman, 'Regulating informational infrastructure: Internet platforms as the new public utilities,' 2 *Georgetown Law and Technology Review* 234 (2018); K. Sabeel Rahman, 'The new utilities: Private power, social infrastructure, and the revival of the public utility concept,' 39 *Cardozo Law Review* 1621 (2018); Pasquale and Bracha, previous n. 6, at 276–78, 299 (arguing, among other things, that dominant search engines should be required to provide nondiscriminatory access to their indices and archives of websites by analogy to public utility regulation of common carriers due to barriers to entry analogous to those in telecom).

155 E.g., Turner Broadcasting System, Inc. v. FCC, 520 U.S. 180, 194, 213–14 (1997); Turner Broadcasting System, Inc. v. FCC, 512 U. S. 622, 643–57 (1994); *id.* at 684 (O'Connor, J., joined by Scalia, J., and Ginsburg, J., dissenting); PruneYard Shopping Center v. Robins, 447 U. S. 74, 88 (1980); *Paxton*, 49 F.4th at 467–69.

156 Verizon v. FCC, 740 F.3d 623, 634, 659 (D.C. Cir. 2014).

157 *United States Telecom Association*, 825 F.3d at 740.

158 Cf., Amalgamated Food Employees Union v. Logan Valley Plaza, 391 U. S. 308, 323 (1968); Police Department of Chicago v. Mosley, 408 U.S. 92, 95–96 (1972); Tinker v.

Des Moines School District, 393 U. S. 503, 512 (1969); Schneider v. State, 308 U. S. 147, 163 (1939); Hudgens v. NLRB, 424 U.S. 507, 525–43 (1976) (Marshall, J., joined by Brennen, J., dissenting).

159 E.g., Rumsfeld v. Forum for Academic and Institutional Rights, Inc., 547 U.S. 47, 65 (2006) ("Nothing about recruiting suggests that law schools agree with any speech by recruiters.").

160 *PruneYard*, 447 U.S. at 88 (when a business is open to the public, any "views expressed by members of the public in passing out pamphlets or seeking signatures for a petition thus will not likely be identified with those of the [business] owner."); cf. *Turner*, 512 U.S. at 644–46, 649 (compelling cable networks to carry broadcast shows does not burden or benefit views or subject matter of any particular type but is rather a restraint on "economic power").

161 *Turner*, 512 U.S. at 662.

162 *Id.* at 644–46, 649.

163 Formal Complaint of Free Press and Public Knowledge against Comcast Corporation, Memorandum Opinion and Order, 23 FCC Rcd. 1308 (2008), *vacated*, Comcast Corp. v. Federal Communications, 600 F.3d 642 (D.C. Cir. 2010); Policy statement, 20 FCC Rcd. 149 6 (2005).

164 E.g., Hannibal Travis, 'The FCC's new theory of the First Amendment,' 51 *Santa Clara Law Review* 417 (2011).

165 E.g., Red Lion v. FCC, 395 U.S. 367 (1969); Prasad Krishnamurthy and Erwin Chemerinsky, 'How Congress can prevent Big Tech from becoming the speech police,' *The Hill* (February 19, 2021), https://thehill.com/opinion/judiciary/539341-how-congress-can-prevent-big-tech-from-becoming-the-speech-police/.

166 Varadarajan, 'The "common carrier" solution,' previous n. 152.

167 Ashutosh Bhagwat, 'Do platforms have editorial rights?', 1 *Journal of Free Speech Law* 97, 124–25 (2021).

168 Airbnb, Inc. v. City and County of San Francisco, 217 F. Supp. 3d 1066 (N.D. Cal. 2016), (citing, inter alia, Pittsburgh Press Co. v. Pittsburgh Comm'n on Human Relations, 413 U.S. 376, 388–89 (1973)).

169 *Pittsburgh Press*, 413 U.S. at 388. See also, *Airbnb*, 217 F. Supp. 3d at 1079.

170 E.g., Patti Buchman, 'Title VII limits on discrimination against television anchorwomen on the basis of appearance,' 85 *Columbia Law Review* 190 (1985).

171 Masterpiece Cakeshop, Ltd. v. Colorado Civil Rights Commission., 138 S.Ct. 1719, 1727 (2018).

172 *Id.* at 1728 ("When it comes to weddings, it can be assumed that a member of the clergy who objects to gay marriage on moral and religious grounds could not be compelled to perform the ceremony without denial of his or her right to the free exercise of religion."). See also, 303 Creative LLC v. Elenis, 143 S. Ct. 2298 (2023).

173 *Masterpiece Cakeshop*, 138 S. Ct. at 1728. See also, *303 Creative*, 143 S. Ct. at 2312–35.

174 E.g., Alternative Thinking Systems v. Simon & Schuster, 853 F. Supp. 791 (S.D.N.Y. 1994); Chodos v. West Publishing Co., 292 F.2d 992 (9th Cir. 2002); Freund v. Washington Square Press, 34 N.U.2d 379 (1974).

175 E.g., Cal. Civ. Code, § 3294, subd. (a) ("In an action for the breach of an obligation not arising from contract, where it is proven by clear and convincing evidence that the defendant has been guilty of oppression, fraud, or malice, the plaintiff, in addition to the actual damages, may recover damages for the sake of example and by way of punishing the defendant."); Amadeo v. Principal Mutual Life Insurance Co., 290 F.3d 1152, 1165 (9th Cir. 2002) (conduct which was not just poor judgment, but reflected defective corporate records, "plainly unreasonable interpretation" of the parties' deal, or "deliberate[ly] restricted" the defendant's factual investigation of the plaintiff's request could be both bad faith and malice for purposes of punitive damages under § 3294).

176 E.g., Shaffer v. George Washington University, 27 F.4th 754, 759, 762, 768–70 (D.C. Cir. 2022) (inquiring into whether university exercised good faith or was unjustly enriched by suspending classes in person during COVID-19 pandemic without providing comparable services or activities, as presenting breach of implied contract or restitution issues for trial); Doe v. University of the Sciences, 961 F.3d 203 (3d Cir. 2020) (holding that private university breached its own documents regarding a fair disciplinary hearing, where fair construed to mean unbiased and equitable and to include right of cross-examining accusers); *Amadeo*, 290 F.3d at 1158 ("There is an implied covenant of good faith and fair dealing in every contract that neither party will do anything which will injure the right of the other to receive the benefits of the agreement.") (quoting Comunale v. Traders & General Ins. Co., 328 P. 2d 198, 200 (Cal. 1958)); Wolf v. Walt Disney Pictures and Television, 76 Cal. Rptr. 3d 585, 597–99 (Cal. Ct. App. 2008) (similar). See also, Freeman v. Howard University College of Medicine, No. 1: 21-cv-02191 (CRC), slip op. (D.D.C. September 16, 2022) (A "plaintiff challenging an academic dismissal must show that there 'was no rational basis for the decision or that it was motivated by bad faith or ill will unrelated to academic performance.'") (citing Chenari v. George Washington Univ., 172 F. Supp. 3d 38, 47 (D.D.C. 2016)); Trustees of Indiana University v. Spiegel, 186 N.E.2d 1151, 1159 n.4 (Ind. Ct. App. 2022) ("Students must prove bad faith in breach-of-contract cases involving matters of academic discipline and academic achievement, in which courts have traditionally granted universities deference, . . . but the Universities cite no precedent requiring proof of bad faith in breach-of-contract cases involving the provision of goods and services in an academic setting."); Matter of Hansbrough v. College of St. Rose, 209 A.D.3d 1168, 1171 (N.Y. App. Div. 2022) (in addressing determinations discontinuing academic programs due to financial hardship, "Deference should be accorded to a college's determination, "and judicial review is circumscribed to whether the [college] failed to substantially comply with its internal rules and whether its decision was arbitrary [and] capricious or made in bad faith."); Nova Southeastern University of Health Sciences, Inc. v. Sharick, 21 So. 3d 41, 42–44 (Fla. 3d Dist. Ct. App. 2009) (concluding that an expelled university student could seek damages in terms of "lost earning capacity" and that the trial would be dedicated to " 'valuing the loss of this degree within the context of an arbitrary, capricious or bad faith deprivation of such' " degree), *review denied*, 36 So.3d 84 (Fla. 2010) (internal citation omitted).

177 E.g., Soldinger v. Northwest Airlines, 51 Cal.App.4th 345, 370 (Cal. Ct. App. 1996) ("Once the employee establishes a prima facie case, then the employer must establish it initiated good faith efforts to accommodate or no accommodation was possible without producing undue hardship."); Beck v. University of Wisconsin Board of Regents, 75 F.3d 1130, 1135 (7th Cir. 1996) (to avoid discriminating unlawfully against disabled individuals, "employer[s] must be willing to consider making changes in its ordinary work rules, facilities, terms, and conditions in order to enable a disabled individual to work. . . . [C]ourts should look for signs of failure to participate in good faith or failure by one of the parties to make reasonable efforts to help the other party determine what specific accommodations are necessary.") (citation and internal quotations omitted); Eidshahen v. Pizza Hut of America, Inc., 115 F. Supp. 2d 279, 284 (D. Conn. 1998) (similar).

178 In re Scholastic Corp. Securities Litigation, 252 F.3d 63, 74, 76 (2d Cir. 2001).

179 E.g., Best Carpet Values, Inc. v. Google LLC, No. 5: 20-cv-04700-EJD, slip op. at § IIID. (N.D. Cal. Sept. 24, 2021) ("Here, Plaintiffs allege that Google's leaderboard and banner ads are commercial speech that misleadingly imply that they endorse Google's ads or were compensated by Google for placing the ads. . . . Therefore, if Plaintiffs prevail in this suit, Google can be enjoined from tethering similar ads to Plaintiffs' websites in the future."); People v. Stanistreet, 29 Cal. 4th 497, 508, 127 Cal. Rptr. 2d 633 (2002) ("knowingly false statements of fact" may be regulated due to the

"potential harm" they cause, and because outlawing this "class of speech" does not threaten viewpoint discrimination) (citing R.A.V. v. St. Paul, 505 U.S. 377, 387–88 (1992)); see also, Int'l Diamond Importers, Inc. v. Oriental Gemco (N. Y.), Inc., 64 F Supp 3d 494, 525 (S.D.N.Y., 2014).

180 HomeAway. com, Inc. v. City of Santa Monica, 918 F. 3d 676, 686 (9th Cir. 2019).

181 *Pittsburgh Press*, 413 U.S. 376.

182 E.g., *NetChoice v. Paxton*, 49 F.4th at 461 (Google, Facebook, and Twitter generally "permit any user who agrees to their boilerplate terms of service to communicate on any topic, at any time, and for any reason."); Murphy v. Twitter, Inc., 60 Cal. App. 5th 12, 23 (Cal. Ct. App., 1st Dist. 2021).

183 E.g., Cohen v. Cowles Media Co., 501 U.S. 663, 670 (1991).

184 Berenson v. Twitter, previous nn. 41, 62. See also, Barnes v. Yahoo!, Inc., 570 F.3d 1096, 1106–9 (9th Cir. 2009). But cf., Divino Group LLC v. Google LLC, No. 19-cv-04749-VKD, slip op. (N.D. Cal. July 5, 2023) (ECF No. 137) (while it could theoretically be breach of contract for YouTube to violate its pledge to treat everyone equally in its Community Guidelines, plaintiffs failed to allege that YouTube violated this pledge in their case); *Murphy v. Twitter*, 60 Cal. App. 5th at 38–39 (declining to bind service to promises not to monitor users or infringe their free speech in light of other provisos about content removal).

185 E.g., *Murphy v. Twitter*, 60 Cal. App. 5th at 38–39. See also, King v. Facebook, Inc., 572 F. Supp. 3d 776 (N.D. Cal. 2021), *aff'd*, 845 F. App'x 691 (9th Cir. 2021); Prager University v. Google LLC, 85 Cal. App. 5th 1022, 1042 (Cal. Ct. App. 6th Dist. 2022). Cf., Prager University v. Google LLC, 951 F.3d 991, 1000 (9th Cir. 2020).

186 Board of Directors of Rotary International v. Rotary Club of Duarte, 481 U.S. 537 (1987).

187 Masterpiece Cakeshop, Ltd. v. Colorado Civil Rights Comm'n, 584 U. S. ___, 138 S.Ct. 1719, 1727 (2018). See also, Hurley v. Irish-American Gay, Lesbian and Bisexual Group of Boston, Inc., 515 U.S. 557, 572 (1995) ("As with many public accommodations statutes across the Nation, . . . [the Massachusetts statute] prohibits discrimination on the basis of 'race, color, religious creed, national origin, sex, sexual orientation . . . , deafness, blindness or any physical or mental disability or ancestry' in 'the admission of any person to, or treatment in any place of public accommodation, resort or amusement.'") (internal citation omitted); *id.* ("Provisions like these are well within the State's usual power to enact when a legislature has reason to believe that a given group is the target of discrimination, and they do not, as a general matter, violate the First or Fourteenth Amendments.").

188 E.g., Boy Scouts of America v. Dale, 530 U.S. 640, 656 (2000); Pauline Trouillard, 'Platforms are not speakers: Why are Facebook and Twitter devoid of First Amendment Rights?,' 19 *Ohio State Technology Law Journal* 257 (2022–2023). See also, 303 Creative LLC v. Elenis, 143 S. Ct. 2298, 2307, 2311–12, 2317–18 (2023); Little Sisters of the Poor Saints Peter and Paul Home v. Pennsylvania, 591 U.S. ___, 140 S. Ct. 2367, 2373, 2377–78, 2391 (2020); cf., National Institute of Family and Life Advocates v. Becerra, 585 U. S. ___, 138 S.Ct. 2361, 2371 (2018); Thomas v. Review Board of Indiana Employment Security Division, 450 U.S. 707, 710, 715–16 (1981); Clay v. United States, 403 U.S. 698 (1971); Tinker v. Des Moines Independent Community School District, 393 U. S. 503, 505–506 (1969). For justices decrying some of these exemptions, see *303 Creative*, 143 S. Ct. at 2322–333, 2338–341 (Sotomayor, J., joined by Kagan, J., and Jackson, J., dissenting); *Becerra*, 138 S. Ct. at 2379, 2388 (Breyer, J., joined by Ginsburg, J., Sotomayor, J., and Kagan, J., dissenting); Irish-American Gay, Lesbian and Bisexual Group of Boston v. Boston, 418 Mass. 238, 242–52, 636 N.E. 2d 1293, 1295–298 (1994) (holding that a parade is a public accommodation and nothing in the expressive purposes relating to it justified excluding gay marchers), *rev'd sub nom. Hurley*, 515 U.S. 557; Martha Minow, 'Not in the

room where it happens: Adversariness, politicization, and *Little Sisters of the Poor*,' 2020–1 *The Supreme Court Review* 35 (2021); Kyle C. Velte, 'Why the Religious Right can't have its (straight wedding) cake and eat it too: Breaking the preservation-through-transformation dynamic in *Masterpiece Cakeshop v. Colorado Civil Rights Commission*,' 36 *Law and Inequality* 67 (2018).

189 *NetChoice v. Moody*, 34 F.4th at 1219–20 & n. 17.

190 E.g., *id.*

191 *Turner Broadcasting*, 512 U.S. at 684 (O'Connor, J., joined by Scalia, J., Thomas, J., and Ginsburg, J., concurring in part).

192 E.g., York Co. v. Central Railroad Co., 70 U.S. 107, 111–13 (1865) ("The law prescribes the duties and responsibilities of the common carrier. He exercises, in one sense, a public employment, and has duties to the public to perform. Though he may limit his services to the carriage of particular kinds of goods and may prescribe regulations to protect himself against imposition and fraud and fix a rate of charges proportionate to the magnitude of the risks he may have to encounter, he can make no discrimination between persons."); *id.* (A railroad owner may not, "by any mere act of his own, avoid the responsibility which the law thus imposes. He cannot screen himself from liability by any general or special notice, nor can he coerce the [consumer] to yield assent to a limitation of responsibility."); *NetChoice v. Moody*, 34 F.4th at 1221 (considering but rejecting the "State's best rejoinder is that because large social-media platforms are clothed with a 'public trust' and have 'substantial market power,' they are (or should be treated like) common carriers.").

193 Hurley v. Irish-American Gay, Lesbian and Bisexual Group of Boston, 515 U.S. 557, 569–70 (1995); see also, Kedroff v. Saint Nicholas Cathedral of Russian Orthodox Church in North America, 344 U.S. 94, 116 (1952).

194 *Turner Broad*casting, 512 U.S. at 677–78 (O'Connor, J., joined by Ginsburg, J., Scalia, J., and Thomas, J., concurring in part and dissenting in part).

195 Smith v. California, 361 U.S. 147, 154 (1959).

196 Kreimer, previous n. 60. Cf. Jack Balkin, 'Old School/New School speech regulation,' 127 *Harvard Law Review* 2296, 2299, 2340–341 (2013) (in 21st century, governments may impose overbroad laws to terrify gatekeepers into chilling and filtering speech by customers of private businesses).

197 Zieper v. Metzinger, 392 F. Supp. 2d 516, 525–26 (S.D.N.Y. 2005) (emphasis and final brackets added, internal citations omitted, other than Supreme Court case cites).

198 Bates v. State Bar of Arizona, 433 U.S. 350, 359–84 (1977).

199 *Id.* at 386–88 (Burger, C.J., dissenting); *id.* at 396–402 (Powell, J., joined by Stewart, J., dissenting).

200 E.g., Braun v. Soldier of Fortune Magazine, Inc., 968 F.2d 1110, 1117–18 (11th Cir. 1992); Eimann v. Soldier of Fortune Magazine, Inc., 880 F.2d 830, 837 (5th Cir. 1989); Backpage.com, LLC v. McKenna, 881 F. Supp. 2d 1262, 1283 (W.D. Wash. 2012); cf. Manual Enterprises, Inc. v. Day, 370 U.S. 478, 492–95 (1962) (in pre-*Bates* case, construing Post Office regulations not to forbid publication advertising "sordid" or "hard core" material unless publisher knew it was obscene, in part to avoid First Amendment issue under *Smith v. California*, 361 U.S. 147, and in part so that advertisers would not be denied "a legitimate and recognized avenue of access to the public," or public be denied some of its " 'access to constitutionally protected matter' ") (quoting *Smith*, 361 U.S. at 153).

201 News & Sun Sentinel Co. v. Bd. of Cty. Comm'rs, 693 F. Supp. 1066, 1072–73 (S.D. Fla. 1987); see also, Penthouse International, Ltd. v. McAuliffe, 610 F.2d 1353 (5th Cir. 1980); Skyywalker Records, Inc. v. Navarro, 739 F. Supp. 578, 598–602 (S.D. Fla. 1990); Council for Periodical Distributors Association v. Evans, 642 F.Supp. 552 (M.D. Ala. 1986), *aff'd*, 827 F.2d 1483 (11th Cir.1987); cf. Backpage.com, LLC v. Dart, 807 F. 3d 229, 230–31 (7th Cir. 2015) ("while [a public official] has a First Amendment right to express his views about [a website or its advertisers], a public

official who tries to shut down an avenue of expression of ideas and opinions through 'actual or threatened imposition of government power or sanction' is violating the First Amendment," and "First Amendment forbids a public official to attempt to suppress the protected speech of private persons by threatening that legal sanctions will at his urging be imposed unless there is compliance with his demands.") (citing *Bantam Books*, 372 U.S. at 64–72); Backpage.com, LLC v. Cooper, 939 F. Supp. 2d 805, 832, 837 (MD Tenn. 2013) ("'The normal method of deterring unlawful conduct is to impose an appropriate punishment on the person who engages in it.'" The court stated that this is preferred to leaving "publishers on the hook for 'offering[to sell advertisements related to [offensive] conduct.") (quoting Bartnicki v. Vopper, 532 U.S. 514, 529–30 (2001)); Backpage.com, LLC v. McKenna, 881 F. Supp. 2d 1262, 1284 (W.D. Wash, 2012) (similar).

202 E.g., Missouri v. Biden, No. 3:22-cv-01213, slip op. (W.D. La. July 4, 2023), https://scholar.google.com/scholar_case?case=14594677694281670394; EU Code of Conduct on countering illegal hate speech online, https://commission.europa.eu/strategy-and-policy/policies/justice-and-fundamental-rights/combatting-discrimination/racism-and-xenophobia/eu-code-conduct-countering-illegal-hate-speech-online_en.

203 Republic of The Gambia v. Facebook, Inc., 575 F. Supp. 3d 8 (D.D.C. 2021); Federal Agency of News LLC v. Facebook, Inc., 432 F. Supp. 3d 1107 (N.D. Cal. 2020); Amirhossein Farzam et al., 'Opinion manipulation on Farsi Twitter,' 13 *Scientific Reports* 333 (2023); Tuğrulcan Elmas, 'Analyzing activity and suspension patterns of Twitter bots attacking Turkish Twitter trends by a longitudinal dataset,' arXiv.org No. arXiv:2304.07907 (2023), https://arxiv.org/pdf/2304.07907.

204 Censorship-Industrial Complex – Shellenberger Testimony, Reclaim the Net (March 9, 2023), pp. 32–34, https://docs.reclaimthenet.org › michael-shellenenberger-twitter-files-congress-testimony.pdf.

205 Daniel Keats Citron, 'Extremist speech, compelled conformity, and censorship creep,' 93 *Notre Dame Law Review* 1035 (2018); Daphne Keller, Who do you sue? State and platform hybrid power over online speech, Hoover Inst., Aegis Series Paper No. 190 (2019), https://www.hoover.org/sites/default/files/research/docs/who-do-you-sue-state-and-platform-hybrid-power-over-online-speech_0.pdf; Daphne Keller, Internet platforms: Observations on speech, danger, and money 18 (Hoover Institution, Aegis Series Paper No. 1807 (2018); Kreimer, previous n. 60; Ira Steven Nathenson, 'Super-intermediaries, code, human rights,' 8 *Intercultural Human Rights Law Review* 19, 19–22, 149–68 (2013) (suggesting that large gatekeepers like Facebook, Twitter, or YouTube start signing on to protecting users' human rights via "Digital Due Process" rules); Joshua A. Kroll et al., 'Accountable Algorithms,' 165 *University of Pennsylvania Law Review* 633, 657–60 (2017) (claiming that transparency of algorithms is the solution); Terrell McSweeny, 'FTC 2.0: Keeping pace with online platforms,' 32 *Berkeley Technology Law Journal* 1027, 1028–030 (2017) (proposing antitrust enforcement by FTC against online platforms); Rahman, 'The New Utilities,' previous n. 154, pp. 1668–670 (proposing fair conduct regulations for Internet giants as if they were railroads or power companies).

206 Richard Rhodes, "Top secret America: The rise of the new American Security State" by Dana Priest and William Arkin, *Washington Post* (October 14, 2011), https://www.washingtonpost.com/entertainment/books/top-secret-america-the-rise-of-the-new-american-security-state-by-dana-priest-and-william-m-arkin/2011/09/30/gIQAvkkUkL_story.html.

207 Project on Intellectual Property and the Public Interest, StyleTalks, YouTube (2019), https://www.youtube.com/watch?v=D7FIYRHbpOU&list=PLuk2SmOxN5RJ8Fx8-ezG6qIgN181Jvq2Q&index=13.

208 E.g., Luke Broadwater, 'US officials who cast doubt on Hunter Biden's laptop face questions,' *The New York Times* (May 17, 2023), p. A18-L; Glenn Diesen, *Russophobia: Propaganda in International Politics* (Springer Nature, 2022), pp. 175–200;

Chuck Grassley, "Big Tech" is censoring conservatives, *The Gazette* (February 28, 2022), https://tinyurl.com/2sesc4vb; Taibbi, previous n. 26 (noting that a former CIA staffer working at Twitter was suspending accounts that covered Russia or highlighted unrest in countries other than Russia, even without technical evidence that the accounts were controlled by Russian government officials or even located in Russia or outside the United States); cf. also, Diana Glebova, Zuckerberg admits Facebook suppressed Hunter Biden Laptop Story ahead of 2020 election, *National Review* (August 26, 2022), https://tinyurl.com/z5v9mwjz; Mike Lee, Big Tech companies falsely claim no bias against conservatives – they may be violating law, *Fox News* (October 29, 2020), https://tinyurl.com/2e7u7sx5; John A. LoNigro, 'Deplatformed: Social network censorship, the First Amendment, and the argument to amend section 230 of the Communications Decency Act,' 37 *Touro Law Review* 427 (2021). Michael Nunez, Former Facebook workers: We routinely suppressed conservative news, *Gizmodo* (May 9, 2016), https://tinyurl.com/4xjdhbn; Michael Rubin, Why does Big Tech censor conservatives and not terrorists, American Enterprise Institute (March 3, 2021), https://tinyurl.com/wx9wm968; Marco Rubio, We must stop Silicon Valley-Democrat collusion before conservatives are silenced for good, *Fox News* (July 28, 2021), https://tinyurl.com/yc8d3nap.

209 Anthony Blinken, Remarks to the Press, U.S. Department of State (October 17, 2022), https://www.state.gov/secretary-antony-blinken-remarks-to-the-press-3; Blinken urges democracies to use technology to help citizens, *Voice of America News* (March 30, 2023), https://www.voanews.com/a/blinken-urges-democracies-to-use-technology-to-help-citizens-/7029475.html; Charles Creitz, Blinken's alleged role in 'Russian disinfo' Hunter letter disqualifies him as Ukraine war point man: Critics, *MSN/Fox News* (May 2023), https://www.msn.com/en-us/news/politics/blinkens-alleged-role-in-russian-disinfo-hunter-letter-disqualifies-him-as-ukraine-war-pointman-critics/ar-AA1ahYQH; U.S. House of Representatives, Judiciary Committee, New Testimony Reveals Secretary Blinken and Biden Campaign Behind the Infamous Public Statement on the Hunter Biden Laptop, April 20, 2023, https://judiciary.house.gov/media/press-releases/new-testimony-reveals-secretary-blinken-and-biden-campaign-behind-infamous; Brooke Signman, Biden Campaign, Blinken orchestrated intel letter to discredit Hunter Biden Laptop Story, Ex-CIA Official says, *Fox News* (April 21, 2023), https://judiciary.house.gov/media/in-the-news/biden-campaign-blinken-orchestrated-intel-letter-discredit-hunter-biden-laptop; U.S. Department of State, Disinformation (2023), https://www.state.gov/subjects/disinformation/; U.S. Department of State, The Global Engagement Center (2023), https://statemag.state.gov/2022/10/1022office/; Taibbi, previous n. 26 (noting role of The Global Engagement Center in urging Twitter to censor content critical of U.S. biological weapons research, that covered China, Iran, or Russia in certain ways, etc.).

210 Felicia Somnez and Amy B. Wang, 'YouTube suspends Ron Johnson for a week after GOP Senator touts questionable drugs to fight COVID-19,' *Washington Post* (June 11, 2021), https://tinyurl.com/ms44ckzz.

211 E.g., Hannah Osborne, Anti-vaxxers feed off Democrats' skepticism of COVID vaccine, *Newsweek* (October 6, 2020), https://www.newsweek.com/anti-vaccine-covid-trust-skepticism-democrat-politicization-1535559; Rubio, previous n. 208. Such statements were amplified as a result of increased coverage of the 2020 political campaigns and public speeches concerning COVID-19 of politicians such as Nancy Pelosi, then-speaker of the House, or Andrew Cuomo, then-governor of New York, or as a result of Google, for example, boosting the relevance of mainstream news sources that cover such politicians or official hearings on such matters as biosecurity.

212 Osborne, previous n. 211.

213 Glenn Greenwald, Ex-CIA Agents Now Occupy Highest-Ranking Positions in Big Tech, Rumble (2023), https://rumble.com/v2zftva-system-update-113.html; Glenn

Greenwald, Spying to censoring: Are the Twitter files a continuation of the Snowden revelations?, *Rumble* (2023), https://rumble.com/v24bmuk-are-the-twitter-files-a-continuation-of-the-snowden-revelations-after-show-.html.

214 E.g., Gabe Kaminsky, Revolving Door: Big Tech staffed with hundreds of ex-DOJ employees amid antitrust battle, *Washington Examiner* (April 1, 2023), https://www.washingtonexaminer.com/policy/technology/big-tech-justice-department-revolving-door-analysis-american-accountability-foundation; Matt Taibbi, The Twitter files: Twitter and the FBI "belly button," *Thread Reader App* (January 3, 2023), https://threadreaderapp.com/thread/1610394197730725889.html; see also, Greenwald, previous n. 213.

215 E.g., Ganesh Sitaraman, 'Economic inequality and constitutional democracy,' in *Constitutional Democracy in Crisis?*, edited by Mark Graber, Sanford Levinson, and Mark Tushnet, (Oxford University Press, 2018), p. 533. See also, Peter Schweitzer, *Secret Empires* (HarperCollins, 2019), ch. 1.

216 Conley, previous n. 61.

217 Glenn Greenwald, Spying to censoring: Are the Twitter files a continuation of the Snowden revelations?, *Rumble* (2023), https://rumble.com/v24ev4a-spying-to-censoring-are-the-twitter-files-a-continuation-of-the-snowden-rev.html. For the inquiries, see U.S House of Representatives, House Permanent Select Committee on Intelligence, House Intelligence Committee Review of Edward Snowden Disclosures, 110th Cong. (2015–2016), https://intelligence.house.gov/uploadedfiles/snowden_report_highlights.pdf; U.S. Privacy and Civil Liberties Oversight Board, Oversight Reports – PCLOB (2023), www.pclob.gov/Oversight; Sarah Eskens, Ot van Daalen and Nico van Eijk. '10 standards for oversight and transparency of national intelligence services,' 8 *Journal of National Security Law and Policy* 553 (2016); David Fahrenthold, With NSA revelations, Sen. Ron Wyden's vague privacy warnings finally become clear, *Washington Post* (July 28, 2013), https://www.washingtonpost.com/politics/after-years-of-obscure-warnings-wyden-gets-sought-after-privacy-debate-in-wake-of-nsa-revelations/2013/07/28/267efd1a-f573–11e2–861b-70461cc1cd24_story.html; see also, n. 37 of Chapter 4.

218 E.g., previous n. 37.

Bibliography

1 *Annals of Congress* 440–54 (1789).

Floyd Abrams, 'First Amendment and Copyright,' 35 *Journal of the Copyright Society* 1 (1987).

Adderly v. Florida, 385 U.S. 39 (1966).

Akhil Amar and Vikram Amar, Guns and the Constitution: Telling the Right Second Amendment Story, Findlaw's Writ, 2001, http://writ.news.findlaw.com/amar/20011102.html.

Akhil Reed Amar, 'Did the Fourteenth Amendment incorporate the bill of rights against states?,' 19 *Harvard Journal of Law and Public Policy* 443 (1996).

Akhil Reed Amar, 'Fourth Amendment first principles,' 107 *Harvard Law Review* 757 (1994).

Akhil Reed Amar, 'Hugo Black and the Hall of Fame,' 53 *Alabama Law Review* 1221 (2002).

Akhil Reed Amar, 'On impeaching Presidents,' 28 *Hofstra Law Review* 291 (1999).

Akhil Reed Amar, 'Original Intent for Liberals (and for Conservatives and Moderates, Too),' Slate Magazine, 2005, www.slate.com/id/2126680/.

Akhil Reed Amar, *The Bill of Rights: Creation and Reconstruction* (Yale University Press, 1998).

Akhil Reed Amar, 'The Bill of rights and the Fourteenth Amendment,' 101 *Yale Law Journal* 1193 (1992).

Akhil Reed Amar, 'The Bill of rights as a constitution,' 100 *Yale Law Journal* 1131 (1991).

Akhil Reed Amar, 'The Supreme Court, 1999 term – foreword: The document and the doctrine,' 114 *Harvard Law Review* 26 (2000).
Akhil Reed Amar, 'The case of the missing Amendments: *R.A.V. v. City of St. Paul*,' 106 *Harvard Law Review* 124 (1992).
David A. Anderson, 'The origins of the press clause,' 30 *UCLA Law Review* 455, 501–06 (1983).
Joel Anderson, 'The "Third Generation" of the Frankfurt School,' 22 *Intellectual History Newsletter* 49 (2000), https://dspace.library.uu.nl/handle/1874/20315.
Annals of Congress, Vol. 3 (1794), https://memory.loc.gov/ll/llac/004/0400/04650933.gif.
Thomas Aquinas, *On Law, Morality, and Politics*, edited by Regan and Baumgarth (Hackett, 1988).
Arkansas Educational Television Commission v. Forbes, 523 U.S. 666, 690 (1998) (Stevens, J., joined by Ginsburg, J., and Souter, J., dissenting).
C. Edwin Baker, 'First Amendment limits on copyright,' 55 *Vanderbilt Law Review* 891 (2002).
Barenblatt v. United States, 360 U.S. 109 (1959).
Becker v. Federal Election Commission, 112 F. Supp. 2d 172 (D. Mass. 2000).
Paul Bedard, 'Voters: Biden's America becoming a "Police State,"' MSN, September 21, 2023, https://msn.com/en-us/news/politics/voters-biden-s-america-becoming-a-police-state/ar-AA1h43Kj.
Paul Schiff Berman, 'Cyberspace and the state action debate: The cultural value of applying constitutional norms to private regulation,' 71 *University of Colorado Law Review* 1263 (2000).
Biden v. Knight First Amendment Institute, 593 U.S. ___, 141 S. Ct. 1220 (2021).
William Blackstone, *Commentaries on the Laws of England*, Vol. 1 (University of Chicago Press, 1979) [1765].
William Blackstone, *Commentaries on the Laws of England*, Vol. 4 (The Clarendon Press, 1770).
Robert M. Bloom and William J. Dunn, 'The Constitutional Infirmity of Warrantless NSA Surveillance: The Abuse of Presidential Power and the Injury to the Fourth Amendment, Boston College Law School Faculty Papers – Paper 163 (2006), http://lsr.nellco.org/bc/bclsfp/papers/163.
Bowers v. Hardwick, 478 U.S. 186 (1986).
Brandenburg v. Ohio, 395 U.S. 444 (1969).
The Bridge Initiative, Victor Orban, https://bridge.georgetown.edu/wp-content/uploads/2019/11/Viktor-Orban-November-2019-factsheet.pdf (updated November 10, 2019).
Byars v. Bluff City News Co., 609 F.2d 843 (6th Cir. 1979).
Cantwell v. Connecticut, 310 U.S. 296 (1940).
Noam Chomsky, *Failed States: The Abuse of Power and the Assault on Democracy* (Metropolitan Books, 2005).
Noam Chomsky, *Rogue States: The Rule of Force in World Affairs* (Haymarket Books, ed. 2015).
Margaret Chon, 'Erasing race?: A critical race feminist view of Internet identity-shifting,' 3 *Journal of Gender Race & Justice* 439 (2000).
Julie Cohen, 'A right to read anonymously: A closer look at "copyright management" in cyberspace,' 28 *Connecticut Law Review* 981 (1996)
Columbia Broadcasting System, Inc. v. Democratic National Committee, 412 U.S. 94 (1973).
The Debates in the Several State Conventions on the Adoption of the Federal Constitution (Elliot's Debates) (1799–1800), Vol. 4 (J.P. Lippincott & Co., 1876).
Richard Delgado, 'Inequality "from the top": Applying an ancient prohibition to an emerging problem of distributive justice,' 32 *UCLA Law Review* 100 (1984).
Dennis v. United States, 341 U.S. 494, 522 (1951) (Frankfurter, J., concurring)).

Divino Group LLC v. Google LLC, No. 19-cv-04749-VKD, slip op. (N.D. Cal. July 5, 2023) (ECF No. 137).
Charlie Eastaugh, *Unconstitutional Solitude: Solitary Confinement and the US Constitution's Evolving Standards of Decency* (Springer, 2017).
Niva Elkin-Koren, 'Cyberlaw and social change: A democratic approach to Copyright law in cyberspace,' 14 *Cardozo Arts & Entertainment Law Journal* 215 (1996).
FCC v. League of Women Voters of California, 468 U.S. 364 (1984).
Federal President Frank-Walter Steinmeier, 75th Anniversary of the End of the 2nd World War, www.bundespraesident.de/SharedDocs/Reden/EN/Frank-Walter-Steinmeier/Reden/2020/05/200508-75th-anniversary-World-War-II.html (last updated May 8, 2020)
'Federalist 84 (Hamilton),' in *The Federalist Papers*, http://press-pubs.uchicago.edu/founders/documents/bill_of_rightss7.html.
'Federalist 43 (Madison),' in *The Federalist Papers*, edited by Clinton Rossiter (Mentor, 1961), pp. 271–72.
Stephen Fraser, 'The conflict between the First Amendment and Copyright law and its impact on the Internet,' 16 *Cardozo Arts & Entertainment Law Journal* 1 (1998).
Freedman v. Maryland, 380 U.S. 51 (1965).
G.A. Res. 2200A(XXI), art. 19(2), adopted Dec. 16, 1966, entered into force March 23, 1976, 999 U.N.T.S. 171.
Garcetti v. Ceballos, 547 U.S. 410 (2006).
Germany's most important book, *Deutschland.de* (April 17, 2019), www.deutschland.de/en/topic/politics/german-basic-law-the-key-facts.
The Global Commission on Drug Policy, The Negative Impact of the War on Drugs on Public Health: The Hidden Hepatitis C Epidemic (2013), pp 11–16.
Julius Goebel, Jr., 'Constitutional history and law,' 38 *Columbia Law Review* 555 (1938).
Mike Godwin, *Cyber Rights: Defending Free Speech in the Digital Age* (Times Books, 1998).
Grundgesetz für die Bundesrepublik Deutschland [GG] [Constitution] July 11, 2012, art. 5, § 1 (Ger.).
Jürgen Habermas, *Between Facts and Norms: Contributions to a Discourse Theory of Law and Democracy*, translated by William Rehg (Wiley, 2018).
Jürgen Habermas, *The Theory of Communicative Action: Reason and the Rationalization of Society*, translated by Thomas McCarthy (Policy Press, 2015).
Kermit L. Hall, *The Magic Mirror: Law in American History* (Oxford University Press, 1998).
Morton J. Horwitz, *The Warren Court and the Pursuit of Justice* (Farrar, Straus, and Giroux, 1999).
In re Fries, 9 F. Cas. 826 (C.C.D. Pa. 1799).
Dorean M. Koenig, 'Joe Camel and the first Amendment: The dark side of copyrighted and trademark-protected icons,' 11 *Thomas M. Cooley Law Review* 803 (1994).
Thomas Jefferson, 'Letter to James Madison, 1789,' in *Writings of Thomas Jefferson*, Vol. 7, edited by Andrew Lipscomb and Albert Ellery Bergh (Thomas Jefferson Memorial Foundation, 1903), p. 450.
Thomas Jefferson, 'Letter to Abigail Adams, 1804,' in *Writings of Thomas Jefferson*, Vol. 9, edited by Andrew Lipscomb and Albert Ellery Bergh (Thomas Jefferson Memorial Foundation, 1903), pp. 28, 42, 49.
Thomas Jefferson, *Notes on the State of Virginia*, 1784, http://press-pubs.uchicago.edu/founders/documents/amendI_religions40.html.
Johnson v. Commission on Presidential Debates. 869 F.3d 976 (D.C. Cir. 2017).
Immanuel Kant, *Of the Injustice of Counterfeiting Books* (Illustrated) (Delphi Classics, 2017) [1785].
Alan J. Koshner, 'The founding fathers and political speech: The First Amendment, the Press and the Sedition Act of 1798,' 6 *Saint Louis University Public Law Review* 395 (1987).
Seth Kreimer, 'Censorship by Proxy: The First Amendment, intermediaries, and the problem of the weakest link,' 155 *University of Pennsylvania Law Review* 11 (2006).

L.L. Bean, Inc. v. Drake Publishers, Inc., 811 F.2d 26 (1st Cir. 1987).
Lamparello v. Falwell, 420 F.3d 309 (4th Cir. 2005).
Arlen W. Langvardt, 'Trademark rights and First Amendment wrongs: Protecting the former without committing the latter,' 83 *Trademark Reporter* 633 (1993).
David Lange, 'Copyright and the constitution in the age of intellectual property,' 1 *Journal of Intellectual Property Law* 119 (1994).
Leonard W. Levy, *Emergence of a Free Press* (Oxford University Press, 1985).
Leonard W. Levy, *Jefferson and Civil Liberties: The Darker Side* (Belknap Press of Harvard University, 1963).
Leonard W. Levy, *Legacy of Suppression: Freedom of Speech and Press in Early American History* (Belknap Press of Harvard University, 1960).
Leonard W. Levy, 'Liberty and the First Amendment: 1790–1800,' 68 *American Historical Review* 22 (1962).
Lawrence Lessig, *Code and Other Laws of Cyberspace* (Basic Books, 1999).
Lawrence Lessig, 'Creative economies,' 2006 *Michigan State Law Review* 33 (2006).
'Letter from Thomas Jefferson to James Madison (December 20, 1787),' The Founders' Constitution, 2005, http://press-pubs.uchicago.edu/founders/documents/v1ch14s30.html?.
'Letter from Thomas Jefferson to James Madison (August 28, 1789),' in *Papers of Thomas Jefferson*, Vol. 15 (1903), p. 367, http://press-pubs.uchicago.edu/founders/documents/amendI_speechs15.html.
'Letter from Thomas Jefferson to President George Washington (September 9, 1792),' in *The Writings of George Washington, Being His Correspondence, Addresses, Messages and Other Papers, Official and Private*, edited by Jared Sparks (Little, Brown and company, 1838), pp. 517–21.
John Locke, *Second Treatise of Government*, edited by C.B. MacPherson (Hackett, 1980[1690]).
Lorain Journal v. United States, 342 U.S. 143 (1951).
Loving v. Virginia, 388 U.S. 1 (1977).
James Madison, 'House Debate, June 8, 1789,' 1 *Annals of Congress*, 440–56 (1794), http://press-pubs.uchicago.edu/founders/documents/amendI_speechs14.html.
James Madison, 'Report on the Virginia resolutions (1798),' quoted in *Elliot's Debates*, Vol. 4 (J.P. Lippincott & Co., 1836), pp. 546–80, 569–71.
Manual Enterprises, Inc. v. Day, 370 U.S. 478 (1962).
Mattel, Inc. v. MCA Records, 296 F.3d 894, 901 (9th Cir. 2002).
Matthew 16:18–19.
Memorial Resolution Adopted by the Bar of the Supreme Court of the United States to Record Our Deep Respect and Affection for Justice William J. Brennan, Jr., https://www.brennancenter.org/programs/programs_cele_memorial.html.
David Meyer, Court tells Facebook: Stop deleting 'offensive' comment, *Vox* (April 13, 2018), https://www.zdnet.com/article/court-tells-facebook-stop-deleting-offensive-comment/.
NAACP v. Button, 371 U.S. 415, 433 (1963).
Ralph Nader and Theresa Amato, 'So you want to run for president? Ha! Barriers to third-party entry,' 90 *National Civic Review* 163 (2001).
Sridevi Nambiar, UN Committee on torture says U.S. must reform its use of solitary confinement, *Solitary Watch* (December 5, 2014), http://solitarywatch.com/2014/12/05/un-committee-against-torture-says-u-s-must-reform-its-use-of-solitary-confinement/.
National Association of Criminal Defense Lawyers, 'The trial penalty: The Sixth Amendment right to trial on the verge of extinction and how to save it,' 13 *Federal Sentencing Reporter* 331 (2018)
New York v. Ferber, 458 U.S. 747 (1982).
New York Times Co. v. Sullivan, 376 U.S. 254 (1964).
Roger K Newman, *Hugo Black* (Pantheon Books, paperback ed. 1997).
John Nichols, *The Genius of Impeachment: The Founders' Cure for Royalism* (The New Press, 2006).

Melville B. Nimmer, 'The right to speak from *Times* to *Time*: First Amendment theory applied to libel and misapplied to privacy,' 56 *California Law Review* 935 (1968).
Nissan Motor Co. v. Nissan Computer Corp., 378 F.3d 1002 (9th Cir. 2004).
Oberlandesgericht Karlsruhe, decision of June 25, 2018, Az. 15 W 86/18.
Oberlandesgericht Munich, decision of August 24, 2018, Az. 18 W 1294/18.
Pernell v. Florida Board of Governors of the State University System, No. 4: 22cv304-MW, slip op. (N.D. Fla. preliminary injunction granted in part Nov. 17, 2022).
Perot v. FEC, 97 F.3d 553, 559 (D.C.Cir. 1996).
Plaintiff's Complaint, Johnson v. Commission on Presidential Debates, No. 15–1580 (RMC) (D.D.C. complaint filed January 8, 2016).
Jack N. Rakove, *Declaring Rights: A Brief History with Documents* (St. Martin's Press, 1998).
Reno v. ACLU, 521 U.S. 844, 868–70 (1997);
Robert D. Richards, *Uninhibited, Robust, and Wide Open: Mr. Justice Brennan's Legacy to the First Amendment* (Parkway, 1994).
Romans 13:1–2,4.
Pamela Samuelson, 'Mapping the digital public domain: Threats and opportunities,' 66 *Law & Contemporary Problems* 147, 169–70 (2003).
San Francisco Arts & Athl. v. United States Olympic Cmte., 483 U.S. 522, 569 (1987) (Brennan, J., dissenting).
Scott v. Sanford, 60 U.S. 393, 564–633 (1857) (Curtis, J., dissenting).
Smith v. California, 361 U.S. 147 (1959).
Smothers v. Gresham Transfer, Inc., 23 P. 2d 333 (Or. 2001).
Daniel J. Solove, 'The First Amendment as criminal procedure,' 82 *New York University School of Law Review* 112 (2007).
Speiser v. Randall, 357 U.S. 513 (1958).
State v. Harlowe, 174 Wash. 227, 24 P. 2d 601 (1933).
Stromberg v. California, 283 U.S. 359 (1931)
Suntrust Bank v. Houghton Mifflin Co., 252 F.3d 1165, *substituted opinion at* 268 F.3d 1257 (11th Cir. 2001).
F.N. Thorpe, *Constitutional History of the United States, 1776–1850*, Vol. 1 (Harper and Brothers, 1898).
Thomas v. Review Bd. of the Indiana Employment Sec. Div., 450 U.S. 707 (1981).
Hannibal Travis, 'Of blogs, ebooks, and broadband: Access to digital media as a First Amendment right,' 35 *Hofstra Law Review* 1519 (2007).
St. George Tucker, *Blackstone's Commentaries*, Vol. 1 (Birch and Small, 1803).
Turner Broadcasting System, Inc. v. FCC, 512 U.S. 622 (1994).
Turner v. US Agency for Global Media, 502 F. Supp. 3d 333 (D.D.C. 2020).
Scott Turow, Scalia the civil libertarian?, *The New York Times* (November 26, 2006), pp. 6-22–6-23.
U.S. Constitution, Amendment I.
U.S. Holocaust Memorial Museum, Liberation of Nazi Camps, Holocaust Encyclopedia, https://encyclopedia.ushmm.org/content/en/article/liberation-of-nazi-camps (last updated February 12, 2021).
Eugene Volokh, 'Crime-facilitating speech,' 57 *Stanford Law Review* 1095, 1137 (2005).
Sophia Waldstein, 'Open-file discovery: A plea for transparent plea-bargaining,' 92 *Temple Law Review* 517 (2019).
White v. Samsung Electronics Am., Inc., 989 F.2d 1512, 1513–14 (9th Cir. 1993) (Kozinski, J., dissenting).
Wendt v. Host Int'l, Inc., 197 F.3d 1284, 1288–89 (9th Cir. 1999).
Thomas Jefferson, *The Works of Thomas Jefferson*, Vol. 8, edited by Paul Leicester Ford (G.P. Putnam's Sons, 1904).

Alfred C. Yen, 'A First Amendment perspective on the idea/expression dichotomy and copyright in a work's "total concept and feel,"' 38 *Emory Law Journal* 393 (1989).
Zacchini v. Scripps-Howard Broad. Co., 433 U.S. 562 (1977).
Diane Leenheer Zimmerman, 'Information as speech, information as goods: Some thoughts on marketplace and the bill of rights,' 33 *William and Mary Law Review* 665, 681 (1992).
Diane Leenheer Zimmerman, 'Is there a right to have something to say? One view of the public domain,' 73 *Fordham Law Review* 297 (2004).

4 The Freedom of Reach

Kingly Power Versus Knowledge Commons

A cliché took hold of debates on Internet freedom over the past five years. Attributed to Renee DiResta, the nostrum is that people have "freedom of speech" but not "freedom of reach."[1] In other words, a speaker does not have the right to reach anyone. Taken to its extreme, does this mean that any account they use can be deleted, their emails can be wiped from servers, their electricity and banking services can be cut off, or they can be made to run the gauntlet or driven into exile as in *Mad Max: Beyond Thunderdome*? They could still exercise the freedom of speech while being marched into the desert backwards on a horse, wearing a giant mask.[2]

The distinction between freedoms of speech and freedoms of reach depends on legal and social theories of dubious validity given our point in time and technological environment. In more contemporary industrial or post-industrial societies, the king's executioner, the hangman, and the guillotine are less of a threat to freedom of speech than social groups and institutions that create more often than they destroy.[3] These disciplines, apparatuses, churches, cliques, guilds, professions, and trusts have been documented as threats to freedom by philosophers, social theorists, jurists, novelists, and filmmakers.

This chapter examines the freedom of reach from three angles. The first is the right to practice a lawful trade, and its corollary, the right to resist domination of the trade. The second is U.S. antitrust history, and its concern for malicious or unreasonable acts. The third is structuralist social theory, for use in understanding whether economic or political power is too concentrated.

The Freedom of Trade Versus Kingly Power

The U.S. Congress, roused to action by complaints against the wealthiest American corporations yet trailing efforts by state attorneys general and state supreme courts, legislated in 1890 on questions of aggregated capital and the unfair exercise of economic power. Senators debated the "trust," a combination, typically of corporations, that controlled or restricted the supply of an article of commerce so as to "fix" its price far in excess of its cost or even consumer demand.[4] High price was but one of the concerns of members of Congress.[5] Another aim of the legislation

DOI: 10.4324/9781003496106-5

was to prevent unfair oppression of the smaller firm and the individual American by the few, the oligarchs:

> It is a sad thought . . . that the present system of production and of exchange is having that tendency which is sure at some not very distant day to crush out all small men, all small capitalists, all small enterprises. This is being done now. We find everywhere over our land the wrecks of small, independent enterprises thrown in our pathway. So now the American Congress and the American people are brought face to face with this sad, this great problem: Is production, is trade, to be taken away from the great mass of the people and concentrated in the hands of a few men who, I am obliged to add, by the policies pursued by our Government, have been enabled to aggregate to themselves large, enormous fortunes?[6]

One objection to the rise of giant enterprises in the United States was that they could "command everybody, laborer, consumer, producer, and everybody else, as the sugar trust and the oil trust." Even when the price of their products fell, "that does not alter the wrong of the principle of any trust; and that . . . is a phrase which covers every combination to get control of the life and the industry and the producing and the consuming classes of the country." The answer, one senator explained, was "to repress and break up and destroy forever the monopolies of that character, because in the long run, . . . [they] come to be tyrannies, grinding tyrannies."[7] Another senator explained that when "great aggregated capital is wielded by a single hand and guided by a single brain, or at least by [many] hands and brains acting in complete harmony and cooperation, . . . wrongs have been perpetrated upon the American people."[8] Among these wrongs were that "the small men engaged in competition with [the trusts] are crushed out," becoming "wretched victims of these great combinations and trusts." A related wrong is the slowing of the improvements that result from many keen competitors vying for a consumer's attention and dollar, "presenting him with wares both skillfully and cheaply made."[9]

Senator John Sherman, after whose name the Anti-trust Act would thereafter be known, emphasized that anti-monopoly and anti-conspiracy law in the commercial context democratizes productive power. "If we will not endure a king as a political power we should not endure a king over the production, transportation, and sale of any of the necessaries of life. If we would not submit to an emperor we should not submit to an autocrat of trade, with power to prevent competition and to fix the price of any commodity."[10] The exponential growth of their wealth, these autocrats, would make "the great mass" of the people virtual servants of "those who have this aggregated wealth at their command."[11]

During the Second Industrial Revolution, the attorneys general of U.S. states fought efforts to bring new technologies under the control of aggregations of capital, which they called trusts. From the mining of coal and salt, to the making of rope or refined sugar or gas for streetlights, state courts heard cases about monopolies and restrictions on trade. As the Pennsylvania Supreme Court observed in a case involving coal in the northern part of that state, such a "combination is criminal whenever the act to be done has a necessary tendency to prejudice the public or to oppress individuals, by unjustly subjecting them to the power of the confederates, and giving effect to the purpose of the latter, whether of extortion or of mischief."[12] It added: "Men can often do by the combination of many what severally no one could accomplish, and even what, when done by one, would be innocent." The Ohio Supreme Court resolved a similar case about the salt trade, writing that when manufacturers combine in an association to control competition in trade: "Courts will not stop to inquire as to the degree of injury inflicted upon the public; it is enough to know that the inevitable tendency of such contracts is injurious to the public."[13] The Illinois Supreme Court observed, in a case involving a secret pact among the grain dealers of a town, that: "So long as competition was free, the interest of the public was safe. The laws of trade, in connection with the right of competition, was all the guaranty the public required, but the secret combination created by the contract destroyed all competition."[14] The U.S. Supreme Court, reviewing these cases and others from a similar time, eventually concluded that combinations among businesses that serve the public, whose operations are imbued with a public interest, cannot be upheld in court.[15] In an earlier case, when the Sherman Anti-trust Act was deemed to have a narrower scope, Justice Harlan surveyed a number of state decisions and opined that undoubtedly a state may, "under the power to regulate its domestic commerce, and for the purpose of protecting its people against fraud and injustice, to make it a public offense, punishable by fine and imprisonment, for individuals or corporations to make contracts, form combinations, or engage in conspiracies, which unduly restrain trade or commerce carried on within its limits."[16]

Since 1890, similar laws have spread throughout the world, and they now cover the vast majority of the world's population in some form or other.[17] The U.S. law itself resembles aspects of the common law of restraints of trade and the Statute of Monopolies passed two centuries earlier.[18]

One might think that these sorts of cases involved only monopolies or price cartels involving all or most of some large industry, such as coal, steel, oil, and the like. However, the state courts have condemned diverse practices using a similar rationale that an association or dominant company had oppressed or arbitrarily treated members of the public or their own competitors.[19]

The federal courts developed the early decisions on oil, steel, the railroads, and tobacco into a complex architecture of fair competition and trade free of conspiracies.[20] Some of the pillars of this edifice included the essential facilities doctrine, a prohibition on tying or monopoly leveraging, limitations on industrial collusion such as group boycotts, and regulation of the duration and scope of trademarks and other controls on dependent firms such as licensees.[21] As to the first of these:

> Four elements are required to establish liability under Section 1 or 2 of the Sherman Act by virtue of the essential facilities doctrine: (1) control of the essential facility by a business or group of businesses; (2) a competitor's inability practically or reasonably to duplicate the essential facility; (3) the denial of the use of the facility to a competitor; and (4) the feasibility of

> providing the facility. *MCI Communications v. American Tel. & Tel. Co.*, 708 F.2d 1081, 1132–33 (7th Cir. 1983). . .. The seminal case under this doctrine is *United States v. Terminal Railroad Assoc.*, 224 U.S. 383 . . . (1912), where a group of railroads acquired ownership over a facility – a huge train station, the only existing railroad bridge, and every connection between the bridge and railroads terminating on either side of the Mississippi River – which constituted the only feasible terminal for rail traffic coming to St. Louis from the West. The Supreme Court ruled that the terminal owners had to make the facility equally accessible to all users. 224 U.S. at 411. . . .
>
> The theory behind the essential facility doctrine rests on the notion of a "bottleneck" in a particular line of business which can be manipulated so as to eliminate competitors. The sole flour mill in a particular region, . . . sports stadiums serving large metropolitan areas, . . . electric power transmission lines, *Otter Tail Power Co. v. United States*, 410 U.S. 366 . . . (1973) and the terminal facility in *Terminal Railroad, supra*, have been found by the courts to be "bottlenecks" whose use was integral to a competitor's survival in a particular industry.[22]

Since the 1970s, the Supreme Court and lower federal courts have attempted to narrow the equal access duties of a "bottleneck" or "essential facility." Between 1984 and 2009 the Supreme Court issued four decisions limiting the antitrust obligations of infrastructure providers.[23] Whatever happened to resisting "kingly" power?

Is Demotion the Main Way that Platforms Compete on "Quality"?

Victims of downranking, shadow-banning, and account suspensions or terminations occasionally file antitrust claims based on their mistreatment by dominant platforms.[24] The platforms often reply that the First Amendment, the Communications Decency Act, and antitrust doctrine protect their role as arbiters of what forms of speech enjoy visibility on millions of Americans' devices.[25] Demotion of offerings is the essence of competition, which involves business judgment, quality control, and positive consumer experiences.[26] Rather than speech critical to a vigorous public debate, words, images, sounds, and videos are mere content to be managed and moderated to balance consumers', advertisers', and regulators' preferences.[27] Facing this frame of reference, which judges and regulators often find appealing, Internet users sometimes shift gears, arguing that the dominant platforms become state actors and violate the U.S. Constitution and fundamental human rights by colluding with current or former government officials to silence disfavored speakers.[28] Elsewhere in this book, I note that judges have responded at times by ignoring the growing evidence of entanglement and symbiosis between large platforms and government agencies, and they simply declare the platforms private and immune from constitutional standards (as well as from many statutory or judge-made standards). Does that also mean that they will be largely exempt from antitrust law when filtering the Internet?

Obviously Disney need not add a DC Comics superhero with a struggling film career (Green Lantern?) into films or comic books about The Avengers. But must a dominant digital brand avoid suppressing or hiding its competitors' applications, services, or devices? This tactic is at the heart of several recent antitrust enforcement actions and proposed legislative enactments, both in the United States and Europe, not to mention elsewhere. Self-preferencing therefore leads to more frequent charges of monopolizing interstate commerce, or a conspiracy to restrain it.[29] Upstarts and also-rans often accuse Big Tech marketplaces and rankings of being unlawfully rigged. Bureaucrats, ministers, and legislators are increasingly taking notice.

Platforms frequently respond to new regulatory efforts aimed at them by invoking three or four theories of how they serve the national interest: (1) they suppress a variety of online harms, thereby contributing to Internet safety and security, a role that would be threatened by new rules;[30] (2) they help their users and small- and medium-sized enterprises (SMEs) access free and low-priced services, and regulations threaten to upend these relationships; (3) they contribute to national competitiveness, especially when it comes to China's growing strength as a market where digital devices and services are designed; and (4) they exercise editorial discretion and set terms of access in the grand traditions of freedom of speech and liberty of contract.[31]

In the United States and in other countries that have imitated its laws, the freedom of a business to decide with whom to deal fairly is not unlimited. Refusals to deal, unfair dealing, and interference with competitors' distribution or marketing efforts could constitute monopolization, a restraint of trade, or a violation of other trade regulations, notably the ban on unfair or deceptive acts or practices.[32] The Trump administration brought one of the most important antitrust cases in recent memory, alleging that Google blocked Bing and other rivals from appearing as the default search engine on iPhones, Android devices, and browsers like Firefox.[33]

Big Tech hurts newer businesses by treating smaller competitors unfairly, whether in google.com results, Android-compatible smartphone screen displays, the App Store, Amazon's home page or "Buy Boxes," or Meta's many apps and interfaces. There are concerns about other companies as well. Europe has taken aim at Apple and Microsoft as well as Google and Amazon. The outgoing chairman of the Senate Judiciary Committee argued in late 2020 for regulation of the deplatforming of newspapers or other users by ubiquitous digital platforms like Twitter.[34]

A key concern of the European Commission as articulated in its abuse of dominance decision on Google Search (Shopping) was that competitor comparison shopping services including those of smaller businesses were subject to the vagaries of algorithmic "demotion," while Google Shopping was not.[35] This sort of self-preferencing in the display of Google Shopping on google.com was objectively unnecessary, disproportionate in its impact on competitors vis à vis any efficiency benefits, or both.[36] Other objections are leveled against the Android and Apple ecosystems' rules, Amazon's tactics in e-commerce, and Meta's user data policies.[37] While the details differ, one recurring theme is the demotion of competitors from some form of visibility or interoperability, such as default installation, high ranking in searches, or platform data access. As the European Commission explains in the Buy Box case, certain platform rules may artificially disfavor users' offerings in comparison to those of the platform's owner.[38]

Contrasting my hypothetical Disney mandate with a requirement of open access to an Internet platform – either as a law governing public accommodations or as a condition of certain privileges such as immunity from republication-based torts or statutory liabilities – reveals why such a comic-book-movie mandate differs from one imposed on a digital communications or directory service. A digital platform operates a place where diverse persons are invited to come and share their own messages, unlike a Disney movie. This may give rise to obligations not to unlawfully discriminate, just as a newspaper that accepts ads from the general public may not publish racially discriminatory ads or racially discriminate in whose ads it publishes.[39] A U.S. district court judge has questioned whether Google has absolute discretion to engage in viewpoint discrimination, whether by virtue of its terms of service or the wording of the First Amendment.[40] Another has noted (although not in his written order) that a platform's discretion to censor must be limited, or racial discrimination by it would also be allowed by the CDA.[41]

The European Commission's proceedings on "illegal" content also propose a path to exercise protocol power to harness digital platforms to national and supranational political objectives.[42] Articles 40–47 of the Digital Services Act establish a Code of Conduct for speech, while Article 34 requires risk assessments on extremely broad issues like crime and mental health on or related to platforms, and Articles 16–17 require removals of content that may be illegal under any national European law, or under such vaguely worded laws as the EU Terrorism Directive.[43] The Act will hold digital platforms liable for more user content unless they are entirely passive regarding it.[44] On the other hand, it may provide guarantees of judicial review in certain circumstances involving deletion of accounts or removal of speech from view.[45]

Figure 4.1 contains a chart of some relevant Internet laws, arranged on two scales: whether the law explicitly or implicitly protects users from loss of access to a platform, and whether it strongly protects users, either in terms of explicit or implicit protection. Thus, a law might strongly protect users but be directed to other subject matter or general principles and therefore do so implicitly. Or it might weakly protect users despite being explicitly designed for that purpose, or implicitly adapted to that scenario or invocation.

U.S. antitrust law is implicitly very protective of Internet users from deplatforming, but it has its loopholes. After an initial, unsuccessful bid to allege that America Online abused its monopoly power over U.S. subscribers by filtering out spam emails,[46] a somewhat more meritorious action targeted the social network Myspace. LiveUniverse claimed that Myspace accounted for the vast majority of visits to a social network, at that time a series of user profiles with updates.[47] The case failed due to difficulty explaining how Myspace's actions harmed *other* networks.[48]

A few years later Facebook was the most engaging website for Internet users and soon to be one of the most-used smartphone apps as well. Still, antitrust claims

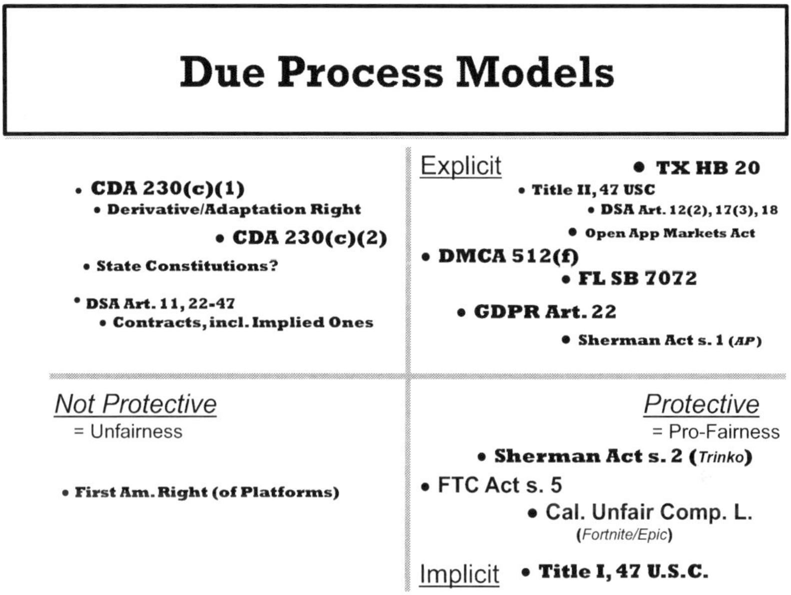

Figure 4.1 A Graphical Representation of Internet Laws Related to Account Protection

against it ran afoul of rules requiring victims of monopolists to prove more than simply the monopolists' refusing to promote them, developing an incompatible dominant offering, or enforcing vague policies or pretextual conduct "strikes."[49] Courts wanted to see more egregious interference with competitors' distribution or product/service, like Microsoft or before that Standard Oil or AT&T perpetrated.

Google, Amazon, and Apple similarly escaped significant oversight as monopolists in this period of time, whether due to the size of the market, strict pleading and proof requirements imposed on victims of monopolists to show harm, or agreeing to abandon their most egregious policies. Google agreed to limit its "scraping" of content from competitive specialized search engines and local guides like Yelp, and it signaled to the FTC that it would not exclude competitors from Double-Click's third-party ad serving marketplace.[50] But it continued to leverage the displays of google.com and the Android menus and screens to drive massive traffic to Google services like Gmail, YouTube, Google Shopping, Google Finance, Google Maps, and Google+. Facebook was allowed to buy Instagram and WhatsApp and to block competitive services such as Vine or MessageMe from using its platform.[51] Apple escaped the bulk of a class action's claims that it manipulated iTunes, its music software and encryption technology, to make rival music store files useless to owners of the dominant iPod digital music players.[52] Amazon prevailed against claims that it blocked independent booksellers from satisfying consumer demand for lower-priced books for the Kindle – the booksellers failed to allege that they would charge less for ebooks than Amazon did, or (for the most part) that it solicited or enjoyed discriminatory discounts from book publishers to the detriment of competition from independent (and physical) booksellers – price-cutting being presumptively beneficial.[53] Although it was not sued for monopolization by Android makers, Apple relented in its efforts to block the Android operating system from emulating aspects of iOS or Android phones and tablets emulating functional features of the iPhone or iPad.[54] It also had to abandon and settle a suit over its practice of increasing eBook prices to entice publishers to use the iBooks and iPad platforms in addition to or instead of Amazon's dominant Kindle and Amazon.com marketplace.[55] Android, too, was pried open to a certain extent to other search engines and video sites, under antitrust pressure.

Google went to trial starting in September 2023 on charges of squelching competition. There is a somewhat credible story that Google has multiple monopolies:

- general Internet searches – about 90%[56];
- licensable mobile device operating systems – about 70%;[57]
- Web browsers – about 66%;[58]
- online video activity –above 50%;[59] and
- search advertisements – about 80%.[60]

Participants and observers see the Google monopolization trial as critical to the future of the demotion as quality frame in Big Tech governance. The case was about "fairness and equal opportunity for all," according to U.S. Attorney General Merrick Garland. It would achieve "economic justice" and "economic freedom" by reining in economic power, just like injunctions halting mergers, which prevent economic giants from getting so large they extract excessive gains from others with whom they deal, like merging publishers avoiding bidding wars with writers, according to Associate Attorney General Vanita Gupta. A follow-on case filed in 2023 would prevent Google from becoming the equivalent of Goldman Sachs owning the New York Stock Exchange, but in online advertising markets rather than securities or commodities markets, with Google obtaining market data quicker than its rivals and boosting its own orders while downgrading others' trades, according to Assistant Attorney General Jonathan Kanter.[61] On the other side, Google argued that it invented more search engine technologies than its rivals, invested more money in competing with them, and was chosen by savvy companies to provide the best experience they could to their users, the purchasers of iPhones and Android devices, led by executives able to protect themselves and their firms – like those at Apple and Samsung.[62]

Malicious Acts Against Open Markets, and the Competition Laws

Filtering people from public spaces is the bane of open markets and democracy. The common law in 1791 has informed competition law and the First Amendment in the United States. When the First Amendment was ratified in that year, excluding male adults from common yet private spaces was ruled to be illegal under the common law.[63] The common law protected the freedom of the individual to practice any lawful trade, contrary to attempts to concentrate the trade and its benefits in a few hands.[64]

Acts by a dominant company, or by a cabal of companies that may or may not control the market by conspiring, may be illegal under competition law. A common inquiry under both U.S. and foreign antitrust laws is whether the disputed acts are designed to reduce competitor's access to the market for reasons other than improving efficiency, reducing cost, or enhancing quality.[65]

The rise of law and economics in the 1970s represented a detour that cut the United States off from the road towards democratic socialism of a European or East Asian variant. A large amount of money flowed into think-tanks, institutes, and both public and corporate media outlets dedicated to neoconservative economic thought. As Ugo Mattei pointed out, European politicians rejected economic efficiency as the chief aim of law, in favor of preserving aspirations to distributive justice. In the United States, however, law and economics became dominant, "beginning in the Reagan years, [as] a full-fledged political agenda and a real industry, capable of flooding with cash any movement that gave cultural prestige to deregulation and other reactionary politics of those years."[66] Politicians used the deceptive label of "deregulation" to refer to these policies, which in fact involved corporate-driven re-regulation of economic sectors.[67] Noam Chomsky has argued that by such means, tens of millions of dollars were spent on propaganda in favor of regimented yet private systems in which Americans were frequently overcharged by corporations for health care, housing, and other essentials of life.[68]

The "Chicago School" tradition of law and economics often proceeds by ignoring studies finding that anti-competitive predation by monopolists and oligopolists against smaller competitors is a reality, and that "unrestricted trade between and among competitors or buyers and sellers is the optimal way to maximize consumer welfare."[69] As one scholar argued, the movement "assumes away most of the elements of the [antitrust] dynamic" by assuming "that buyers are free to choose to deal with whomever they wish or that rivals are already present or poised to enter."[70]

Based on the presumption that the economy corrects itself, so that monopoly power is rare, the U.S. Supreme Court eviscerated U.S. antitrust law starting in 1977. The Chicago School approach found voice in decisions rolling back the established rule that corporations may not seize essential infrastructure and exclude competitors, *Aspen Skiing Corp v. Aspen Highlands Skiing Co*, 472 U.S. 585, 602–03, 608 & n. 39, 611 n. 44 (1985) and *Verizon Communications v. Trinko*, 540 U.S. 398 (2004), curtailing private enforcement of the antitrust laws, *Brunswick Corp. v. Pueblo Bowl-O-Mat, Inc.*, 429 U.S. 477 (1977) and *Illinois Brick v. Illinois*, 431 U.S. 720 (1977), endorsing territorial restraints and other top-down efforts to limit price competition among retailers, *Continental T.V., Inc. v. GTE Sylvania Inc.*, 433 U.S. 36 (1977) and *Leegin Creative Leather Products v. PSKS, Inc.*, 551 U.S. 877 (2007), loosening oversight of agreements among firms on the joint marketing of products or services, *Broadcast Music, Inc. v. CBS, Inc.*, 441 U.S. 1 (1979) and *Texaco, Inc. v. Dagher*, 547 U.S. 1 (2006), and permitting corporations that exclude competitors and later raise prices due to their resulting economic power to win cases by alleging some short-term benefits to consumers during the period of exclusion, *Matsushita Electrical & Industrial Co. v. Zenith Radio Corp.*, 475 U.S. 574 (1986).[71]

Lower courts took note and followed suit, with some of the lower-court judges who parroted Chicago School rhetoric being promoted to Supreme Court justice. Federal judges on the U.S. Courts of Appeals, a surprising number of which ended up as U.S. Supreme Court justices, seemingly competed to whittle away the pre-1980s precedents of the Supreme Court establishing duties to deal fairly or equally with one's competitors and various members of the public. For example, Justices Ruth-Bader Ginsburg, Samuel Alito, and Brett Kavanaugh, sitting on the D.C. Circuit Court of Appeals, issued or joined such rulings.[72] Justice Breyer wrote one on the First Circuit, and Justice Gorsuch on the Tenth.[73] Other justices who became influential for such decisions and were mentioned as Supreme Court material included Judges Frank Easterbrook and Diane Wood, along with Judges Robert Bork and Douglas Ginsburg, whose nominations were scuttled by Senate Democrats in the 1980s.[74]

Despite its growing influence, the Chicago School "economics of the brick-and-mortar world" may not be suited to the contemporary Internetworked economy. The Chicago School tends to focus on the "free rider problem" and the divergence between private and social cost in distributing products.[75] This focus helps to justify restrictive contracts that undermine the freedom of retailers and distributors to cut prices. It looks kindly on large market shares obtained in part by intellectual-property rights or bargaining disparities, because scholars and judges excuse a monopolist or price-fixer for recouping its high fixed costs. With the Internet, however, the economics of digital distribution promise to avoid the need for quality-control at the level of the chain, franchise, or distribution network by using feedback mechanisms, digital previews, and virtual competition among vendors.[76]

Chicago School thinking aids actors with market power who would like to suppress price-cutting competition to boost investment returns without incurring antitrust liability.[77] According to Matt Stoller, from the 1890s to the 1910s and again from 1940 to 1970, courts and attorneys general of the United States viewed with suspicion rising concentration in which "the industrial life of a country passes into the hands of relatively a few individuals," creating "power over the direction of public affairs [that] exceeds the power confided by the people to their elected representatives in the government itself."[78] This era of antimonopoly thought faded as Chicago School theories of antitrust took over, destroying a pillar of Sherman Act prosecutions of the giant trusts – the doctrine that strategic price cutting in order to weaken key competitors and impel them to sell out or quit the game is exclusionary.[79] Mergers and acquisitions, once viewed as a race to the bottom as a lessening of competition in one market causes responsive concentration in other markets, came to be celebrated as mechanisms of moving capital and personnel to their highest-valued users, unless the government could tread a narrow path to show a sharp, unjustified rise in concentration.[80]

Hipster antitrust came to be the term for a revival of interest in small, decentralized industries and subsectors as a way of preventing excessive inequalities of wealth and corruption of the political process. Excessive bigness creates inequalities within and across firms, and contributes to the capture of regulatory institutions and legislatures themselves.[81] Net neutrality was a distant concern for many businesses online, way behind unfair boilerplate and rules foisted upon them by platforms with the power to ban or downrank them.[82] The original framers of the Sherman Act and the FTC Act realized this, but their vision was lost in a fog of charts of supply, demand, and price that a new economic priesthood used to awe and sedate the courts.

Hipster antitrust has its counterparts in distributive political theories. John Médaille and other "distributivists" have argued that socialists diagnosed the inequalities arising from unfair allocation of property rights as a fundamental economic problem, but they proposed precisely the wrong solution: a denial of property to any but the State. The distributivist solution is to subdivide and spread property throughout human realms. In this way, bureaucratic control by both commissars and capitalist bosses will be blunted, and as many persons as possible will have the freedom to reject labor contracts based on the possibility of having recourse to property income. Moreover, a "wider distribution of property is not so much about what the government should do as about what it should stop doing: bolstering wealth accumulation" by a few "through subsidies, privileges, tax breaks, monopolies, externalized costs, and the like."[83]

With the rise of AI, the causes of wealth and power differentials may be supercharged. AI leaders like Microsoft, OpenAI, Facebook, Google, Amazon, and Tesla enjoy generous tax deductions and government largesse.[84] Prior to recent years, some of them imposed restraints on competition with near impunity. They often extended little recourse to people harmed by enhanced surveillance or regulation of economic activity, or censorship of public debates. They often bought or partnered with firms that should be disciplining their conduct as to privacy, consumer protection, freedom of speech, or dispute resolution procedures.

Douglas Rushkoff argues that critiques of digital media miss the point because new applications and platforms produce economic value, meaningful employment, and ways of communicating digitally. The problem, he explains, is that as the process of primitive accumulation by territorial expansion and resource extraction winds down, capitalism must find value in existing industries and their disruption. This disruption used to happen over many years and even decades, as shopping malls or Wal-Mart stores devastated Main Street economies. Once supercharged with digital efficiencies, corporations such as Amazon.com or Uber can perform similar feats in a matter of months or a few years. These new digital superpowers create a tenth as many jobs as the legacy enterprises did, leaving a growing number of people with no way to participate, so they express their anger through left- or right-wing politics rather than the "centrism" he favors. The solution, he suggests, is diversification of the legal structures governing digital firms, with public-interest organizational charters that would allow managers to value quality of service, community health, or workforce numbers and not simply shareholder value. Corporations often invest their revenue in ways that are not as socially valuable as small startups and teams of inventors. Passive income is valorized even by the tax code, which often taxes producing economic value through labor more harshly than extracting it from the economy and storing it in share prices or cash accounts flush with dividend payments.[85]

Rushkoff sees worker-owned firms, in which property is more widely distributed than in founder-dominated public corporations, as enabling "highly reciprocal, peer-to-peer, worker-owned, and community-defined marketplaces."[86] Crowdfunding outside banks, minting currencies outside financial systems, collaborating horizontally on writings outside of publishers, and exchanging value as equals will forge a more "sustainable prosperity."[87]

Peter Fraser points to automation as making human labor obsolete. Political economy could respond in several ways: liberate people from the necessity of labor, maintain a hierarchical distribution of income that doles out the essentials of life in exchange for unnecessary labor, or create new scarcities or intensify old ones to make labor important again (as in postwar reconstruction, for example). The economic base could include a vast increase in wealth and free access to virtually unlimited necessities of life, or continued scarcity and market-traded exchange as before, especially if new sources of energy and new labor-saving machines are not shared across geographies. Carcerality will remain important because in what "the sociologist Bryan Turner calls 'enclave society', . . . 'governments and other agencies seek to regulate spaces and, where necessary, to immobilize flows of people, goods and services' by means of 'enclosure, bureaucratic barriers, legal exclusions and registrations.'"[88] Criminal prohibitions and both digital and social filters stand guard over abundance: "Gated communities, private islands, ghettos, prisons, terrorism paranoia, biological quarantines; together, these amount to an inverted global gulag, where the rich live in tiny islands of wealth strewn around an ocean of misery."[89]

Slavoj Žižek makes a related point in terms of critical social theory. Corporations such as Microsoft earn fabulous profits and make their founders rich by disrupting and extracting value from social processes of communicating knowledge in standard document formats. Efficiencies of this kind threaten to make other types of workers – typesetters, printers, distributers of paper in various forms – obsolete. The benefits of digitization inflict costs in terms of making jobs redundant. Eventually most workers could be fired, but many are kept on as a kind of surplus bourgeoisie, earning surplus wages paid for with the surplus rents appropriated from common labors. When economic changes or cyclical fluctuations threaten even the position of these intellectual and cultural workers, in which category Žižek includes artists and journalists as well as lawyers, protests emerge in the form of Occupiers, Tea Partiers, MAGA voters, and Bernie Bros who organize themselves "against the threat of being reduced to proletarians." Some might place the "color revolutions" of the post-Soviet space, the "Arab Spring," and Iranian protest movements especially in 2009 and 2022 in a similar category. Citing Hardt and Negri but prefiguring the journalistic enthusiasm for Piketty's *Capital in the Twenty First Century*, Žižek observes that this "proletarianisation of the lower salaried bourgeoisie is matched at the opposite extreme by the irrationally high remuneration of top managers and bankers (irrational since, as investigations have demonstrated in the U.S., it tends to be inversely proportional to a company's success)."[90] While the declining living standards of the lower and lower-middle classes abated a bit in the years just prior to the pandemic and during the massive expansion in the money supply and in government budgets that characterized its middle phase, the issue of stagflation took center stage again in 2022 and 2023 and as the world looked towards recessions in 2024.

Zĭzek critiques social media for privatizing knowledge, culture, and other "commons" and calls for knowledge's redistribution in a revived "communism" (or commons-ism, to avoid the baggage of communism as an organized party doctrine) as a response.[91] Yanis Varoufakis writes of "technofeudalism" as an extractive relationship with knowledge and culture: "almost everyone produces for free the capital stock of large corporations. That is what it means to upload stuff on Facebook."[92] Alongside making Internet speech useful to economic and political elites, docile platforms channel many users into the system of carcerality.[93] They regularly make communications ordinarily treated as private available to governments who have not gone to a judge for a warrant, even though the text of laws calls for warrants.[94] They "use hard-to-detect tracking techniques to follow individuals across a variety of apps, websites, and devices," and while this data collection is limited in many ways against governmental access and exploitation, the data collected is vulnerable to the risk of governmental abuse.[95] The Digital Services Act in Europe and various data localization and backdoor wiretapping schemes in the world's major and minor powers will ensure a constant flow of speaker data to police forces.[96]

A Return to Structuralism

Continental European philosophy, even prior to Althusser, seemed to pick up on the insights of U.S. competition law and economics. Franz Neumann, affiliated with the Frankfurt School for Social Research, argued that traditional capitalism was giving way in the 20th century to monopoly capitalism, which took an extreme form in the National Socialist regime in Germany and Austria. In monopoly capitalism, freedom of contract and freedom of trade come under assault by large institutions and "collectivism," so that the freedoms of speech and assembly start to melt away as well.[97] Althusser, who was focused on ideology and repressive state institutions, analyzed structures within the state that shape everyone's lives, namely the ideological state apparatuses and repressive state apparatuses.[98] While there are overlaps (particularly in the relationship between judges and police), the ideological apparatuses include media, jurisprudence, politics, religion, the family, and education, while the repressive institutions include police, armies, and jailers.[99] The ideological state apparatuses reproduce the power structures of a society, the "relations of production" such as the tribal, the feudal, etc.[100]

A return to structuralism may have consequences for the study of platform docility. In Foucault's work on the prison, for example, one theme is tactical analysis of practices and institutions, through which we learn how and why possibilities for human experience were suppressed. This revised version of Friedrich Nietzsche's "genealogy of morals" reveals the origins of divides between the permissible and impermissible, and the strategies by which these impermissible realms of experience and debate are co-opted if not eradicated.[101] Such a genealogy explores why not only the incarcerated, but apparently free and unconstrained subjects, limit their own possibilities. Foucault narrates one approach (that of early modern France) to producing this restrained subjectivity using coercive technologies and allied apparatuses.

Looking at digital platforms through a structuralist lens may reveal new aspects of the history and implications of platform docility. Structuralism examines the efforts of governments to wield power and spread ideology throughout society. It casts doubt on an atomistic view of governmental versus commercial interests. Something like "military-civilian fusion," which is more often associated with the People's Republic of China, may be driving censorship in an age of docile platforms, mobilized by states to serve military and securitization interests, invisibly.

Finally, structuralism may have implications for the application of the First Amendment and its counterparts in the International Convention on Civil and Political Rights (ICCPR), the European Convention on Human Rights (ECHR), and similar enactments in national and trans-national laws. The assumption of some courts in First Amendment cases is that unless there is a paper trail of direct orders from the state to a digital platform, there is no unconstitutional entanglement or participation of the state in private censorship. Section 230 of the CDA is an example of disciplinary power in Foucault's sense, and a repressive state apparatus in Althusser's. In one of its applications, it mobilizes and incentivizes platforms to remove offensive and suspicious speech, regularizing and normalizing the Internet itself, by preventing many Internet users from challenging their deplatforming. In this way, states trample upon the human right to seek and receive information of all kinds regardless of medium chosen or national frontiers.

The Senate's Subcommittee on Competition Policy, Antitrust, and Consumer Rights once witnessed a bid to amplify the impact of the CDA by further threatening Internet platforms with substantial penalties for not demoting vaguely defined "harmful" speech. Its Chair, Senator Amy Klobuchar of Minnesota, introduced bipartisan legislation to do this, called the Nudging Users to Drive Good Experiences on Social Media (Social Media NUDGE) Act. She explained that "we know that social media platforms have repeatedly put profits over people, with algorithms pushing dangerous content that hooks users and spreads misinformation."[102] The bill's introduction was an opportunity to transition from the disciplinary model of CDA Section 230 to a "protocol" power model of algorithmic intervention. Online censorship could morph into an even more innocuous and undetectable form, that of protecting users from addiction and bad nudges. The universe of statements that are readable or watchable on social media could become predictable in the manner that the intoxicants on sale at 7-Eleven are, or the investments at E*TRADE are. The effort received a slight boost from the disclosures by Frances Haugen, boosted many times over by *The Wall Street Journal*, CNN, Fox News, and other corporate media.[103] It has yet to change U.S. law.

Notes

1 Renee DiResta, Free speech is not the same as free reach, *Wired* (August 30, 2018), https://www.wired.com/story/free-speech-is-not-the-same-as-free-reach.
2 This is how the first act of the third *Mad Max* movie closes. It was written by George Miller and Terry Hayes and co-directed by Miller and George Ogilvie. Hayes also co-wrote *Mad Max: The Road Warrior* (1981).
3 John Stuart Mill, *On Liberty* (Longman, Roberts & Co., 4th ed. 1869), ch. 3 (noting one aspect "of public opinion, [which is] peculiarly calculated to make it intolerant of any marked demonstration of individuality. The general average of mankind are not only moderate in intellect, but also moderate in inclinations: they have no tastes or wishes strong enough to incline them to do anything unusual, and they consequently do not understand those who have, and class all such with the wild and intemperate whom they are accustomed to look down upon.").
4 21 *Congressional Record* 137 (1889) (statement of Sen. Turpie).
5 Ibid., pp. 1457–58 (statement of Sen Jones); ibid., p. 1768 (statement of Sen. George); 21 Congressional Record 4098 (1890) (statement of Rep. Taylor); ibid., pp. 4102 (1890) (statement of Rep. Fithian).
6 21 *Congressional Record* 2598 (1890) (statement of Sen. George).
7 Ibid., p. 2726 (statement of Sen. Edmunds).
8 Ibid., p. 3147 (statement of Sen George).
9 Ibid., p. 4102 (statement of Rep. Fithian).
10 Ibid., p. 2457 (statement of Sen. Sherman).
11 Ibid., p. 2462 (statement of Sen. Sherman) (quoting statement of Sen. George).
12 Morris Run Coal Co. v. Barclay Coal Co., 68 Pa. St. 173, 183–187 (1871) (internal citation and quotation marks omitted).
13 Salt Co. v. Guthrie, 35 Ohio St. 666, 672 (1880).
14 Craft v. McConoughy, 79 Ill. 346, 349, 350 (1875).
15 Gibbs v. Consolidated Gas Co. of Baltimore, 32 U.S. 411, 412 (1888).
16 United States v. E.C. Knight Co., 156 U.S. 1, 32 (1895) (Harlan, J., dissenting).
17 E.g., Silvia Beltrametti, 'Capturing the transplant: US antitrust law in the European Union,' 48 *Vanderbilt Journal of Transnational Law* 1147 (2015); R.S. French, In Hope of Convergence: A Regional Perspective on Competition Law, Paper Presented to 2009 Competition Law Conference, Sydney, Australia (May 23, 2009), https://www.hcourt.gov.au/assets/publications/speeches/current-justices/frenchcj/frenchcj-23may09.pdf; Spencer Weber Waller, 'The Omega Man or the isolation of US antitrust law,' 52 *Connecticut Law Review* 123 (2020).
18 E.g., Standard Oil Co. (Indiana) v. United States, 283 U.S. 162, 169–70 & n.2 (1931) (monopolies); United States v. Arnold, Schwinn & Co., 388 U.S. 365, 391 (1967) (Stewart, J., joined by Harlan, J., dissenting) (restraints of trade) (citing Mitchel v. Reynolds, 1 P. Wms. 181, 24 Eng. Rep. 347 (1711)); United States v. Addyston Pipe & Steel Co., 85 F. 271, 283–284 (6th Cir. 1898).
19 E.g., Eastman Kodak Co. v. Image Technical Servs., Inc., 504 U.S. 451 (1992) (copier repair services); FTC v. Indiana Fed'n of Dentists, 476 U.S. 447 (1990) (dental services); Aspen Skiing Co. v. Aspen Highlands Skiing Corp., 472 U.S. 585 (1985) (Colorado destination downhill skiing resorts); NCAA v. Board of Regents of the University of Oklahoma, 468 U.S. 85 (1984) (collegiate football exhibitions on television); International Boxing Club v. United States, 348 U.S. 236 (1955) (professional boxing exhibitions at championship level); Lorain Journal Co. v. United States, 342 U.S. 143 (1951) (local advertising); Fashion Originators' Guild of America v. FTC, 312 U.S. 457 (1941) (fashion dresses); Caribbean Broad. Sys. Ltd. v. Cable & Wireless PLC, 148 F.3d 1080 (D.C. Cir. 1998) (broadcasting for entertainment); Wilk v. American Medical Association, 895 F.2d 353 (7th Cir. 1990) (offering treatment of back and neck

pain); Simon-Whelan v. The Andy Warhol Foundation for the Visual Arts, Inc., 2009–1 Trade Cases P 76,657, 2009 WL 1457177 (S.D.N.Y. 2009) (art authentication services); U.S. Football League v. National Football League, 634 F. Supp. 1155 (S.D.N.Y. 1986) (professional football leagues); Creative Trading Co., Inc. v. Larkin-Pluznick-Larkin, Inc., 75 N.Y.2d 830, 552 N.Y.S.2d 558 (1990), *adopting dissenting opinion in* 148 A.D.2d 352, 539 N.Y.S.2d 1 (1st Dep't 1989) (exhibition booths); Neri's Land Imp., LLC v. J.J. Cassone Bakery, Inc., 65 A.D.3d 1312, 886 N.Y.S.2d 202 (2d Dep't 2009) (bakeries); Cox v. Microsoft Corp., 778 N.Y.S.2d 147 (N.Y. App. Div. 1st Dep't 2004) (computer operating systems); Sands v. Ticketmaster-N.Y., Inc., 616 N.Y.S.2d 362 (N.Y. App. Div. 1st Dep't 1994) (event tickets); American Dental Cooperative, Inc. v. Attorney General of State of New York, 514 N.Y.S.2d 228 (N.Y. App. Div. 1st Dep't 1987) (dental services).

20 United States v. United States Steel Corp., 251 U.S. 417 (1920); United States v. Terminal Railroad Assoc., 224 U.S. 383 (1912); United States v. American Tobacco Co., 221 U.S. 106 (1911). See also, United States v. American Tobacco Co., 328 U.S. 781 (1946); United States v. Socony-Vacuum Oil Co., 310 U.S. 150, 226 (1940); United States v. Aluminum Co. of America, 148 F.2d 416, 427–32 (2d Cir. 1945).

21 E.g., *Eastman Kodak*, 504 U.S. 451 (leveraging product monopoly into service monopoly); *Indiana Federation of Dentists*, 476 U.S. 447 (collusion); United States v. Topco Associates, Inc., 405 U.S. 596 (1972) (collusion and trademark controls); Timken Roller Bearing Co. v. United States, 341 U.S. 593 (1951) (similar); Motion Picture Patents Co. v. Universal Film Manufacturing Co., 243 U.S. 502 (1917) (tying); (essential facilities and monopoly leveraging/control of retailers' choices); Beverage Management, Inc. v. Coca-Cola Bottling Corp., 653 F.Supp. 1144, 1156–57 (S.D. Ohio 1986).

22 *Beverage Management*, 653 F. Supp. at 1151, 1154, 1156–57.

23 Pacific Bell Telephone Co. v. Linkline Communications, 555 U.S. 438 (2009); *Trinko*, 540 U.S. 398; Atlantic Richfield Co. v. USA Petroleum Co., 495 US 328, 331–32, 338–45 (1990); Jefferson Parish Hospital Dist. No. 2 v. Hyde, 466 U.S. 2 (1984).

24 *See, e.g.,* Best Carpet Values, Inc., v. Google LLC, No. 5:20-cv-04700-EJD, slip op. at 27–29 (N.D. Cal. September 24, 2021) (ECF No. 41) (rejecting unfair competition claim against Google for actions akin to abuse of monopoly power); Epic Games, Inc. v. Apple, Inc., No. 4:20-cv-05640-YGR, 2020 WL 5073937 (N.D. Cal. mot. for prelim. inj. denied August 24, 2020) ("serious questions" raised as to whether Apple charged sufficiently high fees to app developers to have an anticompetitive effect; court stated that it anticipated that plaintiff app developer's experts would so opine), *further proceedings at* 493 F. Supp. 3d 817 (N.D. Cal. 2020) (finding insufficient evidence that app developer would succeed on Sherman Act theory against Apple to enjoin Apple from terminating developer's app on that basis, but finding "serious questions" as to whether Apple had an app distribution monopoly with respect to apps coded for iOS devices); HiQ Labs, Inc. v. LinkedIn Corp., 485 F. Supp. 3d 1137, 1152 (N.D. Cal. 2020) (dismissing virtually all of plaintiff's monopolization theories based on power leveraging, and stating that leveraging is insufficient without illegal conduct); Sayre v. Google, Inc. No. No. C 19–02247 WHA, 2019 WL 6036703, at § 1.C. (N.D. Cal. November 14, 2019) ("Anticompetitive conduct involves electing to forgo short-run benefits because of an interest in reducing competition in the long run by harming smaller competitors.") (citing Verizon Communs., Inc. v. Law Offices of Curtis V. Trinko, LLP, 540 U.S. 398, 408 (2004)); Dreamstime.com, LLC v. Google, LLC, 470 F. Supp. 3d 1082, 1084 (N.D. Cal. 2020) (noting that court had dismissed stock image service's downranking/misranking claim against search engine under monopolization theory because Google's conduct was not deliberately designed to harm plaintiff), *prior proceedings at* Dreamstime.com, LLC v. Google, LLC, No. C 18–01910 WHA, 2019 WL 2372280, at *2 (N.D. Cal. June 5, 2019) (declining to dismiss earlier version of downranking claim against Google, noting that discovery was needed), *prior proceedings*

at 2019 WL 341579 (N.D. Cal. January 28, 2019) (dismissing monopolization claim but not breach of contract claim, even though contract governed access to a program – Adwords – which plaintiff claimed that defendant manipulated to exclude plaintiff from the market for licensing photos); HiQ Labs, Inc. v. LinkedIn Corp., 273 F. Supp. 3d 1099, 1118 (N.D. Cal. 2017) ("'The Sherman Act prohibits companies from leveraging monopoly power to 'foreclose competition or gain a competitive advantage, or to destroy a competitor.' . . . There is . . . a plausible inference that LinkedIn terminated HiQ's access to its public member data in large part because it wanted exclusive control over that data for its own business purposes; as noted earlier, HiQ faces an existential threat.") (quoting Otter Tail Power Co. v. United States, 410 U.S. 366, 377 (1973)); e-Ventures Worldwide, LLC v. Google, Inc., 188 F. Supp. 3d 1265, 1276–77 (M.D. Fla. 2016) ("Here, plaintiff has alleged the Google removed its websites from its search results for anticompetitive and punitive reasons. . .. Google disagrees with these allegations, but at this stage of the proceedings these allegations are sufficient to allege deceptive acts or unfair practices" under the Florida Unfair and Deceptive Trade Practices Act); Kickflip, Inc. v. Facebook, Inc., 999 F. Supp. 2d 677, 689 (D. Del. 2013) (denying motion to dismiss claim that Facebook created a new market in virtual currency services for social networking and eliminated defendant from it by banning defendant from its platform); Tucker v. Apple Computer, Inc., 493 F. Supp. 2d 1090, 1099 (N.D. Cal. 2006) (if Apple unnecessarily modified its iPod to make it incompatible with competitive online music stores to iTunes, that would be exclusionary and anticompetitive conduct by a firm adequately alleged to be a monopolist in at least two areas), *further proceedings at* In re Apple iPod iTunes Antitrust Litig., 796 F. Supp. 2d 1137, 1144–47 (N.D. Cal. 2011); Caldera, Inc. v. Microsoft Corp., 72 F. Supp. 2d 1295, 1317 (D. Utah 1999) (holding that claim was stated against Microsoft for "a clandestine campaign to eliminate DR DOS from the market by a variety of tactics, none of which alone supports a Sherman Act violation but the aggregation of which results in prohibited predatory conduct.").

25 E.g., Domen v. Vimeo, Inc., 6 F. 4th 245 (2d Cir. 2021) (citing *e-Ventures*, 188 F. Supp. 3d 1265; National Numismatic Certification, LLC v. eBay, Inc., No. 6:08-cv-42-Orl-19GJK, 2008 WL 2704404 at *24 (M.D. Fla. July 8, 2008)), *withdrawn*, 2021 WL 4399692 (2d Cir. Sept. 23, 2021); *Best Carpet Values*, slip op. (citing Zhang v. Baidu. Com, Inc., 10 F. Supp. 3d 433, 439 (S.D.N.Y. 2014); Langdon v. Google, Inc., 474 F. Supp. 2d 622, 629 (D. Del. 2007); Search King, Inc. v. Google Tech., Inc., 2003 WL 21464568, at *4 (W.D. Okla, May 27, 2003)).

26 Cf., Aurelien Portuese, When demotion is competition: Algorithmic antitrust, Concurrences N°2–2018/SSRN (2018), https://papers.ssrn.com/sol3/papers.cfm?abstract_id=3188776.

27 Maggie Clark, CCIA sponsored event: Content moderation & removal at scale, *CCIA* (2018), https://www.ccianet.org/2018/01/content-moderation-removal-at-scale/.

28 E.g., Prager Univ. v. Google LLC, No. 17-CV-06064-LHK, 2018 WL 1471939, at *8 (N.D. Cal. Mar. 26, 2018), *aff'd*, 951 F.3d 991 (9th Cir. 2020); Sikhs for Justice, Inc. v. Facebook, Inc., 697 Fed. App'x 526 (9th Cir. 2017); Rutenberg v. Twitter, Inc., No. 4:21-cv-0548, slip op. (N.D. Cal. April 9, 2021); Federal Agency of News LLC v. Facebook, Inc., 432 F. Supp. 3d 1107 (N.D. Cal. 2020); Ebeid v. Facebook, Inc., No. 18-CV-07030-PJH, 2019 WL 2059662, at *6 (N.D. Cal. May 9, 2019); Nyabwa v. Facebook, No. 2:17-CV-24, 2018 WL 585467, at *1 (S.D. Tex. January 26, 2018); Shulman v. Facebook.com, No. CV 17–764 (JMV), 2017 WL 5129885, *4 (D.N.J. November 6, 2017); Kinderstart.com LLC v. Google, Inc., No. C06–2057 JFRS, 2007 WL 831806, *13–15 (N.D. Cal, March 16, 2007).

29 Frank Pasquale, Internet nondiscrimination principles revisited, Brooklyn Law School, Legal Studies Paper No. 655 (2020), https://papers.ssrn.com/sol3/papers.cfm?abstract_id=3634625.

30 'Editorial, new big tech rules will harm conservatives,' *L.A. Daily News* (January 27, 2022), p. 11 (arguing that if Big Tech took a "hands-off approach to content, "it would turn these sites into the equivalent of your email spam folder or what's found on the uncontrolled dark web."); Bilal Sayyed, Grassley/Klobuchar regulations on companies would hurt tech competition, consumers, *Des Moines Register*/WestlawNext (December 14, 2021), https://1.next.westlaw.com (subscription required).
31 E.g., Computer and Communications Industry Association [CCIA], National Security Issues Posed by House Antitrust Bills (2022), https://www.ccianet.org/2021/09/ccia-whitepaper-identifies-national-security-risks-posed-by-house-bills-targeting-u-s-tech-companies/; Brief of Applicants NetChoice, LLC and CCIA, NetChoice, LLC v. Paxton, No. 22–555 (U.S. brief filed May 13, 2022); Heather Greenfield, CCIA responds to manager's amendment to controversial antitrust bill, *CCIA* (2022), https://www.ccianet.org/2022/05/ccia-responds-to-managers-amendment-to-controversial-antitrust-bill/. On editorial discretion, see previous notes 25, 28 for examples where platforms successfully made this argument or a similar one.
32 E.g., 15 U.S.C. §§ 1–2.
33 Plaintiffs' Pre-Trial Brief, at 5–6, United States v. Google, No. 1:20-cv-03010-APM (D.D.C. brief filed September 8, 2023).
34 WATCH: Twitter and Facebook CEOs testify in Senate hearing, *The Washington Post/YouTube* (2020), https://www.youtube.com/watch?v=9nwnYPclano (Sen. Lindsey Graham proposing to revise CDA's Section 230 to limit the power of digital platforms to halt the sharing of information and the selective fact-checking of political content, while preserving its role of allowing platforms to reduce the spread of terrorist or child abuse material); JUST IN: Lindsey Graham slams Facebook, Twitter over 'New York Post' Hunter Biden article, *YouTube* (October 15, 2020), https://www.youtube.com/watch?v=D-QTGLd4x3I.
35 Case T-612/17, Google and Alphabet v. Commission (Google Shopping), ECLI: EU:T:2021:763.
36 Ibid.; Elias Deutscher, 'Google Shopping and the Quest for a Legal Test for Self-preferencing Under Article 102 TFEU,' 6 *European Papers* 1345–1361 (2021).
37 E.g., European Commission, Press release IP/20/2077 – Antitrust: Commission sends Statement of Objections to Amazon for the use of non-public independent seller data and opens second investigation into its e-commerce business practices (2020), https://ec.europa.eu/commission; European Commission, Press release IP/22/2764, Press release Antitrust: Commission sends Statement of Objections to Apple over practices regarding Apple Pay (2022), https://ec.europa.eu/commission; European Commission, Press release IP/21/2061, Antitrust: Commission sends Statement of Objections to Apple on App Store rules for music streaming providers (2021), https://ec.europa.eu/commission, European Commission, Press release IP/20/1073, Antitrust: Commission opens investigations into Apple's App Store rules (2020), https://ec.europa.eu/commission; European Commission, Antitrust: Commission opens investigation into possible anti-competitive conduct of Amazon, (July 17, 2019), https://ec.europa.eu/commission/presscorner/detail/en/IP_19_4291; House Subcommittee Report, previous n. 108, at 268–330; Autorità garante della Concorrenza e del Mercato [Italian Competitive Markets Authority], Press release A528 – Antitrust – Amazon fined over € 1,128 billion for abusing its dominant position (2021), https://www.en.agcm.it; Competition and Markets Authority (CMA) [of the United Kingdom of Great Britain and Northern Ireland], Press release – CMA investigates Facebook's use of ad data (2021), https://www.gov.uk; Deutscher Bundeskartellamt, Press release 080/2020, KVR 69/19, Federal Court of Justice provisionally confirms allegation of Facebook abusing dominant position (2020).
38 European Commission, Statement by Executive Vice-President Vestager on Statement of Objections to Amazon for the use of non-public independent seller data and second investigation into its e-commerce business practices (November 10, 2020),

p. 2. The case concluded with Amazon's commitment to use nondiscriminatory conditions to display a default or "Featured Offer," and to display equal descriptive information for at least one qualifying alternative offer. E.g., Commitments to the European Commission, Case Nos. COMP/AT.40462 and COMP/AT.40703 – Amazon (December, 2022), https://ec.europa.eu/competition/antitrust/cases1/202252/AT_40462_8825091_8265_4.pdf.

39 E.g., Pittsburgh Press Co. v. Pittsburgh Commission on Human Relations, 413 U.S. 376 (1973). See also, 303 Creative LLC v. Elenis, 143 S. Ct. 2298, 2326 n.6 (2023) (Sotomayor, J., joined by Kagan J., and Jackson, J., dissenting) (a trader or artisan like an ironsmith had a duty of care resulting from holding himself or herself out to the public as being prepared to serve any member of the public) (citing, inter alia, Lane v. Cotton, 88 Eng. Rep. 1458, 1464 (K. B. 1701) (Holt, C. J.); William Blackstone, *Commentaries on the Laws of England*, Vol. 3 (The Clarendon Press, 1768), p. 164; Joseph Story, *Commentaries on the Law of Bailments* §§ 495, 591 (Little, Brown and Company, 1837); 1 T. Parsons, *Law of Contracts* (1853), pp. 639, 643, 649; M. Konvitz and T. Leskes, *A Century of Civil Rights* (1961), pp. 155–157; Edward Adler, 'Business Jurisprudence,' 28 *Harvard Law Review* 135, 156 (1914)).

40 *e-Ventures*, 188 F. Supp. 3d 1265.

41 Alex Berenson, Lifting the kimono (uh-oh, trigger alert) a little more on *Berenson v. Twitter*, Substack (July 1, 2022), https://alexberenson.substack.com/p/lifting-the-kimono-uh-oh-trigger; but see, Berenson v. Twitter, Inc., No. C 21–09818 WHA, slip op. (N.D. Cal. April 29, 2022).

42 European Commission, Recommendation on Measures to Effectively Tackle Illegal Content Online, C(2018) 117 final.

43 Regulation on a Single Market for Digital Services, arts. 16–47, *Official Journal* L 277 (27 October 2022), pp. 1–102; Gabriela Zanfir-Fortuna and Vasileios Rovilos, EU'S Digital Services Act just became applicable: outlining ten key areas of interplay with the GDPR, Future of Privacy Forum (August 31, 2023), https://fpf.org/blog/eus-digital-services-act-just-became-applicable-outlining-ten-key-areas-of-interplay-with-the-gdpr/.

44 EU Digital Services Act will restructure tech services, *Oxford Analytica* (2022), https://www.emerald.com/insight/content/doi/10.1108/OXAN-DB270191/full/html; Murdoch Watney, 'Regulation of social media intermediary liability for illegal and harmful content,' 9 *European Conference on Social Media* 194 (2022).

45 Regulation on a single market for digital services and amending Directive 2000/31/EC (Digital Services Act), arts. 16–27, COM/2020/825, *Official Journal* L 277 (October 27, 2022).

46 *America Online, Inc.*, 948 F. Supp. 436.

47 LiveUniverse, Inc. v. Myspace, Inc., No. CV 06–6994 AHM (RZx), 2007 WL 6865852 (N.D. Cal. June 4, 2007), *aff'd*, 304 Fed. App'x 554 (9th Cir. 2008); Shin-Ru Cheng, "Entry barriers: The role of big data in the online networking market,' 69 *Drake Law Review* 487 (2021).

48 *LiveUniverse v. Myspace*, 304 Fed. App'x 554; Spencer Weber Waller, 'Antitrust and social networking,' 90 *North Carolina Law Review* 1771, 1794 (2010–2011).

49 One court found: "The facts as alleged in the complaint do not support the conclusion that Facebook's preclusion of Sambreel's products from being viewed on its own website harms the process of competition and consumer welfare." Sambreel Holdings LLC v. Facebook, Inc., 906 F. Supp. 2d 1070, 1082 (N.D. Cal. 2012). Another concluded that: "If Facebook has the right to manage access to and use of its website, then there can be nothing anticompetitive about taking legal action to enforce that right." Facebook, Inc. v. Power Ventures, Inc., No. C 08–5780 JW, 2010 WL 3291750, at*14 (N.D. Cal. July 20, 2010). A Myspace decision had found, prior to these two Facebook judgments, that just as a dominant camera manufacturer can produce a new model that is not interoperable with a competitor's film or models, a website can refuse to deal with

a competitor and decline to produce a compatible version of its own interface to help the plaintiff's interface or website succeed. *Myspace*, 394 Fed. App'x 554, 554–557. The judges in this case explained that they could not see "how Myspace's actions *on its own website* can reduce consumers' choice or diminish the quality of their experience on other social networking websites-" *Id.* at 557 (emphasis in original).

50 Melissa Lippman, Yelp accuses Google of breaking search bias vows to FTC, *Law360* (September 12, 2017), https://www.law360.com/articles/962892/yelp-accuses-google-of-breaking-search-bias-vows-to-ftc; U.S. Federal Trade Comm'n, Google Inc. File No. 111–0163 (January 3, 2013), https://www.ftc.gov; FTC, Press Release, Federal Trade Commission closes Google/DoubleClick investigation (December 20, 2007), https://www.ftc.gov.

51 New York v. Facebook, Inc., 549 F. Supp. 3d 6, 17–21 (D.D.C. 2021), *aff'd sub nom.* New York v. Meta Platforms, Inc., No. 21–7078, slip op. (D.C. Cir. April 27, 2023). Vine and MessageMe, "after promising early growth, faltered shortly after losing [their] access" to Facebook's application programming interfaces, which allow Facebook users to find Facebook friends when using apps connected to the Facebook platform, for example to share videos, play games, or send more private or media-rich messages. *See id.* at 18–19.

52 In re Apple iPod iTunes Antitrust Litigation, 796 F. Supp. 2d 1137, 1143–44 (N.D. Cal. 2011), *further proceedings at* No. 05-CV-0037 YGR, slip op. (N.D. Cal. September 26, 2014) (limiting case to Apple's alleged manipulation of iTunes to thwart a competitor's efforts to achieve music store compatibility with iPods), *jury verdict for defendant* (N.D. Cal. December 16, 2014).

53 Bookhouse of Stuyvesant Plaza, Inc. v. Amazon.com, 985 F. Supp. 2d 612, 612–19 (S.D.N.Y. 2013) (Kindle); Intimate Bookshop, Inc. v. Barnes & Noble, Inc., 88 F. Supp. 2d 133, 139–40 (S.D.N.Y. 2000) (secret rebates). Still, Amazon abandoned aspects of its pricing policies for sellers when governments plausibly objected. Makena Kelly, Amazon silently ends controversial pricing agreements with sellers, *The Verge* (March 11, 2019), www.theverge.com/2019/3/11/18260700/amazon-anti-competitive-pricing-agreements-3rd-party-sellers-end.

54 Dan Levine, Apple, Google settle smartphone patent litigation, *Reuters* (May 16, 2014), www.reuters.com. Compare, Apple Inc. v. Samsung Electronics Co., Ltd., 786 F. 3d 983 (Fed. Cir. 2015) (Apple tried to claim Lanham Act rights in smartphones with rounded edges etc.).

55 United States v. Apple, Inc., 791 F.3d 209 (2d Cir. 2015); House Subcommittee Report, previous n. 108, p. 333 (Apple paid $450 million to settle antitrust claims).

56 Plaintiffs' Pre-Trial Brief, *Google*, previous n. 33, at 5; see also, Inform, Inc. v. Google, Inc. No. 1:19-cv-05362-JPB (N.D. Ga. first amended complaint filed October 9, 2020) (citing Google Inc., 2019 Annual Report on Form 10-k, htttps://www.vox.com/2017/3/14/14890122/google-search-ad-market-share-growth; Statcounter, Search engine market share, https://gs.statcounter.com/search-engine-market-share).

57 Ibid. (citing Statcounter, OS market share mobile, worldwide, https://gs.statcounter.com/os-market-share/mobile/worldwide).

58 Ibid. (citing Statcounter, Browser market share, https://gs.statcounter.com/browser-market-share).

59 Plaintiff's Complaint, 37, 63, 193, Rumble, Inc. v. Google, LLC, No. 21-cv-00229-HSG (N.D. Cal. complaint filed 2021).

60 Plaintiffs' Pre-Trial Brief, *Google*, previous n. 33, p. 5.

61 CNET Highlights, WATCH: DOJ announce antitrust enforcement against Google – LIVE, *YouTube* (2023), https://www.youtube.com/watch?v=sNL62LaUQ1U.

62 Brian Fung, Landmark Google trial opens with sweeping DOJ accusations of illegal monopolization, *CNN* (September 12, 2023), https://www.cnn.com/2023/09/12/tech/google-antitrust-lawsuit-government-trial-duplicate-2/index.html.

63 Standard Oil Co. v. United States, 221 U.S. 1, 54 (1911) ("[B]y the common law monopolies were unlawful because of their restriction upon individual freedom of contract and their injury to the public."). *See also*, Butchers' Union Slaughter-House & Live-Stock Landing Co. v. Crescent City Live-Stock Landing and Slaughter House Co., 111 U.S. 746, 761 (1884) (Bradley, J., concurring) (declaring an "incontrovertible proposition of both English and American public law, that all mere monopolies are odious and against common right"); People ex rel. Peabody v. Chicago Gas Trust Co., 130 Ill. 268, 294 (1889) ("All grants creating monopolies are made void by the common law.") (citing Darcy v. Allein (The Case of Monopolies), 77 Eng. Rep. 1260 (K.B. 1602)); *id.* at 293 ("Whatever tends to create a monopoly is unlawful as being contrary to public policy.") (citing Morris Run Coal Co. v. Barclay Coal Co. 68 Pa. St. 173 (1871); Craft v. McConoughy, 79 Ill. 346 (1875); Central R.R. Co. v. Collins, 40 Ga. 582 (1869); Hazelhurst v. Savannah R.R. Co. 43 Ga. 13 (1871); Trans. Co. v. Pipe Line Co. 22 W. Va. 600 (1883)); State v. Nebraska Distilling Co., 29 Neb. 700, 715 (1890) ("Whatever tends to destroy competition and create a monopoly is contrary to public policy and therefore unlawful.") (citing *Morris Run Coal Co.*, 68 Pa. 173; *McConoughy*, 79 Ill. 346; *Collins*, 40 Ga. 582; *Hazelhurst*, 43 Ga. 13; *Pipe Line Co.*, 22 W. Va. 600; People v. Chicago Gas Trust Co., 130 Ill. 268 (1889); Richardson v. Buhl, 77 Mich. 632 (1889)); People v. North River Sugar Ref. Co., 121 N.Y. 582, 625 (1890) (ordering dissolution of corporation at common law because "if corporations can combine . . . , without limit to the magnitude of the aggregation, a tempting and easy road is opened to enormous combinations, vastly exceeding in number and in strength and in their power over industry any possibilities of individual ownership; and the State by the creation of the artificial persons constituting the elements of the combination, and failing to limit and restrain their powers, becomes itself the responsible creator [of them]"); State ex rel. Attorney Gen. v. Standard Oil Co., 30 N.E. 279, 289–90 (Ohio 1892) (unlawful for "many separate interests [to be] united under one management, form a virtual monopoly through the power acquired of so controlling the production and price of petroleum and its products, as to destroy competition" because: "Monopolies have always been regarded as contrary to the spirit and policy of the common law.") (citing *Darcy v. Allein*, 77 Eng. Rep. 1260); The East India Co. v. Sandys (The Great Case of Monopolies), 10 St. Tr. 371, 538 (1683) ("[T]hough monopolies are forbidden, yet that cannot be understood to be so universally true, (as no general law can ever be) that it should in no respect, and upon no occasion or emergency whatsoever, admit of any exception or limitation."); The Cloth Workers of Ipswich, 78 Eng. Rep. 147, 148 (K.B. 1615) ("It was agreed by the Court, that the King might make corporations . . . but thereby they cannot make a monopoly for that is to take away free-trade, which is the birthright of every subject."); *Darcy v. Allein*, 77 Eng. Rep. at 1260–69 (common law invalidated attempt to convey national monopoly over manufacture or importation of playing cards); James Madison, 'Monopolies. Perpetuities. Corporations. Ecclesiastical Endowments.,' *in Writings*, edited by Jack Rakove (Library of America, 1999), p. 756 (U.S. Constitution restricted official monopolies to "two cases, the authors of Books, and of useful inventions"); Edward Grant Buckland, 'Combinations and trusts,' 16 *New Englander and Yale Review* 241 (1890) ("In the infancy of this nation, the disposition was to regard with suspicion any approach to facilitating corporate organization. . . . The old memories of English monopolies still lingered."); Edward Coke, *Institutes of the Laws of England*, Vol. 3 (facsimile ed., 1985) [1641], p. 181 ("[A]ll Grants of Monopolies are against the ancient and fundamentall laws of this Kingdome.").

64 Yick Wo v. Hopkins, 118 U.S. 356, 370 (1886) (law conferring upon city government the "arbitrary power" to withhold the right to carry on a trade violated Equal Protection Clause: "[T]he very idea that one man may be compelled to hold . . . any material right essential to the enjoyment of life, at the mere will of another, seems to be intolerable in

any country where freedom prevails, as being the essence of slavery itself."); Beall v. Beck, 2 F. Cas. 1111, 1114 (C.C. D.C. 1829) ("Wherever the privilege of [a] landlord would destroy a lawful trade or occupation which is useful to the public, it is restrained by law."); Corfield v. Coryell, 6 F. Cas. 546 (No. 3, 230) (C.C.E.D. Pa. 1825) (law restricting any person not an "actual inhabitant and resident" of New Jersey from practicing fisherman's trade violated Privileges and Immunities Clause of the Constitution because it restricted ability of citizens of the United States "to acquire . . . property," "pursue and obtain happiness," and engage in a lawful "trade, agriculture, [or] professional pursuit"); City of Memphis v. Winfield, 27 Tenn. 707, 709–10 (1848) (striking down discriminatory curfew imposed on African-Americans as contrary to their "liberty" because "in cities, very often, the most profitable employment is to be found in the night"); *Darcy v. Allein*, 77 Eng. Rep. at 1269 (monopolies contrary to the "benefit and liberty of the subject"); Magna Charta, art. 41 (1215), https://www.uni-bielefeld.de/lili/personen/fleischmann/archwise04/32_hse_magnacarta.htm?support_person=bskpvvjs6odvmb1b2u9ah9jrh1 ("All merchants are to be safe and secure . . . to buy and sell free from all maletotes [impositions] by the ancient and rightful customs."); James Madison, 'Property,' *in Writings of James Madison, Volume IV: 1829–1836* (J.P. Lippincott Co., 1867), p. 475 ("That is not a just government, nor is property secure under it, where arbitrary restrictions, exemptions, and monopolies deny to a part of its citizens that free use of their faculties, and free choice of their occupations . . ."); William Blackstone, *Commentaries on the Laws of England*, Vol. 1 (1765), p. *427 ("At the common law, every man might use what trade he pleased."); Sir Edward Coke, *The second part of the institutes of the laws of England: containing the exposition of many ancient and other statutes*, vol. 1 (W. Clarke & Sons, 1809), p. 47 ("Generally all monopolies are against this great charter [Magna Charta], because they are against the liberty and freedome of the subject, and against the law of the land."); Timothy Sandefur, 'The Common Law Right to Earn a Living,' VI *The Independent Review* 69, 70 (2002) ("In 1377, the court struck down a royal monopoly on the sale of wine in London that had been granted to a man named John Peachie. The court held this grant to violate the right of free trade.").

65 E.g., Viamedia, Inc. v. Comcast Corp., 951 F.3d 429,451–52 (7th Cir. 2020); United States v. Microsoft, Inc., 264 F.3d 34, 50–51 (D.C. Cir. 2001); Linkline Communications, Inc. v. SBC California, Inc., 503 F.3d 876, 881 (9th Cir. 2007), *rev'd sub nom.* Pacific Bell Telephone Co. v. Linkline Communications, 555 U.S. 438 (2009); Blix, Inc. v. Apple, Inc., No. 19–1869-LPS, slip op. (D. Del. motion to dismiss granted July 9, 2021); *FTC v. Facebook*, 560 F. Supp. 3d at 12–13. Compare, Pierre LaRouche and Maarten Pieter Schinkel, 'Continental Drift in the Treatment of Dominant Firms,' in *The Oxford Handbook of International Antitrust Economics*, edited by D. Daniel Sokol and Roger D. Blair (Oxford University Press, 2015), pp. 159–63, 181–84.

66 Ugo Mattei, *The rise and fall of law and economics: An essay for Judge Guido Calabresi*, 64 Maryland Law Review 220 (2005), http://digitalcommons.law.umaryland.edu/cgi/viewcontent.cgi?article=3365&context=mlr.

67 Hannibal Travis, 'The FCC's New Theory of the First Amendment,' 51 *Santa Clara Law Review* 417, 428–30, 445 (2011).

68 E.g., Noam Chomsky, The Clinton vision, *Z Magazine* (October 28, 1993), https://www.worldmedia.com/archives/articles/z9312-clinton-vision.html.

69 Eliot G. Disner, 'Antitrust law: The Chicago School meets the real world,' *Los Angeles Lawyer*, March 2002, pp. 14–15, 17.

70 Jonathan L. Rubin, American Antitrust Institute, Response to Public Consultation on the European Commission Directorate-General for Competition Discussion Paper on the Application of Article 82 of the Treaty to Exclusionary Abuses (March 31, 2006), p. 8, https://www.antitrustinstitute.org/recent2/491.pdf.

71 William Page, 'The Chicago School and the evolution of antitrust: Characterization, antitrust injury, and evidentiary sufficiency,' 75 *Virginia Law Review* 1221 (1989);

Jonathan Baker, 'A preface to post-Chicago antitrust,' *in Post-Chicago Developments in Antitrust Law*, edited by Antonio Cucinotta, Roberto Pardolesi and Roger van den Bergh (Edward Elgar, 2002) p. 72. See also, Einer Elhauge and Damien Geradin, *Global Competition Law and Economics* (Bloomsbury, 2011); David Schwartzman, *The Japanese Television Cartel: A Study Based on* Matsushita v. Zenith (University of Michigan Press, 1993); W. Kip Viscusi, Joseph Harrington, and John Vernon, *Economics of Regulation and Antitrust* (The MIT Press, 2005), pp. 319–20.

72 E.g., Rothery Storage & Van Co. v. Atlas Van Lines, Inc., 792 F.2d 210 (D.C. Cir. 1986) (Bork, J., joined by Ginsburg, J., with Wald, J., concurring); LePage's Inc. v. 3M, 324 F.3d 141, 169–82 (3rd Cir. 2003) (Greenberg, J., joined by Alito, J., and Scirica, J., dissenting); Mathews v. Lancaster General Hospital, 87 F.3d 624 (3d Cir. 1996) (Scirica, J., joined by Alito, J., and Weis, J.). Cf. Comcast Cable Communications, LLC v. FCC, 717 F.3d 982, 987–994 (Kavanaugh, J., dissenting) (contending that federal communications law relating to cable networks should be narrowly construed as with recent Sherman Act cases involving vertical restraints, and so as not to deny editorial discretion of cable network providers as to which channels to license from channel providers).

73 Justice Gorsuch, for example, emphasized that refusing ever to deal with a monopolist's competitor or customer is lawful; it is only the termination of a course of dealing that antitrust law requires, and moreover "the monopolist's discontinuation of the preexisting course of dealing must suggest a willingness to forsake short-term profits to achieve an anti-competitive end." *Novell*, 731 F.3d at 1075 (Gorsuch, J.); *see also id.* at 1072–73. Justice Breyer maintained that locking up 50% of the market with a long-term contract with onerous noncancellation clause was neither exclusionary under Section 2 nor unreasonable under Section 1 of the Sherman Act. Barry Wright Corp. v. ITT Grinnell Corp., 724 F. 2d 227, 237–40 (1st Cir. 1983) (Breyer, J.). See also, Kartell v. Blue Shield of Massachusetts, Inc., 749 F. 2d 922, 922–25 (1st Cir. 1984) (Breyer, J.) (holding that Sherman Act not violated by "Blue Shield payment-schedule amounts," which district court found to "interfere with the doctors' freedom to set higher prices for more expensive services and discourages them from developing and offering patients more expensive (and perhaps qualitatively better) services."); Auburn News Co., Inc. v. Providence Journal Co., 659 F. 2d 273 (1st Cir. 1981) (Bownes, J., joined by Breyer J., and Campbell, J.) (vacating preliminary injunction against dominant local newspaper prohibiting it from refusing to deal with independent distributors who competed with its wholly-owned distributor subsidiary).

74 Covad Communications Co. v. Bell Atl. Corp., 398 F.3d 666, 675 (D.C. Cir. 2005) (Ginsburg, J.); Rothery Storage & Van Co., v. Atlas Van Lines, Inc., 792 F.2d 210, 214–215 (D.C. Cir. 1986) (Bork, J.) (opining that, even though Supreme Court has often held group boycotts of competitors to be automatically illegal, they should be found legal as being "common and entirely beneficial business arrangements"); Reifert v. South Cent. Wisconsin MLS Corp., 450 F.3d 312 (7th Cir. 2006) (Flaum, J., joined by Wood, J., and Kanne, J.); Wallace v. International Business Machines Corp., 467 F.3d 1104 (7th Cir. 2006) (Easterbrook, J.); Elliott v. United Center, 126 F. 3d 1003 (7th Cir. 1997) (Wood, J.); Paddock Publications, Inc. v. Chicago Tribune Co., 103 F.3d 42 (7th Cir. 1996) (Easterbrook, J.); Olympia Equip. Leasing Co. v. Western Union Telegraph Co., 797 F.2d 370, 379–80 (7th Cir. 1986) (Posner, J.); see also, Douglas H. Ginsburg, Wikipedia (2023), https://en.wikipedia.org/wiki/Douglas_H._Ginsburg (citing Associated Press, 'Drug furor forces Ginsburg's withdrawal,' *Spokesman-Review (Spokane, Washington)*, Nov. 8, 1987, p. A1, and Associated Press, 'Bork loses by 58–42 Senate vote,' *Eugene Register-Guard*, Oct. 24, 1987, p. 1A); Bill Mears, Supreme Court possibilities if Obama is reelected, *CNN* (October 1, 2012), https://edition.cnn.com/2012/09/30/politics/court-obama-list/index.html (mentioning Judge Wood along with Judge Easterbrook and Judge Posner as intellectual heavyweights and Supreme Court material who teach part-time at the University of Chicago).

75 Raymond Shih Ray Ku, 'The creative destruction of copyright: Napster and the new economics of digital technology,' 69 *University of Chicago Law Review* 263, 301–5 (2002).

76 Ibid.

77 Matt Stoller, *Goliath: The 100-Year War between Monopoly Power and Democracy* (Simon & Schuster, 2019), pp. 359–422; Tim Wu, *The Curse of Bigness: Antitrust in the New Gilded Age* (Columbia Global Reports, 2018), pp. 87–107, 190–200.

78 Matt Stoller, How powerful ideas can shape society: Aaron Director and the triumph of nihilism, *ProMarket* (September 17, 2019), https://www.promarket.org/2019/09/17/how-powerful-ideas-can-shape-society-aaron-director-and-the-triumph-of-nihilism/.

79 Ibid. See also, Stoller, *Goliath*, previous n. 77, pp. 237–56, 362.

80 Stoller, *Goliath*, previous n. 77, pp. 376–82; see also, Jonathan B. Baker and Carl Shapiro, 'Reinvigorating horizontal merger enforcement,' in *How the Chicago School Overshot the Mark: The Effect of Conservative Economics on U.S. Antitrust*, edited by Robert Pitofsky (Oxford University Press, 2008), pp. 235–37, 244–69, 284–85.

81 Wu, *The Curse of Bigness*, previous n. 77, pp. 1–10, 87–107; see also, Amy Klobuchar, *Antitrust: Taking on Monopoly Power from the Gilded Age to the Digital Age* (Knopf, 2021); Stoller, *Goliath*, pp. 407–56; Christopher S. Yoo, 'Hipster antitrust: New bottles, same old w(h)ine?,' *CPI Antitrust Chronicle, April* (2018), pp. 20–25. The origins of the term "hipster" in the moniker is a little ambiguous between old and retro, as in anachronistic in an era of advanced economic thought, and radical urban leftist, as the dominant connotation on social media. E.g., Friso Bostoen, Platform neutrality: Hipster antitrust or logical next step? (Part I), *KU Leiven Center for IT and IP (CITIP) Blog* (December 12, 2017), https://www.law.kuleuven.be/citip/blog/platform-neutrality-hipster-antitrust-or-logical-next-step-part-i/ ("old" ideas make up the school of thought, according to Joshua Wright's thread on Twitter); Nitasha Tiku, Do not mistake Orrin Hatch for #HipsterAntitrust, *Wired* (August, 3, 2017), https://www.wired.com/story/orrin-hatch-antitrust-hipster-antitrust/ (quoting Senator Orrin Hatch Office, Just say no to #HipsterAntitrust (August 3, 2017) [links followed by picture of middle-aged man in arguably hip urban getup]).

82 Friso Bostoen, Platform neutrality: Hipster antitrust or logical next step? (Part II), *KU Leiven Center for IT and IP (CITIP) Blog* (December 14, 2017), https://www.law.kuleuven.be/citip/blog/platform-neutrality-hipster-antitrust-or-logical-next-step-part-ii/. See also, Friso Bostoen, 'Competition law in the peer-to-peer economy,' in *The Platform Economy*, edited by Bram Devolder (Intersentia, 2019), pp. 143–72.

83 John Médaille, A return to a political economy based on distributed property, *P2P Foundation* (August 11, 2012), http://blog.p2pfoundation.net/a-return-to-a-political-economy-based-on-distributed-property/2012/08/11.

84 E.g., Klobuchar, previous n. 81, pp. 196–203, 254, 282, 455; Mazzucato, previous n. 11.

85 Douglas Rushkoff, Interview [The growth trap: The agenda with Steve Paiken on CBC], *YouTube* (April 20, 2016), https://www.youtube.com/watch?time_continue=1117&v=yUGzUktP7jg; Douglas Rushkoff, Medium – How growth became the enemy of prosperity and how to fix it, *Rushkoff.com* (2017), https://www.rushkoff.com/medium-douglas-rushkoff-growth-became-enemy-prosperity-fix/; Douglas Rushkoff, *Throwing Rocks at the Google Bus: How Growth Became the Enemy of Prosperity* (Penguin, 2017), pp. 49–94.

86 Rushkoff, *Throwing Rocks*, pp. 225–26.

87 Ibid.

88 Peter Fraser, Four futures, *Jacobin Magazine* (December 13, 2011), https://jacobinmag.com/2011/12/four-futures

89 Ibid.

90 Slavoj Žižek, 'The revolt of the salaried bourgeoisie,' 34 *London Review of Books* 9 (2012), pp. 9–10. See also Thomas Piketty, *Capitalism in the Twenty-First Century*

(2017), pp. 397–422, 658–62. Piketty wrote of a "super-manager" who extracts an outsized share of the fruits of economic expansion. Ibid., pp. 397–405.
91 *In Defense of Lost Causes* (Verso, 2008), p. 429.
92 Techno-Feudalism is taking over, *Project Syndicate* (June 28, 2021), https://www.project-syndicate.org/commentary/techno-feudalism-replacing-market-capitalism-by-yanis-varoufakis-2021-06.
93 *Cf.* Glossary: Carcerality, *Purdue University*, https://www.purdue.edu/critical-data-studies/collaborative-glossary/carcerality.php (suggesting that carcerality extends the presence of the jail outside its walls, placing persons at a constant risk of incarceration, often without having committed a crime).
94 E.g., Brendan Sasso, 'Digital due process: The government's unfair advantage under the Stored Communications Act,' 8 *Virginia Journal of Criminal Law* 35 (2020).
95 Electronic Information Privacy Center, Social Media Privacy, https://epic.org/issues/consumer-privacy/social-media-privacy/.
96 E.g., Digital Services Act, arts. 11, 18, 22–23, 28, 34–37, 40.
97 *Behemoth: The Structure and Practice of National Socialism, 1933–1944* (Ivan R. Dee, 2009), p. 44.
98 E.g., David Walton, *Doing Cultural Theory* (SAGE Publications Ltd., 2012).
99 Louis Althusser, 'Ideology and ideological state apparatuses: Notes towards an investigation,' in *Lenin and Philosophy*, edited by Louis Althusser (Monthly Review Press, 1971), pp. 128–48.
100 Ibid.; see also, Louis Althusser, *On the Reproduction of Capitalism: Ideology and Ideological State Apparatuses*, translated by G.M. Goshgarian (Verso, 2014).
101 Michel Foucault, 'Nietzsche, genealogy, history,' in *Language, Counter-Memory, Practice*, edited by Donald Bouchard, translated by Sherry Simon (1977), p. 150; Michel Foucault, 'Theatrum philosophicum,' in *ibid.*, p. 191; Michel Foucault, 'What is Enlightenment?', *in The Foucault Reader*, edited by Paul Rabinow (1984), p. 57.
102 Klobuchar, Lummis Introduce Bipartisan Legislation, U.S. Senator Amy Klobuchar (2022), https://www.klobuchar.senate.gov/public/index.cfm/2022/2/klobuchar-lummis-introduce-bipartisan-legislation-to-address-problems-in-social-media-algorithms.
103 E.g., Giancarlo Frosio and Christoph Geiger, 'Taking Fundamental Rights Seriously in the Digital Services Act's Platform Liability Regime,' 29 *European Law Journal* 31 (2023).

Bibliography

15 U.S.C. §§ 1–2.

303 Creative LLC v. Elenis, 600 U.S. 570, 603, 143 S. Ct. 2298, 2322 (2023) (Sotomayor, J., joined by Kagan J., and Jackson, J., dissenting).

Edward Adler, 'Business jurisprudence,' 28 *Harvard Law Review* 135 (1914).

Louis Althusser, 'Ideology and ideological state apparatuses: Notes towards an investigation,' in *Lenin and Philosophy*, edited by Louis Althusser (Monthly Review Press, 1971), pp. 128–48.

American Dental Cooperative, Inc. v. Attorney General of State of New York, 514 N.Y.S.2d 228 (N.Y. App. Div. 1st Dep't 1987).

Apple Inc. v. Samsung Electronics Co., Ltd., 786 F. 3d 983 (Fed. Cir. 2015).

Aspen Skiing Co. v. Aspen Highlands Skiing Corp., 472 U.S. 585 (1985).

Atlantic Richfield Co. v. USA Petroleum Co., 495 U.S. 328 (1990).

Louis Althusser, 'Ideology and ideological state apparatuses: Notes towards an investigation,' in *Lenin and Philosophy*, edited by Louis Althusser (Monthly Review Press, 1971).

Louis Althusser, *On the Reproduction of Capitalism: Ideology and Ideological State Apparatuses*, translated by G.M. Goshgarian (Verso, 2014).

Auburn News Co., Inc. v. Providence Journal Co., 659 F. 2d 273 (1st Cir. 1981) (Bownes, J., joined by Breyer J., and Campbell, J.).

Autorità garante della Concorrenza e del Mercato [Italian Competitive Markets Authority], Press release A528 – Antitrust – Amazon fined over € 1,128 billion for abusing its dominant position (2021), www.en.agcm.it.

Jonathan Baker, 'A preface to post-Chicago antitrust,' in *Post-Chicago Developments in Antitrust Law*, edited by Antonio Cucinotta, Roberto Pardolesi, and Roger van den Bergh (Edward Elgar, 2002), p. 72.

Jonathan B. Baker and Carl Shapiro, 'Reinvigorating horizontal merger enforcement,' in *How the Chicago School Overshot the Mark: The Effect of Conservative Economics on U.S. Antitrust*, edited by Robert Pitofsky (Oxford University Press, 2008), pp. 235–85.

Barry Wright Corp. v. ITT Grinnell Corp., 724 F. 2d 227 (1st Cir. 1983) (Breyer, J.).

Beall v. Beck, 2 F. Cas. 1111 (C.C. D.C. 1829).

Silvia Beltrametti, 'Capturing the transplant: US antitrust law in the European Union,' 48 *Vanderbilt Journal of Transnational Law* 1147 (2015).

Alex Berenson, 'Lifting the kimono (uh-oh, trigger alert) a little more on *Berenson v. Twitter*,' Substack, July 1, 2022, https://alexberenson.substack.com/p/lifting-the-kimono-uh-oh-trigger.

Berenson v. Twitter, Inc., No. C 21–09818 WHA, slip op. (N.D. Cal. April 29, 2022).

Best Carpet Values, Inc., v. Google LLC, No. 5:20-cv-04700-EJD, slip op. (N.D. Cal. September 24, 2021).

Beverage Management, Inc. v. Coca-Cola Bottling Corp., 653 F.Supp. 1144 (S.D. Ohio 1986).

William Blackstone, *Commentaries on the Laws of England*, Vol. 1 (The Clarendon Press, 1765).

William Blackstone, *Commentaries on the Laws of England*, Vol. 3 (The Clarendon Press, 1768).

Blix, Inc. v. Apple, Inc., No. 19–1869-LPS, slip op. (D. Del. motion to dismiss granted July 9, 2021).

Bookhouse of Stuyvesant Plaza, Inc. v. Amazon. Com, 985 F. Supp. 2d 612 (S.D.N.Y. 2013).

Friso Bostoen, Platform neutrality: Hipster antitrust or logical next step? (part I), *KU Leiven Center for IT and IP (CITIP) Blog* (December 12, 2017), www.law.kuleuven.be/citip/blog/platform-neutrality-hipster-antitrust-or-logical-next-step-part-i/.

Friso Bostoen, Platform neutrality: Hipster antitrust or logical next step? (part II), *KU Leiven Center for IT and IP (CITIP) Blog* (December 14, 2017), https://www.law.kuleuven.be/citip/blog/platform-neutrality-hipster-antitrust-or-logical-next-step-part-ii/.

Friso Bostoen, 'Competition law in the peer-to-peer economy,' in *The Platform Economy*, edited by Bram Devolder (Intersentia, 2019), pp. 143–72.

Edward Grant Buckland, 'Combinations and trusts,' 16 *New Englander and Yale Review* 241 (1890).

Central R.R. Co. v. Collins, 40 Ga. 582 (1869).

Butchers' Union Slaughter-House & Live-Stock Landing Co. v. Crescent City Live-Stock Landing and Slaughter House Co., 111 U.S. 746, 761 (1884) (Bradley, J., concurring).

Caldera, Inc. v. Microsoft Corp., 72 F. Supp. 2d 1295 (D. Utah 1999).

Caribbean Broad. Sys. Ltd. v. Cable & Wireless PLC, 148 F.3d 1080 (D.C. Cir. 1998).

Noam Chomsky, The Clinton vision, *Z Magazine* (October 28, 1993), https://www.world-media.com/archives/articles/z9312-clinton-vision.html.

City of Memphis v. Winfield, 27 Tenn. 707 (1848).

Maggie Clark, CCIA sponsored event: Content moderation & removal at scale, *CCIA* (2018), https://www.ccianet.org/2018/01/content-moderation-removal-at-scale/.

The Cloth Workers of Ipswich, 78 Eng. Rep. 147 (K.B. 1615).

CNET Highlights, 'WATCH: DOJ Announce Antitrust Enforcement against Google – LIVE,' YouTube, 2023, www.youtube.com/watch?v=sNL62LaUQ1U.

Sir Edward Coke, *Institutes of the Laws of England*, Vol. 3 (facsimile ed., W.S. Hein Company, 1986) [1641].
Craft v. McConoughy, 79 Ill. 346 (1875).
Sir Edward Coke, *The Second Part of the Institutes of the Laws of England: Containing the Exposition of Many Ancient and Other Statutes*, Vol. 1 (W. Clarke & Sons, 1809).
Comcast Cable Communications, LLC v. FCC, 717 F.3d 982, 987–994 (Kavanaugh, J., dissenting).
Competition and Markets Authority (CMA) [of the United Kingdom of Great Britain and Northern Ireland], Press Release – CMA Investigates Facebook's Use of ad Data, 2021, https://www.gov.uk.
Computer & Communications Industry Association [CCIA], National Security Issues Posed by House Antitrust Bills (2022), https://www.ccianet.org/2021/09/ccia-whitepaper-identifies-national-security-risks-posed-by-house-bills-targeting-u-s-tech-companies/.
21 *Congressional Record* 137 (1889) (statement of Sen. Turpie).
21 *Congressional Record* 1457–58 (1889) (statement of Sen. Jones).
21 *Congressional Record* 1768 (1889) (statement of Sen. George).
21 *Congressional Record* 2457 (1889) (statement of Sen. Sherman).
21 *Congressional Record* 2462 (1889) (statement of Sen. Sherman) (quoting statement of Sen. George).
21 Congressional Record 2598 (1889) (statement of Sen. George).
21 *Congressional Record* 2726 (1889) (statement of Sen. Edmunds).
21 *Congressional Record* 3147 (1889) (statement of Sen. George).
21 *Congressional Record* 4098 (1890) (statement of Rep. Taylor).
21 *Congressional Record* 4102 (1890) (statement of Rep. Fithian).
Corfield v. Coryell, 6 F. Cas. 546 (C.C.E.D. Pa. 1825) (No. 3,230).
Covad Communications Co. v. Bell Atlantic Corp., 398 F.3d 666 (D.C. Cir. 2005) (Ginsburg, J.).
Cox v. Microsoft Corp., 778 N.Y.S.2d 147 (N.Y. App. Div. 1st Dep't 2004).
Craft v. McConoughy, 79 Ill. 346 (1875).
Creative Trading Co., Inc. v. Larkin-Pluznick-Larkin, Inc., 75 N.Y.2d 830, 552 N.Y.S.2d 558 (1990), *adopting dissenting opinion in* 148 A.D.2d 352, 539 N.Y.S.2d 1 (1st Dep't 1989).
Darcy v. Allein (The Case of Monopolies), 77 Eng. Rep. 1260 (K.B. 1602).
Deutscher Bundeskartellamt, Press release 080/2020, KVR 69/19, Federal Court of Justice provisionally confirms allegation of Facebook abusing dominant position (2020).
Renee DiResta, Free speech is not the same as free reach, *Wired* (August 30, 2018), https://www.wired.com/story/free-speech-is-not-the-same-as-free-reach.
Eliot G. Disner, Antitrust law: The Chicago School meets the real world, *Los Angeles Lawyer* (March 2002), pp. 14–7.
Domen v. Vimeo, Inc., 6 F.4th 245 (2d Cir. 2021), *withdrawn*, 2021 WL 4399692 (2d Cir. Sept. 23, 2021).
Dreamstime.com, LLC v. Google, LLC, 470 F. Supp. 3d 1082 (N.D. Cal. 2020), *prior proceedings at* Dreamstime.com, LLC v. Google, LLC, No. C 18–01910 WHA, 2019 WL 2372280 (N.D. Cal. June 5, 2019), *prior proceedings at* 2019 WL 341579 (N.D. Cal. Jan. 28, 2019).
Case T-612/17, Google and Alphabet v. Commission (Google Shopping), ECLI:EU:T:2021:763.
Electronic Information Privacy Center, Social Media Privacy, https://epic.org/issues/consumer-privacy/social-media-privacy/.
Elias Deutscher, 'Google shopping and the quest for a legal test for self-preferencing under article 102 TFEU,' 6 *European Papers* 1345 (2021).
e-Ventures Worldwide, LLC v. Google, Inc., 188 F. Supp. 3d 1265 (M.D. Fla. 2016).
The East India Co. v. Sandys (The Great Case of Monopolies), 10 St. Tr. 371 (1683).
Eastman Kodak Co. v. Image Technical Servs., Inc., 504 U.S. 451 (1992).
Ebeid v. Facebook, Inc., No. 18-CV-07030-PJH, 2019 WL 2059662 (N.D. Cal. May 9, 2019).

'Editorial, New Big Tech rules will harm conservatives,' *L.A. Daily News* (January 27, 2022), p. 11.
Einer Elhauge and Damien Geradin, *Global Competition Law and Economics* (Bloomsbury, 2011).
Elliott v. United Center, 126 F. 3d 1003 (7th Cir. 1997) (Wood, J.).
Epic Games, Inc. v. Apple, Inc., No. 4:20-cv-05640-YGR, 2020 WL 5073937 (N.D. Cal. mot. for prelim. inj. denied August 24, 2020), *further proceedings at* 493 F. Supp. 3d 817 (N.D. Cal. 2020), *aff'd in part,* 67 F.4th 946 (9th Cir. 2023).
EU Digital Services Act will restructure tech services, *Oxford Analytica* (2022), https://www.emerald.com/insight/content/doi/10.1108/OXAN-DB270191/full/html
European Commission, Press release IP/19/4291, Antitrust: EC opens formal investigation against Amazon (July 17, 2019), https://ec.europa.eu/commission/presscorner/detail/en/IP_19_4291.
European Commission, Press Release IP/20/1073, Antitrust: Commission Opens Investigations into Apple's App Store Rules (2020), https://ec.europa.eu/commission.
European Commission, Press release IP/20/2077 – Antitrust: Commission sends Statement of Objections to Amazon for the Use of Non-public Independent Seller Data and Opens Second Investigation into Its E-commerce Business Practices (2020), https://ec.europa.eu/commission.
European Commission, Press release IP/21/2061, Antitrust: Commission sends Statement of Objections to Apple on App Store rules for music streaming providers (2021), https://ec.europa.eu/commission.
European Commission, Press release IP/22/2764, Press release Antitrust: Commission sends Statement of Objections to Apple over practices regarding Apple Pay (2022), https://ec.europa.eu/commission.
European Commission, Antitrust: Commission opens investigation into possible anti-competitive conduct of Amazon (2019), https://ec.europa.eu/commission.
Fashion Originators' Guild of America v. FTC, 312 U.S. 457 (1941).
Federal Agency of News LLC v. Facebook, Inc., 432 F. Supp. 3d 1107 (N.D. Cal. 2020).
R.S. French, In hope of convergence: A regional perspective on competition law, Paper Presented to 2009 Competition Law Conference, Sydney, Australia (May 23, 2009), https://www.hcourt.gov.au/assets/publications/speeches/current-justices/frenchcj/french-cj23may09.pdf.
Michel Foucault, 'Nietzsche, genealogy, history,' in *Language, Counter-Memory, Practice*, edited by Donald Bouchard, translated by Sherry Simon (Cornell University Press, 1977), p. 150.
Michel Foucault, 'Theatrum philosophicum,' in *Language, Counter-Memory, Practice*, edited by Donald Bouchard, translated by Sherry Simon (Cornell University Press, 1977), p. 191.
Michel Foucault, 'What is Enlightenment?,' in *The Foucault Reader*, edited by Paul Rabinow (Pantheon Books, 1984), p. 57.
Peter Fraser, Four futures, *Jacobin Magazine* (December 13, 2011), https://jacobinmag.com/2011/12/four-futures.
Giancarlo Frosio and Christoph Geiger, 'Taking Fundamental Rights Seriously in the Digital Services Act's Platform Liability Regime,' 29 *European Law Journal* 31 (2023).
FTC v. Indiana Federation of Dentists, 476 U.S. 447 (1990).
Brian Fung, Landmark Google trial opens with sweeping DOJ accusations of illegal monopolization, *CNN* (September 12, 2023), https://www.cnn.com/2023/09/12/tech/google-antitrust-lawsuit-government-trial-duplicate-2/index.html.
German Alliance Ins. Co. v. Lewis, 233 U.S. 389 (1914).
Gibbs v. Consolidated Gas Co. of Baltimore, 32 U.S. 411 (1888).
Douglas H. Ginsburg, Wikipedia (2023), https://en.wikipedia.org/wiki/Douglas_H._Ginsburg.
Glossary: Carcerality, *Purdue University*, https://www.purdue.edu/critical-data-studies/collaborative-glossary/carcerality.php.

Google Inc., 2019 Annual Report on Form 10-k, htttps://www.vox.com/2017/3/14/14890122/google-search-ad-market-share-growth.
Heather Greenfield, CCIA responds to manager's amendment to controversial antitrust bill, *CCIA* (2022), https://www.ccianet.org/2022/05/ccia-responds-to-managers-amendment-to-controversial-antitrust-bill/.
Hazelhurst v. Savannah R.R. Co. 43 Ga. 13 (1871).
HiQ Labs, Inc. v. LinkedIn Corp., 485 F. Supp. 3d 1137 (N.D. Cal. 2020).
HiQ Labs, Inc. v. LinkedIn Corp., 273 F. Supp. 3d 1099 (N.D. Cal. 2017), *aff'd*, 937 F.3d 985 (9th Cir. 2019), vacated and remanded on other grounds, LinkedIn Corp. v. HiQ Labs, Inc., 593 U.S. ___, 141 S. Ct. 2752 (2021).
In re Apple iPod iTunes Antitrust Litigation, 796 F. Supp. 2d 1137 (N.D. Cal. 2011), *further proceedings at* No. 05-CV-0037 YGR, slip op. (N.D. Cal. Sept. 26, 2014), *jury verdict for defendant* (N.D. Cal. Dec. 16, 2014).
Ingate v. Christie, 3 Car. & K. 61, 63, 175 Eng. Rep. 463 (N. P. 1850).
International Boxing Club v. United States, 348 U.S. 236 (1955).
Intimate Bookshop, Inc. v. Barnes & Noble, Inc., 88 F. Supp. 2d 133 (S.D.N.Y. 2000).
In re Apple iPod iTunes Antitrust Litig., 796 F. Supp. 2d 1137 (N.D. Cal. 2011).
Jefferson Parish Hospital Dist. No. 2 v. Hyde, 466 U.S. 2 (1984).
Makena Kelly, Amazon silently ends controversial pricing agreements with sellers, *The Verge* (March 11, 2019), https://www.theverge.com/2019/3/11/18260700/amazon-anti-competitive-pricing-agreements-3rd-party-sellers-end.
Kickflip, Inc. v. Facebook, Inc., 999 F. Supp. 2d 677 (D. Del. 2013).
Kinderstart.com LLC v. Google, Inc., No. C06–2057 JFRS, 2007 WL 831806, *13–15 (N.D. Cal. Mar. 16, 2007).
Inform, Inc. v. Google, Inc. No. 1:19-cv-05362-JPB (N.D. Ga. first amended complaint filed Oct. 9, 2020).
JUST IN: Lindsey Graham slams Facebook, Twitter over 'New York Post' Hunter Biden article, *YouTube* (October 15, 2020), www.youtube.com/watch?v=D-QTGLd4x3I.
Amy Klobuchar, *Antitrust: Taking on Monopoly Power from the Gilded Age to the Digital Age* (Knopf, 2021).
Raymond Shih Ray Ku, 'The creative destruction of copyright: Napster and the new economics of digital technology,' 69 *University of Chicago Law Review* 263 (2002).
Milton Konvitz and Theodore Leskes, *A Century of Civil Rights* (Columbia University Press, 1961).
Lane v. Cotton, 88 Eng. Rep. 1458 (K. B. 1701) (Holt, C. J.).
Langdon v. Google, Inc., 474 F. Supp. 2d 622 (D. Del. 2007).
Pierre LaRouche and Maarten Pieter Schinkel, 'Continental Drift in the Treatment of Dominant Firms,' in *The Oxford Handbook of International Antitrust Economics*, edited by D. Daniel Sokol and Roger D. Blair (Oxford University Press, 2015), pp. 159–84.
Dan Levine, Apple, Google settle smartphone patent litigation, *Reuters* (May 16, 2014), https://www.reuters.com.
Linkline Communications, Inc. v. SBC California, Inc., 503 F.3d 876 (9th Cir. 2007), *rev'd sub nom.* Pacific Bell Telephone Co. v. Linkline Communications, 555 U.S. 438 (2009).
Melissa Lippman, Yelp accuses Google of breaking search bias vows to FTC, *Law360* (September 12, 2017), https://www.law360.com/articles/962892/yelp-accuses-google-of-breaking-search-bias-vows-to-ftc.
LePage's Inc. v. 3M, 324 F.3d 141, 169–82 (3rd Cir. 2003) (en banc) (Greenberg, J., joined by Alito, J., and Scirica, J., dissenting).
LiveUniverse, Inc. v. Myspace, Inc., No. CV 06–6994 AHM (RZx), 2007 WL 6865852 (N.D. Cal. June 4, 2007), *aff'd*, 304 Fed. App'x 554 (9th Cir. 2008).
Lorain Journal Co. v. United States, 342 U.S. 143 (1951).
Mad Max: Beyond Thunderdome (1985), written by George Miller and Terry Hayes, and directed by George Miller and George Ogilvie.

Mad Max: The Road Warrior (1981), written by Terry Hayes, George Miller, and Brian Hannant, and directed by George Miller.
James Madison, 'Monopolies. Perpetuities. Corporations. Ecclesiastical Endowments.,' in *Writings*, edited by Jack Rakove (Library of America, 1999), p. 756.
James Madison, 'Property,' in *Writings of James Madison, Volume IV: 1829–1836* (J.P. Lippincott Co., 1867), p. 475.
Magna Charta, art. 41 (1215), https://www.uni-bielefeld.de/lili/personen/fleischmann/archwise04/32_hse_magnacarta.htm?support_person=bskpvvjs6odvmb1b2u9ah9jrh1.
Mathews v. Lancaster General Hospital, 87 F.3d 624 (3d Cir. 1996) (Scirica, J., joined by Alito, J., and Weis, J.).
Ugo Mattei, 'The rise and fall of law and economics: An essay for Judge Guido Calabresi,' 64 *Maryland Law Review* 220 (2005), http://digitalcommons.law.umaryland.edu/cgi/viewcontent.cgi?article=3365&context=mlr.
Bill Mears, Supreme Court possibilities if Obama is reelected, *CNN* (October 1, 2012), https://edition.cnn.com/2012/09/30/politics/court-obama-list/index.html.
John Médaille, A return to a political economy based on distributed property, *P2P Foundation* (August 11, 2012), http://blog.p2pfoundation.net/a-return-to-a-political-economy-based-on-distributed-property/2012/08/11.
John Stuart Mill, *On Liberty* (Longman, Roberts & Co., 4th ed. 1869).
Mitchel v. Reynolds, 24 Eng. Rep. 347 (Q.B. 1711).
Morris Run Coal Co. v. Barclay Coal Co., 68 Pa. St. 173 (1871).
Motion Picture Patents Co. v. Universal Film Manufacturing Co., 243 U.S. 502 (1917).
Kartell v. Blue Shield of Massachusetts, Inc., 749 F. 2d 922 (1st Cir. 1984) (Breyer, J.).
Franz Neumann. *Behemoth: The Structure and Practice of National Socialism, 1933–1944* (Ivan R. Dee, 2009).
Nyabwa v. Facebook, No. 2:17-CV-24, 2018 WL 585467 (S.D. Tex. Jan. 26, 2018).
Neri's Land Imp., LLC v. J.J. Cassone Bakery, Inc., 65 A.D.3d 1312, 886 N.Y.S.2d 202 (2d Dep't 2009).
NCAA v. Board of Regents of the University of Oklahoma, 468 U.S. 85 (1984).
National Numismatic Certification, LLC v. eBay, Inc., No. 6:08-cv-42-Orl-19GJK, 2008 WL 2704404 (M.D. Fla. July 8, 2008).
New York v. Facebook, Inc., 549 F. Supp. 3d 6 (D.D.C. 2021), *aff'd sub nom*. New York v. Meta Platforms, Inc., 66 F.4th 288 (D.C. Cir. 2023).
Olympia Equip. Leasing Co. v. Western Union Telegraph Co., 797 F.2d 370 (7th Cir. 1986) (Posner, J.).
Paddock Publications, Inc. v. Chicago Tribune Co., 103 F.3d 42 (7th Cir. 1996) (Easterbrook, J.).
Otter Tail Power Co. v. United States, 410 U.S. 366 (1973).
Pacific Bell Telephone Co. v. Linkline Comm., 555 U.S. 438 (2009).
William Page, 'The Chicago School and the evolution of antitrust: Characterization, antitrust injury, and evidentiary sufficiency,' 75 *Virginia Law Review* 1221 (1989).
Theophilus Parsons, *Law of Contracts*, vol. 1 (Little, Brown, and Co., 1853).
Frank Pasquale, Internet nondiscrimination principles revisited, Brooklyn Law School, Legal Studies Paper No. 655 (2020), https://papers.ssrn.com/sol3/papers.cfm?abstract_id=3634625.
People ex rel. Peabody v. Chicago Gas Trust Co., 130 Ill. 268 (1889).
People v. North River Sugar Ref. Co., 121 N.Y. 582, 625 (1890).
Richardson v. Buhl, 77 Mich. 632 (1889).
Thomas Piketty, *Capitalism in the Twenty-First Century* (Harvard University Press, 2017).
Pittsburgh Press Co. v. Pittsburgh Comm'n on Human Relations, 413 U.S. 376 (1973).
Plaintiff's Complaint, Rumble, Inc. v. Google, LLC, No. 21-cv-00229-HSG (N.D. Cal. complaint filed 2021).
Plaintiffs' Pre-Trial Brief, United States v. Google, No. 1:20-cv-03010-APM (D.D.C. brief filed September 8, 2023).

Aurelien Portuese, When demotion is competition: Algorithmic antitrust, Concurrences N°2–2018/SSRN (2018), https://papers.ssrn.com/sol3/papers.cfm?abstract_id=3188776.

Prager Univ. v. Google LLC, No. 17-CV-06064-LHK, 2018 WL 1471939 (N.D. Cal. March 26, 2018), *aff'd*, 951 F.3d 991 (9th Cir. 2020).

Regulation on a single market for digital services and amending Directive 2000/31/EC (Digital Services Act), COM/2020/825, *Official Journal L* 277 (October 27, 2022), pp. 1–102.

Reifert v. South Cent. Wisconsin MLS Corp., 450 F.3d 312 (7th Cir. 2006) (Flaum, J., joined by Wood, J., and Kanne, J.).

Rothery Storage & Van Co. v. Atlas Van Lines, Inc., 792 F.2d 210 (D.C. Cir. 1986) (Bork, J., joined by Ginsburg, J., with Wald, J., concurring).

Jonathan L. Rubin, American Antitrust Institute, Response to Public Consultation on the European Commission Directorate-General for Competition Discussion Paper on the Application of Article 82 of the Treaty to Exclusionary Abuses (March 31, 2006), https://www.antitrustinstitute.org/recent2/491.pdf.

Douglas Rushkoff, Interview [The growth trap: The agenda with Steve Paiken on CBC], *YouTube* (April 20, 2016), https://www.youtube.com/watch?time_continue=1117&v=yUGzUktP7jg.

Douglas Rushkoff, Medium – How growth became the enemy of prosperity and how to fix it, *Rushkoff.com* (2017), https://www.rushkoff.com/medium-douglas-rushkoff-growth-became-enemy-prosperity-fix/.

Douglas Rushkoff, *Throwing Rocks at the Google Bus: How Growth Became the Enemy of Prosperity* (Penguin, 2017).

Rutenberg v. Twitter, Inc., No. 4:21-cv-0548, slip op. (N.D. Cal. Apr. 9, 2021).

Salt Co. v. Guthrie, 35 Ohio St. 666, 672 (1880).

Sambreel Holdings LLC v. Facebook, Inc., 906 F. Supp. 2d 1070, 1082 (N.D. Cal. 2012).

Timothy Sandefur, 'The common law right to earn a living,' VI *The Independent Review* 69 (2002).

Sands v. Ticketmaster-N.Y., Inc., 616 N.Y.S.2d 362 (N.Y. App. Div. 1st Dep't 1994).

Brendan Sasso, 'Digital due process: The government's unfair advantage under the Stored Communications Act,' 8 *Virginia Journal of Criminal Law* 35 (2020).

Sayre v. Google, Inc. No. No. C 19–02247 WHA, slip op. at 1.C. (N.D. Cal. Nov. 14, 2019).

Bilal Sayyed, Grassley/Klobuchar regulations on companies would hurt tech competition, consumers, Des Moines Register/*WestlawNext* (December 14, 2021), https://1.next.westlaw.com (subscription required).

David Schwartzman, *The Japanese Television Cartel: A Study Based on* Matsushita v. Zenith (University of Michigan Press, 1993).

Search King, Inc. v. Google Tech., Inc., 2003 WL 21464568, at *4 (W.D. Okla. May 27, 2003).

Senator Orrin Hatch Office, Just say no to #HipsterAntitrust (August 3, 2017), https://www.twitter.com.

Shulman v. Facebook.com, No. CV 17–764 (JMV), 2017 WL 5129885 (D.N.J. Nov. 6, 2017).

Sikhs for Justice, Inc. v. Facebook, Inc., 697 Fed. App'x 526 (9th Cir. 2017).

Simon-Whelan v. The Andy Warhol Foundation for the Visual Arts, Inc., 2009–1 Trade Cases P 76,657, 2009 WL 1457177 (S.D.N.Y. 2009).

Standard Oil Co. v. United States, 221 U.S. 1 (1911).

Standard Oil Co. (Indiana) v. United States, 283 U.S. 162 (1931).

Statcounter, Search Engine Market Share (2020), https://gs.statcounter.com/search-engine-market-share.

Statcounter, Browser Market Share (2020), https://gs.statcounter.com/browser-market-share.

Statcounter, OS market share mobile, worldwide (2020), https://gs.statcounter.com/os-market-share/mobile/worldwide.

State ex rel. Attorney Gen. v. Standard Oil Co., 30 N.E. 279 (Ohio 1892).

State v. Nebraska Distilling Co., 29 Neb. 700 (1890).

Matt Stoller, *Goliath: The 100-Year War Between Monopoly Power and Democracy* (Simon & Schuster, 2019).

Matt Stoller, How powerful ideas can shape society: Aaron Director and the triumph of nihilism, *ProMarket* (September 17, 2019), https://www.promarket.org/2019/09/17/how-powerful-ideas-can-shape-society-aaron-director-and-the-triumph-of-nihilism/.

Joseph Story, *Commentaries on the Law of Bailments* (Charles C. Little and James Brown, 1837).

Nitasha Tiku, Do not mistake Orrin Hatch for #HipsterAntitrust, *Wired* (August 3, 2017), https://www.wired.com/story/orrin-hatch-antitrust-hipster-antitrust/.

Timken Roller Bearing Co. v. United States, 341 U.S. 593 (1951).

Trans. Co. v. Pipe Line Co. 22 W. Va. 600 (1883)).

Hannibal Travis, 'The FCC's new theory of the First Amendment,' 51 *Santa Clara Law Review* 417 (2011).

Tucker v. Apple Computer, Inc., 493 F. Supp. 2d 1090 (N.D. Cal. 2006).

U.S. Football League v. Nat'l Football League, 634 F. Supp. 1155 (S.D.N.Y. 1986).

United States v. Addyston Pipe & Steel Co., 85 F. 271 (6th Cir. 1898).

United States v. Aluminum Co. of America, 148 F.2d 416 (2d Cir. 1945).

United States v. American Tobacco Co., 221 U.S. 106 (1911).

United States v. American Tobacco Co., 328 U.S. 781 (1946).

United States v. Arnold, Schwinn & Co., 388 U.S. 365 (1967) (Stewart, J., joined by Harlan, J., dissenting).

United States v. Apple, Inc., 791 F.3d 209 (2d Cir. 2015).

United States v. E.C. Knight Co., 156 U.S. 1, 18–46 (1895) (Harlan, J., dissenting).

United States v. Microsoft, Inc., 264 F.3d 34 (D.C. Cir. 2001).

United States v. Socony-Vacuum Oil Co., 310 U.S. 150 (1940)

United States v. Terminal Railroad Assoc., 224 U.S. 383 (1912).

United States v. United States Steel Corp., 251 U.S. 417 (1920).

United States v. Topco Assocs., Inc., 405 U.S. 596 (1972).

Wallace v. International Business Machines Corp., 467 F.3d 1104 (7th Cir. 2006) (Easterbrook, J.).

Yanis Varoufakis, Techno-feudalism is taking over, *Project Syndicate* (June 28, 2021), https://www.project-syndicate.org/commentary/techno-feudalism-replacing-market-capitalism-by-yanis-varoufakis-2021-06.

W. Kip Viscusi, Joseph Harrington, and John Vernon, *Economics of Regulation and Antitrust* (The MIT Press, 2005).

Spencer Weber Waller, 'Antitrust and social networking,' 90 *North Carolina Law Review* 1771 (2010–2011).

Spencer Weber Waller, 'The omega man or the isolation of US antitrust law,' 52 *Connecticut Law Review* 123 (2020).

David Walton, *Doing Cultural Theory* (2012).

WATCH: Twitter and Facebook CEOs testify in Senate hearing, The Washington Post/*YouTube* (2020), https://www.youtube.com/watch?v=9nwnYPcIano.

Murdoch Watney, 'Regulation of social media intermediary liability for illegal and harmful content,' 9 *European Conference on Social Media* 194 (2022).

Wilk v. American Medical Association, 895 F.2d 353 (7th Cir. 1990).

Tim Wu, *The Curse of Bigness: Antitrust in the New Gilded Age* (Columbia Global Reports, 2018).

Verizon Communs., Inc. v. Law Offices of Curtis V. Trinko, LLP, 540 U.S. 398 (2004).

Viamedia, Inc. v. Comcast Corp., 951 F.3d 429 (7th Cir. 2020).

Yick Wo v. Hopkins, 118 U.S. 356 (1886).

Christopher S. Yoo, 'Hipster antitrust: New bottles, same old w(h)ine?,' *CPI Antitrust Chronicle*, April, 2018, pp. 20–25.

Gabriela Zanfir-Fortuna and Vasileios Rovilos, EU's Digital Services Act just became applicable: Outlining ten key areas of interplay with the GDPR, *Future of Privacy Forum* (August 31, 2023), https://fpf.org/blog/eus-digital-services-act-just-became-applicable-outlining-ten-key-areas-of-interplay-with-the-gdpr/.

Zhang v. Baidu.com, Inc., 10 F. Supp. 3d 433 (S.D.N.Y. 2014).

Slavoj Žižek, *In Defense of Lost Causes* (Verso, 2008).

Slavoj Žižek, 'The revolt of the salaried bourgeoisie,' 34 *London Review of Books* 9(2012), pp. 9–10.

5 Locking the Web "Open"

Paths to a Neutral Online Environment

In this final chapter, brief summaries of several paths forward are presented. Downranking and demotion algorithms and practices challenge legal and social norms in several ways.

There are at least seven paths to ensuring a free and open Internet in the 21st century, despite the rise of dominant websites and apps, coordinated inauthentic activity, and bad-faith deplatforming. The first path has perhaps the oldest roots, and it involves regulating monopoly and oligopoly power. Some threats to fair competition are the domain of antitrust law.

The second path involves the First Amendment more directly. It grows out of a recent ruling addressing encouragement or pressure from the federal government directed to websites or apps and winning their cooperation in censoring citizens.

The third and fourth paths involve the ability to legislate neutral or evenhanded treatment. The Federal Communications Commission or FCC might have the authority to remove barriers to small businesses succeeding in the online environment, perhaps including some form of platform neutrality. Alternatively, a form of net neutrality for websites and apps might exist at the level of the U.S. states, or at varying national or regional levels in other countries. Arbitrary or discriminatory conduct can be a violation of duties owed to the public by either a private deputy of the state or as a common carrier under the First Amendment, state anti-deplatforming law, or international human rights law. There may also be a state constitutional right to use private property for purposes of speech or petitioning the powerful for relief, or a state statutory right to be protected from arbitrary or discriminatory suppression of one's identity or viewpoint.

The Section 230 privilege could be revised to better fulfill its purpose of promoting the development of the Internet for the benefit of the American people by requiring viewpoint-neutrality in content moderation, or clarifying its actual scope as not applying to removals of user content that is not excessively violent, lewd, harassing, and the like. A new version of net neutrality could cover gatekeeper websites, apps, and devices as well as broadband firms. The chapter touches on how it could be set up by the FCC, the FTC, the European Commission, or a new e-commerce or digital-services agency in the United States.

The fifth and sixth paths relate to federal policies outside the constitutional or communications law areas. At the federal level, there are at least two purposes or

DOI: 10.4324/9781003496106-6

aims that federal law implements in this area: ensuring free and fair elections where candidates access the public sphere without media or technology barons gifting favored candidates the most screen time, and promoting creativity and innovation through the intellectual-property system in ways that are carefully calibrated to prevent rightsholders from aggregating too much power over the media. Disguised political campaign contributions in the form of boosting or throttling partisan electoral communications could undermine a public's right to free and fair elections, while intervention in altering or mutilating authors' or videographers' bodies of work undermines the rights of creators.

One final path forward requires a change in technical or business models as well as legal standards. The distributed Web (DWeb or Web3) and the metaverse could be domains of less centralized and more open forms of commerce and communication than Web2 giants can offer. As ranking and sharing technologies, computing power, digital storage, and community standards come to be developed by consensus and a cooperative approach, the radically egalitarian promise of the early Internet gets revived.

A Right to a Fair Deal Online?

Despite some setbacks since the 1960s in establishing an antitrust duty to deal fairly with others, the duty to interconnect or remain interoperable may be emerging with surprising strength. In four cases involving Apple Computer, federal courts addressed a dominant device and content provider's assertions that it had no duty to deal with its rivals. The first case involved Apple supposedly controlling digital music distribution by making iPods incompatible with rival licensed music download services, and making its iTunes music service files incompatible with devices that competed with the iPod, like Microsoft's or Sony's.[1] The second case dealt with Apple arranging with AT&T for exclusivity of the iPhone on the AT&T network for a period of years, inhibiting competition between AT&T and other networks for data services in particular for the iPhone. The third was about Apple refusing to license its Mac operating system to manufacturers of personal computers that compete with those of Apple, including its relatively expensive MacBook. And the fourth resulted from the infamous dispute between Epic Games, the company behind the Fortnite gaming phenomenon, and Apple's App Store bundling of app distribution services to an in-app purchasing transactions system designed to extract 30% of the revenue from gaming upgrades, subscriptions, and the like.

In the iPod case, the court found that the monopoly share of the iPod and iTunes had been adequately stated, although only part of the lawsuit ended up going to a jury trial, which Apple won. The court's opinion provides support for an antitrust duty on the part of an entertainment-distribution ecosystem to compete reasonably or at least without malice towards its rivals:

> Plaintiff has alleged that Apple deliberately makes music sold at [iTunes Music Store] incompatible with its competitors' digital music players (Compl. ¶ 14) – that is, Apple deliberately chooses to forego sales of digital media

> files at its asking price. Plaintiff also alleges that Apple deliberately makes the iPod unable to play music sold at its competitors' online music stores through the use of "crippleware." (Compl. ¶¶ 15, 38.) The inference is that Apple deliberately foregoes iPod sales to prospective customers who have purchased digital media files from other vendors and want a digital media player on which they can place these files. By so doing, Plaintiff alleges that Apple has been able to charge iPod purchasers a supracompetitive price and has deterred iPod purchasers from even considering doing business with its music and video competitors. (Compl. ¶¶ 54–55.) Plaintiff has alleged facts that, if proven, could establish that Apple was acting with "anticompetitive malice" rather than "competitive zeal."

Most recently, the relatively large size and health of alternative gaming platforms meant that Epic Games was not likely to show that Apple unlawfully abused its monopoly on supplying apps for iPhones or iPads, or that it had adopted unnecessarily restrictive rules for the "monetization" of apps.[2] These alternative platforms included the Xbox and the Sony PlayStation; the court also considered the varied benefits of the App Store's curated and more secure marketplace for apps, compared to a free-for-all of downloads. Similarly, an iPhone exclusivity case and a MacOS licensing case turned out favorably from Apple's point of view.[3]

The *Epic Games* lawsuit has an additional wrinkle, however, which points to one path forward relating to fair dealing challenges to Big Tech practices. In it, the court noted that state antitrust law is older than and just as valid as federal law. A developer might not have a claim under either federal law or California law against a technology company like Apple for setting up an App Store and a developer commission that restricts developers from distributing their apps in the most beneficial or remunerative ways from their point of view.[4] It may, however, have a claim against platform policies that increase developer costs, result in bloated platform profits, restrict competition among developers, and impede the flow of information about apps from developers to consumers. Developers, in short, might have a right under state law to steer customers acquired on one platform to another one, or to another payment system. Imposing anti-steering or information-suppressing rules as an app store seems to violate the spirit of the antitrust laws and therefore to be an unfair method of commerce under state law.[5]

There is hope that a fairness regime in terms of how authors and app developers contact their audiences could be revived under federal law as well. A judge in Washington, DC, hearing the FTC's case against Facebook for not sharing its platform and then expanding its control to WhatsApp, Instagram, and other potential competitors, discussed the current state of the law:

> [Courts have ruled that] "the monopolist's discontinuation of the preexisting course of dealing must suggest a willingness to forsake short-term profits to achieve an anti-competitive end," . . . rather than to advance a valid business purpose. See also *Covad Commc'ns Co. v. Bell Atl. Corp.*, 398 F.3d 666, 675 (D.C. Cir. 2005) (to prevail on refusal-to-deal claim, plaintiff "will have to prove [that defendant's] refusal to deal caused [defendant] short-term

> economic loss"). The cases, and the leading treatise, offer a demanding gloss on this prong of the test: . . . whether the cessation of dealing was "irrational but for its tendency to harm competition," . . . ; and [whether there was] "an unexplained, apparently irrational change in an established course of dealing."[6]

This ruling provides some basis, although one not easy to invoke, for challenging exclusion from a platform or marketplace. Some kind of arbitrary or unreasonable decision must have been made. The standard is not all that dissimilar to those regarding good faith content moderation under Section 230 of the CDA or good faith exercise of contractual rights, e.g. by a college.

Going forward, it remains to be seen whether the discussion in Facebook exhausts federal antitrust law's guarantees of open competition to the startup, the business customer, or the rival. An economic sacrifice test for monopolization, although it is good law due to Supreme Court opinions, makes little sense. Why should a monopoly be illegal only when it is unprofitable and therefore irrational? This turns on its head the original purpose of antitrust, which was to rein in the aggregations of capital that were crushing competitors, holding customers hostage, and corrupting our institutions.

Scholars have proposed many alternative accounts of "better monopolization standards," prior to or other than the "sacrifice test."[7] Einer Elhauge maintains that while antitrust law may not "impose some general common carrier duty of nondiscrimination on all monopolists," it does and should prohibit monopolists from strategically and anticompetitively denying access to rivals to parts of their facilities or properties; this prohibition would not apply to monopolists' own executive offices or research and development facilities, but to facilities or properties that monopolists open up or lease to members of the public.[8] A sacrifice test will not capture enough of this type of illegal exclusion because buyers or subscribers will not have a strong incentive to boycott the monopolist's unfair conduct, and the monopolist will not need to offer discounts that deny it any profit in order to persuade them.[9] Eleanor Fox has argued that the United States has departed from its core concern with economic power and dynamic market structures, and that much of the trust placed by the sacrifice test in dominant firms to promote the public interest may be misplaced.[10] Marshall Steinbaum and Maurice Stucke advance the "effective competition" standard, which would protect actual competition from its limitation by firms exercising "significant market power," including limitation by low-cost denials of access to technological platforms.[11] Lina M. Khan recenters infrastructure's role in antitrust history and argues for the principle that antitrust law should separate the owners of infrastructure from the dynamic markets it supports, such as shippers on railroads or sellers on Amazon.[12]

One glimmer of hope that fair dealing by tech titans might be assured to their rivals, at least, came in a decision in the monopolization case brought by the online video sharing platform Rumble against Google. Antitrust law considers the cumulative or synergistic effect of exclusionary tactics such as downranking a competitor's website or tying one's own apps up into a bundle that must be taken together. In response to Google's argument that neither offering preferential displays or rankings to one's own apps or websites, nor asking customers to accept a bundled software product, is absolutely illegal in itself, the court declared:

> [Plaintiff asserts, first,] that YouTube controls 73% of global online video activity . . . . And second, Plaintiff alleges among other things that Defendant, with no valid business purpose or benefit to users, designs its search engine algorithms to show users YouTube links instead of links to its competitors' sites . . . . According to Plaintiff, "Rumble and consumers (e.g. content creators) are disadvantaged, and competition is harmed, in the defined market because Google provides self-preferencing search advantages to its wholly-owned YouTube platform as a part of its scheme to maintain its monopoly power, and to reap a monopolist's financial rewards." . . .
>
> The only authority Defendant cites for the premise that a court can disaggregate a single Section 2 cause of action into subtheories, then scrutinize and potentially dismiss some subtheories without dismissing the entire cause of action, comes from two unpublished district court cases. . . . [T]he sort of parsing urged by Defendants is at least arguably in tension with the Supreme Court's direction that Sherman Act plaintiffs "should be given the full benefit of their proof without compartmentalizing the various factual components and wiping the slate clean after scrutiny of each." . . . This is especially true given the Ninth Circuit's holding that "even though [a] restraint effected may be reasonable under Section 1, it may constitute an attempt to monopolize forbidden by Section 2 if a specific intent to monopolize may be shown."[13]

The court in the FTC's and 46 U.S. states' case against Facebook reached a somewhat contrary decision, finding that a monopolist's course of conduct must be broken down and a court must test each unilateral act to see whether antitrust law's prohibition of monopolies and attempts to monopolize make it unlawful.[14] The FTC, the 46 states joining it in the Facebook suit, and the court in *Rumble* raise valid questions as to whether this atomistic approach is inconsistent with Supreme Court precedent. Appeals courts will no doubt weigh in on this before too long.[15]

Even under the rather pro-monopolist approach of the federal courts hearing the U.S. states' Facebook case, the discretion of a Big Tech monopoly in banning content or apps is not unlimited. Despite noting that there is no general duty to deal with rivals under the Sherman Act, the court emphasized that aspects of the case failed because Facebook was not alleged to have discriminated against authors or developers for using multiple platforms (sometimes called "multi-homing") or to have revoked an app's or website's access to its interfaces or facilities with an anti-competitive motive.[16] The court suggested that "conditional dealing" with rivals or certain customers might be a form of monopolization, so that the FTC or others (like the states or the rivals themselves) might have had a claim if Facebook had enforced policies to block its rivals' use of *other* platforms, in rules governing how these rivals could use the Facebook platform.[17]

Manipulating the display of websites or apps, by excluding competitors' links, icons, or menu options, or downranking them while leaving them available somewhere, can be anticompetitive conduct. In *United States v. Microsoft Corp.*, a key aspect of the monopolization and tying theories advanced by the Justice Department was that Microsoft used its copyright licenses for Windows 95/98, Windows ME, and later Windows XP to hobble Netscape's efforts to find low-cost ways to secure prime placement for its icons on users' computers.[18] The courts concluded that Microsoft's expressive interest in its copyrighted software was no basis to justify its exclusion of competing software's icons or menu options.[19] As the district court stated:

> Even constitutional privileges confer no immunity when they are abused for anticompetitive purposes. . . . Microsoft's conduct is effectively explained by its foreboding that OEMs would pre-install and give prominent placement to [browser software] like Navigator that could attract enough developer attention to weaken the applications barrier to entry. . . .
>
> Microsoft's bundling practices caused Navigator's usage share to drop substantially from 1995 to 1998, and that as a direct result Netscape suffered a severe drop in revenues from lost advertisers, Web traffic[, etc.] . . . [its] agreements prohibited [computer makers] from ever modifying or deleting any part of Windows, despite the [makers] expressed desire to be allowed to do so. . . . As a result, [computer makers] were generally not permitted, with only one brief exception, to satisfy consumer demand for a browserless version of Windows 95 without Internet Explorer. . . . Similarly, Microsoft refused to license Windows 98 . . . unless [makers] also agreed to abstain from removing the icons for Internet Explorer from the desktop. . . . [It made a] deliberate and purposeful choice to quell incipient competition.[20]

A judge across the country in San Francisco also reached a different conclusion from the one in *Facebook*, as to whether a social network had to share user data with a rival firm. This decision, involving LinkedIn and a human-resources data firm called HiQ, emphasized the infrastructure aspect of large databases as affecting fair competition. HiQ uses LinkedIn profiles and updates to provide services regarding employee qualifications, mobility, and compensation.[21] It argues that LinkedIn and platforms like it should not be able to "leverage" their massive user base to unfairly disadvantage rivals who need access to information about a social network. The courts agreed in part,

> The Sherman Act prohibits companies from leveraging monopoly power to "foreclose competition or gain a competitive advantage, or to destroy a competitor." . . . In this case, HiQ plausibly asserts that LinkedIn enjoys a position as the dominant power in the market of professional networking. Furthermore, HiQ has presented evidence that LinkedIn is seeking to compete with HiQ in the market of data analytics[, where HiQ] helps employers understand what skills the members of their workforces possess. There is thus a plausible inference that LinkedIn terminated HiQ's access to its public member data in large part because it wanted exclusive control over that data for its own business purposes; as noted . . . , HiQ faces an existential

> threat. That inference is supported by the timing of the commencement of its employer product which appears to coincide roughly with its terminating HiQ's access.[22]

Filtering out or blocking a rival's access to a public-facing facility or resource (in other words not the monopolist's executive headquarters or the like) is harmful monopoly leveraging.[23]

The General Court of the European Union has likewise concluded that when a dominant firm targets its rival's Internet traffic for throttling, this can be a form of illegal monopolization. The Treaty on the Functioning of the European Union acts like a Sherman Act for Europe, limiting tactics that abuse a "dominant position," which is something like monopoly power (but may extend somewhat further than how U.S. courts would define a monopoly).[24]

> As regards the effects of the practice at issue on competition, the General Court recalls that an abuse of a dominant position exists where the dominant undertaking, through recourse to methods different from those governing normal competition, hinders the maintenance of the degree of competition in the market or the growth of that competition, and that that may be established merely by demonstrating that its conduct is capable of restricting competition. . . . [A]fter having measured the actual effects of the conduct concerned on comparison shopping services' traffic from Google's general results pages, the Commission had a sufficient basis for showing as it did that that traffic accounted for a large share of their total traffic, that that share could not be effectively replaced by other sources of traffic, such as advertising (AdWords) or mobile applications, and that the potential outcome was the disappearance of comparison shopping services, less innovation on their market and less choice for consumers, characteristic features of a weakening of competition.[25]

With this 2021 decision of the Court of Justice of the European Union, self-preferencing may be a limited power of dominant websites or apps, rather than a general or absolute right. The question arose as the European Commission challenged Google's exclusion of other websites from some of the benefits of the Android ecosystem, including a default search box, a default app, default status on the default Web browser, protection from uninstallation, etc. After strongly defending its defaults, Google admitted that this kind of exclusion could not go on forever. It agreed in 2021 to allow a choice screen for search engines on the Android platform, although default options for competitive video apps, search widgets, etc. may take longer to arrive.[26]

According to a press release by FairSearch, allied businesses and other groups arguing for transparency and innovation, the problems with Google's proposals regarding search choice are:

> The Google proposal entirely excludes any choice of browsers.
>
> So Google continues to profit from its illegal behavior, both from existing users and from browsers.

> Alternatives to Google search are chosen using StatCounter, a global measure inherently biased toward Google that gives it an unfair edge in small markets. . . .
>
> And Google's announcement remains fundamentally flawed and falls well short of truly addressing the devastating effects of its anticompetitive behaviour.
>
> For example:
>
> 1. Google's announcement does nothing to address the problem of consumer preference for browsers, allowing Google to perpetuate a proven infringement.
> 2. Google's announcement for the search choice screen would only apply to new users, taking effect in September. The millions of existing users Google acquired by illegal conduct would continue to suffer without true choice, gaining nothing. In other words, Google will continue to profit from conduct the Commission found to be unlawful.
> 3. The revised choice screen relies indiscriminately on the identification of alternatives based on StatCounter, which . . . is ill-suited for smaller markets, rather than alternatives adapted to and focused on each local market.[27]

This concession represented a move towards platform neutrality, initially at the operating system level but perhaps also at the browser or settings level.[28] In this regard, it was similar to Google's stance – as an upstart – regarding the alleged bullying of some websites by Microsoft, Verizon, or other dominant companies of the 2000s. Google called non-neutrality by these firms destructive to "innovation," the Internet user's online "experience," and " 'consumer choice.' "[29]

Google's concession to the EU was echoed years later when Amazon proposed a settlement with the EU that would "end [its] preferential treatment for itself and treat sellers equally when ranking their offers for the 'Buy Box' on its website that generated the bulk of its sales."[30] Most recently, Google is poised to settle antitrust claims involving threats or discrimination against Android app developers who avoid the 30% Play Store app commission, brought by the 50 states, the Commonwealth of Puerto Rico, and the District of Columbia.[31] The FTC and the attorneys general of 17 states announced in September 2023 that they would seek an injunction against Amazon favoring its own products over higher-quality or lower-priced ones from Amazon marketplace sellers, tying Amazon.com search rankings and "Buy Box" displays to sellers' use of Amazon fulfillment services and restrictive contracts. The plaintiffs might even seek to break apart some of Amazon's empire, such as deliveries vs. the marketplace.[32]

Tying and monopoly leveraging are concepts that help explain much of the contemporary jurisprudence relating to Big Tech's limitations on the freedom of commerce and right to earn a living.[33] The trial court in the U.S. government's case against Microsoft concluded that the operating system Windows was inefficiently priced at a high level and that new competitors like Netscape were at risk of exclusion from the market: "a company able to leverage its substantial power in the [operating system] market in order to force consumers to accept a tie of partial substitutes [like Microsoft's browser Internet Explorer] is thus able to spread inefficiency from one market to the next . . . , and thereby 'sabotage a nascent technology,'" in the case of Netscape a potential laptop run on a browser suite, much like the Chromebook eventually became.[34] An appeals court largely agreed, warning that Microsoft's agreements with other hardware and software companies could have "a significant effect in preserving its monopoly; they help keep usage of [Netscape's] Navigator below the critical level necessary for Navigator or any other rival to pose a real threat to Microsoft's monopoly."[35] Now, the Department of Justice suggests that some Google ads may be priced at an artificially high level, and the FTC says products or services ranked highly or recommended by Amazon may be of lower quality or higher price.[36] Both cases allege manipulation of various ranking or recommendation algorithms.[37]

Another case that potentially involved misuse of software copyright licenses to disadvantage rivals, specifically photocopier repair and maintenance businesses, was *Image Technical Services, Inc. v. Eastman Kodak Co.*[38] In that case, the court held that it could be exclusionary conduct to "ma[k]e a conscious choice to change an established pattern of distribution to the detriment of a competitor."[39] Under *Kodak* and *Microsoft*, restricting competitors' access to part of a company's own market or commercial ecosystem may amount to the unlawful leveraging of monopoly power.[40] As noted in Chapter 1, the House Judiciary Committee's subcommittee report charged that Google and Facebook are leveraging market power in some areas into others, and that Amazon essentially leveraged a monopoly in general-purpose online goods marketplaces to gain power over e-commerce fulfillment (performance and delivery) of third-party marketplace online retail sales, or it possibly leveraged a fulfillment monopoly into market power that it initially lacked in online retail marketplaces.[41] As of this writing, the exclusion of Microsoft Bing from certain Apple devices is the subject of a monopolization trial brought by the United States and all 50 states, the Commonwealth of Puerto Rico, and the District of Columbia.[42] The FTC may also appeal a trial court ruling that it could not challenge Facebook's denial of access to its platform to competitors who emulated or improved upon the functions of Facebook or its app.[43] Thus, changing Android or Facebook Platform policies to the detriment of a company like Rumble or Parler (rivals of YouTube in some ways) or Vine (a rival of Instagram and Facebook particularly as to videos) may harm competition.[44]

Product or function cloning is an underdeveloped theory of monopoly leveraging or vertical exclusionary conduct. A "copy-acquire-kill" strategy arguably goes back to Standard Oil and the original trusts; today it is associated with Alphabet and Meta, or Google and Facebook, as they bought firms like DoubleClick and Instagram.[45] The background of the Microsoft antitrust case was that, perceiving a threat from standalone browsers such as Netscape Navigator, Microsoft acquired and further developed Internet browser technology that it could offer itself and bundle with Windows. Similarly, platforms that refused Facebook's attempts to buy them, such as Twitter and Snapchat, saw their functionalities cloned by aspects of Facebook's and Meta's suite of apps.[46] As noted previously, the FTC, along with many attorneys general including those of New York and California, engaged in a lengthy investigation of product listing rankings and recommendations on Amazon's online marketplace platform.[47] The investigation examined Amazon's use of third-party sellers' data to launch its own branded products. Amazon's founder and then-CEO, Jeff Bezos, stated the company maintains a policy against using seller-specific data, but he could not guarantee that the policy had never been broken.[48] The House Judiciary Committee's subcommittee report suggested that the policy had been violated in at least some cases,[49] but breach of a policy does not always rise to the level of unlawful exclusion.[50] The FTC and the states may, however, bring up this evidence in conjunction with algorithmic manipulation or contractual restrictions as part of a course of conduct, as in Rumble/Google.

A final antitrust theory that could protect rivals from inauthentic competitors is the restraint of trade, the unreasonable group boycott, or the collusive refusal to deal. Contemporary courts sometimes infer an illegal conspiracy among competitors against the public by permitting consumers or victim firms to submit evidence that leading companies in fact "coordinate their conduct simply by observing and reacting to the moves of their competitors."[51] Such "business behavior is admissible circumstantial evidence from which the fact finder may infer [an illegal] agreement" to restrict the freedom of trade.[52] Watching and mimicking another leading company's policies may give rise to antitrust liability for collusion when there is evidence of a sufficiently concentrated or distorted industry such as "(1) a common rational motive to conspire . . . ; (2) a concentrated degree of inter-firm communications . . . ; (3) the performance of actions that are against a defendant's own business interest without collective involvement . . . ; (4) evidence of coercion . . . ; and (5) market phenomena that may only be attributed to concerted action."[53] Inauthentic business activity, that which makes the most sense as part of a collusive industry strategy to squelch disruptive entrants and uninhibited competition, could be prohibited under antitrust law under a boycott or restraint theory.[54] Like the movie theater chains, the music licensing bodies, and the stock markets before them, the Big Tech companies might be persuaded to adopt a common approach towards creators, users accused of policy violations, or the freedom of expression more generally, and thus trigger antitrust rules.[55]

A variety of congressional hearings, legal complaints, and press reports (including Twitter/X threads) have alleged that inter-firm communications in the Big Tech sector result in collective decision-making on the flagging and suppressing of lawful content, sometimes on grounds of partisanship or speaker viewpoint. While there has been little interest on the part of antitrust enforcers at the federal, state, or international level to explore this possibility, it is another way in which the Web or the Internet could be locked open, when the powerful guard the entry gate. An agreement to rig online discourse, which would otherwise be in the interest of a digital platform to keep open, makes more sense as a concerted effort to carve up and govern a lucrative sector.

A Civil Right to Platform Neutrality?

In order to overcome the state action hurdle to imposing First Amendment duties of private platforms, Internet users typically rely on the "public function" or "public forum" doctrines, but they have typically failed. Less commonly, Internet users point to evidence that dominant Internet firms have conspired with government officials, whether domestic or foreign, to disfavor certain views or imagery and to delete the accounts of Americans communicating them to others. Under established First Amendment doctrine, "state action" may exist not only when public officials engage in censorship, but also when private individuals or firms suppress speech due to the "encouragement" or involvement of officialdom.[56]

With the Fifth Circuit's decision in *Missouri v. Biden*, the stage is set for members of the U.S. public to challenge government entanglement with AI filters of private platforms.[57] Entanglement is a familiar concept from First Amendment law of religious neutrality, which would prohibit, for example, the federal government from misusing an educational or cultural program to intervene into questions of spiritual doctrine and religious faith, thereby favoring one sect over another.[58]

The question arises whether the White House may intrude into the governance of journalistic, historical, or scientific debates online, even though it should not do so in religious debates to promote one sect over others. As discussed earlier in this book, *Bantam Books* and cases like it from *Skyywalker Records* and *Zieper* to *Backpage* and *NRA* look upon government encouraging businesses to censor private citizens' access to books, music, or digital content as a violation of the First Amendment.[59] The Biden administration argues that private action does not become state action for constitutional purposes simply because the government recommends or even organizes such private action.[60] Whoever in the government has information about a website or social media post that should be banned, it says, may send the link to the appropriate platform for execution of the ban.[61] Likewise, Facebook, Google, Amazon, and Twitter argue that receiving federal requests for action and being heavily regulated does not mean that they are state actors.[62]

Users of the Big Tech platforms argue that if the government adopts a consciously permissive approach to private conduct that is threatening to constitutional rights, e.g., immunizing it, this is state action. For example, Congress singling out one form of speech for special vulnerability to "private censorship" was state action to which the First Amendment applied, not private action under an immunity.[63] Similarly, when Congress authorized *private* alcohol and drug tests administered by private railroads as to employees suspected of safety concerns, this was not private action in a Fourth Amendment case.[64] In *Bantam Books*, soliciting private action and thanking private actors for it was state action.[65] In another case, it was recognized that governments may act unconstitutionally by adopting certain private sector rules as government policy; private firms may also act unconstitutionally as policy instruments.[66]

The law in this area tends to focus on the "private censorship" case, *Denver Area*, which is especially relevant because it was from the same era of hostility to adult content and LGBT speech that gave us the CDA. Two judges in California, however, have found the case not to support striking down Section 230 of the CDA to the extent it immunizes deplatforming or shadow-banning social media users. They reason that the CDA immunizes all activities in the nature of publishing or not publishing on the part of Internet intermediaries, not only those relating to a specific content or viewpoint. However, they ignore much of the language of Section 230, specifically the subsection title, statement of federal policy, and text of

Section 230.[67] These provisions were and are clearly intended to encourage private censorship of a specific type of content, like the "indecent" LGBT speech at issue in one of the two cases and the offensive viewpoints at issue in the other one.[68] Political dissent was an obvious target of one of the bill's authors, Representative Chris Cox, who read an article about Prodigy Services being treated like a publisher for defamation purposes because it edited user posts, and he worried whether Prodigy would stop censoring uncivil discourse: "It struck me that if that rule was going to take hold then the internet would become the Wild West and nobody would have any incentive to keep the internet civil," he said.[69] While standards of civility are appropriate for a classroom or a legislative debate, public discourse is allowed to be strident, harsh, personal, and offensive.[70]

Whether considered as solicitation, encouragement, covert action, authorization or immunization for acting as entwinement, or implicit threats or virtual orders, a recommendation and negotiation or agreement on the response to it compromises the integrity of private judgment.

Even if there is not always a clear penalty for private actors not doing the act found to be state action, a persistent pressure to act distorts the autonomy of actors and tilts the playing field.

If, as *Bantam Books* and cases like it state, government threats or encouraging words may make private action part of a pattern of state action, a victim of Internet censorship should be able to sue the private actor for collusion, whether on a theory of conspiracy between government official(s) and the private actor, joint action, or apparent or express agency to act for the state.

Is Platform Neutrality for "Red States" and Net Neutrality for "Blue States"?

Frank Pasquale conceives of platform neutrality as a protection of private commerce and the public sphere from concentrations of revenue, control, and data visibility in the largest digital services, or intermediaries.[71] He observes that, like the Digital National Council of France and its leader, Axelle Lemaire, a French official in 2015, policymakers might view platform neutrality as a guarantee of Internet openness to free speech and artistic or other posts.[72] As the French competition authority announced in 2019, the dominance of an advertising service makes smaller companies vulnerable to "unfair" or erratic treatment and desperate to maintain their accounts.[73]

Barack Obama famously intoned that there is no "red" America and "blue" America, referring to the political maps coded for statewide elections victories: there is the "United" States of America.[74] In terms of protecting the open Internet, however, there is an emerging partisan divide between red – or Republican-dominated – states and blue states – those dominated by the Democratic Party.[75] Two prominent Republican states enacted platform neutrality or nondiscrimination principles that the U.S. Supreme Court took up in 2024, while ten states that tend to vote for Democratic presidents and senators have enacted net neutrality laws.[76] A Republican president, George W. Bush, eliminated aspects of net neutrality (while introducing others via his FCC nominees), while a Democratic president, Mr. Obama, famously pushed net neutrality into law, only to see it undone by an appointee of his successor, the Republican Donald J. Trump.[77]

Blue state law-school centers and think-tanks are generally enthusiastic about platform censorship, or non-neutral "content moderation," but they are opposed to egregious violations of net neutrality, or telecom censorship.[78] Stanford Law School, for example, is the source of much commentary, calling platform neutrality "wacky" if not "grim," but it was the home of prominent net neutrality advocates Lawrence Lessig (who left for Harvard) and Mark Lemley, as well as Barbara van Schewick, the author of a book on net neutrality as an important design principle, entitled *Internet Architecture and Innovation* (MIT Press, 2010).[79] Platform neutrality is seen as introducing Nazis, terrorists, and a "flood of garbage" to the Internet,[80] while net neutrality is praised for protecting "online ideas and commerce that . . . pose a threat to network owners."[81] The lawfulness of offensive content that is typically censored by platforms is deemed to be irrelevant, while lawfulness of Internet content is at the core of net neutrality.[82]

In challenging platform neutrality, companies like Meta and Twitter tend to bring up Nazis and terrorist-related accounts and emphasize that they do not want to host them. Platforms say that if they are allowed to engage in automated or human-run censorship systems, they will remove and are already taking down such "awful content." Facebook emphasizes terrorism and "violent or graphic content," while Twitter also appears to emphasize spam, violence, and other sources of "offens[e]."[83] The track record of these companies, however, establishes that Nazi and terrorist materials such as Hitler or bin Laden speeches, images of swastikas or ISIS logos, etc. remain available on social media and in books to those who truly want to find them.[84] Nazi and jihadist speeches – not to mention graphic or violent content relating to World War II or the many "wars" on terrorism – can easily be found online or even using cable television, DVDs, or books. Hitler's *Mein Kampf* can be bought in Germany to read in German.[85] Western scholars, legislators, and reporters regularly discuss the contents of al Qaeda, Taliban, Hamas, or ISIS magazines, press conferences, videos, and websites. Even when platform sites do not themselves host such videos or images, they link to places like CNN or Amazon.com that have them.

Content moderation advocates like former Twitter CEO Jack Dorsey claim that they consider "severity of potential harm," but this does not stand up to much scrutiny either.[86] Violent threats by politicians and military leaders are often transmitted across all kinds of digital media, and during or just before extremely destructive military and paramilitary campaigns.[87] Politicians and diplomats of a number of countries accused of genocide, aggression, torture, war crimes, and suppressing democracy or even killing environmental, labor, or indigenous rights activists often have social media accounts and enjoy wide distribution of their remarks and speeches in online video repositories. That is not even to mention other violent rhetoric such as that in the entertainment media; many people have been killed in incidents believed by U.S. prosecutors to be "directly related" to violent music lyrics, and even the artists themselves in some genres fall victim in violence in significant numbers.[88] A number of victims have filed court papers claiming that heavy metal or rap music (like Slayer's music or *Cop Killer*), movies featuring school shootings or massacres (like *The Basketball Diaries* or *Natural Born Killers*), violent video games (like *Doom*), and even occult art and board games (like *Dungeons & Dragons*) contributed to the murder or suicide of their loved ones, but the works remain online.[89] Two major waves of violent films, in the 1970s and early 1990s, and waves of violent video games, in the mid-1990s and mid-2000s, raised questions as to whether "unbalanced individuals" would have "morbid fantasies" and become copycats.[90]

There is every indication that banning disfavored views or representations of harm could backfire. Drug dealing, terrorist speech, Nazi speech, QAnon theories, vaccine skepticism, support of Donald J. Trump for President of the United States, skepticism about the 2020 election's results, advocacy of anorexia or suicide: all of these categories were supposed to be banned on social media and/or television, but speech on all of these themes remains quite common. This is consistent with the observation that the Internet and perhaps television witness a "Streisand effect," where trying to restrict a message piques curiosity and engagement.[91]

Hate speech is not defined well virtually anywhere.[92] British law is looked to by some as a model, as the United States has mostly hate crime enhancements for non-speech conduct, rather than (enforceable) hate speech laws proper.[93] States like Florida are beginning to follow Britain's lead by, for example, making it a felony to project hateful images onto buildings, accost people like Jewish worshippers approaching synagogues, or distribute hateful "litter" such as flyers.[94] Sites like Twitter appear to borrow from human rights law and aspects of French law in distinguishing advocacy of racial hatred from contextualized depictions of it as in films, or hateful slurs used in anger from the same slurs used to "reappropriate" them.[95] Both U.S. and international case law and U.N. experts question whether hate can be defined with the specificity needed to protect the freedom of expression, given historic problems with religious insult laws such as blasphemy and political insult laws such as seditious libel or simply sedition (sometimes known as counterrevolution, insulting the leader, or insulting God via His minister the leader).[96]

Article 19 of the International Covenant on Civil and Political Rights guarantees freedom of opinion and the freedom of expression, including the right to seek, receive, and impart information and ideas of all kinds regardless of frontiers. The Human Rights Committee, charged with oversight of this article, insists that laws on hate or other prohibited expressions be truly necessary, clarified in advance, and applied in a nondiscriminatory way, three requirements which it is very difficult for a policy to meet.[97] Race or public order laws may need to be applied differently depending on the place or manner of expression, for example a courtroom versus a classroom versus a public street versus a fiction book or dramatic play.[98] A UN Plan of Action of Hate Speech does not distinguish between fiction versus nonfiction works, or personal stalking versus general publications, or interpersonal animosity versus intergroup hate, whereas the United States may distinguish between interpersonal disputes and impermissible racial or religious discrimination, raising the question whether free expression and due process (in the sense of advance notice and clear framing) would be trampled upon by implementation of the UN plan on social media or video sites.[99] Moreover, the plan mentions identity factors as defining hateful motives but does not limit such factors to immutable or inheritable ones.[100] It could therefore be hate speech to incite hatred of hateful people, Nazis, terrorists, etc.

The Digital Services Act (DSA) suffers from similar difficulties with its provision on rapid removal of demeaning expressions.[101] This will inevitably lead to overblocking. Given the massive potential fines under the DSA, the result could be a comprehensive system of prepublication censorship of social media, online videos, and search engines. As one institutional critic of the DSA explains:

> States should not require platforms to undertake proactive monitoring or filtering of content. Maintaining a prohibition on general monitoring is critical to protecting individuals' right to privacy and the filtering of content pose unique risks to freedom of expression. If these are required, there is a risk of creating a situation where all content may need to be potentially approved before it is published.[102]

AI will be inevitably the predominant mechanism for complying with such duties.[103] Without legislation, and probably even with it, users will not understand the AI that deletes speech.[104] Unless governments confine their definitions of prohibited hate speech to the zone contemplated by human-rights covenants and charters, there will be politicized misuse of the AI systems, leading to censorship of protected political, cultural, and scientific expression.[105] The fine for noncompliance with the illegal content provisions of the DSA could result in fines of $20 billion or more for some giant multinationals, and illegal content may include ("false") news reports.[106]

While there are some differences between net neutrality and platform neutrality, there are significant similarities that might break down some of the partisanship associated with them. First, both principles are about keeping the Internet open. Consider how a recent speech by a Biden administration appointee and the FCC's Chair, Jessica Rosenworcel, supports this point:

> [F]or everyone, everywhere to enjoy the full benefits of the internet age, internet access should be more than just accessible and affordable. The internet also needs to be open – and that is what I want to focus on today.
>
> The internet's open design is revolutionary. It means creating without permission, building community beyond geography, organizing without physical constraints, consuming content you want when and where you want it, and cultivating ideas not just around the corner but around the world.
>
> I believe it is essential that we sustain this foundation of openness – and that is why, for as long as I have served on the FCC, I have supported net neutrality.[107]

In that, both neutrality regimes share something with antitrust law, which (as explained by the DOJ's Jonathan Kanter and FTC's Lina Khan, among many other advocates and authorities) prevents lines of commerce from being locked up.[108] Indeed, the Obama-era FCC defended net neutrality from First Amendment attacks using antitrust jurisprudence.[109] This antitrust function has long been bipartisan and multinational, with the Reagan administration famously breaking up AT&T and Republican Teddy Roosevelt and Democrat Woodrow Wilson pushing forward a progressive vision of fair competition overcoming giant trusts.[110] The high water mark of fair competition principles was reached in a long bipartisan era from Franklin Delano Roosevelt to Lyndon Baines Johnson, with Republican Dwight D. Eisenhower sandwiched in the middle alongside a Democratic Congress.[111]

A law that seems extraordinarily well-suited to implementing both platform neutrality and net neutrality is Section 5 of the FTC Act. It promotes the basic policies of personal autonomy, economic deconcentration, and anti-domination and anti-collusion under the Sherman Act, but without being as technical as Sherman Act doctrines have become.[112] Thus, as the FTC explained in 2022, unfair conduct

> may be coercive, exploitative, collusive, abusive, deceptive, predatory, or involve the use of economic power of a similar nature. It may also be otherwise restrictive or exclusionary, depending on the circumstances. . . .
>
> [It] tends to foreclose or impair the opportunities of market participants, reduce competition between rivals, limit choice, or otherwise harm consumers.[113]

Using Section 5, the courts can advance the vision of Louis Brandeis and other architects of the FTC that economic liberty shall be preserved by shielding the weak from the strong.[114] The "industrial menace" of unequal treatment of "existing or putative competitors" is the target.[115] As the legislative history explains, unfair methods of competition "shut out competitors who, by reason of their efficiency, *might* otherwise be able to continue in business and prosper."[116]

Misleading or manipulated rankings systems threaten the spirit of the antitrust laws by impairing competition on the merits of product or service appeal to the public, and preventing high-quality or more efficient creators from gaining their fair share of audiences. A monopoly may be maintained, or an effective competitor boycotted and restrained, by false statements in letters, advertisements, or algorithmic output.[117] Even when antitrust violations are less likely, conduct with respect to rankings (such as shadow-banning) may have a negative impact not justified by positive aims or results. When the effects fall into net negative territory, an act or practice may be unfair under federal and state law.[118]

A second similarity between net neutrality and viewpoint neutrality is interference with the independent judgment of the service provider called upon by the law to be more neutral. Like the platforms affected by state laws passed in Texas or Florida, the Internet service providers claimed an editorial right to edit user speech. They had some basic rules about viruses and other illegal or offensive material, and even more controversial rules protecting themselves from activities like Wi-Fi sharing or certain voice over Internet competition.[119] Yet they do not edit most websites or emails for offensiveness, decency, graphic violence, or other subjective criteria. Like the Google and Meta algorithms, broadband providers do not "somehow exercise substantive, discretionary review akin to newspaper editors."[120] Newspapers are very much unlike search engines or social media sites in that they author most of their articles.[121]

A third similarity is that the First Amendment justifies both net neutrality and viewpoint neutrality on the basis that the corporation's interest in earning revenue by carrying most but not all offensive or indecent content is outweighed by the interest of individuals in an open Web. A free speech interest may often be too weak to outweigh another person's interest in being served, especially when proclaiming a message different from and opposed to that person is peripheral to a company or service provider's message or beliefs. For example, it is not enough to strike down a law on First Amendment grounds to say that the application of the law will require a group to undergo more meetings at which views with which it disagrees are expressed (such as views on foreign affairs, school prayer, or voting rights). Instead, to strike down the law it may need to be shown that admitting or providing services in a public place to persons expressing disagreeable views will change the organization's *own* speech in its "content or impact."[122] Even if a person has a message to proclaim or harbors a belief that is contrary to that of the person served, the right to articulate that message or live according to that belief must sometimes give way to other interests, like the compelling state interest in equal treatment in public places. Under ministerial, conscientious-objector, and First Amendment exemptions from laws, the state interest may be overridden by a person's or a group's "basic goals."[123] Unless one's own basic mission or personal impact is distorted or lost, the law may demand that an expressive association deal with or serve a customer or other person. For example, a shopping center hosting diverse stores and customers may be compelled to allow campaigners to picket or solicit on its private property.[124]

Dissenting from the denial of US Telecom Association's petition for rehearing en banc, then-Judge Brett Kavanaugh reached a different conclusion both as to ISPs and presumably as to platforms:

> Under the Supreme Court's landmark decisions in *Turner Broadcasting System, Inc. v. FCC*, 512 U.S. 622, 114 S.Ct. 2445, 129 L.Ed.2d 497 (1994), and *Turner Broadcasting System, Inc. v. FCC*, 520 U.S. 180, 117 S.Ct. 1174, 137 L.Ed.2d 369 (1997), the First Amendment bars the Government from restricting the editorial discretion of Internet service providers, absent a showing that an Internet service provider possesses market power in a relevant geographic market. Here, however, the FCC has not even tried to make a market power showing. Therefore, under the Supreme Court's precedents applying the First Amendment, the net neutrality rule violates the First Amendment. . . .
>
> [T]he Supreme Court emphasized and relied on the Government's market power showing when the Court upheld the must-carry requirements. See *Turner Broadcasting II*, 520 U.S. at 196–208, 117 S.Ct. 1174 (controlling

> opinion of Kennedy, J.). Indeed, . . . Justice Breyer specifically disagreed with the Court's emphasis on market power as the justification for the must-carry law. Justice Breyer would have held that the Government's interest in promoting a multiplicity of voices sufficed to satisfy intermediate scrutiny. . . . But the Court did not go that route.[125]

In 2016, however, the D.C. Circuit concluded that broadband providers do not have a First Amendment right to block lawful content or applications in violation of net neutrality. There is little similarity between net neutrality and forcing a cable provider to add five more channels to a basic cable package of 20 channels, as in *Turner Broadcasting*, or a newspaper to give scarce space on one or two opinion pages to the politicians it attacks, as in *Miami Herald.*

> Equal access obligations . . . have long been imposed on telephone companies, railroads, and postal services, without raising any First Amendment issue. See *Denver Area Educational Telecommunications Consortium, Inc. v. FCC*, 518 U.S. 727, 739, 116 S.Ct. 2374, 135 L.Ed.2d 888 (1996) (plurality opinion) (noting that the "speech interests" in leased channels are "relatively weak because [the companies] act less like editors, such as newspapers or television broadcasters, than like common carriers, such as telephone companies"). . . . The Supreme Court has explained that the First Amendment comes "into play" only where "particular conduct possesses sufficient communicative elements," that is, when an "intent to convey a particularized message [is] present, and in the surrounding circumstances the likelihood [is] great that the message would be understood by those who viewed it," [public carriers] merely facilitate the transmission of the speech of others rather than engage in speech in their own right.[126]

Internet platforms might be slightly different from broadband Internet services if they are traditionally editing their available content like a newspaper:

> In contrast to newspapers and cable companies, the exercise of editorial discretion is entirely absent with respect to broadband providers subject to the Order. Unlike with the printed page and cable technology, broadband providers face no such constraints limiting the range of potential content they can make available to subscribers. Broadband providers thus are not required to make, nor have they traditionally made, editorial decisions about which speech to transmit.[127]

However, the Fifth Circuit made similar findings that the D.C. Circuit did as to broadband providers not being real editors, but with respect to the large Internet platforms:

> The Platforms are nothing like the newspaper in *Miami Herald.* Unlike newspapers, the Platforms exercise virtually no editorial control or judgment. The Platforms use algorithms to screen out certain obscene and spam-related

> content. And then virtually everything else is just/posted to the Platform with zero editorial control or judgment. "Something well north of 99% of th[is] content . . . never gets reviewed further. The content on a site is, to that extent, invisible to the [Platform]." *NetChoice, LLC v. Moody*, 546 F. Supp. 3d 1082, 1092 (N.D. Fla. 2021). Thus the Platforms, unlike newspapers, are primarily "conduit[s] for news, comment, and advertising." *Miami Herald*, 418 U.S. at 258, 94 S.Ct. 2831. And that's why the Supreme Court has described them as "the modern public square." *Packingham*, 137 S. Ct. at 1737; *see also Biden v. Knight First Amend. Inst.*, 593 U.S. ___, 141 S. Ct. 1220, 1224, 209 L.Ed.2d 519 (2021) (Thomas, J., concurring) (noting Platforms are also "unlike newspapers" in that they "hold themselves out as organizations that focus on distributing the speech of the broader public").[128]

Another suggestion that is often made is that platform neutrality is a taking or expropriation of private property.[129] That theory lacks traction under existing law, although it is difficult to predict how the law will evolve in the decades to come. A rule prohibiting this or that commercial practice is not a confiscation of property or an expropriation of a business.[130] The courts have, for example, "consistently affirmed that States have broad power to regulate housing conditions in general and the landlord-tenant relationship in particular without paying compensation for all economic injuries that such regulation entails."[131] That is not a confiscation or taking, any more than other land use restrictions or mandates such as the wage laws or health-insurance mandates. "Limitations on how a business generally open to the public may treat individuals on the premises are readily distinguishable from regulations granting a right to invade property closed to the public."[132] If any interference with physical "server space" constituted a confiscation of property, any antidiscrimination or consumer protection rule would be unconstitutional under the Fifth Amendment as requiring the storage of, for example, the emails of a racial or religious group that the website proprietor wished to exclude. Home sellers would be free to discriminate on grounds of race or religion, rather than be forced to sell to a person who would embark upon a permanent physical occupation of their property without just compensation for the taking.

User Rights Versus Platforms' First Amendment Interests

On May 2, 2021, Florida's Republican governor, Ron DeSantis, signed a "first-of-its-kind" law to regulate deplatforming, particularly of political candidates and "journalistic enterprises." The law, S.B. 7072, was based on the premise that certain very large social media platforms "should be treated similarly to common carriers."[133] In order not to totally erase platforms' terms of service and independent discretion, the law permitted them to apply content "moderation" standards, as long as they did so consistently.[134] However, candidates for statewide or local political office in Florida would not be subject to ordinary content moderation – even if consistent – so any deplatforming of them would be subject to a fine of $250,000 per day. This provision was pretty clearly targeted at the deplatforming of former President Donald Trump by Facebook, Twitter, and YouTube on the ground that his statements on January 6, 2021, contributed to a risk of offline harm including the U.S. Capitol riot or coup attempt that injured many Capitol police officers and allegedly threatened the lives of several public officials.[135] Another section seemed geared to shadow-banning or deprioritizing certain political candidates, or in other words failing to feature or rank the words or images of those candidates as prominently as their opponents' content. A third section prohibits certain platforms from removing or appending fact-checks or warnings to the stories or videos of a "journalistic enterprise" – such as the *New York Post*'s famous stories about the contents of Hunter Biden's laptop and the Biden family's links to various wealthy foreigners.[136] Perhaps the most revolutionary provision would allow social media users to opt out of algorithmic content prioritization and presentation, and see posts by other users of the platform *chronologically*.[137]

In late May 2021, NetChoice, LLC and the Computer & Communications Industry Association sued several Florida officials, notably Attorney General Ashley Brooke Moody. The suit, filed in federal court in northern Florida where the State of Florida's capital is located, sought a quick ruling that the law violated the First Amendment to the United States Constitution as applied to the State of Florida by the Fourteenth Amendment, as well as the Constitution's Commerce Clause and a law enacted by Congress pursuant to it, the Communications Decency Act of 1996, 47 U.S.C. § 230.[138] The plaintiffs' members include not only Facebook, Twitter, and YouTube, but also platforms like AOL, Amazon.com, Airbnb, eBay, Etsy, Expedia, Hotels.com, PayPal, Pinterest, and TikTok. The lawsuit described them all as "online businesses who share the goal of promoting free speech and free enterprise on the Internet."[139]

The challenge made numerous points but had three or four emphases. First, the law unconstitutionally singled out "Silicon Valley" businesses while expressly exempting conglomerates with similar platform business units as long as they owned a theme park in the State of Florida. The Disney and NBC Universal theme parks in Orlando, a region that numerous members of the Florida legislature represent, were obviously in view here. Second, the definitions of political candidates and journalistic enterprises were so broad, and the obligations of consistency and chronological presentation for some users so onerous and burdensome, as to unconstitutionally violate the freedoms of speech and of the press under the First and Fourteenth Amendments. Third, Section 230 of the Communications Decency Act expressly states that a provider of an interactive computer service should never be held liable for voluntary and good-faith efforts to restrict "objectionable" user speech, whether it be obscene, lewd, excessively violent, harassing, or otherwise offensive.[140] Finally, the Florida law's various standards were unconstitutionally vague, uncertain, and in breach of the right to equal protection of the laws.[141]

The United States District Court for the Northern District of Florida agreed with the Big Tech companies that the Florida law failed First Amendment scrutiny, conflicted with a federal statute designed to encourage removal of offensive speech, and was hopelessly ambiguous and imprecise.[142] The way that the Florida law imposed special disabilities on large platforms, and extended special rights to political candidates and journalistic enterprises, triggered "strict scrutiny," shifting the burden to the Florida officials to establish a "compelling state interest" for the law's provisions and, moreover, that the provisions were narrowly tailored to serve those interests.[143] Moreover, the carve-out for platforms under common ownership with a theme park was a content-based law that required strict scrutiny. The court concluded that it was not a compelling interest to place all candidates for all statewide office, as well as certain journalistic enterprises, on a "level playing field" in terms of social media. In support, it cited a U.S. Supreme Court decision striking down Florida's "right of reply" law regulating newspapers' attacks on political candidates during election season, another decision holding that parade organizers had a First Amendment right to exclude a gay rights group that was otherwise qualified to participate, and a third decision declining to allow California to force a public utility to carry the messages of a utility regulation activist group with whose messages the utility disagreed.[144] Finally, it cited a decision of the Supreme Court striking down an Arizona law that did not prohibit or require any speech but provided matching funds to political candidates in proportion to their opponents' fundraising for campaign advertisements, thereby penalizing the speech of the richer candidates in the Court's view.[145]

In addition, the court agreed that the Florida law conflicted with the CDA and had to give way under the Supremacy Clause of the U.S. Constitution. The purpose of that law was to permit – and encourage – "computer service providers to establish standards of decency without risking liability for doing so."[146] The court found the federal law's rejection of liability for removal of objectionable speech applicable to the Florida law's attempt to protect politicians and victims of deplatforming, inconsistent platform censorship, and "shadow-banning."[147] CDA Section 230, on the other hand, promotes deplatforming, including of disfavored political candidates, and including arbitrary or inconsistent deplatforming, in the view of some judges.[148]

In July 2021, the Florida officials filed their notice of the state's intent to appeal the injunction to the United States Court of Appeals for the Eleventh Circuit.[149] The state argued that under Supreme Court case law, state governments and even federal agencies may require private enterprises to open up their facilities to speakers with whom they disagree, even vehemently. In one case, the Supreme Court ruled that the State of California could require shopping malls to allow certain persons to speak freely in them, despite the malls' claim to have editorial freedom based on ownership.[150] In the other, the Court rejected a challenge to federal laws restricting federal funding to law schools that refused to allow military recruiters operate in the schools' recruiting events, a refusal that some law schools justified on the grounds that the military discriminated against gay, lesbian, and bisexual persons, among other sexual minorities.[151] The Florida officials regard these cases as opening a space for compelled access to certain facilities, especially where there is a clear way for the public to distinguish the speaker from the facility's operator, such as distinguishing activists in a mall from mall security or officials, or distinguishing recruiters from law school faculty or deans. There was little chance, in the state's view, that users of Twitter or YouTube would confuse political candidates like Donald Trump or journalistic enterprises like the *New York Post* with the platform's owners or officials.

The Eleventh Circuit found that the platforms must prevail in their challenge to Florida's anti-deplatforming law. The law burdened Facebook, TikTok, Twitter, and YouTube too much, it ruled. These platforms have a right of editorial expression, which they exercise by removing "content" that they judge to be contrary to their community standards.[152] In a critical passage, the curt distinguished other laws, such as anti-discrimination laws, federal spending rules, or state constitutional laws, which might force a private actor to host or tolerate expression with which it disagrees:

> The first decision to which the State points, *PruneYard*, is readily distinguishable. There, the Supreme Court affirmed a state court's decision requiring a privately owned shopping mall to allow members of the public to circulate petitions on its property. 447 U.S. at 76–77, 88, 100 S.Ct. 2035. In that case, though, the only First Amendment interest that the mall owner asserted was the right "not to be forced by the State to use [its] property as a forum for the speech of others." *Id.* at 85, 100 S.Ct. 2035. The Supreme Court's subsequent decisions . . . cabined *PruneYard.* [There was no] . . . concern that access to this area might affect the shopping center owner's exercise of his own right to speak: the owner did not even allege that he objected to the content of the pamphlets." 475 U.S. at 12, 106 S.Ct. 903 (plurality op.); *see also id.* at 24, 106 S.Ct. 903 (Marshall, J., concurring in the judgment) ("While the shopping center owner in *PruneYard* wished to be free of unwanted expression, he nowhere alleged that his own expression was hindered in the slightest."). . . . Because NetChoice asserts that S.B. 7072 interferes with the platforms' own speech rights by forcing them to carry messages that contradict their community standards and terms of service, *PruneYard* is inapposite. . . .
>
> In [*Rumsfeld*], the Supreme Court upheld a federal statute – the Solomon Amendment – that required law schools, as a condition to receiving federal funding, to allow military recruiters the same access to campuses and students as any other employer. 547 U.S. at 56, 126 S.Ct. 1297. The . . . Court held that the law didn't implicate the First Amendment because it "neither limit[ed] what law schools may say nor require[d] them to say anything." *Id.* at 60, 126 S.Ct. 1297 . . . [¶] [This case] isn't controlling here because social-media platforms warrant First Amendment protection on both of the grounds that the Court held that law-school recruiting services didn't. . . . [¶] S.B. 7072 interferes with social-media platforms' own "speech" within the meaning of the First Amendment. Social-media platforms, unlike law-school recruiting services, are in the business of disseminating curated collections of speech.[153]

The court, unfortunately, disregarded more factually similar Supreme Court opinions, involving the fairness doctrine in FCC broadcast television and radio law, and the ability of the press to exclude upstart newspapers from news-sharing systems like the Associated Press.[154] Eugene Volokh and Donald M. Falk argue that these cases no longer stand (or never stood) for the idea that a company can be forced under antitrust law to publish content with which it editorially disagrees, consistent with the First Amendment.[155] At least two cases they cite, however, required a party either to change its own governing document or to generate new documents protected by the First Amendment (like litigation briefs) in order to comply with antitrust obligations.[156] The expressive harm is much less serious than that when a big company simply has to be a conduit for other speakers, rather than altering publications issued in its own name.

It is conceivable that, on appeal, the Supreme Court could accept Florida's view that a rule compelling a person to open up property to others desiring to speak on certain topics does not violate the First Amendment, at least where the law is not impossibly vague and does not force the property owner to speak or refrain from speaking on its own behalf.[157] For example, the Court might draw heavily from the following analysis in a 2006 Supreme Court opinion:

> "[I]t has never been deemed an abridgment of freedom of speech or press to make a course of conduct illegal merely because the conduct was in part initiated, evidenced, or carried out by means of language, either spoken, written, or printed." *Giboney v. Empire Storage & Ice Co.*, 336 U. S. 490, 502 (1949). Congress, for example, can prohibit employers from discriminating in hiring on the basis of race. The fact that this will require an employer to take down a sign reading "White Applicants Only" hardly means that the law should be analyzed as one regulating the employer's speech rather than conduct. See *R. A. V. v. St. Paul*, 505 U. S. 377, 389 (1992) ("[W]ords can in some circumstances violate laws directed not against speech but against conduct"). Compelling a law school that sends scheduling e-mails for other recruiters to send one for a military recruiter is simply not the same as forcing a student to pledge allegiance [to the flag when the student or a parent objects to this].[158]

The justices might have to adopt narrowing or clarifying constructions of some terms in the statute, however, to avoid unconstitutionally chilling the freedoms of speech and of the press pending the trial on the statute's constitutionality and validity. As the lower courts pointed out in *NetChoice v. Moody*, mandates of "consistent" application of terms of service, like bans on efforts to "prioritize" content by or about one candidate at the expense of another, are rules subject to various interpretations.[159] Alternatively, the justices might suggest that the merits of the parties' contentions get examined more closely in a trial, during which the State of Florida would offer evidence that its anti-deplatforming law serves important interests, imposes a minimal burden on platforms' speech, and is not overbroad in effect.[160]

On the issue of federal preemption and the Supremacy Clause, it is possible that the Supreme Court will agree with Florida officials that enjoining the law is premature until the state enforces it, and its enforcement punishes "good faith" conduct against "objectionable" material, i.e. conduct shielded from state regulation by the federal CDA. A more controversial ruling would be that the Florida law is at least partially valid because CDA Section 230 does not cover bad faith removals, or even because Section 230 does not cover any removal or demonetization of non-obscene, non-violent discourse.[161] Some courts other than those in Florida reject the use of Section 230 to cover speech that is not indecent, obscene, harassing, or excessively violent.[162] An even more complex question is whether the CDA is itself unconstitutional for encouraging and emboldening social media and e-commerce platforms to carry out the (capricious) intention of Congress to cleanse the Internet of offensive and indecent speech.[163] The district court in *NetChoice* cited the Supreme Court's important 1997 decision on this act of Congress, specifically for the proposition that Big Tech platforms have First Amendment rights. The 1997 decision, however, may also stand for the premise that Congress passed a web of provisions designed to censor and control Internet speech, including the statute being used by the NetChoice plaintiffs to wipe out significant user protections.[164]

Several pieces of proposed legislation might dramatically transform the statutory landscape, and perhaps also the constitutional one. In Congress, the American Choice and Innovation Online Act, which received a vote of approval by the House Judiciary Committee in June 2022, is part of a package of competition law reforms; it would restrict certain forms of "discrimination" or deprioritization – as of a video platform or social media app disadvantaged by Alphabet/Google – when such conduct affects "business users."[165] An official with one of the plaintiffs in the *NetChoice* litigation warns that this provision could have a similar effect to the Florida anti-deplatforming law, at least in some cases.[166] Republican members of Congress have proposals more targeted to platform censorship than to competition law, but because Republicans are currently in the minority, these would be on hold until at least one house of Congress changes party control and Republicans push through a bill, perhaps using it as a bargaining chip while giving the Democrats in the White House or the other chamber a win. One such proposal would classify certain Big Tech platforms as public places where viewpoint discrimination is banned.[167]

While some of these proposals have political and arguably constitutional problems of their own, they may have advantages over the Florida Internet platform law in terms of definitional and substantive clarity – and a federal provenance. They also have certain counterparts in the European Union and other regions; in Europe, most notably, the Digital Services Act (DSA) would protect freedom of expression by allowing users to challenge deplatforming decisions.[168]

A Human Right to Maximize Internet Access for Human Development

The DSA would increase transparency and some user rights in the event of the removal of user speech or algorithmic manipulation of its availability or visibility. As the transparency model discussed in Chapter 1 contemplates, regulated entities must disclose "information on any policies, procedures, measures and tools used for the purpose of content moderation, including algorithmic decision-making and human review, as well as the rules of procedure of their internal complaint-handling system." They also have to disclose "significant changes made to terms and conditions, for instance when they modify the rules on information that is permitted on their service," or other modifications to permitted uses.[169]

The DSA goes beyond the transparency model, however, in requiring actions on behalf of users. Among other things: (1) when a platform decides that information provided by users will be removed to comply with law or the service's conditions of use, it must inform the user or other person impacted by the decision; (2) this disclosure must be "clear and easily comprehensible" and include the "reasons for its decision and the available possibilities for redress to contest the decision;" (3) the identity of any person or entity who complained about the information should be provided to the user where necessary to contest the decision, such as in intellectual property disputes; (4) the user should have a chance to participate in a challenge or out-of-court dispute settlement of such disputes, settlement "by certified bodies that have the requisite independence, means and expertise to carry out their activities in a fair, swift and cost-effective manner;" and (5) the fees charged for dispute settlement "should be reasonable, accessible, attractive, inexpensive for consumers and proportionate, and assessed on a case-by-case basis" and the user "should not be prevented from initiating judicial proceedings in relation to the same dispute.[170]

The DSA is not a full nondiscrimination or fair treatment framework. It does contemplate fair resolution of disputes and other protection of users from discrimination, however, so it may represent an improvement of the law in some parts of the United States in this one regard. Some of its provisions only apply to "designated" "gatekeepers," the "very large" search engines, social media apps, and app stores that much assess and report on/respond to risks to freedom of expression, elections, or health and safety occasioned by their AI or algorithmic rankings.[171] In addition, such large platforms must offer users an option for the recommendation of websites, apps, or social posts that is not based on user profiling as one of its "main parameters."[172]

The United States may see new administrative or legislative proposals to ensure sustainable user access to digital services and ranking systems. There may be renewed enthusiasm for such a law if, as is quite possible, the FTC loses its Facebook or Amazon case, the DOJ loses its Google case, and state attorneys general lose their bid for an injunction against the Biden administration threatening and encouraging social-media censorship. The former chairman of the Senate Judiciary Committee has argued for regulation aimed at the deplatforming of newspapers or other users by ubiquitous digital platforms; while discrimination in favor of newspapers or even news might be suspect, some form of framework that disproportionately benefits newsgatherers and opinionmakers as delivering public speeches may be imaginable. Various bipartisan proposals would limit platform or "gatekeeper" power over app downloads and transactions, or online innovation more generally, or focus on mergers and acquisitions by Big Tech.[173] A key concern of the European Commission as articulated in its abuse of dominance decision on Google Search (Shopping) was that competitor comparison shopping services (including those of smaller businesses) were subject to the vagaries of algorithmic "demotion," while Google Shopping was not. This sort of self-preferencing in the display of Google Shopping on google.com was objectively unnecessary, disproportionate in its impact on competitors vis à vis any efficiency benefits, or both. Other forms of downranking or account removal demanded by U.S. officials are neither necessary to protect the public nor viewpoint-neutral in practice.[174]

The regulation of digital marketplaces to promote the principles of equal access and consumer choice could evolve in one of several ways. For one thing, courts and other institutions such as justice departments and competition commissions could elaborate on existing legal norms concerning fairness and equal treatment. Alternatively, national legislatures or transnational ones such as the European institutions are amending competition law to target loopholes in the treatment of self-preferencing, refusals to deal, "shared" monopolies and monopsonies, or conglomerate mergers and acquisitions. This approach may be easier in Europe than in the United States due to the institutional design and political divisions in the latter, but a targeted effort to tailor or revive the "essential facilities" doctrine as the House antitrust subcommittee suggested holds some promise to empower upstart firms, the DOJ, and the FTC. The United States nearly passed one or more domain-specific laws that would prohibit harmful denials of equitable access to a digital platform's prime spaces of visibility and profitability, such as U.S. proposals for the separation of platforms and commerce or the European Digital Markets Act (DMA). The Open App Markets Act enjoyed some support in the U.S. Senate, and a House antitrust subcommittee proposed codifying an essential facilities doctrine.[175] A more modest reform might be to enhance digital antitrust enforcement by lessening the burden borne by the government and private parties to show market or monopoly power in a "two-sided market" and shifting the burden to large firms to prove that an acquisition of a (nascent?) competitor does not lessen competition or tend towards monopoly. The FTC is reinvigorating its enforcement of the prohibition of unfair acts and practices, which has the drawback of being vague but the potential virtue of considering the benefits of the speech that a platform disallows.[176] The challenge will be to avoid the arbitrariness that regulation may impose, while hearing unpopular voices about how apps and websites are being unfairly targeted and excluded from achieving prominence.

Whether or not the Supreme Court upholds the Texas or Florida approach to deplatforming and shadow-banning, in whole or in part, the U.S. states will no doubt be active in this area. Requiring evidence of market power, an impact on the broader public, a nexus to an approaching election, or a certain size of platform could temper the adverse impact of state laws restricting user bans on smaller platforms with smaller legal staffs. A small claims court or no-action letter proceeding, funded by the public, might be beneficial. It would be a place where a platform or its user could quickly have disputes about the legality of user posts or apps decided in some form of arbitration or administrative proceeding. Meanwhile, the states could be rigorous in avoiding discrimination among speakers that might reveal content or viewpoint preferences on legislators' part, other than the preference for openness and fair treatment.[177] For example, they could implement existing state constitutional rights on the part of persons to speak freely despite private censors, and to use private property to speak or petition those in power for reforms.[178]

Things of Value: Big Tech and Fair Elections Law

In the Netflix series *House of Cards*, Season 4 features a contested presidential election between a Democratic incumbent and a Republican challenger during a war on terror. The challenger "owns" the head of a search engine, in the series, and uses it to obtain an advantage. Knowing more than anyone else about what people are searching for online, and what they may want a candidate to say, could be priceless. The story arc raised a question for reviewers: what if real candidates pry open backdoors into search engines and manipulate elections this way?[179]

There should be a law, right? Would not stealth aid to candidates – involving huge repositories of nonpublic information and data on engagement with ads and political topics – upend the playing field between rivals for elected office, potentially putting the worse candidate in power?

At the federal level, there is a very long section in the law concerning voting and elections. One section states that candidates should not accept certain contributions from corporations, and corporations should not make them. The Federal Elections Commission (FEC) interprets the ban on contributions widely, sort of like the federal bribery statute, which covers "anything of value" even if it is not cash or cash equivalents like checks.[180] After *Citizen's United v. FEC*, it is questionable whether providing information to a candidate and speech in their favor (such as attack ads or fake news powered by bots amplifying articles' popularity) can be prohibited at all.[181] Yet advocacy groups and FEC commissioners argue that receiving in-kind support from a U.S. company or foreign government, for example, violates elections laws.[182] There is an exemption for media corporations, further complicating both the statutory and the First Amendment framework governing in-kind support for presidential or legislative candidates.[183]

Third-party candidates and victims of unfair presidential primaries have been complaining about in-kind contributions for many years. Their pleas for a level playing field were rebuffed.[184] For years, media corporations and primary and general election debate organizers have arguably been giving some candidates disproportionate minutes and hours of television coverage, fawning and slanted debate questions, biased moderator interventions, and other unfair benefits.[185]

The question may arise someday as to whether the discriminatory denial of social media, search engine, online video, messaging, or other services could be a regulated campaign contribution. Complex questions may arise concerning purchase at the going rate, donated use of prime digital facilities or placement, bad-faith demotion or demonetization of other candidates, and the like. This is another quite powerful, if limited, route to achieve communicative freedom. Observers of certain foreign elections in particular are acutely aware that lack of access to state media, state control over private media, and denial of candidate access to coverage can result in unfairness.[186] In the United States, the FEC is concerned that giving away facilities and employees' time and attention to a candidate could be a "thing of value," which election law should control.[187] Under international and hopefully under U.S. law, there should be nothing that prevents "parties and the candidates from freely presenting their views and qualifications, or [that] prevents the voters from learning and discussing them or from casting their vote free of fear of retribution."[188]

A National Guarantee of Advanced Communications Services?[189]

The Open Internet Coalition has endorsed efforts by the FCC to reach a commonsense clarification of its authority to promote open and widely accessible high-speed Internet service.[190] Its members included Amazon, eBay, Facebook, Google, Netflix, Sony Electronics, TiVo, and Twitter.[191] Prior to a D.C. Circuit ruling in a major case, a coalition of Internet industry leaders such as Jeff Bezos of Amazon, Eric Schmidt of Google, and Mark Zuckerberg of Facebook wrote the FCC to express their view that: "For most of the Internet's history, FCC rules have ensured that consumers have been able to *choose the content and services they want* over their Internet connections."[192] Academic experts have reached similar conclusions.[193]

Congress declared that the FCC "shall encourage the deployment on a reasonable and timely basis of advanced telecommunications capability to all Americans" with "measures that promote competition in the local telecommunications market, or other regulating methods that remove barriers to infrastructure investment."[194] The Supreme Court has held that "the Commission remains free to impose special regulatory duties on [cable Internet providers] under its Title I ancillary jurisdiction."[195]

Comcast itself invited these conclusions by reassuring the Supreme Court that it should uphold the FCC's early 2000s deregulatory orders because "the FCC retained *Chevron* discretion in classifying cable modem service,"[196] so that " 'the Supreme Court would be bound under *Chevron* to defer to the [agency] rule.' "[197] Subsequently, Comcast reassured a lower court that was hearing a private case against the company that "[a]ny inquiry into whether Comcast's [peer-to-peer] management is unlawful falls squarely within the FCC's subject matter jurisdiction."[198] The Supreme Court only rejected a challenge to the FCC's deregulatory orders of the early 2000s on the grounds that Title I ancillary jurisdiction could still be used.[199]

In 2010, the D.C. Circuit noted that Section 706 is a "mandate" but rejected it as a source of authority over broadband based on the FCC's own prior binding order disclaiming Section 706 as a source of its power, in 1998.[200] The court indicated that the FCC could overrule that prior order as long as it did not do so silently.[201] The Telecommunications Act of 1996 grants the FCC "significant, albeit not unfettered, authority and discretion to settle on the best regulatory or deregulatory approach to broadband."[202]

It is possible that the right to advanced digital services only applies to wired and wireless broadband and not to information services or platforms (sometimes called edge providers). Congress defined advanced telecommunications capability to include "high-speed, switched, broadband telecommunications capability that enables users to originate and receive high-quality voice, data, graphics, and video telecommunications using any technology."[203] Prior to *Comcast*, the D.C. Circuit distinguished an "information service" from a "telecommunications" service and rejected the notion that Congress had intended broadband to go unregulated by declaring it an "information service" in the same category as electronic publishing or e-mail that required few licenses to operate.[204] In 2010, the D.C. Circuit ruled that the FCC lacked the jurisdiction to issue open Internet rules, specifically those applicable to blocking or throttling peer-to-peer file sharing protocols.[205] The court held that several statutory delegations of authority to the FCC to monitor and improve competition, including competition in providing "advanced telecommunications capability," efficient public telecommunications networks, and wire and radio communication, did not constitute subject-matter jurisdiction for the FCC to regulate Comcast's attempts to interfere with the proper operation of the Internet.[206]

In 2018, the FCC placed broadband in virtually the same category as information services like Google or LexisNexis, but continued to regulate it particularly as to anticompetitive conduct under a "light touch" Title I approach.[207] The commission noted that it has authority to regulate Internet services that are not common carriers, and to "identify and eliminat[e] . . . market entry barriers for . . . small businesses in the provision and ownership of telecommunications services and information services, or in the provision of parts or services to providers of telecommunications services and information services."[208] Although proper administrative procedures would have to be followed, the FCC could use this provision to implement some form of platform neutrality. If it applies to information services, it could have a broader scope than Section 706.

Net neutrality and platform neutrality laws safeguard the freedom to innovate in a dynamic economy. The FCC argued in 2008 that disfavoring specific Internet protocols or practices " 'damages the Internet as a whole,' including the ability of entrepreneurs to enter the market with new Internet services."[209] The agency cited testimony from one of the architects of the Internet that "[t]he Internet's open, neutral architecture has proven to be an enormous engine for market innovation, economic growth, social discourse, and the free flow of ideas."[210] Analogously, one of the objectives of the fairness doctrine was to compel the opening up of the broadcast airwaves to persons and organizations desiring to develop formats and content relating to "coverage of public issues" and "broadcast news and commentary."[211]

Big Tech companies, such as Amazon, eBay, Google, Intel, Microsoft, and Yahoo! have agreed that net neutrality is needed to protect innovation from the power of infrastructure companies to favor their own Internet services, and to pick winners and losers by charging higher fees or providing degraded service to the "losers."[212] In antitrust terms, non-neutrality represents a bundling of content or applications/formats with access to the underlying network, whether it is a television station, residential cable, or telephone network. The danger of such bundling is that it will force consumers to accept a bundled product they do not want or that does not satisfy their needs with a bundling product that they cannot cheaply or easily do without, like a scarce broadcast frequency or high-speed Internet connection.[213] It could be an illegal restraint of trade or monopolistic practice under the Sherman Act or an unfair method of competition under the FTC Act. Most advanced economies have governments that compel the unbundling of local telephone networks from broadband access service because of the danger of monopoly leveraging, reduced output, and unnecessarily high prices.[214] In 2005, three dissenting justices concluded that: "Under its undefined and sparingly used 'ancillary' powers, the Commission might conclude that it can order cable companies to 'unbundle' the telecommunications component of cable-modem service."[215]

Google and other platforms have opined that enforceable provisions banning discrimination by broadband providers are needed to prevent them from squashing potential competition in video programming (YouTube or Netflix), text and images (Google, Instagram, or Flickr), online investing (Ameritrade), or telephony (Skype or Zoom).[216] Although Internet discrimination might be profitable for infrastructure companies, it would threaten the existence of the upstart and initially undercapitalized firms that make new options like these possible.[217] The antitrust and telecommunications laws aim to accelerate the pace of technological advances by stamping out market power over essential infrastructure such as oil pipelines, gas lines, electrical wires, telephone networks, or computer operating systems.[218] Permitting Internet discrimination frustrates these objectives, whether by telecommunications firms or platforms. As the House Judiciary Committee declared in a report on proposed legislation, the leveraging of market power undermines competition, restrains the freedom of trade, and impairs consumers' access to various forms of content or services delivered over the Internet.[219]

Suppressing or downranking a website or app would not always be an appropriate topic of antitrust enforcement. One court suggested that where a platform does not provide an app or site of the type it demoted or disparaged, this is not the type of injury antitrust law prevents.[220] Another court, by contrast, found that "disabling and disparaging its competitors' products and services" or "using [a platform's] control over [its] dominant ad auction to preference its own offerings and disadvantage those of rivals" might be subject to antitrust alongside contractual and compatibility issues more akin to those in *United States v. Microsoft*.[221]

Antitrust authority over platforms might be more apparent than FCC authority, but the latter might have benefits as well. Digital-era cases at the Supreme Court and some Courts of Appeal have been somewhat skeptical of private antitrust suits for interrupting high-speed Internet access or merging TV and cellular/Internet companies. Strangely, one of the cases described by the Supreme Court as pushing the boundaries of antitrust enforcement in a pro-consumer direction involved luxurious Aspen ski resorts.

Other cases involving robust antitrust rules tend to involve sporting events and associations of laborers or professionals rather than technology companies, despite the involvement of the Supreme Court, the DOJ, and/or the FTC historically with railroads, electricity, radio stations, business computers, microchips, and personal computer software.[222] There are also significant challenges to an antitrust suit against Meta or Alphabet/Google/YouTube, including the question of whether they compete with one another so as not to be monopolies, not to mention difficulties pursuing small companies like TikTok or X (formerly known as Twitter and available at twitter.com).[223] Unlike AT&T, Microsoft, or IBM, some services of Meta or Alphabet are free to consumers, and consumers and publishers can monetize services acquired by Facebook (like Instagram or WhatsApp) or Google (like YouTube) better than they could in 2014 and without paying anything, e.g., by becoming influencers, seeking patrons, or pursuing offline deals.[224] Neither WhatsApp nor YouTube was profitable in 2011, and WhatsApp didn't even have ads at the time of acquisition in 2014, in stark contrast to AT&T in 1979 or Microsoft in 1999.[225]

The Federal Power to Promote Science and Innovation[226]

Congress has the power to promote the progress of knowledge and technology.[227] One of the ways it achieves this is by recognizing the rights of visual artists to receive credit for their art and giving artists remedies against third parties modifying or destroying art in certain circumstances.[228] Thus, the United States joined other countries in having "limited *moral rights* of attribution and integrity to authors of narrowly defined works of visual arts."[229] The United States and the international community have agreed that the right of privacy is one involving control over publicity, as well as legal rights against misrepresentation, unfair competition, and the like; having privacy rights for persons whose images or words are distorted or purloined carries out the United States' duties under a treaty containing moral rights, the Berne Convention.[230]

Just because a person is banned from a website or app where they have many followers does not mean the person is no longer visible on that platform. Rather, their speech, art, and ideas may continue to circulate there in garbled or patchy form. If the integrity of authorship is to mean anything, there is a case for allowing a person to insist that their authentic work not get deleted from a place where the work and its author are in conversation with thousands of other minds. Therefore, some scholars argue that the moral right of integrity should provide some sort of remedy against those unfair, malicious, bad faith, or deceptive acts of deplatforming that allow users other than the author to use and misuse censored speech. As one of them explains:

> The essence of the right of integrity is to put a check on a publisher's abusive claim as an active speaker or a discretionary editor – it "embodies the author's right to decide what is [the] 'final' or 'official' version of the work."
>
> Moral rights have equal importance for both fiction and non-fiction or factual works. They add gravity to people's expression and their thought and, in the gray sea of information that is the Internet, moral rights thus offer "the hope of culture and ritual of authorship to persist in the human development."[231]

This is the flip side of another important principle, that an author or artist has no obligation to display or sell a work they think is unfinished or botched.[232] The principle (as Methaya Sirichit, the author of the previous passage, recognizes) is not one that would bar any form of quotation, transformation, satire, or parody; it is about preservation and authorial control.[233] Where another author or performer enters into a true dialogue with a work, adding some expression or exercise of judgment to it, their speech interests come into play as well. It is a situation more like adding Community Notes on X than deleting or demonetizing accounts.

Reconceiving a right against deplatforming or shadow-banning as a right of authorial integrity could be critical if CDA Section 230 is interpreted very broadly. Such an interpretation might preempt state anti-deplatforming laws that are not intellectual property laws.[234] A law that vindicates the marketability of individual names, images, and creations is potentially exempt from Section 230, whether it is a federal law or a state one.[235]

Building a Decentralized Web (and Internet Devices) Together

Decentralized Web or DWeb advocates believe that the next generation of websites and apps will be much more decentralized, and this will contribute to preserving civil liberties.[236] Four principles articulated by some of the movement's participants are relevant here:

> We aim for peer-to-peer relationships, rather than hierarchical control and power imbalance.
>
> Our technologies must minimize surveillance and manipulation of people's behavior, and optimize for social benefits and empower individuals to determine how and why their data is used. . . .
>
> We believe that decentralized technologies will be most beneficial to society when the rewards and recognition of their success, monetary or otherwise, are distributed among those who contributed to that success.
>
> If that is infeasible, proportionate benefit should flow to the community at large.[237]

Web3 could offer some of the same benefits, and some DWeb developers also call themselves Web3 developers. Web3 would be decentralized services, often blockchain-based but generally dedicated to enhancing choice and decreasing dominant firms' power by replacing authentication by services such as Facebook with alternative social graphs and application platforms.[238] While it is beyond the scope of this book, some of the proposed legislation or enforcement action analyzed earlier in this chapter might aid Web3 projects to obtain fair competition with Web2.[239]

As George Gilder argues, the "financial establishment" hated the rise of cryptocurrencies that could power alternative app stores, but crypto platforms like Ethereum could "unbundle" money and markets from concentrations of data, user accounts, advertisers, and resulting economic power.[240] This "cryptocosm" could break down barriers between rival data hoards and incompatible applications, empowering users to distribute control of the Web more fully.[241]

So far, many DWeb and Web3 services have not taken off.[242] The Metaverse is a bust so far.[243] Part of the problem may be how much money is locked up in the traditional banking system and legacy industries, which view Web3 and decentralization with suspicion or hostility.[244] Another problem may be the self-preferencing and exclusionary conduct of the tech giants. Either way, it will be some years before DWeb-style decentralization takes off, but this may be a liberating possibility. As Brewster Kahle, founder of the Internet Archive, asks, what if we construct a new Web where the old one once was, but less censored, more fun, and, when necessary and with the benefit of more speaker control, more private? We will have locked the Web "open."[245]

Notes

1 Tucker v. Apple Computer, Inc., 493 F. Supp. 2d 1090 (N.D. Cal. 2006).

2 Epic Games, Inc. v. Apple Inc., 493 F. Supp. 3d 817, 845 (N.D. Cal. August 24, 2021) (noting that Apple had "produced evidence that its security features are more effective than its competitors, a basis on which it competes. Thus, the dispute likely comes down to whether these features and Apple's monetization can be achieved through less anti-competitive means."), *further proceedings at* 559 F. Supp. 3d 898, 1003–005, 1011–013, 1034 (N.D. Cal. 2021). But see, United States of America's Unopposed Mot. for Leave to Partic. in Oral Arg., Epic Games, Inc. v. Apple, Inc., No. 21–16506 & 21–16695 (9th Cir. September 16, 2022) (ECF No. 188) (arguing that trial court in *Epic Games* had improperly failed to balance properly anticompetitive effects of Apple's platform policies against its stated and procompetitive justifications and wrongly restricted the scope of Section 2's prohibition on willful maintenance of monopolies in interstate commerce when it came to high App Store fees).

3 In the AT&T exclusivity case, despite some mixed results partially favorable to consumers' theory that Apple and AT&T had colluded unlawfully to limit competition for lower-priced data and voice service for iPhones bought when AT&T was the only carrier to offer them, certification of a class of consumers to seek recovery of some percentage overcharge by AT&T and/or Apple was denied because of problems with the consumers' economic expert. E.g., In re Apple & A T & T M Antitrust Litigation, 596 F. Supp. 2d 1288 (N.D. Cal. 2008); Ward v. Apple Inc., No. 12-cv-05404-YGR, slip op. (N.D. Cal. class certification denied February 16, 2018), *aff'd*, No. 18–16016, 2019 WL 5957405 (9th Cir. November 13, 2019). In the Mac OS case, the court simply held that Apple had no duty to deal with potential manufacturers of Apple-compatible computers on PC-style hardware unless "Mac OS" was distinct from the larger operating system market so that Apple would be dominant and accrue the duties of a monopolist. Apple, Inc. v. Psystar Corp., 586 F. Supp. 2d 1190, 1198–203 (N.D. Cal. 2008), *subsequent proceedings at* 673 F. Supp. 2d 931 (N.D. Cal. 2009), *aff'd*, 658 F.3d 1150 (9th Cir. 2011).

4 *Epic Games*, 493 F. Supp. 3d at 1051, 1053–54, *aff'd in pertinent part*, 73 F.4th 785.

5 *See id.* at 1054–55.

6 *FTC v. Facebook*, 560 F. Supp. 3d at 23–24 (quoting *Novell*, 731 F.3d at 1076; Phillip E. Areeda and Herbert Hovenkamp, *Antitrust Law: An Analysis of Antitrust Principles and Their Application* ¶ 772d3 (4th ed. 2020), p. 233).

7 The sacrifice test was rarely referred to as such in the 20th century.

8 'Defining better monopolization standards,' 56 *Stanford Law Review* 253, 285, 311–14 (2003) (citing Aspen Skiing Co. v. Aspen Highlands Skiing Corp., 472 U.S. 585, 603 (1985); Otter Tail Power Co. v. United States, 410 U.S. 366, 368–72 (1973); *Lorain Journal*, 342 U.S. 143; Griffith v. United States, 334 U.S. 100 (1948)).

9 Ibid. See also, Thomas G. Krattenmaker and Steven C. Salop, 'Anticompetitive exclusion: Raising rivals' costs to achieve power over price,' 96 *Yale Law Journal* 209 (1986).

10 Eleanor M. Fox, 'An antitrust fable – A tale of predation,' *Concurrences* No 3–2008, September 2008, https://www.concurrences.com/en/review/issues/no-3-2008; Eleanor M. Fox, 'The battle for reform of US antitrust law,' 11 *Journal of Antitrust Enforcement*

179 (2023); Eleanor M. Fox, 'Monopolization and abuse of dominance: Why Europe is different,' 59 *The Antitrust Bulletin* 129 (2014); Eleanor M. Fox, 'The efficiency paradox,' in *How the Chicago School Overshot the Mark: The Effect of Conservative Economic Analysis on US Antitrust*, edited by Robert Pitofsky, pp. 77–88 (Oxford University Press, 2008), pp. 84, 87–88.

11 'The effective competition standard: A new standard for antitrust,' 86 *University of Chicago Law Review* 595, 602, 606–09 (2019).

12 Lina M. Khan, 'Amazon's antitrust paradox,' 126 *Yale Law Journal* 710 (2016); Lina M. Khan, 'The separation of platforms and commerce,' 119 *Columbia Law Review* 973 (2019). See also, Lina M. Khan, 'Section 5 in action: reinvigorating the FTC Act and the rule of law,' 11 *Journal of Antitrust Enforcement* 149, 151–52 & n. 6 (2023) (arguing that the FTC may arrest exercises of economic power short of monopolization or cartel behavior, because under Section 5 of the FTC Act, " 'Congress advisedly left the concept [of unfair methods of competition] flexible . . . [and] designed it to supplement and bolster the Sherman Act and the Clayton Act[,] [so as] to stop . . . acts and practices [in their incipiency] which, when full blown, would violate those Acts[,] . . . as well as to condemn as 'unfair methods of competition' existing violations of them' ") (quoting FTC v. Motion Picture Advertising Service Co., 344 U.S. 392, 394–95 (1953)).

13 Rumble, LLC v. Google, LLC, No. 21-cv-00229-HSG, 2022 WL 3018062, at *2–3 (N.D. Cal. July 29, 2022) (internal citations omitted) (quoting Continental Ore Co. v. Union Carbide & Carbon Corp., 370 U.S. 690, 699 (1962); United States v. Columbia Steel Co., 334 U.S. 495, 531–32 (1948); LePage's Inc. v. 3M, 324 F.3d 141 (3d Cir. 2003); California Computer Products, Inc. v. International Business Machines Corp., 613 F.2d 727, 737 (9th Cir. 1979)).

14 New York v. Facebook, 549 F. Supp. 3d 6, 28–29 (D.D.C. 2021), *aff'd sub nom.* New York v. Meta Platforms, Inc., 66 F.4th 288 (D.C. Cir. 2023).

15 Cf., *id.* at 28–29 (citing *Microsoft*, 253 F.3d at 34, 78, as raising but not resolving issue). The D.C. Circuit, in affirming dismissal of the states' antitrust case against Facebook's platform policies, did not address the course of conduct theory from *Rumble, 3M*, and *California Computer Products v. IBM*, despite the district court's discussion of the states raising the theory against Facebook's acts, although it did – in a footnote–adopt some related reasoning of the district court. 66 F.4th 288.

16 *New York v. Facebook*, 549 F. Supp. 3d at 20–25, 31–34.

17 *Id.* at 33. The D.C. Circuit cast some doubt on this analysis in broadly stating that Facebook did not have a duty to deal with apps with whom it did not provide services to voluntarily in the past, but it also noted that if Facebook had revoked access or terminated an arrangement with an app that still needed access to the Facebook Platform and continued refusing to deal with the app to the time of trial, an injunction might serve an antitrust goal. 66 F.4th 288.

18 United States v. Microsoft Corp., 253 F.3d 34, 58 (D.C. Cir. 2001).

19 *Id.* at 63 (D.C. Cir. 2001) (en banc) (deeming it just as "frivolous" to argue that property rights in baseball bats justify attacks with them, as to argue that proprietary interest in copyrighted software, and copyright owner's right to prevent derivative works from being prepared from it, would justify antitrust violations involving such software and denial of access to its interface on part of competitors); Elhauge, previous n. 8, at 276 (arguing that finding that "patent and copyright statutes simply trump antitrust duties to deal" would be wrong because other "property right[s]," for example in ski slopes or other lands, do not override antitrust obligations). But see, Novell, Inc. v. Microsoft Corp., 731 F.3d 1064, 1074 (10th Cir. 2013) (Gorsuch, J.) ("Even a monopolist generally has no duty to share . . . its intellectual or physical property with a rival."); *FTC v. Facebook*, 560 F. Supp. 3d at 24 ("[I]t is clear off the bat that Facebook's adoption of a policy of not offering API access to competitors did not, standing alone, violate Section 2. . . . [A] monopolist has no duty to deal with its competitors, and a refusal to

do so is generally lawful even if it is motivated, as Verizon's was in *Trinko*, by a desire . . . [to] impede the growth of existing ones") (citing *Trinko*, 540 U.S. at 407)).

20 United States v. Microsoft Corp., 87 F. Supp. 2d 30, 41, 49–50 (D.D.C. 2000) (citing Lorain Journal Co. v. United States, 342 U.S. 143, 155–56 (1951)), *aff'd*, 253 F.3d 34.

21 Brief for Appellees, at 3–10, HiQ Labs, Inc. v. LinkedIn, Corp., NO. 17–16783 (9th Cir. brief filed November 20, 2017).

22 HiQ Labs, Inc. v. LinkedIn Corp., 273 F. Supp. 3d 1099, 1117–18 (N.D. Cal. 2017) (internal citation omitted) (citing Otter Tail Power Co. v. United States, 410 U.S. 366, 377 (1973)), *aff'd*, 938 F.3d 985 (9th Cir. 2019).

23 See also, Brief for Appellees, at 49–51, *HiQ*, previous n. 21 (arguing that such leveraging may constitute attempted monopolization and an unreasonable vertical exclusivity arrangement) (citing ZF Meritor, LLC v. Eaton Corp., 696 F.3d 254, 270 (3d Cir. 2012); *Microsoft*., 253 F.3d at 71; Clear Connection Corp. v. Comcast Cable Communications Management, LLC, 149 F. Supp. 3d 1188, 1197 (E.D. Cal. 2015); Pecover v. Electronic Arts Inc., 633 F. Supp. 2d 976, 984 (N.D. Cal. 2009)).

24 European Union, Consolidated Version of the Treaty on the Functioning of the European Union, art. 102, 13 December 2007, 2008/C 115/01; European Union, Treaty of Lisbon Amending the Treaty on European Union and the Treaty Establishing the European Community, art. 102, *Official Journal* (C 306/1) of 17 December 2007. 2007/C 306/01. See also, Maureen Ohlhausen, U.S. – E.U. Convergence: Can We Bridge the Atlantic? Remarks at the 2016 Georgetown Global Antitrust Symposium Dinner The Metropolitan Club (2016), https://www.ftc.gov.

25 Press Release, General Court of the European Union, General Court largely dismisses Google's action against the decision of the Commission finding that Google abused its dominant position by favouring its own comparison shopping service over competing comparison shopping services [Google and Alphabet v. Commission (Google Shopping)] (November 10, 2021), https://content.mlex.com/Attachments/2021-11-10_VU85MP244SUWSF43/CP210197EN.pdf.

26 Pablo Ibáñez Colomo, 'What is an abuse of a dominant position? Deconstructing the prohibition and categorizing practices,' in *Research Handbook on Abuse of Dominance and Monopolization*, edited by Pınar Akman, Or Brook, and Konstantinos Stylianou (Edward Elgar, 2023), p. 100. See also, Aoife White and Stephanie Bodoni, 'The Story Behind Google's Secret Offer to Settle EU's Android Probe,' Bloomberg News, July 22, 2018, http://bqprime.com/author/28716/aiofe-white.

27 FairSearch statement: Google's flawed proposal, *Fairsearch.org* (June 17, 2021), https://fairsearch.org/fairsearch-statement-googles-flawed-proposal/ (bolding omitted). Although the Android.com announcement is dated two years later than this criticism, it appears that the browser and StatCounter policies were as stated by FairSearch, as of June 2023. There is also some browser choice, contrary to FairSearch's rather sweeping suggestion that there is not any.

28 E.g., Google takes Android search blow in Russia, *BBC* (April 17, 2017), https://www.bbc.com/news/technology-39623343 ("In addition, Google has promised to develop a tool to make it easy for users to change their device's default search engine."); Sarah Perez, Google Reaches $7.8 million settlement in its android antitrust case in Russia, *Techcrunch* (April 17, 2017), https://techcrunch.com/2017/04/17/google-reaches-7-8-million-settlement-in-its-android-antitrust-case-in-russia/ (Russia's Federal Antimonopoly Service placed details on its website about an "out-of-court settlement" with Google whereby, in addition to Android choices, it "must develop an active 'choice window' for the Chrome browser which will allow users to pick their preferred default search engine.").

29 Sundar Pichai, Browsers powered by user choice, *Google Public Policy Blog* (February 24, 2009), https://publicpolicy.googleblog.com/2009/02/browsers-powered-by-user-choice.html; see also, Alan Davidson, A joint policy proposal for an open internet, *Google Public Policy Blog* (August 9, 2010), https://publicpolicy.googleblog.

com/2010/08/joint-policy-proposal-for-open-internet.html; Google and Verizon Joint Submission on the Open Internet, FCC GN Docket No. 09–191, FCC WC Docket No. 07–52 (January 4, 2010), https://docs.fcc.gov/public/attachments/DOC-317413A1.pdf (arguing, among other things, that "[w]hen a person accesses the Internet, he or she should be able to connect with any other person that he or she wants to – and that other person should be able to receive his or her message."); Richard Whitt, What do we mean by "net neutrality"?, *Google Public Policy Blog* (June 16, 2007), https://publicpolicy.googleblog.com/2007/06/what-do-we-mean-by-net-neutrality.html; cf. also, Scott Cleland, Google's ad blocking exposes the company's hypocrisy on net neutrality, *The Hill* (April 21, 2017), https://thehill.com/blogs/pundits-blog/technology/329920-googles-ad-blocking-exposes-the-companys-hypocrisy-on-net/ ("Since 2006, Google has been a well-known corporate leader, funder, and vocal proponent of the net neutrality movement.").

30 Foo Yun Chee, 'Amazon may have to tweak proposals for ending business practices probes,' EU's vestager says, *Reuters* (September 16, 2022), https://www.reuters.com. Previously, Amazon committed to the EU that it would not impose anticompetitive contractual commitments on marketplace sellers not to offer lower prices off Amazon. E.g., Plaintiffs' Complaint, at 8, 88, FTC v. Amazon, No. 2:23-cv-01495 (W.D. Wash. complaint filed September 26, 2023); E-book MFNs and related matters, ¶ 36, Commission Decision of 4 May 2017, Case AT.40153, C(2017) 2876 final, https://ec.europa.eu/competition/antitrust/cases/dec_docs/40153/40153_4392_3.pdf.

31 E.g., New York State Attorney General, Attorney General James releases statement on settlement in principle with Google (September 6, 2023), https://ag.ny.gov/press-release/2023/attorney-general-james-releases-statement-settlement-principle-google.

32 Plaintiffs' Complaint, FTC v. Amazon, No. 2:23-cv-01495 (W.D. Wash. Complaint filed Sept. 26, 2023). See also, Jon Brodkin, FTC files "the big one," a lawsuit alleging Amazon illegally maintains monopoly, *Ars Technica* (September 23, 2023), https://arstechnica.com/tech-policy/2023/09/ftc-files-the-big-one-a-lawsuit-alleging-amazon-illegally-maintains-monopoly/; Dara Kerr, FTC Chair Lina Khan's lawsuit isn't about breaking up Amazon, for now, *NPR* (September 28, 2023), https://www.npr.org/2023/09/28/1202205683/amazon-lina-khan-lawsuit-monopoly-prices-sellers-shoppers.

33 E.g., United States v. Loew's, 371 U.S. 38, 45 (1962); *LePage's*, 324 F.3d at 162; Multistate Legal Studies, Inc. v. Harcourt Brace Jovanovich Legal and Professional Publications, Inc., 63 F.3d 1540, 1543–48 (10th Cir. 1995); Roberts v. Elaine Powers Figure Salons, Inc., 708 F.2d 1476, 1478–79 (9th Cir. 1983); CollegeNet, Inc. v. Common Application, Inc., 355 F. Supp. 3d 926, 953–58 (D. Or. 2018); Tele Atlas N.V. v. NAVTEQ Corp., 2008 WL 4911230, at *3–4 (N.D. Cal. November 13, 2008).

34 United States v. Microsoft Corp., 87 F. Supp. 2d 30, 51 & n.6 (D.D.C. 1999) (quoting III Phillip E. Areeda and Herbert Hovenkamp, *Antitrust Law* ¶ 1746.1d (Supp. 1999), p. 495).

35 United States v. Microsoft, 253 F.3d 34, 71 (D.C. Cir. 2001).

36 E.g., Office of Public Affairs, U.S. Department of Justice, Justice Department sues Google for monopolizing digital advertising technologies (January 23, 2023), https://www.justice.gov/opa/pr/justice-department-sues-google-monopolizing-digital-advertising-technologies (lawsuit alleges, among other things, "inflating advertising costs, reducing revenues for news publishers and content creators"); Plaintiffs' Complaint, at 7, 10–11, *FTC v. Amazon*, previous n. 30. See also, Bobby Allyn, DOJ sues Google, seeking to break up online advertising business, *NPR* (January 24, 2023), https://www.npr.org/2023/01/24/1151055903/doj-files-second-antitrust-suit-against-google-seeks-to-break-up-its-ad-business; Linah Mohammad, Patrick Jarenwattananon, and Ari Shapiro, FTC Chair Lina Khan breaks down the case against Amazon, *WLRN* (September 28, 2023), https://www.npr.org/2023/09/27/1202128274/ftc-chair-lina-khan-breaks-down-the-lawsuit-against-amazon.

37 E.g., Plaintiffs' Complaint, at 10–11, *FTC v. Amazon*, previous n. 30 (alleging a sort of shadow-banning or abuse strike system where trending low-priced offerings might be suppressed by one or more Amazon algorithms); Office of Public Affairs, U.S. Department of Justice, previous n. 36 (DOJ antitrust lawsuit against Google – joined by states by April 2023 – alleged Google was "[m]anipulating auction mechanics across several of its products to insulate Google from competition, deprive rivals of scale, and halt the rise of rival technologies."). See also, Mohammad, Jarenwattananon, and Shapiro, previous n. 36 (FTC Chair Lina Khan contends that Amazon marketplace sellers must refuse to offer lower prices on other sites like eBay or Wal-Mart, and must use Amazon's fulfillment services, if they want to reach a critical mass of Amazon.com or Amazon app shoppers in search results); Devin Coldewey, What is Amazon's [redacted] 'Project Nessie' algorithm?, *TechCrunch* (September 26, 2023), https://techcrunch.com › 2023/09/26 › what-is-amazons-redacted-project-nessie-algorithm (suggesting that Amazon's "small, seemingly arbitrary changes to price we see on items – up by a few cents today, down by a few tomorrow" are a target of FTC's complaint as allowing Amazon to control competition by "increasing or decreasing the price as needed based on the immense amount of sales data they have access to" and preventing excessive or abusive discounting via a product search results algorithm which it "heavily manipulates in favor of certain sellers").

38 125 F.3d 1195 (9th Cir. 1997).

39 *Id.* at 1211 (citing *Aspen Skiing*, 472 U.S. at 602–5). A narrower reading of this case as being limited to suddenly withdrawing aftermarket repair parts from the market to build a service monopoly is also advanced by some defendants.

40 Epic Games, Inc. v. Apple, Inc., No. 4:20-cv-05640-YGR, 2020 WL 5073937 (N.D. Cal. mot. for prelim. inj. denied August 24, 2020) ("serious questions" raised as to whether Apple charged sufficiently high fees to app developers to have an anticompetitive effect; court stated that it anticipated that plaintiff app developer's experts would so opine), *further proceedings at* 493 F. Supp. 3d 817 (N.D. Cal. prelim. inj. granted in part, denied in part October 9, 2020) (finding insufficient evidence that app developer would succeed on Sherman Act theory against Apple to enjoin Apple from terminating developer's app on that basis, but finding "serious questions" as to whether Apple had an app distribution monopoly with respect to apps coded for iOS devices); HiQ Labs, Inc. v. LinkedIn Corp., 273 F. Supp. 3d 1099, 1118 (N.D. Cal. 2017) ("'The Sherman Act prohibits companies from leveraging monopoly power to 'foreclose competition or gain a competitive advantage, or to destroy a competitor.' . . . There is . . . a plausible inference that LinkedIn terminated HiQ's access to its public member data in large part because it wanted exclusive control over that data for its own business purposes; as noted earlier, HiQ faces an existential threat.") (quoting Otter Tail Power Co. v. United States, 410 U.S. 366, 377 (1973)); Tucker v. Apple Computer, Inc., 493 F. Supp. 2d 1090, 1099 (N.D. Cal. 2006) (if Apple unnecessarily modified its iPod to make it incompatible with competitor music stores to iTunes, that would be exclusionary and anticompetitive conduct), *further proceedings at* In re Apple iPod iTunes Antitrust Litig., 796 F. Supp. 2d 1137, 1144–47 (N.D. Cal. 2011); *cf.* Sayre v. Google, Inc. No. No. C 19–02247 WHA, slip op. at 1.C. (N.D. Cal. November 14, 2019) ("Anticompetitive conduct involves electing to forgo short-run benefits because of an interest in reducing competition in the long run by harming smaller competitors.") (citing Verizon Communs., Inc. v. Law Offices of Curtis V. Trinko, LLP, 540 U.S. 398, 408 (2004)); E-Ventures Worldwide, LLC v. Google, Inc., 188 F. Supp. 3d 1265, 1276–77 (M.D. Fla. 2016) ("Here, plaintiff has alleged the Google removed its websites from its search results for anticompetitive and punitive reasons. . . . Google disagrees with these allegations, but at this stage of the proceedings these allegations are sufficient to allege deceptive acts or unfair practices under [Florida Unfair and Deceptive Trade Practices Act]."). *But see* HiQ Labs, Inc. v. LinkedIn Corp., 485 F. Supp. 3d 1137 (N.D. Cal.

2020) (dismissing virtually all of plaintiff's monopolization theories based on power leveraging and stating that leveraging is insufficient without illegal conduct).

41 House Subcommittee Report, previous n. 104, at 277.

42 United States v. Google LLC, Nos. 20-cv-3010 (APM), 20-cv-3715 (APM), slip op. (D.D.C. August 3, 2023) (noting that main monopolization complaint involves only 38 states). See also, New York State Attorney General, Attorney General James releases statement on settlement in principle with Google (September 6, 2023), https://ag.ny.gov/press-release/2023/attorney-general-james-releases-statement-settlement-principle-google; Cozen O'Connor, Google reaches settlement with AGs from 50 states, D.C., and PR on Google Play Store antitrust allegations, *JD Supra* (September 8, 2023), https://www.jdsupra.com/legalnews/google-reaches-settlement-with-ags-from-6180878/.

43 *FTC v. Facebook*, 560 F. Supp. 3d at 21–30 (holding that FTC had not pleaded that Facebook had " 'significantly limited' the 'opportunities for [competitors] to enter into or remain in [the] market' for personal-social-networking services, as is required for Section 2 liability," for example by prohibiting Facebook app developers from releasing versions for other social networks, or revoking access to Facebook functionality on the part of competing social networks who had enjoyed such access before Facebook deemed them to be a threat) (quoting *Microsoft*, 253 F.3d at 69, and *Trinko*, 540 U.S. at 407–9). The FTC apparently did not appeal with the states led by New York because it obtained a trial date on some FTC claims, while the states had all claims dismissed. 66 F.4th 288.

44 Facebook reportedly restricted Vine's access to the Facebook Platform for replicating Facebook functionality. In 2020, Google changed its Play Store policies regarding subscriptions and other digital sales in a way that makes it difficult for apps like Parler or Rumble for Android to allow content creators to receive tips though an app's own in-app payment system. Mishaal Rahman, Google clarifies in-app billing requirements, says using third-party app stores will be easier in Android 12, *XDA* (October 5, 2020), https://www.xda-developers.com/google-play-store-in-app-billing-clarity-android-12-third-party-app-stores/; Rumble, Rumble doesn't allow tips in app due to App/Play Store fees (~30%), *X* (December 29, 2022), https://twitter.com/rumblevideo/status/1608510784296087552. Google also banned Parler for allowing speech related to election disputes or contemporaneous violence, even though such speech – and images of the violence itself – were widely circulated on YouTube, cable news channels, and even C-Span, which were not banned. E.g., Nico Grant, Parler returns to Google Play Store, *The New York Times* (September 2, 2022), https://www.nytimes.com/2022/09/02/technology/parler-google-play.html; see also, James Bisbee et al., 'Election fraud, YouTube, and public perception of the legitimacy of president Biden,' 1 *Journal of Online Trust and Safety* 3 (2022), https://tsjournal.org/index.php/jots/article/download/60/24; Matthew Childs, Cody Buntain, Milo Trujillo, and Benjamin Horne, 'Characterizing YouTube and Bitchute content and mobilizers during us election fraud discussions on Twitter,' in *Proceedings of the 14th ACM Web Science Conference 2022* (2023), pp. 250–259, https://arxiv.org/pdf/2203.16274; Prerna Juneja, Md Momen Bhuiyan, and Tanushree Mitra, 'Assessing enactment of content regulation policies: A post hoc crowd-sourced audit of election misinformation on YouTube,' in *Proceedings of the 2023 CHI Conference on Human Factors in Computing Systems,* edited by Albrecht Schmidt et al. (CHI, 2023), pp. 1–22; Kevin Roose, YouTube cracks down on QAnon conspiracy theory, citing offline violence, *The New York Times* (October 15, 2020), https://www.nytimes.com/2020/10/15/technology/youtube-bans-qanon-violence.html. For cable and C-Span coverage, see CNN, Shockingly disappointing: "Tapper rebukes Trump's election speech," *YouTube* (November 4, 2020), https://youtu.be/ovLKZFNm-8M; Fox News, Tucker: We heard you. it's hard to trust anything. Here's what we know, *YouTube* (November, 2020), https://youtu.be/R5ki6S-WsKU; User clip: Ted Cruz objections to Arizona electors, *C-SPAN.org* (January 6, 2021),

https://www.c-span.org/video/?c4933761/user-clip-ted-cruz-objections-arizona-electors; User clip: Sydney released the Kraken, *C-SPAN.org* (November 19, 2020), https://www.c-span.org/video/?c4924423/user-clip-sydney-released-kraken.

45 Sarah Frier, *No Filter: The Inside Story of Instagram* (Simon & Schuster, 2021), p. 281.

46 Ibid., pp. 46–49, 86, 110, 148, 198, 215–16, 226, 282; see also, S. Duke, Copy, acquire, kill: How Facebook stays on top, *The Times* (July 31, 2020), https://www.thetimes.co.uk/article/copy-acquire-kill-how-facebook-stays-on-top-w2f8lxvv6; House Subcommittee Report, previous n. 104, at 14–15. On the attempted acquisitions, see Plaintiffs' Complaint, ¶ 73, FTC) v. Facebook, Inc., No. 20–3590 (D.D.C. complaint filed December 9, 2020).

47 Plaintiffs' Complaint, at 15, *FTC v. Amazon*, previous n. 30; Brent Kendall, Justice Department to open broad, new antitrust review of Big Tech companies, *The Wall Street Journal* (July 23, 2019), https://www.wsj.com/articles/justice-department-to-open-broad-new-antitrust-review-of-big-tech-companies-11563914235; Kim Lyons, Prosecutors are investigating Amazon's treatment of third-party sellers, *TheVerge.com* (August 3, 2020), https://www.theverge.com/2020/8/3/21352990/new-york-california-ftc-amazon-investigation-marketplace; John D. McKinnon, FTC aims new task force at Big Tech, *The Wall Street Journal* (February 26, 2019), www.wsj.com/articles/ftc-aims-new-task-force-at-big-tech-11551209556?mod=article_inline; Spencer Soper and Ben Brody, Amazon probed by U.S. antitrust officials over marketplace, *Washington Post* (September 17, 2019), https://www.washingtonpost.com/business/on-small-business/amazon-probed-by-us-antitrustofficials-over-marketplace/2019/09/11/c5cfcb4c-d474–11e9–8924–1db7dac797fb_story.html.

48 Lyons, previous n. _47.

49 House Subcommittee Report, previous n. 104, at 268.

50 *Cf.* Dreamstime.com, LLC v. Google, LLC, No. C 18–01910 WHA, 2019 WL 2372280, at *2 (N.D. Cal. June 5, 2019) (declining to dismiss downranking/misranking claim under monopolization theory, noting that discovery was needed), *prior proceedings at* 2019 WL 341579 (N.D. Cal. January 28, 2019) (dismissing monopolization claim but not breach of contract claim, even though contract governed access to a program – Adwords – which plaintiff claimed that defendant manipulated to exclude plaintiff from the market for licensing photos), *further proceedings at* 470 F. Supp. 3d 1082, 1084 (N.D. Cal. 2020) (noting that court had dismissed monopolization claim because Google's conduct was not deliberately designed to harm plaintiff). But see, Apple Inc. v. Samsung Elecs. Co., No. 11-CV-01846-LHK, 2011 WL 4948567, at *4 (N.D. Cal. October 18, 2011) (certain "intentionally false promises" may be anticompetitive); Michael A. Carrier, Don't die! How biosimilar disparagement violates antitrust law, 115 Northwestern University Law Review Online 119, 140–45 (2020) (describing how materially false statements of fact to detriment of a vigorous direct competitor amount to monopolization); see generally, Michael A. Carrier and Rebecca Tushnet, 'An antitrust framework for false advertising,' 106 *Iowa Law Review* 1841 (2021). If you are confused by my parentheticals to *Dreamstime.com*, you have reason to be; the plaintiff switched its theory and seemingly abandoned in June 2019 one theory that the district court had allowed to proceed. *See* Def.'s Reply Br. in Supp. of Mot. for Summ. Judg., at 1–3, *Dreamstime.com*, No. 3L18-CV-0910-WHA.

51 Theatre Enterprises, Inc. v. Paramount Film Distribution Corp., 346 U.S. 537, 540–541 (1954). See also, Continental Ore Co. v. Union Carbide & Carbon Corp., 370 U.S. 690, 699 (1962) (conduct that might be lawful by one company acting in isolation may be evidence of unlawful collusion when other firms act in concert or collusion in a similar way: "the character and effect of a conspiracy are not to be judged by dismembering it and viewing its separate parts, but only by looking at it as a whole"); In re Medical X-Ray Film Antitrust Litigation, 946 F.Supp. 209, 218 (E.D.N.Y.1996) (holding that

"seemingly innocent or ambiguous behavior can give rise to a reasonable inference of conspiracy in light of the background in which the behavior takes place."); Masters v. Wilhelmina Modeling Agency, 2004 WL 594396 (S.D.N.Y. March 23, 2004) (same).

52 *Paramount*, 346 U.S. at 540–41.

53 In re Nasdaq Market-Makers Antitrust Litigation, 894 F.Supp. 703, 713 (S.D.N.Y.1995).

54 E.g., FTC v. Cement Institute, 333 U.S. 683, 683–93, 718–21 (1948) (collusive control over pricing system in industry could be illegal combination of companies in restraint of trade under Sherman Act, 15 U.S.C. § 1); Associated Press v. United States, 326 U.S. 1, 4, 15–18 (1945) (affirming injunction against "a combination and conspiracy in restraint of trade and commerce in news among the states" in form of members of news sharing association using their property and joint business decisions to " 'unduly hinder or obstruct the free and natural flow of commerce in the channels of interstate trade.' ") (internal citation omitted); United States v. Terminal Railroad Association, 224 U.S. 383, 410–12 (1912) (railroads could not use their private property rights and trade association collusively to control commerce across the United States); Official Airline Guides, Inc. v. FTC, 630 F.2d 920, 926 (2d Cir. 1980) ("[I]n *Silver v. New York Stock Exchange*, 373 U.S. 341, 347–49, 364 . . . (1963), the Court held that the New York Stock Exchange and its members violated Section 1 of the Sherman Act when they jointly denied nonmember broker-dealers access to private wire services with certain Exchange members."); see also, JTC Petroleum Co. v. Piasa Motor Fuels, 190 F.3d 775, 780 (7th Cir. 1999) (if some sellers worked together to control prices by boycotting low-cost seller, this could be an illegal restraint); Movie 1 & 2 v. United Artists Communications, Inc., 909 F.2d 1245, 1247–48, 1255–56 (9th Cir. 1990) (similar); Oltz v. St. Peter's Community Hosp., 861 F.2d 1440, 1450 (9th Cir. 1988) (if doctors seized control of surgery market in a Montana community, excluding some options that might benefit consumers, court found that hospital might have conspired illegal with its non-employee doctors); Intellective, Inc. v. Massachusetts Mutual Life Insurance Co., 190 F. Supp. 2d 600 (S.D.N.Y. 2002) (collusion to control insurance policy issuance by excluding plaintiff could be actionable). Cf. also, United States Football League v. National Football League, 634 F. Supp. 1155, 1175, 1182 (S.D.N.Y. 1986) (collusion by teams in dominant National Football League against new football league could be actionable).

55 Cf. Order Modifying Judgment, United States v. American Society of Composers, Authors and Publishers, No. 41-cv-1395, slip op. (S.D.N.Y. November 14, 1997); Arenson v. Board of Trade of City of Chicago, 372 F. Supp.1349 (N.D. Ill/1973); *Paramount*, 346 U.S. at 540–41; United States of America v. Paramount Pictures, Inc., 85 F.Supp. 881 (S.D.N.Y. 1949); Alden-Rochelle, Inc. v. ASCAP, 80 F. Supp. 888 (S.D.N.Y. 1948); see also, Plaintiff's Memorandum in Support of the Application to Modify the Consent Judgment, United States v. ASCAP, No. 42–245 (S.D.N.Y. memorandum filed July 29, 1997); Settlement Agreement, Radio Music License Committee, Inc. v. SESAC Inc., et al., No. 12-cv-05807 (E.D. Pa. filed September 2017), http://dehayf5mhw1h7.cloudfront.net/wp-content/uploads/sites/893/2017/09/22194517/Final-SESAC-RMLC-Settlement-Agreement.pdf; Comments of the Radio Music License Committee, Inc. and the Television Music License Committee, LLC at 8–10 (August 6, 2014), https://www.justice.gov/atr/page/file/1082141/download; Comments of PandoraMedia, Inc. In Response to the Department of Justice's Review of the ASCAP and BMI Consent Decrees at 26–27 (August 6, 2014), https://www.justice.gov/sites/default/files/atr/legacy/2014/08/27/307973.pdf.

56 E.g., Bantam Books, Inc. v. Sullivan, 372 U.S. 58, 62–72 (1963). A Federal Judicial Center civil rights litigation (Section 1983) manual refers to encouragement and other collusion between government officials and private actors as interfering with civil rights under "color of law," which is broader than "the law." *Section 1983 Litigation, Third Edition*, edited by Karen Blum and Kathryn Urbonya (Federal Judicial Center,

1998), pp. 5–12. *Brentwood Academy v. Tennessee Secondary School Athletic Association*, 531 U.S. 288 (2001) and its progeny refer to various theories of collusion: agency (private actor doing public official's bidding), willful joint activity (public and private person work together), significant covert encouragement (from public official to private person), and entwinement (between public agency and private entity). In copyright or patent law, for example, there are many ways in which one person becomes liable for the acts of another that are mutually beneficial or encouraged or aided by the party who does not act directly. It seems fair to say that when significant encouragement of/entwinement in the violation itself happens, rather than just encouragement of the private actor to exist as a regulated firm, then the private action may violate the constitution. *Compare*, *Section 1983 Litigation*, pp. 5–12, *with*, Manhattan Community Access Corp. v. Halleck, 587 U.S. ___, 139 S. Ct. 1921 (2019).

57 Missouri v. Biden, 83 F.4th 350 (5th Cir. 2023), *partially withdrawn on petition for rehearing*, 2023 WL 6425697 (5th Cir. Oct. 3, 2023), *stayed and cert granted sub nom.* Murthy v. Missouri, 144 S. Ct. 7 (2023); see also, Kennedy v. Biden, No. 3:23-CV-00381, 2024 WL 625327, at *9-10 (Feb. 14, 2024).

58 Walz v. Tax Commission, 397 U.S. 664, 668 (1970) (equating entanglement with religion with its sponsorship by the state, or state involvement in it); *id.* at 694 (opinion of Harlan, J.) (noting that "government involvement in religious life that, as history teaches us, is apt to lead to strife and frequently strain a political system to the breaking point."). But see, Kennedy v. Bremerton School Dist., 597 U.S. ___, 142 S. Ct. 2407, 2428 (2022) (apparently limiting consideration of entanglement in First Amendment establishment clause cases to entanglements that are historically unusual or unanticipated by "Founding Fathers").

59 E.g., National Rifle Association v. Vullo, 49 F.4th 700, 715 (2d Cir. 2022) (under *Zieper*, "[a]lthough government officials are free to advocate for (or against) certain viewpoints, they may not encourage suppression of protected speech in a manner that 'can reasonably be interpreted as intimating that some form of punishment or adverse regulatory action will follow the failure to accede to the official's request.'") (internal citations omitted); Mathis v. Pacific Gas and Elec. Co., 75 F.3d 498 (9th Cir. 1996) (private company policy barring illegal drug use or sales was ruled to be state action after federal commission threatened enforcement meetings, orders, or license suspensions if policy was not adopted voluntarily); National Rifle Association of America v. Cuomo, 350 F. Supp. 3d 94, 112–14 (N.D.N.Y. 2018) (under *Bantam* and *Backpage*, virtual orders to private entities and implicit demands on them violate the First Amendment) (citing *Bantam Books*, 372 U.S. at 68; *Backpage.com*, 807 F.3d at 233–35; *Zieper*, 474 F.3d at 66).

60 E.g., Application for a Stay of Injunction, at 7–37, Murthy v. Missouri, No. 23A-243 (S. Ct. application filed September 2023).

61 Ibid.

62 E.g., Daniels v. Alphabet, No. 20-cv-04687-VKD, 2021 WL 1222166 (N.D. Cal. March 31, 2021) (that officials "wanted certain kinds of videos removed and [plaintiff's] videos fell within that category" was not enough to infer state action in plaintiff's case, involving YouTube videos on riots of 2020 and manipulation of bat coronaviruses in laboratories); see also, Rutenburg v. Twitter, Inc., No. 21–16074, 2022 WL 1568360 (9th Cir. May 18, 2022); Hall v. Meta, Inc., Civil No. 3: 22-cv-03063-TLB, 2022 WL 1810962 (W.D. Ark. December 14, 2022), *adopted by* slip op. (W.D. Ark. January 4, 2023), https://archive.org/details/gov.uscourts.arwd.67207/gov.uscourts.arwd.67207.6.0.pdf; Berenson v. Twitter, Inc., No. C 21–09818 WHA, 2022 WL 1289049 (N.D. Cal. April 29, 2022); Informed Consent Action Network v. YouTube LLC, 582 F. Supp. 3d 712 (N.D. Cal. 2022); Doe v. Google LLC, No. 5:20-cv-07502-BLF, 2021 WL 4864418 (N.D. Cal. Oct. 19, 2021), *aff'd*, No. 21–16934, 2022 WL 17077497 (9th Cir. November 18, 2022).

63 Denver Area Educational Telecommunications Consortium, Inc. v. FCC, 518 U.S. 727, 760–766 (1996) (striking down a statute that merely "*permits* a cable operator to prevent transmission of 'patently offensive' programming, in this case on public access channels") (emphasis in original). See also, *id.* at 830–81 n. 14 (Thomas, J., joined by Rehnquist, J., and Scalia, J.) (seemingly recognizing that to encourage removal of lawful speech violates free speech: "§ 10(d) of the 1992 Act, 47 U. S. C. § 558 . . . lifts cable operators' immunity for obscene speech, forces or encourages operators to ban indecent speech. *Because Congress could directly impose an outright ban on obscene programming*, . . . petitioners' encouragement argument is meritless.") (emphasis added).

64 E.g., Skinner v. Railway Labor Executives' Assn., 489 U.S. 602 (1989). And private action is like state action where the private party uses state procedures. E.g., *Cowles Media*, 501 U.S. 663; Lugar v. Edmondson Oil Co., 457 U.S. 922 (1982).

65 372 U.S. 58.

66 E.g., National Collegiate Athletic Assn. v. Tarkanian, 488 U.S. 179, 194 (1988). See also, Lebron v. National Railroad Passenger Corporation, 513 U.S. 374, 384, 395–96 (1995) (private corporation was state actor for constitutional purposes where federal government used it to carry out policy to "relieve private railroads of their passenger-service obligations and provide intercity and commuter rail passenger service"); Smith v. NCAA, 266 F.3d 152, 160 (3d Cir. 2001) (courts "have treated a nominally private entity as a state actor when it is entwined with governmental policies" or "when a public entity receiving federal dollars has delegated control to a private actor") (citations and internal quotation marks omitted); Demarest v. Athol/Orange Cmty. TV, Inc., 188 F. Supp. 2d 82, 90–92 (D. Mass. 2002) ("'[C]onduct that is formally "private" may become so entwined with governmental policies or so impregnated with a governmental character as to become subject to the constitutional limitations placed upon state action.'") (quoting Evans v. Newton, 382 U.S. 296, 299 (1965)).

67 Huber v. Biden, No. 21-cv-06580-EMC, 2022 WL 827248 (N.D. Cal. March 18, 2022), *aff'd*, No. 22-15443, 2022 WL 17818543 (9th Cir. Dec. 20, 2022); Divino Group, LLC v. Google LLC, No. 19-CV-04749-VKD, 2021 WL 51715, at *7 (N.D. Cal. January 6, 2021).

68 "No provider or user of an interactive computer service shall be held liable on account of . . . any action voluntarily taken in good faith to restrict access to or availability of material that the provider or user considers to be obscene, lewd, lascivious, filthy, excessively violent, harassing, or otherwise objectionable, whether or not such material is constitutionally protected." 47 U.S.C. § 230(c)(2)(A). *Huber* actually quotes this language, then loses sight of it in following *Divino Group* to the mistaken conclusion that CDA Section 230(c) is neutral as to content. The subsection title is: "[p]rotection for 'Good Samaritan' blocking and screening of *offensive material*." The statement of congressional policy states that this may be about "children's access to *objectionable or inappropriate* online material." The presidential signing ceremony likewise emphasized that the Internet challenges "our values and make it more difficult for parents to raise their children. Children sometimes are exposed to images parents don't want them to see." Telecommunications Bill Signing (February 8, 1996), https://www.c-span.org/video/?69814-1/telecommunications-bill-signing. A later presidential statement focuses on this one issue as well: "our Constitution allows us to help parents by enforcing this Act to prevent children from being exposed to *objectionable material* transmitted through computer networks." The White House, Office of the Press Secretary, Statement by the President (June 12, 1996), https://clintonwhitehouse6.archives.gov/1996/06/1996-06-12-president-on-communications-decency-act-decision.html (emphasis added). A regulation that targets offensive speech is, of course, neither content neutral nor viewpoint neutral. E.g., Iancu v. Brunetti, 139 S. Ct. 2294,

2296 (2019); Reno v. American Civil Liberties Union, 521 U.S. 844 (1996); Texas v. Johnson, 491 U.S. 397, 417 (1989).

69 Matt Reynolds, The strange story of section 230, the obscure law that created our flawed, broken internet, *Wired UK* (March 24, 2019), https://web.archive.org/web/20210105000234/www.wired.co.uk/article/section-230-communications-decency-act.

70 E.g., Texas v. Johnson, 491 U.S. 397, 414 (1989); NAACP v. Claiborne Hardware Co., 458 U.S. 886, 910 (1982); Watts v. United States, 394 U.S. 705, 708 (1969).

71 'Platform neutrality: Enhancing freedom of expression in spheres of private power,' 17 *Theoretical Inquiries in Law* 487, 488 (2016).

72 Ibid., Quoting Conseil National Numerique, Platform Neutrality: Building An Open and Sustainable Digital Environment (2014), https://www.cnnumerique.fr/wp-content/uploads/2014/06/PlatformNeutrality_VA.pdf, and citing Axelle Lemaire, Which digital strategy for France and Europe in an age of disruption?, London School of Economics (2015), https://web.archive.org/web/20180309173049/www.lse.ac.uk/newsAndMedia/videoAndAudio/channels/publicLecturesAndEvents/player.aspx?id=2998.

73 Decision 19-D-26 of December 19, 2019 regarding practices in the advertising sector (Gibmedia), *Authorité de le concurrence*, https://www.autoritedelaconcurrence.fr/sites/default/files/attachments/2020-04/19d26_en.pdf; Press Release, Authorié de le concurrence, Decision 19-D-26 of December 19, 2019 regarding practices in the advertising sector (Gibmedia) (April 2020), https://www.autoritedelaconcurrence.fr/en/decision/regarding-practices-implemented-sector-online-search-advertising-sector.

74 C-SPAN: Barack Obama Speech at 2004 DNC Convention, C-SPAN/YouTube (2008) [2004], https://www.youtube.com/watch?v=eWynt87PaJ0&pp=ygUVbm8gcmVkIGFtZXJpY2Egc3BlZWNo.

75 In addition to Florida and Texas, reliable Republican-voting states at the presidential and senatorial level in 2016 and 2020, platform neutrality has been proposed in Republican-leaning states during presidential elections, such as Iowa, Missouri, Ohio, and Oklahoma, as well as 2016 toss-up but Democratic-voting (in 2020) New Hampshire, which has two Democratic senators after a Democrat won a very close vote in 2016. E.g., Brief of Amici Curiae State of Ohio et al., at 11–12, NetChoice, LLC v. Moody, No. 22–277 (U.S. brief filed October 2022), https://www.supremecourt.gov/DocketPDF/22/22-277/243634/20221021135207159_NetChoice%20Amicus.PDF.

76 The states that tend to vote Democratic and have net neutrality statutes are California, Colorado, Maine, Oregon, Vermont and Washington. Net Neutrality Responses by State, *Ballotpedia* (2019), https://ballotpedia.org/Net_neutrality_responses_by_state. Except for Colorado and Montana, net neutrality appears to be a strictly coastal phenomenon, excluding the eastern coast south of New Jersey. Rich men south of Camden apparently did not favor it. One exception is Puerto Rico, a commonwealth of the United States that has a net neutrality law. National Conference of State Legislators, Net Neutrality 2022 Legislation, https://www.ncsl.org/technology-and-communication/net-neutrality-2022-legislation. Hawaii, Montana, New Jersey, New York, and Rhode Island have net neutrality executive orders. Executive Order No. 175: Ensuring Net Neutrality Protections for New Yorkers, N.Y. Comp. Codes R. & Regs. tit. 9 § 8.175 (2018); Klint Finley, States and cities keep the battle for net neutrality alive, *Wired* (January 23, 2018), https://www.wired.com/story/states-and-cities-keep-the-battle-for-net-neutrality-alive; Governor's Office, State of Rhode Island, Executive Order 18–02 (2018), https://governor.ri.gov/executive-orders/executive-order-18-02; Katherine Landergan, Murphy order requires New Jersey to establish net neutrality, *Politico* (February 5, 2018), www.politico.com/states/new-jersey/story/2018/02/05/murphy-order-requires-new-jersey-to-establish-net-neutrality-protections-236837; State of Hawaii Office of Enterprise Technology Services, Governor's News Release: Governor Ige signs executive order to protect net neutrality in Hawaii (February 5, 2018), https://ets.hawaii.gov/governors-news-release-governor-ige-signs-executive-

order-to-protect-net-neutrality-in-hawaii/. The states with executive orders tend to vote Democratic in presidential elections except for Montana.

77 E.g., National Cable and Telecommunications Association v. Brand X Internet Services, 545 U.S. 967, 973–75 (2005) (involving 2002 repeal of aspects of cable regulation helpful for net neutrality); ACA Connects v. Bonta, 24 F.4th 1233 (9th Cir. 2022); Time Warner Telecommunications, Inc. v. FCC, 507 F.3d 205 (2d Cir. 2007) (involving Appropriate Framework for Broadband Access to the Internet over Wireline Facilities, Report and Order and Notice of Proposed Rulemaking, 20 FCC Rcd. 14853, 14855, 14862 (2005)).

78 For the think-tanks and nonprofits based in California or New York, see Brief of Amici Curiae the Electronic Frontier Foundation, Wikimedia, et al. in Support of Petitioners, NetChoice, LLC v. Moody, No. 21–720 (U.S. brief filed May 2022), https://www.eff.org/document/eff-amicus-brief-netchoice-v-florida; Brief of ACLU, Reporters Committee for Freedom of the Press, et al. in Support of Petitioners, *Moody* (U.S. brief filed May 2022), https://www.supremecourt.gov/DocketPDF/21/21A720/225626/20220517163128468_RCFP%20Netchoice%20v%20Paxton%20Vacate%20Stay%20for%20Filing%20PDF%20A.pdf. Cf. also, Pasquale, 'Platform neutrality,' previous n. 71, p. 498. Two notable exceptions to the trend I can identify are Columbia Law School's Law School's Center for Law and Liberty, and the nonprofit the New Civil Liberties Alliance, both strongly associated with law professor Phillip Hamburger, who is a strong supporter of platform neutrality. E.g., Brief of Amicus Curiae Phillip Hamburger, *Moody* (U.S. brief filed May 2022), https://www.supremecourt.gov/DocketPDF/22/22-277/243763/20221024133439836_Moody%20v%20NetChoice%20Petition-Stage%20Amicus%20FINAL.pdf.

79 E.g., Daphne Keller, Posting to X (September 17, 2022), https://twitter.com/daphnehk/status/1570952595623268353; Monica Schreiber, Stanford Cyber Policy Center Panel Dissects Four SCOTUS Cases with Major Implications for Internet Platforms (February 22, 2023), https://law.stanford.edu/stanford-lawyer/articles/stanford-cyber-policy-center-panel-dissects-four-scotus-cases-with-major-implications-for-internet-platforms/. See also, Barbara van Schewick, Letter to Marlene Dortch, Secretary, FCC, GN Docket Nos. 14–28, 10–127 (FCC letter filed February 18, 2015).

80 Daphne Keller, Lawful but awful? Control over legal speech by platforms, governments, and internet users, *University of Chicago Law Review Online* (June 28, 2022), https://lawreviewblog.uchicago.edu/2022/06/28/keller-control-over-speech/.

81 Lawrence Lessig and Ben Scott, Public must fight to maintain net neutrality, *San Francisco Chronicle* (April 17, 2008), https://www.sfgate.com/opinion/article/Public-must-fight-to-maintain-net-neutrality-3219226.php.

82 E.g., Mozilla Corp. v. FCC, 940 F.3d 1, 64 (D.C. Cir. 2019).

83 Malena Dailey, Content Moderation by the Numbers, NetChoice (2022), pp. 4–6, https://netchoice.org/wp-content/uploads/2021/11/Content-Moderation-By-The-Numbers-v5.pdf.

84 E.g., Google (2023), https://www.google.com/search?q=hitler+speech+site%3Ainstagram.com & https://www.google.com/search?q=hitler+speech+site%3Afacebook.com#ip=1; Osama bin Laden tells the reasons of declaring jihad [etc.], *Facebook* (2022), https://www.facebook.com. Twitter essentially admitted this even prior to the X Corp. rebrand by stating that swastikas or other Nazi or hateful symbols may be shown on the platform in a photo or video if not included in live video, profile pictures, or account bios. E.g., Twitter, Help Center (April 2022), https://web.archive.org/web/20220415192155/https://help.twitter.com/en/rules-and-policies/hateful-conduct-policy.

85 Hitler, Mein Kampf: Eine kritische Edition – Amazon.de (2023), https://www.amazon.de/Hitler-Mein-Kampf-Eine-kritische/dp/3981405234.

86 E.g., Social Media Content Moderation, *C-Span* (2020), https://www.c-span.org/video/?476686-1/social-media-content-moderation (at minute 41). Michael Schellenberger

emphasizes the linguistic drift and slippery slope problems with grouping terrorism with other problems into something known as "harm":

> Importantly, the bar for bringing military-grade government monitoring and speech-countering techniques has moved from "counterterrorism" to "countering extremism" to countering simple misinformation, otherwise known as being wrong on the Internet. The government no longer needs a predicate of calling you a terrorist or an extremist to deploy government resources to counter your political activity. The only predicated need is the simply the assertion that the opinion you expressed on social media is wrong. These efforts extend to influencing and even directing conventional news media organizations. Since 1971 when the *Washington Post* and *The New York Times* elected to publish classified Pentagon Papers about the war in Vietnam journalists have understood that we have a professional obligation to report on leaked documents whose contents are in the public interest. Yet in 2020 the Aspen Institute and Stanford Cyber Policy Center urged journalists to "break the Pentagon Papers Principle" and not cover leaked information to prevent the spread of disinformation. Government-funded censors frequently invoke the specter of real-world harm to justify their needs for censorship, but the censors define harm for more expansively than the Supreme Court does. Increasingly the censors say that their goal is to restrict information that [making quotes with fingers] delegitimizes governmental, industrial, and news media organizations. That mandate is so sweeping that it could easily censor criticism from any part of the status quo from elected officials to institutions to laws.

Ibid. (minutes 23 to 26).

87 E.g., John Hendel, Iran leader's "saber rattling" doesn't violate our policies, *Politico* (October 28, 2020), https://www.politico.com/news/2020/10/28/twitter-ceo-iran-tweets-ok-433259. See also, Sara Bazoobandi, 'Populism, jihad, and economic resistance: Studying the political discourse of Iran's supreme leader,' *Digest of Middle East Studies* (2023), https://onlinelibrary.wiley.com/doi/pdf/10.1111/dome.12303; Michael Rubin, Why does Big Tech censor conservatives and not terrorists, *American Enterprise Institute* (March 3, 2021), https://tinyurl.com/wx9wm968.

88 Deena Zaru, Battle brews over drill rap in NYC after killings of 2 aspiring NYC rappers spark debate about a controversial rap genre, *ABC News* (February 15, 2022), https://abcnews.go.com/US/killings-aspiring-nyc-rappers-spark-debate-controversial-rap/story?id=82798514; WUSA9, "Drill rap" playing a role in maryland murders, prosecutors say, *YouTube* (July 3, 2023), https://www.youtube.com/watch?v=0Wo0cgNFjCw.

89 E.g., Sanders v. Acclaim Entertainment, Inc., 188 F. Supp. 2d 1264 (D. Colo. 2002); James v. Meow Media, Inc., 90 F. Supp. 2d 798 (W.D. Ky. 2000), *aff'd*, 300 F. 3d 683 (6th Cir. 2003); Pahler v. Slayer, No. CV 79356, 2001 WL 1736476 (Cal. Super. Ct., San Luis Obispo County, 2001). See also, Jacqueline B. Helfgott, *Copycat Crime: How Media, Technology, and Digital Culture Inspire Criminal Behavior and Violence* (Bloomsbury, 2023), pp. 155–172; George Lipsitz. 'The Hip Hop Hearings,' in *Generations of Youth: Youth Cultures and History in Twentieth-Century America*, edited by Joe Alan Austin, Michael Nevin Willard (New York University Press, 1998), pp. 395–415.

90 E.g., British Board of Film Classification, Annual Report (1992), pp. 6–7, 16–17, https://darkroom.bbfc.co.uk/original/9d1cc41183b62e0e5564c92fd28e57f4:91b2c085b0870d853e37a664ff379a12/bbfc-annual-report-1992.pdf (referring to early 1990s wave including *Reservoir Dogs* [later topped in some ways by *Pulp Fiction*] and *Romper Stomper* [later echoed in its themes by *American History X*], and even *Batman* [later topped by *The Dark Knight*] and *Lethal Weapon 2*); The BBFC in the 1970s, British Board of Film Classification, https://www.bbfc.co.uk/education/university-students/bbfc-history/the-1970s (mentioning *A Clockwork Orange* (1973), *Emmanuelle* (1973), and *The Texas Chain Saw Massacre* (1974) as part of a trend: "The 1970s did indeed see the release of a number of provocative films, in particular those

that linked sex and violence."); Helfgott, previous n. 89, pp. 158–59 (1979 film *The Warriors*). On copycats, but in the U.S. context, see Rice v. Paladin Enterprises, Inc., 128 F.3d 233, 254–66 (4th Cir. 1997), *cert. denied*, 523 U.S. 1074 (1998) (referring to a book in the post-home video but pre-social media period).

91 E.g., Robby Soave, *Tech Panic: Why We Shouldn't Fear Facebook and the Future* (Simon & Schuster, 2021).

92 Nadine Strossen argues that hate speech laws vary dramatically in terms of their breadth and required mental state of guilty intent, while quoting many vague terms that the laws use such as demeaning/disrespectful/intolerant, noting that Human Rights Watch calls some of these laws "draconian," and observing that social scientists argue that what is hurtful speech is subjective as well as "situational" or dependent on context. *Hate: Why We Should Resist It with Free Speech, Not Censorship* (Oxford University Press, 2018), pp. 108–12, 124, 137.

93 E.g., Raphael Cohen-Almagor, *Confronting the Internet's Dark Side: Moral and Social Responsibility on the Free Highway* (Cambridge University Press, 2015), pp. 233–34 (discussing Public Order Act (1936), § 5; Public Order Act (1986), § 17; Race Relations Act (1965), § 6); Race Relations Act (1976), https://www.legislation.gov.uk/uksi/2003/1626/contents/made (accessed on August 20, 2022); Race Relations (Amendment) Act (2000), https://www.legislation.gov.uk/ukpga/2000/34/contents (accessed on August 20, 2022); Theatres Act (1968), § 5, https://www.google.com/books/edition/The_Public_General_Acts_and_the_Church_A/JnYaAQAAMAAJ; Video Recordings Bill, Parliamentary Debates (Hansard). House of Commons (January 6, 2010). col. 183, https://web.archive.org/web/20110604192116/www.parliament.the-stationery-office.co.uk/pa/cm200910/cmhansrd/cm100106/debtext/100106-0005.htm#10010649000001 (Video Recordings Act (1984) stopped distribution of some films or games containing "gross violence" by establishing British Board of Film Classification and prohibiting sale of items without classification from it). There are extreme instances in which hate speech utterances may be tortious without a violent act, where there is emotional distress, intimidation or stalking, an assault, or an invasion of privacy. E.g., Brerit Brogaard, Should hate speech be free speech?, *Psychology Today The Superhuman Mind Blog* (March 29, 2019), https://www.psychologytoday.com/us/blog/the-superhuman-mind/201903/should-hate-speech-be-free-speech (citing, inter alia, Gersh v. Anglin, No. 9:2017-cv-0050, slip op. (D. Mont. November 2018); Joseph v. Scalione, No. #84113459 (Fla. Civil Ct., 11th Judicial Circuit 2019)).

94 Danielle Seat, New bill could criminalize recent antisemitic propaganda, *WPTV News Channel 5 West Palm* (June 26, 2023), https://www.wptv.com/news/state/new-bill-could-criminalize-recent-antisemitic-propaganda.

95 Twitter, Help Center, previous n. 84.

96 E.g., Amal Clooney and Philippa Webb, 'The right to insult in international law,' 48 *Columbia Human Rights Law Review* 1 (2017); European Court of Human Rights, Gündüz v. Turkey, December 4, 2003, Appl. No. 35071/97; European Court of Human Rights, Handyside v. United Kingdom, December 7, 1976, Appl. No. 5493/72, para. 49; Rabat Plan of Action, https://www.un.org/en/preventgenocide/adviser/pdf/Rabat_draft_outcome.pdf. See also, Bernard A. Ramundo, "Counterrevolutionary crimes" under the laws of the Soviet Union, A.M. Thesis, City College of New York (1957). Article 19 of the International Covenant on Civil and Political Rights views free opinion and speech formation "indispensable conditions for the full development of the person." Thus, "when a State party imposes restrictions," such laws must "not put in jeopardy the right itself." Laws should be clear so that there is no "unfettered discretion for the restriction of freedom of expression on those charged with its execution." General Comment No. 34, United Nations UN Doc. No. CCPR/C/GC/34 (September 12, 2011), pp. 1, 6. Those that protect a particular community should not ignore "the form of expression at issue as well as the means of its dissemination. For instance, the value placed by [human rights law] upon uninhibited expression is particularly high in the circumstances of public debate in a democratic society concerning figures in the

public and political domain." Ibid., p. 8. A UN Plan of Action of Hate Speech arguably does not distinguish between protected disrespectful opinions and illegal acts, and may stigmatize persons holding certain opinions contrary to the human right of freedom of opinion under Article 19 (ICCPR). Ibid., pp. 2–3. Compare, U.N. Secretary-General, Say #NoToHate (2023), https://www.un.org/en/hate-speech. Defamation laws should not be applied to opinions and the strictures of the criminal law should not be applied to ordinary defamation or "the display of a lack of respect for a religion or other belief system." Ibid., p. 12.

97 General Comment No. 34, UN Doc. No. CCPR/C/GC/34 (September 12, 2011).

98 Ibid., 31.

99 U.N. Secretary-General, Say #NoToHate (2023), www.un.org/en/hate-speech.

100 Ibid. See also, Clooney and Webb, previous n. 97, p. 31.

101 Joan Barata et al., *Unravelling the Digital Services Act package*, translated by Julie Mamou et al. (European Audiovisual Observatory, 2022), pp. 26–27, https://rm.coe.int/iris-special-2021-01en-dsa-package/1680a43e45.

102 Global Partners Digital, UN special rapporteur on freedom of opinion and expression: Report on disinformation consultation (February 18, 2021), p. 9, https://www.ohchr.org/sites/default/files/Documents/Issues/Expression/disinformation/2-Civil-society-organisations/Input-for-report-on-disinformation-GPD-Submission.pdf.

103 Ibid., p. 6 (DSA permits "algorithmic decision-making"). The report observes:

> Companies continue to use automated processes for content modeation, whether required by law or not, and this is likely to increase the scale of erroneous removals of content. It has been widely observed that AI is at a very nascent stage when it comes to analyzing speech and can only accurately identify a small number of categories of speech which don't require an assessment of context or other nuances – unlike disinformation. These issues are compounded by a lack of sufficient transparency by platforms on decisions surrounding content moderation, political advertising and use of recommender systems.

Ibid., p. 3. See also, Niamh Coghlan et al., Special Rapporteur on the Promotion and Protection of the Right to Freedom of Opinion and Expression: A Report by Students at Leiden Law School, pp. 25–27, 34, 45–53, https://www.ohchr.org/sites/default/files/Documents/Issues/Expression/disinformation/3-Academics/Leiden-University-Law-School.pdf (exploring impacts on parody, satire, criticism of public policy, and news reporting).

104 U.N. Special Rapporteur on Freedom of Opinion and Expression, 'Promotion and protection of the right to freedom of opinion and expression', A/73/348, August 29, 2018, paras. 12, 42, 60; U.N. Special Rapporteur on Freedom of Opinion and Expression, 'Promotion and protection of the right to freedom of opinion and expression', A/74/486, October 9, 2019, paras. 6–7, 31–33.

105 U.N. Special Rapporteur on the Promotion and Protection of the Right to Freedom of Opinion and Expression, Statement at the 47th Session of the Human Rights Council, https://www.ohchr.org/en/press-briefing-notes/2021/07/statement-irene-khan-special-rapporteur-promotion-and-protection. The rapporteur, Irene Khan, observes: "States have resorted to disproportionate measures such as Internet shutdowns or to broad, vaguely defined laws that criminalize, chill or censor online speech, or compel social media platforms to remove content without a judicial process." She also observes that while governments perhaps including the European Union may ban disinformation, some people spread false facts by mistake and: "Opinions, beliefs, uncertain knowledge and other forms of expression like parody and satire do not easily fall into a binary analysis of truth and falsity." AI filters are often "unable to capture nuance," she added. Disinformation and freedom of opinion and expression, Report of the Special Rapporteur on the promotion and protection of the right to freedom of opinion and expression, Irene Khan, UN Doc. No. A/HRC/47/25 (April 13, 2021), p. 3, https://www.

undocs.org/Home/Mobile?FinalSymbol=A%2FHRC%2F47%2F25&Language=E&DeviceType=Desktop&LangRequested=False.

106 Giancarlo Frosio and Christoph Geiger, 'Taking Fundamental Rights Seriously in the Digital Services Act's Platform Liability Regime,' 29 *European Law Journal* 33 (2023) (reporting that fines may equal 6% of global turnover, which in case of Amazon or Apple could exceed $500 billion in 2025); see also, Victor Claussen, 'Fighting hate speech and fake news. The Network Enforcement Act (NetzDG) in Germany in the context of European legislation,' 3 *Media Laws* 110, 118 (2019); Coghlan et al., previous n. 103. Indeed, the German law prohibiting fake news as treasonous data or false data seems to be the model for parts of the DSA. E.g., Quentin Fontaine, The German NetzDG: A model for future online speech regulation in the European Union?. Master's degree thesis, Faculté de droit et de criminologie, Université catholique de Louvain (2020), p. 54.

107 FCC Chairwoman Jessica Rosenworcel, Remarks at The National Press Club in Washington, DC (September 26, 2023), https://www.fcc.gov/document/fcc-chairwoman-rosenworcels-net-neutrality-remarks.

108 E.g. previous n. 32.

109 In the Matters of Formal Complaint of Free Press and Public Knowledge Against Comcast Corp. for Secretly Degrading Peer-to-Peer Applications, 23 FCC Rcd. 13028, 13040, 13053 & n.203 (2008); Brief for the Federal Respondents, Comcast v. FCC, No. 17–498 (D.C. Cir. brief filed April 2018).

110 See generally, Stoller, *Goliath*.

111 E.g., ibid.; see also, United States v. Philadelphia National Bank, 374 U.S. 321 (1963); FCC v. Allentown Broadcasting Corp., 349 U. S. 358, 361–362 (1955); Theatre Enterprises, Inc. v. Paramount Film Distributing Corp., 346 U.S. 537 (1954); FTC v. Motion Picture Advertising Service Co., 344 U.S. 392 (1953); *Lorain Journal*, 342 U.S. 143; Timken Roller Bearing Co. v. United States, 341 U.S. 593 (1951).

112 E.g., FTC v. Brown Shoe, 384 U.S. 316, 321 (1966); Pan American World Airways v. United States, 371 US 296, 306–08 (1963).

113 FTC, Policy Statement Regarding the Scope of Unfair Methods of Competition Under Section 5 of the Federal Trade Commission Act (Nov. 2022), https://www.ftc.gov (citing, inter alia, Fashion Originators' Guild of America v. FTC, 312 U.S. 457, 466 (1941); In re Coca-Cola Co., 117 F.T.C. 795, 915 (1994); Consent Order, Statement in Support of Consent, In the Matter of Intel Corp., File No. 061–0247 (Dkt. 9341) (July 28, 2010)).

114 Daniel Crane, Antitrust's unconventional politics, 104 Virginia Law Review Online 118 (2018), https://virginialawreview.org/articles/antitrusts-unconventional-politics/.

115 Ibid. (citing United States v. Columbia Steel Co., 334 U.S. 495, 534–36 (1948) (Douglas, J., joined by Murphy, J., Black, J., and Rutledge, J., dissenting).

116 51 *Congressional Record* 12,146 (1914) (emphasis added).

117 E.g., *Microsoft*, 253 F.3d at 76–77 (deceptive statements relating to potentially competitive software platform); National Association of Pharmaceutical Manufacturers v. Ayerst Laboratories, 850 F.2d 904, 916 (2d Cir. 1988) (misleading statement regarding drugs in letter to pharmacists); Simon-Whelan v. The Andy Warhol Foundation for the Visual Arts, Inc., 2009–1 Trade Cases ¶ 76,657, 2009 WL 1457177 (S.D.N.Y. 2009) (statement regarding art authentication that impaired competition in market for genuine works of a famous artist, Andy Warhol); United States Football League v. National Football League, 634 F. Supp. 1155, 1175, 1182 (S.D.N.Y. 1986) (false statement regarding upstart football league); Analysis of Proposed Consent Order to Aid Public Comment: In the Matter of Intel Corp., FTC Dkt No. 9341 pp. 5–6 (powerful chip manufacturer allegedly misstated potential performance advantages of other chips); In re Coleco Industries, 111 F.T.C. 651 (1989) (misleading statements as to relative timing of availability of products on market); In re Xerox Corp., 86 F.T.C. 364 (1975) (another timing of availability matter); see also, American Professional Testing Service, Inc. v. Hancourt Brace Jovanovich Legal and Professional Publications, Inc.,

108 F.3d 1147, 1150–52 (9th Cir. 1997) (misleading statement that provider of another bar review course was financially unstable); David L. Aldridge Co. v. Microsoft Corp., 995 F. Supp. 728 (S.D. Tex. 1998) (misleading statement regarding quality of upstart software company); Maurice E. Stucke, 'When a monopolist deceives,' 76 *Antitrust Law Journal* 823 (2010) (surveying such cases).

118 E.g., FTC, Policy Statement, previous n. 113; Backhaut v. Apple, Inc., 74 F. Supp. 3d 1033, 1051 (N.D. Cal. 2014) (state law) (citing McKell v. Washington Mutual, Inc., 142 Cal. App. 4th 1457, 1473 (Cal. Ct. App. 2d Dist. 2006)).

119 E.g., Hannibal Travis, 'Of blogs, ebooks, and broadband: Access to digital media as a First Amendment right,' 35 *Hofstra Law Review* 1519 (2006); Tim Wu, 'Network neutrality, broadband discrimination,' 2 *Journal on Telecomm. and High Technology Law* 141 (2003); Christopher S. Yoo, 'Free speech and the myth of the Internet as an unintermediated experience,' 78 *George Washington Law Review* 697 (2009).

120 *NetChoice v. Paxton*, 49 F.4th at 460 n.8. See also, *id.* at 459–60 ("'Something well north of 99% of th[is] content . . . never gets reviewed further. The content on a site is, to that extent, invisible to the [Platform].'") (quoting *NetChoice, LLC v. Moody*, 546 F. Supp. 3d at 1092); *id.* at 460 (Platforms have told their users: 'We try to explicitly view ourselves as not editors. . . . We don't want to have editorial judgment over the content that's in your feed.'") (internal citations omitted); *id.* (Platforms have "told the public that they 'may not monitor,' 'do not endorse,' and 'cannot take responsibility for' the content on their Platforms"); *id.* (Platforms have "told Congress that their 'goal is to offer a platform for all ideas'" and "told courts – over and over again – that they simply 'serv[e] as conduits for other parties' speech.'"); *US Telecom Association*, 825 F.3d at 741 (FCC "concluded that broadband providers 'exercise little control over the content which users access on the Internet' and 'allow Internet end users to access all or substantially all content on the Internet, without alteration, blocking, or editorial intervention,' thus 'display[ing] no such intent to convey a message in their provision of broadband Internet access services.'") (internal citation omitted); *id.* (FCC found "end users 'expect that they can obtain access to all content available on the Internet, without the editorial intervention of their broadband provider.'"); Pasquale, 'Platform neutrality,' previous n. 71, p. 495 (sometime starting in 2004, Google started explaining offensive search results as not being result of its editorial preferences, in response to criticisms); Eugene Volokh and Donald M. Falk, 'First Amendment protection for search engine search results,' 8 *Journal of Law, Economics and Policy* 883, 886–88 (2011) (noting that a search engine does not generate the websites or their addresses or snippets that it displays in search results, in paper commissioned by Google, but not intended for attribution to it).

121 E.g., Pasquale, 'Platform neutrality,' previous n. 71, p. 503.

122 E.g., Roberts v. United States Jaycees, 468 U.S. 609, 627–28 (1984); see also, Boy Scouts of America v. Dale, 530 U.S. 640, 657–58 (2000) (requiring proof that regulation challenged under First Amendment contradicts regulated entity's "'belief in moral values and [that the entity] uses its activities to encourage the moral development'" of people in that direction) (internal citation omitted); *id.* at 683 (Stevens, J., joined by Souter, J., Ginsburg, J., and Breyer, J., dissenting) (for entities to mount First Amendment challenge a law, they must show the "law would require [them] 'to abandon their basic goals.'") (internal citation omitted); Green v. Miss US of America, LLC, 533 F. Supp. 3d 978, 997 (D. Or. 2021) (requiring inclusion of transgender contestants to disrupt "the core expressive purpose of its pageants" for plaintiff beauty pageant to have a First Amendment claim involving not including transgender contestants); Pauline Trouillard, 'Social media platforms are not speakers. Why are Facebook and Twitter devoid of First Amendment rights?', 19 *Ohio State Technology Law Journal* 257 (2022).

123 Board of Directors of Rotary International v. Rotary Club of Duarte, 481 U.S. 537, 548–49 (1987). See also, *Roberts*, 468 U.S. at 628 ("[E]ven if enforcement of the [law]

causes some incidental abridgment of the Jaycees' protected speech, that effect is no greater than is necessary to accomplish the State's legitimate purposes. As we have explained, acts of invidious discrimination in the distribution of publicly available goods, services, and other advantages cause unique evils that government has a compelling interest to prevent."). Cf. also, *303 Creative*, 143 S. Ct. at 2340 (Sotomayor, J., joined by Kagan, J., and Jackson, J., dissenting) ("A content-neutral equal-access policy is 'a far cry' from a mandate to 'endorse' a pledge chosen by the Government."); *id.* at 2326 n.6 (noting that at common law, "the duty to serve all comers . . . came from a business's act of holding itself out to the public as ready to serve anyone who would hire it."); Hosanna-Tabor Evangelical v. EEOC, 565 U.S. 171,188–89 (2012) (exemption from employment law relating to religious mission of a group); Meyer v. Nebraska, 262 U.S. 390, 399 (1923) (Fourteenth Amendment guarantees "right of the individual to . . . worship God according to the dictates of his own conscience, and generally to [engage in] the orderly pursuit of happiness" in freedom).

124 Sears, Roebuck & Co. v. San Diego County District Council, 25 Cal. 3d 317, 326–27, 599 P. 2d 676 (Cal. 1979) (citing, inter alia, Schwartz-Torrance Investment Corp. v. Bakery & Confectionery Workers' Union, 61 Cal. 2d 766, 771, 394 P. 2d 921 (Cal. 1964)). The Supreme Court of California concluded that "First Amendment principles" dictate that "persons may circulate initiative petitions on shopping center property even though the challenged activity did not involve a labor dispute." *Id.* at 327. An initiative is like a referendum in California. A California appellate court has also suggested that the same principles might allow political organizing in a single-store location like a megastore that has assumed the role of a shopping mall but lacks the diverse tenants of the latter. Waremart, Inc. v. Progressive Campaigns, Inc., 102 Cal. Rptr. 2d 392, 398 (Cal. Ct. App., 3d Dist. 2000), *depublished and review granted*, 19 P. 3d 1128 (Cal. 2001), *review dismissed and cause remanded*, 45 P. 3d 1161 (Cal. 2002). Another case found that there is no right under California law to speak or distribute literature in the parking lots of a private medical clinic because "[u]nlike a large shopping mall or . . . public sidewalks," a medical clinic offers "no significant opportunity to disseminate ideas." Allred v. Harris, 14 Cal. App. 4th 1386, 1391 (Cal. Ct. App., 4th Dist. 1991). This rationale suggest that political speech should be allowed on platforms where ideas are exchanged.

125 US Telecom Ass'n v. FCC, 855 F.3d 381, 418, 433 (D.C. Cir. 2017) (Kavanaugh, dissenting from denial of petition for rehearing en banc).

126 US Telecom Association v. FCC, 825 F.3d 674, 740–41 (D.C. Cir. 2016) (internal citations omitted by ellipses) (quoting Texas v. Johnson, 491 U.S. 397, 404 (1989); Spence v. Washington, 418 U.S. 405, 410–11 (1974)).

127 *Id.* at 743.

128 NetChoice, LLC v. Paxton, 49 F.4th 439, 459–60 (5th Cir. 2022) (footnote omitted).

129 E.g., Ilya Somin, Why the Florida and Texas social media laws violate the takings clause, *The Volokh Conspiracy* (September 17, 2022), https://reason.com/volokh/2022/09/17/why-the-florida-and-texas-social-media-laws-violate-the-takings-clause/.

130 E.g., PruneYard Shopping Center v. Robins, 447 U.S. 74, 79–80 (1980); Young v. American Mini Theatres, Inc., 427 U.S. 50, 62–63 (1976); FPC v. Texaco Inc., 417 U.S. 380, 391–392 (1974); Covington & Lexington Turnpike Road Co. v. Sandford, 164 U.S. 578, 597 (1896).

131 Loretto v. Teleprompter Manhattan CATV Corp., 458 U.S. 419, 440 (1982).

132 Cedar Point Nursery v. Hassid, 141 S. Ct. 2063, 2077 (2021).

133 S.B. 7072, 2021 Leg. (Fla. 2021), *codified at* Fla. Stat. §§ 108.072, 287.137, 501.2041. The minimum size of a covered platform would be at least 100 million global users or $100 million in annual revenue, far fewer/less than needed to capture, for example, Twitter ($3.7B/year).

134 *Id.*

135 Impeachment Related Publications | GovInfo (2020), https://www.govinfo.gov/collection/impeachment-related-publications (last visited August 2, 2022). See also, Oversight Board upholds Facebook's decision to suspend Donald Trump's accounts, *Meta* (May 2021), https://about.fb.com/news/2021/05/facebook-oversight-board-decision-trump/ (last visited Aug. 2, 2021).
136 Katie Benner, Kenneth P. Vogel, and Michael S. Schmidt, Hunter Biden paid tax bill, but federal investigation goes on, *The New York Times* (December 9, 2020), https://web.archive.org/web/20210215004026/www.nytimes.com/2020/12/09/us/politics/hunter-biden-tax-investigation.html (last visited August 2021).
137 Fla. Stat. § 501.2041(f)(2).
138 Plaintiff's Complaint, NetChoice, LLC v. Moody, No. 4:21cv220-RH (N.D. Fla. complaint filed May 2021) (ECF No. 1), https://netchoice.org/wp-content/uploads/2021/05/NetChoice-CCIA-Complaint-for-Declaratory-and-Injunctive-Relief-5.27.21.pdf.
139 *Id.* ¶ 32.
140 47 U.S.C. § 230(c)(2).
141 NetChoice, LLC v. Moody, 546 F. Supp. 3d 1082, 1075, 1094–95 (N.D. Fla. 2021).
142 See *id.* at 1093–95.
143 See *id.*
144 See *id.* at 1091–93 (citing Miami Herald Publishing Co. v. Tornillo, 418 U.S. 241 (1974); *Hurley*, 515 U.S. 557; Pacific Gas & Electric Co. v. Public Utilities Commission of California, 475 U.S. 1 (1986)).
145 See *id.* at 1095 ("Leveling the playing field – promoting speech on one side of an issue or restricting speech on the other – is not a legitimate state interest") (citing Arizona Free Enterprise Club v. Bennett, 564 U.S. 721, 749–50 (2011)). Also of potential relevance is a more recent Supreme Court decision permitting New York to give public access cable channels to a private corporation which then excluded critics of the network from using its channels. The Court there recognized that private corporations have "rights to exercise editorial control over speech and speakers on their properties or platforms." Manhattan Community Access Corp. v. Halleck, 139 S. Ct. 1921, 1932 (2019). See also, Divino Group LLC v. Google LLC, No. 19-cv-04749-VKD, 2021 WL 51715 (N.D. Cal. January 6, 2021).
146 Domen v. Vimeo, Inc., 991 F.3d 66, 73 (2d Cir. 2021); *NetChoice*, 546 F. Supp. 3d at 1089–93.
147 *NetChoice*, 546 F. Supp. 3d at 1089–93.
148 See *id.* at 1089–90.
149 NetChoice, LLC v. Moody, No. 4:21cv220-RH-MAF (N.D. Fla. notice of appeal filed July 12, 2021) (ECF No. 115).
150 *PruneYard*, 447 U.S. 74.
151 Rumsfeld v. FAIR, 547 U.S. 47 (2006).
152 NetChoice, LLC v. Moody, 34 F.4th 1196 (11th Cir. 2022).
153 *Id.* at 1215–16.
154 Red Lion Broadcasting Co. v. FCC, 395 U.S. 367 (1969) (holding that First Amendment does not protect private censorship from appropriate regulation of resulting power over public debate and exchanges of views on public issues and political candidates); *Associated Press*, 326 U.S. at 32–33, 38–39, 49 (Roberts, J., joined by Jackson, C.J., dissenting) (dissent opposed antitrust regulation of the press, arguing that "any regulation of this major source of information, in the light of the constitutional guarantee of free speech, should be closely and jealously examined by the courts," but noted that majority's ruling allowed a decree to force members of Associated Press to share their news and "literary product" with other papers); cf., United States v. National Ass'n. of Realtors, 2006–2 Trade Cases ¶ 75,499, 2006 WL 3434263, at *24–25 (N.D. Ill. 2006) ("[P]recedent further reflects that a group of market participants cannot immunize 'arrangements or combinations designed to stifle competition . . . by adopting a [group]

membership device accomplishing that purpose.'") (quoting *Associated Press*, 326 U.S. at 19).

155 Volokh and Falk, previous n. 120, p. 895–99.

156 Ibid. (citing FTC v. Superior Court Trial Lawyers Association, 493 U.S. 411 (1990); National Society of Professional Engineers v. United States, 435 U.S. 679 (1978)). See also, *Superior Court Trial Lawyers Association*, 493 U.S. at 444 (while prohibited conduct concerned a boycott, it was a boycott of specific attorney-client relationships that did not involve enough compensation for lawyers to them provide effective representation); *National Society of Professional Engineers*, 435 U.S. at 697 ("Just as an injunction against price fixing abridges the freedom of businessmen to talk to one another about prices, so too the injunction in this case must restrict the Society's range of expression on the ethics of competitive bidding."); National Association for Advancement of Colored People v. Button, 371 U.S. 415, 420, 438–40 (1963) (recognizing attorney speech as protected particularly where constitutional rights are involved in the cases as being protected by First Amendment even if done for a fee); Greenberg v. Haggerty, 491 F. Supp. 3d 12, 25–30 (E.D. Pa. 2020) (similar).

157 Even the court issuing the injunction against the Florida law stated: "*FAIR* and *Pruneyard* establish that compelling a person to allow a visitor access to the person's property, for the purpose of speaking, is not a First Amendment violation, so long as the person is not compelled to speak, the person is not restricted from speaking, and the message of the visitor is not likely to be attributed to the person." *NetChoice v. Moody*, 546 F. Supp. 3d at 1093. Similarly, the Eleventh Circuit conceded that just as the FCC can compel cable television networks to save broadcast television channels by carrying the channels on cable lineups, so Florida "could argue that S.B. 7072 ensures that political candidates and journalistic enterprises are able to communicate with the public, see Fla. Stat. §§ 106.072(2); 501.2041(2)(f), (j)." *NetChoice v. Moody*, 34 F.4th at 1228 (citing *Turner Broad.*, 512 U.S. at 662). It did not, however, agree with this argument, given candidates' access to other media besides digital platforms, and the alleged overbreadth or ambiguity of Florida law's sections 106.072(2) and 501.2041(2). *See id.* at 1228–229.

158 *Rumsfeld*, 547 U.S. at 62.

159 *NetChoice v. Moody*, 546 F. Supp. 3d at 1086–95.

160 Defendants' Answer, NetChoice, LLC v. Moody, No. 4:21cv220-RH (ECF No. 118) (N.D. Fla. answer filed July 15, 2021).

161 The Florida officials pointed out that the principal provision relied upon by NetChoice, the CCIA, and the district court to immunize Internet intermediaries from state-law regulation is about removing obscene, indecent, harassing or violent content, and that to the extent that the provision also covers removal of "otherwise objectionable" material, the word *objectionable* should be construed to mean something similar to obscene or highly violent. Defendant's Response to Motion for Leave to File Motion for Preliminary Injunction, at 9–10, *NetChoice*, No. 4:21cs2290RH (N.D. Fla. resp. filed June 15, 2021) (ECF No. 79) (citing 47 U.S.C. § 230(c)(2)(A)). As one court in Florida concluded, moreover, an Internet search engine or other platform may not be immune from state statutory liability when it did not act in good faith. E-ventures Worldwide, LLC v. Google, Inc., 188 F. Supp. 3d 1265, 1273 (M.D. Fla. 2016). Good faith would appear to be a fact-intensive question that requires depositions and discovery of documents, precluding a resolution on a motion to dismiss or motion for judgment on the pleadings before a trial. E.g., Google LLC v. Oracle America, Inc., 141 S. Ct. 1183, 1204 (2021); Christian v. Rhode, 41 F.3d 461 (9th Cir. 1994).

162 E.g., Song fi Inc. v. Google, Inc., 108 F. Supp. 3d 876, 883 (N.D. Cal. 2015) (citing Goddard v. Google, Inc., No. C 08–2738 JF (PVT), 2008 WL 5245490, at *6 (N.D. Cal. Dec. 17, 2008); National Numismatic Certification, LLC v. eBay, Inc., No. 6:08-cv-42-Orl-19GJK, 2008 WL 2704404, at *25 (M.D. Fla. July 8, 2008)). Eric Goldman and Jess Miers, 'Online account terminations/content removals and the benefits of Internet

services enforcing their house rules,' 1 *Journal of Free Speech Law* 191 (2021). Cf. also, Apollomedia Corp. v. Reno, 19 F. Supp. 2d 1081 (N.D. Cal. 1998) (interpreting term indecent to mean obscene), *aff'd*, 1998 WL 853216, *amended by* 526 U.S. 1071 (1998); U.S. v. Landham, 251 F.3d 1072, 1085–86 (6th Cir. 2001) (federal statutes referring to filthy or indecent material must be interpreted as banning only that which is obscene).

163 Defendants' Response to Motion for Leave to File Motion for Prelim. Injunction, at 9–12, *NetChoice v. Moody*, No. 4:21cs2290RH (N.D. Fla. resp. filed June 15, 2021) (ECF No. 79).

164 Reno v. American Civil Liberties Union, 521 U.S. 844 (1997). For expositions of this argument that the tech platforms are somehow complicit in congressional censorship of the Internet, see Defendants' Response, *NetChoice v. Moody*, previous n. 161, at 11–14; Sam Husseini, When government and Big Tech collude against the First Amendment: An interview with Nadine Strossen, *Counterpunch* (July 30, 2021), https://www.counterpunch.org/2021/07/30/when-government-and-big-tech-collude-against-the-first-amendment-an-interview-with-nadine-strossen.

165 H. 381, 117th Cong. (2021), www.congress.gov/bill/117th-congress/house-bill/3816/text?r=43&s=1 (last visited August 2, 2021).

166 Arthyr Sidney, House Antitrust Nondiscrimination Bill May Require Covered Platforms to Host Discrimination, DisCo – Project Disruptive Competition (July 27, 2021), https://tinyurl.com/sidneydisco (last visited August 2, 2021). See also https://www.tinyurl.com/sidneybio2021.

167 U.S. House of Representatives, Energy and Commerce Committee Republican Staff, Big Tech Accountability Platform (April 15, 2021), https://republicans-energycommerce.house.gov/wp-content/uploads/2021/04/2021.04.15-Big-Tech-Memo-Staff-Legislative-Concepts.pdf (last visited August 2, 2021).

168 'Regulation on a Single Market for Digital Services,' *Official Journal L* 277, October 27, 2022, pp. 1–102.

169 Ibid., preamble (45) and arts. 16–17, 24.

170 Ibid., preamble (54)-(55), (59) and art. 21.

171 Ibid., arts. 33–43; see also, Natasha Lomos, Europe names 19 platforms that must report algorithmic risks under DSA, *TechCrunch* (April 25, 2023), https://techcrunch.com/2023/04/25/europe-names-19-platforms-that-must-report-algorithmic-risks-under-dsa/; Marc Wiggers and Robin Struijlaart, Commission aims to introduce traffic lights for the digital sector, *Kluwer Competition Law Blog*, http://competitionlawblog.kluwercompetitionlaw.com/2020/12/17/commission-aims-to-introduce-traffic-lights-for-the-digital-sector-detailed-regulation-for-the-digital-sector-instead-of-genuine-ex-ante-enforcement.

172 Regulation on a single market for digital services, previous n. 168, art. 38; ibid., preamble (94); Lomos, previous n. 171. The profiling referred to seems to include account IDs or usernames, and device identifiers, so much of it may be covered.

173 E.g., Open App Markets Act, S. 2710, 117th Cong. (2022); American Innovation and Choice Online Act, S. 2992, 117th Cong. (2022); Lauren Feiner, Senate committee votes to advance major tech antitrust bill, *CNBC* (January 20, 2022), https://www.cnbc.com/2022/01/20/senate-committee-votes-to-advance-major-tech-antitrust-bill.html; Lauren Feiner, Senate Committee advances bill targeting Google and Apple's app store profitability, *CNBC* (February 3, 2022), https://www.cnbc.com/2022/02/03/senate-committee-advances-open-app-markets-act.html; House Subcommittee Report, previous n. 104, p. 1 (objecting to development that "each platform now serves as a gatekeeper over a key channel of distribution . . . [,] can pick winners and losers throughout our economy . . . [and may] abuse [its resulting power] by charging exorbitant fees, imposing oppressive contract terms, and extracting valuable data from the people and businesses that rely on them"); ibid., p. 8 ("market participants analogized Google to a gatekeeper that is extorting users for access to its critical distribution

channel, even as its search page shows users less relevant results."); ibid., p. 29 ("numerous businesses [have] described how dominant platforms exploit this gatekeeper power to dictate terms and extract concessions that third parties would not consent to in a competitive market"); ibid., p. 81 ("App Store and Play Store are dominant distribution channels and can exert gatekeeper power over their platforms, [which] has the potential to distort competition, lead to discrimination," etc.); ibid., p. 156 ("Google's documents show that Google adjusted its search algorithm to automatically elevate the ranking of some of Google's services above those offered by rivals."); ibid. (Google "added a 'cooccurring [sic] sites' signal to bias ourselves towards triggering [in other words, probably to uprank Google sites] when a local-oriented aggregator site (i.e. Citysearch) shows up in the Web results.'") (quoting internal Google document); ibid., pp. 158–59 (one "search provider stated that, after Google purchased its rival, Google demoted the provider in search rankings while vaulting [i.e. upranking?] those of its rival [which Google had acquired]"); ibid., p. 160 ("'Without explanation or recourse, Google can deliver a fatal blow to a website's search ranking visibility.'" One U.K.-based shopping service wrote that: "'An unjustified Google search penalty, whether imposed anticompetitively or in error, has the power to cause grave and irreparable harm to virtually any online business.'"); ibid., p. 263 ("Amazon repeatedly refers to its power to delist [another] company's product if Amazon's services are not prominent enough on" Amazon Alexa's Internet of Things or "smart home" ecosystem); ibid., p. 302 ("In 2019, *The Wall Street Journal* and *The New York Times* both conducted extensive investigations and reported that Apple appeared to be favoring its apps in the App Store search results."). For the former chairman of the Senate Judiciary Committee, Chuck Grassley, and his proposal, see Nihal Krishan, Major anti-big tech 'self-preferencing' bill headed to senate floor, *The Washington Examiner* (January 20, 2022), https://www.washingtonexaminer.com/policy/technology/major-anti-big-tech-self-preferencing-bill-headed-to-senate-floor#google_vignette; Tech CEOs descend on Congress to block antitrust bill, *Politico* (June 17, 2022), https://login.politicopro.com/?redirect=https%3A%2F%2Fsubscriber.politicopro.com%2Fnewsletter%2F2022%2F06%2Ftech-ceos-descend-on-congress-to-block-antitrust-bill-00040430.

174 E.g., *Missouri v. Biden*, 2023 WL 5821788.

175 E.g., previous n. 108; see also, House Subcommittee Report, previous n. 108, pp. 14, 336–342; cf. also, ibid., pp. 1, 5, 9, 26, 33, 102, 138, 161, 210, 323.

176 15 U.S.C. § 45 (2006); FTC, Policy Statement Regarding the Scope of Unfair Methods of Competition (November 2022), https://www.ftc.gov.

177 *NetChoice, LLC v. Moody*, 546 F. Supp. 3d 1082; cf. also, Eric Goldman and Jess Miers, Regulating internet services by size, *CPI Antitrust Chronicle* (May 2021), pp. 1, 3, https://www.competitionpolicyinternational.com/wp-content/uploads/2021/05/3-Regulating-Internet-Services-by-Size-By-Eric-Goldman-Jess-Miers.pdf ("[P]ending bills would reduce or eliminate Section 230 for large services. Other proposals at the federal and state level would impose greater duties on big Internet services.") (footnotes omitted).

178 E.g., Elijah O'Kelley, 'State constitutions as a check on the New Governors: Using state Free Speech clauses to protect social media users from arbitrary political censorship by social media platforms,' 68 *Emory Law Journal* 111 (2019). In this book, I do not focus on this route, as it has been called into question even where a state constitution seems to support it in unambiguous terms, textually speaking. E.g., Domen v. Vimeo, Inc., 433 F. Supp. 3d 592, 606–07 (S.D.N.Y. 2020), *aff'd*, 991 F.3d 663 (2d Cir. 2021); HiQ Labs, Inc. v. LinkedIn Corp., 273 F. Supp. 3d 1099, 1116–17 (N.D. Cal. 2017), *aff'd and remanded on other grounds*, 938 F.3d 985 (9th Cir. 2019), *vacated and remanded on other grounds*, 141 S. Ct. 2752 (2021), *reaffirmed on remand*, 31 F.4th 1180 (9th Cir. 2022); Prager University v. Google LLC, No. 19CV340667, 2019 Cal. Super. LEXIS 2034, at *17 (Cal. Super. Ct. November 19, 2019), *aff'd*, 85 Cal. App. 5th 1022 (Cal. Ct. App. 6th Dist. 2022). There is a great deal of support for

this route to platform neutrality in case law I do discuss, however, such as *PruneYard, Sears, NetChoice v. Paxton*, and even *Waremart* and *Allred*, not to mention *Red Lion, US Telecom Association, Pittsburgh Press*, and *303 Creative*.

179 Jack O'Keefe, Conway has a secret weapon on "House of Cards," *Bustle* (March 4, 2016), https://www.bustle.com/articles/146074-what-is-pollyhop-on-house-of-cards-the-search-engine-poses-a-very-real-threat; see also, Jen Chaney, "House of cards" Season 4, Episode 7: Rock star candidate, *nytimes.com* (March 8, 2016), https://www.nytimes.com/2016/03/08/arts/television/house-of-cards-season-4-episode-7.html; Alexandra Watt, PollyHop has a unique 'HoC' connection, *Bustle* (March 22, 2016), https://www.bustle.com/articles/148363-why-is-pollyhop-so-dangerous-on-house-of-cards-frank-underwood-is-not-happy-about-the. The actions of Conway's Democratic Party rival, incumbent Frank Underwood, raised another question: what if the White House used national-security surveillance to develop lists of voters to target with campaign messages, or to generate messages from patterns in private communications, or (to make it more analogous to what the fictional candidate Conway did) to review and analyze reams of user profiles or the copies of emails or other direct messages sent or received via big platforms to decide which rivals to arrest or hurt? E.g., Aidan Macallan on "house of cards": A storyline recap, *Heavy* (May 29, 2017), https://heavy.com/entertainment/2017/05/aidan-macallan-house-of-cards-refresher-recap/.

180 18 U.S.C. § 201(b); see also, 52 U.S.C. § 30101(8) (definition of thing of value); *id.* §§ 30116, 30125(a)(1) (prohibited contribution statutes); 2 U.S.C.A. § 441i(a)(1) (Supp. 2003) (another prohibited contribution statute); Campaign Legal Ctr. v. FEC, 31 F.4th 781, 784–88 (D.C. Cir. 2022); Ready for Ron v. FEC, No. 22–3282 (RDM), 2023 WL 3539633 (D.D.C. May 17, 2023); George D. Brown, '*McConnell* and the criminalization of politics,' 5 *Virginia Journal of Criminal Law* 1 (2017).

181 E.g., Richard Hasen, *Cheap Speech: How Disinformation Poisons our Politics – And How to Cure It* (Yale University Press, 2022), p. 211–12 (citing Citizens United v. FEC, 558 U.S. 310 (2010)).

182 E.g., Code of Federal Regulations, 11 C.F.R. § 109.21 (2023); Ready for Ron, slip op., previous n. 180; FEC, Advisory Opinion 2022–12, Ready for Ron; Administrative Complaint, Buchanan v. CPD, FEC Docket MUR # 4987 (FEC complaint filed Mar. 20, 2000); Administrative Complaint, RNC v. Twitter, FEC Docket MUR #7821 (FEC complaint filed Oct. 16, 2020), https://www.fec.gov/files/legal/murs/7821/7821_01.pdf; Administrative Complaint, Woodhouse v. Carson, FEC Docket MUR # 6989 (FEC complaint filed Nov. 2015), http://americandemocracy.org/wp-content/uploads/CARSON-FEC-COMPLAINT_001.pdf; Republican National Committee, RNC sends letter to FEC on Twitter censorship, *GOP.com* (December 20, 2022), https://gop.com/press-release/rnc-sends-letter-to-fec-on-twitter-censorship; Brian Slodysko, How Trump's Ukraine call could violate campaign finance laws, *Associated Press* (September 25, 2019), https://apnews.com/article/560b20b139d943969e17c82eda77ca8d. But see, Reader's Digest Association v. FEC, 509 F. Supp. 1210, 1215 (S.D.N.Y. 1981); FEC, Advisory Opinion 2014–20, Make Your Laws PAC; FEC, MUR # 5928, Kos Media LLC (September 4, 2007), https://www.fec.gov/updates/fec-resolves-two-matters-involving-internet-activity-applies-media-exemption-to-political-blogs/; FEC, MUR # 7821, Twitter (September 13, 2021); FEC, MURs # 7207, 7268, 7274 & 7623, Donald J. Trump for President, *FEC* (February 15, 2022), https://www.fec.gov/updates/week-of-february-14-18-2022/; FEC, MURs # 7645, 7663, and 7705, Donald J. Trump, *FEC* (August 31, 2022), https://www.fec.gov/updates/week-of-august-29-september-2-2022/.

183 Hasen, previous n. 181, p. 212 (citing *Citizens United*, 558 U.S. at 551–53); FEC, MUR # 5928, previous n. 182.

184 E.g., Perot v. FEC, 97 F.3d 553, 559 (D.C. Cir. 1996) (suggesting that court might not limit discretion of Commission on Presidential Debates to exclude third-party candidate from televised debates, even if he led in the three-way polls at one point in 1992,

because "staging the debates" and "choosing debate participants" might be part of the commission's "First Amendment rights."); Becker v. FEC, 112 F. Supp. 2d 172, 184–85 (D. Mass. 2000) (finding continuation of Commission on Presidential Debates' system of corporation and major-party control over major presidential debates to be in the public interest despite argument of third party supporters that corporations and parties were "stifling" and "shunting" third parties and their candidates' speech), *aff'd*, 230 F. 3d 381 (1st Cir. 2000); Buchanan v. Federal Election Commission, 112 F. Supp. 2d 58, 61, 65–7, 70–6 (D.D.C. 2000) (despite third party candidate's argument that only two major parties had fair chance to compete to win presidency, FEC and private debate staging groups had to be given "latitude" that makes this happen).

185 E.g., Plaintiffs' Complaint, at 21, In the Matter of Commission on Presidential Debates, FEC Docket MUR # 6869 (FEC complaint filed September 10, 2014), https://www.shapiroarato.com/wp-content/uploads/2015/03/Complaint-against-the-CPD-9.10.14.pdf

186 E.g., Organization on Security and Cooperation in Europe, International Election Observation Mission, Türkiye, General Elections (May 14, 2023), pp. 17, https://www.osce.org/files/f/documents/6/2/543543.pdf (noting that public broadcaster in Turkey did not provide impartial coverage of all parties as required by law in 2023, and that media environment in general was unfair, with private broadcasters favoring the incumbent about 1.5 to 1).

187 Ellen Weintraub, Chair, FEC, The law of a "thing of value," *FEC* (October 2019), htps://www.fec.gov/resources/cms-content/documents/2019-10-ELW-the-law-of-a-thing-of-value.pdf. This receives the most attention with respect to foreign nationals because Section 30121(1)(A) of title 52 purports to regulate in a differential manner how foreign nationals may give any things of value in regard to a federal election. There is a question of where First Amendment coverage extends in a territorial sense, and whether U.S. courts in this area ignore international human rights, as they often do. But absent First Amendment issues, a domestic corporation or individual might unlawfully evade contribution limits in an analogous way.

188 OSCE, previous n. 186, p. 13, n. 56 (quoting OSCE, Copenhagen Document (1990), ¶ 7.7). See also, International Covenant on Civil and Political Rights, art. 25, 99 U.N.T.S. 171, entered into force March 23, 1976 (every citizen has the right to vote in elections without unreasonable restrictions in a way that free expression of will of the electors is reflected in outcome).

189 Parts of this section were previously published in 'The FCC's new theory of the First Amendment,' 51 *Santa Clara Law Review* 417 (2011), or in 'Neutralizing the Open Internet,' in *Cyberspace Law: Censorship and Regulation of the Internet*, edited by Hannibal Travis (Routledge, 2013), p. 209.

190 Open Internet Coalition, OIC supports FCC notice of inquiry and third way approach, *Internet Archive* (June 16, 2010), https://web.archive.org/web/20110105132045/www.openinternetcoalition.com/index.cfm?objectid=7587D410-89EB-11DF-A6BC000C296BA163.

191 Open Internet Coalition, Who we are, *Internet Archive* (2010), https://web.archive.org/web/20110105131040/www.openinternetcoalition.com/index.cfm?objectid=6C43DDC0-5C6A-11DF-9E27000C296BA163 (last visited October 4, 2023).

192 155 *Congressional Record* S10614–01, S10618–19 (October 21, 2009) (emphasis added).

193 Austin Carr, FCC pushes for net neutrality and internet regulation: What happens next? [Update], *Fast Company* (May 6, 2010), https://web.archive.org/web/20110719163741/www.fastcompany.com/1639209/fcc-pushes-for-net-neutrality-and-internet-regulation-what-happens-next; Tim Wu, Is net neutrality dead?, *Slate* (April 13, 2010), https://www.slate.com/id/2250700/.

194 47 U.S.C. § 1302(a) (2006).

195 National Cable and Telecommunications Association v. Brand X Internet Servs., 545 U.S. 967, 996 (2005).

196 "*Chevron* discretion" refers to a federal agency's power to adopt reasonable interpretations of ambiguous statutes, reasonable being defined in contrast to arbitrary, capricious, or contrary to the statute's text. Chevron U.S.A., Inc. v. Natural Resources Defense Council, Inc., 467 U.S. 837, 842–43 (1984); American Council on Education v. FCC, 451 F.3d 226, 231–32 (D.C. Cir. 2006); U.S. Telecom Association v. FCC, 227 F.3d 450, 457 (D.C. Cir. 2000).

197 Brief for Cable-Industry Petitioners at 34, National Cable and Telecomms. Ass'n v. Brand X Internet Servcs., 545 U.S. 967 (2005) (Nos. 04–277 & 04–281) (quoting Satellite Broad. and Communs. Ass'n v. Oman, 17 F.3d 344, 348 (11th Cir. 1994)). Comcast was technically not a party to this brief, but it is a member company of the National Cable and Telecommunications Association, which was. *See* Press Release, Nat'l Cable Telecomms. Ass'n, Comcast's Brian Roberts Elected Chairman of NCTA Board: Other NCTA Board Members Elected; Executive Committee Named, April 11, 2005, http://web.archive.org/web/20060322001325/www.ncta.com/press/press.cfm?PRid=595&showArticles=ok.

198 Comcast Corp. v. FCC, 600 F.3d 642, 647 (D.C. Cir. 2010) (quoting Defendant's Memorandum of Law in Support of Motion for Judgment on the Pleadings at 10, Hart v. Comcast of Alameda, Inc., No. 07–6350 (N.D. Cal. June 25, 2008), 2008 WL 2610787).

199 The order at issue was primarily contained in *Inquiry Concerning High-Speed Access to the Internet Over Cable and Other Facilities*, 17 FCC Rcd. 4798, 4802–4803 ¶ 9 (2002), but the Court also addressed the order in *Appropriate Framework for Broadband Access to the Internet over Wireline Facilities*, 17 FCC Rcd. 3019, 3030, ¶ 20 (2002).

200 See *id.* at 658 (quoting 47 U.S.C. § 1302(a) (2006), and Deployment of Wireline Servs. Offering Advanced Telecomms. Capability, 13 FCC Rcd. 24012, 24047, ¶ 77 (1998)).

201 See *id.* at 659 ("Because the Commission has never questioned, let alone overruled, that understanding of Section 706, and because agencies 'may not . . . depart from a prior policy sub silentio,' the Commission remains bound by its earlier conclusion that Section 706 grants no regulatory authority.'") (citation omitted) (quoting FCC v. Fox Television Stations, Inc., 129 S. Ct. 1800, 1811 (2009)).

202 Ad Hoc Telecomms. Users Committee v. FCC, 572 F.3d 903, 906–07 (D.C. Cir. 2009). *See also Comcast*, 600 F.3d at 659.

203 Pub. L. 104–104, § 706(c)(1), 110 Stat. 56, 153 (1996) (reproduced at note under 47 U.S.C. § 157).

204 American Council of Education v. FCC, 451 F.3d 226, 228 (D.C. Cir. 2006) (Internet access was not an "information service" but a "telecommunications service" subject to "an express delegation of authority to the agency to elucidate a specific provision of the statute by regulation" as FCC's "reasonable policy choice[s]") (quoting Chevron U.S.A., Inc. v. NRDC, Inc. 467 U.S. 837, 843–45 (1984)).

205 Comcast Corp. v. FCC, 600 F.3d 642, 645 (D.C. Cir. 2010) ("We begin – and end – with Comcast's jurisdictional challenge.").

206 See *id.* at 648, 651–52, 658–60.

207 In the Matter of Restoring Internet Freedom, FCC WC Docket No. 17–108 (FCC report and order January 4, 2018), *further proceedings at* Docket No. 17–108 (FCC report on remand October 27, 2020).

208 *Id.* ¶ 232 (quoting 47 U.S.C. § 257(a)).

209 In the Matters of Formal Complaint of Free Press and Public Knowledge Against Comcast Corporation for Secretly Degrading Peer-to-Peer Applications, *23 FCC Rcd. 13028*, 13040 (2008).

210 *Id.*, p. 13040 n. 94 (citing *Net Neutrality: Hearing Before the S. Comm. on Commerce, Sci., and Transp.*, 109th Cong. 2 (2006) (statement of Vinton G. Cerf, Vice President and

Chief Internet Evangelist, Google, Inc.), https://web.archive.org/web/20090227173250/http://frwebgate.access.gpo.gov/cgi-bin/getdoc.cgi?dbname=109_senate_hearings&docid=f:30115.pdf [hereinafter Cerf, Net Neutrality].

211 The Handling of Public Issues Under the Fairness Doctrine, 48 F.C.C. 2d 1, 1–7 (1974).

212 739 H.R. Rep. No. 109–541 (2006); Cerf, Net Neutrality, previous n. 210; Travis, 'Of Blogs, eBooks, and Broadband,' previous n. 119; Jackie Wattles, Net neutrality repeal: Facebook, Amazon, Netflix and internet providers react, *CNN Money* (December 14, 2017), https://money.cnn.com/2017/12/14/technology/business/fcc-net-neutrality-reactions/index.html.

213 FTC v. Motion Picture Advertising Co., 344 U.S. 392, 395 (1953); LePage's Inc. v. 3M, 324 F.3d 141 (3d Cir. 2003); Conwood Co. v. United States Tobacco Co., 290 F.3d 768 (6th Cir. 2002); United States v. Microsoft, 253 F.3d 34, 34–35, 70–97 (D.C. Cir. 2001); United States v. Dentsply International, 2003 U.S. Dist. LEXIS 14139, *191 (D. Del. August 8, 2003); In re Beltone Electronics Corp., 100 F.T.C. 68, 204 (1982); Phillip E. Areeda & Herbert Hovenkamp, *Antitrust Law* ¶ 1703g2 (Aspen Publishers, 1991), pp. 51–52.

214 E.g., Rob Friedan, 'Network Neutrality or Bias? – Handicapping the Odds for a Tiered and Branded Internet,' 29 *Hastings Communications and Entertainment Law Journal* 171 (2006).

215 *Brand X*, 545 U.S. at 1014 (Scalia, J., joined by Ginsburg, J., and Souter, J., dissenting).

216 E.g., H.R. Rep. No. 109–541, at 10–11 (2006) (describing SBC' s declared intention not to allow Google to access AT&T's Internet subscribers "for free"; SBC later merged with AT&T); Cerf, Net Neutrality, previous n. 210 (describing Google's concerns about Internet discrimination); H.R. Rep. No. 110–95, at 2 (2008) ("We never would have had a Google search engine or YouTube videos or Daily Kos blogs if pa[y] to play had been our national policy."); Financial Services Roundtable, Statement in Support of Net Neutrality, in H.R. Rep. No. 110–95, at 51 (2008); Internet Freedom Preservation Act of 2008: Hearing on H.R. 5353 Before the U.S. H. Comm. on Energy and Commerce, Subcomm. on Telecomms. and the Internet, 110th Cong. (2008) (statement of Ben Scott, Policy Director, Free Press) (describing Skype as a peer-to-peer voice conversation program at risk from Comcast's policy of blocking peer-to-peer applications); Erika Morphy, House Committee shoots down net neutrality clause, *E-Commerce Times* (April 27, 2006), https://www.ecommercetimes.com/story/50219.html?wlc=1253664286 (according to a consultant to Flickr, the photo sharing service, called it "a high-bandwidth offering – just the sort of Internet service that could be impacted by a lack of net neutrality.").

217 Brett M. Frischmann and Barbara van Schewick, 'Network Neutrality and the economics of an information superhighway: A reply to Professor Yoo,' 47 *Jurimetrics* 383 (2007).

218 E.g., 15. U.S.C. § 1 (2006) (condemning unreasonable restraints of trade affecting any part of interstate commerce); 15 U.S.C. § 2 (2006) (condemning attempts or conspiracies to monopolize any part of interstate commerce); Chicago Gas-Light & Coke Co. v. People's Gas-Light & Coke Co., 121 Ill. 530, 13 N.E. 169 (1887) (condemning monopoly in gas lines of Chicago); U.S. Telephone Co. v. Central Union Telephone Co., 171 F. 130 (C.D. N.D. Ohio W.D. 1909) (condemning anticompetitive restrictions against local telephone companies); Standard Oil Co. v. United States, 221 U.S. 1 (1911) (condemning monopolization of oil infrastructure of the United States under antitrust laws, especially 15 U.S.C. § 2); Otter Tail Power Co. v. United States, 410 U.S. 366 (1973) (condemning monopolization of electrical infrastructure to detriment of smaller providers and their customers under same section); United States v. AT&T, 524 F. Supp. 1336 (D.D.C. 1981) (condemning monopolization of telephone network), *further proceedings at* 552 F. Supp. 131 (D.D.C. 1982), *aff'd sub nom.* Maryland v. United States, 460 U.S. 1001 (1983), *vacated sub nom.* United States v. W. Elec. Co.,

No. 82–5192 (HHG), 1996 WL 255904 (D.D.C. Apr. 11, 1996); *Microsoft*, 253 F.3d at 34–35, 70–97 (condemning monopolization of PC-compatible operating system market); Memorandum of Points and Authorities in Support of the Alliance for Competition in Telecommunications for Amicus Curiae and Intervenor Status, United States v. Verizon, No. 1:05CV02103 (D.D.C. brief filed May 4, 2006), ("When the software monopolist Microsoft stated its intention to charge a 'vigorish' – the slang term for a bookie's or loan shark's cut – on every transaction over the Internet, the Antitrust Division initiated a lawsuit to break up the company."); see also, Public Utility Commission of Texas, 13 FCC Rcd. 3460, ¶ 1 (1997) (Telecommunications Act of 1996 intended to accelerate rapidly the deployment of advanced telecommunications and information technologies).

219 H.R. Rep. No. 109–541, at 7, 11–13 (2006). See also, Inform Inc. v. Google LLC, No. 21–13289, slip op. § III.B., 2022 WL 3703958 (11th Cir. August 26, 2022) (plaintiff had antitrust standing to challenge whether Google had excluded it from market for digital advertising by disparaging it, disabling it, contractually limiting it, or not preferring it).

220 Coronavirus Reporter v. Apple, Inc., No. 21-cv-05567-EMC, slip op. at § IV.A.1 (N.D. Cal. February 2, 2022), *prior proceedings at* Coronavirus Reporter v. Apple Inc., No. 21-cv-5567, 2021 WL 5936910 (N.D. Cal. November 30, 2021).

221 *Inform Inc*., previous n. 219, § III.B.

222 E.g., National Collegiate Athletic Assn. v. Alston, 594 U.S. ___, 141 S. Ct. 2141, 2147 (2021) (collusion against intercollegiate "student-athletes") (citing NCAA v. Oklahoma, 468 U.S. 85, 104 n. 27 (1984)); Aspen Skiing Co. v. Aspen Highlands Skiing Corp., 472 U.S. 585, 587, 594–97 (1985) (affirming jury verdict regarding monopolization of for "market for downhill skiing services in Aspen"); International Boxing Club of N. Y., Inc. v. United States, 358 U.S. 242, 249–50 (1959) (upholding case against anticompetitive activity in "promotion of championship boxing contests in contrast to all professional boxing events"); Elizabeth Wilkins, Director, FTC Office of Policy and Planning, Keynote remarks: Rethinking antitrust (2023), p. 2 & n. 10, www.ftc.gov (citing, inter alia, Sandeep Vaheesan, 'Accommodating capital and policing labor: Antitrust in the two Gilded Ages,' 78 *Maryland Law Review* 766, 767–771 (2019)).

223 Cf., United States v. Google LLC, --- F. Supp. 3d ----, Nos. 20-cv-3010 (APM), 20-cv-3715 (APM), 2023 WL 4999901, at *8 (D.D.C. August 3, 2023) ("Advertisers can purchase online advertisements in a variety of ways. The three most notable are: (1) directly from online content publishers, like *The New York Times*, (2) directly from online platforms like Google, Amazon, Facebook, and Microsoft through 'native tools' or 'interface tools,' and (3) through an SEM tool.") (internal citation omitted); *Kinderstart.com*, 2006 WL 3246596 (suggesting larger digital advertising market may exist, rather than plaintiff's proposed search engine advertising market). See generally, Ohio v. American Express Co., 138 S. Ct. 2274, 2285 (2018) (holding that "relevant market is defined as 'the area of effective competition,'" usually "the 'arena within which significant substitution in consumption or production occurs.'") (internal citations omitted); Coronavirus Reporter v. Apple, Inc., No. 21-cv-05567-EMC, slip op. at § IV.A.1 (N.D. Cal. February 2, 2022) (when it comes to market for smartphone apps, such a "relevant market must be 'two-sided' because [Apple's] App Store 'functions as an intermediary between the respective sides – app developers and end users'") (quoting Reilly v. Apple Inc., 578 F. Supp. 3d 1098, 1111 n.3 (N.D. Cal. 2022)); *FTC v. Facebook*, 560 F. Supp. 3d at 19 ("The overall revenues earned by [Facebook or Instagram] cannot be the right metric for measuring market share here, as those revenues are all earned in a separate market – viz., the market for advertising."); *id.* at 18 ("As the above market-definition analysis underscores, however, the market at issue here is unusual in a number of ways, including that the products therein are not sold for a price, meaning that [personal social networking] services earn no direct revenue from

users."); SC Innovations, Inc. v. Uber Technologies, Inc., 434 F. Supp. 3d 782 (N.D. Cal. 2020) (Uber argued that competitor's antitrust suit had to be dismissed for inadequacy of allegation of two-sided market involving drivers and passengers, but court rejected as "fact intensive" issue).

224 E.g., Hannibal Travis, 'The freedom of influencing,' 77 *Miami Law Review* 388 (2023).

225 E.g., *New York v. Facebook*, 549 F. Supp. 3d at 17–18; Wu, *The Curse of Bigness*, previous n. 77, p. 123. See also, Peter Bell, *Creating Commercial Music: Advertising * Library Music * TV Themes * and More* (Berklee Press, 2020).

226 Parts of this section were previously published as 'WIPO and the American Constitution: Thoughts on a new treaty relating to actors and musicians,' 16 *Vanderbilt Journal of Entertainment and Technology Law* 45 (2013).

227 U.S. Const., art. I, § 8, cl. 8; United States v. Martignon, 346 F. Supp. 2d 413 (S.D.N.Y. 2004), *vacated*, 492 F.3d 140 (2d Cir. 2007).

228 17 U.S.C. § 106A; see also, Kelley v. Chicago Park District, 635 F.3d 290 (7th Cir. 2011); Cohen v. G&M Realty, L.P., 320 F. Supp. 3d 421 (E.D.N.Y. 2018), *aff'd sub nom.* Castillo v. G&M Realty L.P., 950 F.3d 155 (2d Cir. 2020).

229 U.S. Copyright Office, Waiver of Moral Rights in Visual Artworks: Executive Summary (1996) (emphasis added), https://www.copyright.gov/reports/exsum.html; *see also* U.S. Copyright Office, Annual Report of the Register of Copyrights (1995), *available at* https://www.copyright.gov/reports/annual/archive/ar-1995.pdf.

230 Sirichit, previous n. 146, p. 130 (citing Berne Convention for the Protection of Literary and Artistic Works, art. 6*bis*, July 24, 1971, 25 U.S.T. 1341, 828 U.N.T.S. 221).

231 Ibid., p. 133 (quoting Carlo Lavizzari, Moral rights in the 21st century – A perspective from the standpoint of publishers of literary works, Contribution to ALAI [Association Littéraire et Artistique Internationale] Congress Brussels (September 18–19, 2014), p. 2, https://web.archive.org/web/20161124174040/http://alai2014.org/IMG/pdf/d2_-_s3_-_1520_-_lavrizzari.pdf (last visited Oct. 10, 2023), and Guy Pessach, 'Deconstructing disintermediation: A skeptical copyright perspective,' 31 *Cardozo Arts and Entertainment Law Journal* 833, 841 (2013), and citing Drummond v. Altemus, 60 F. 334, 339 (E.D. Pa. 1894)).

232 Ibid., p. 92 (citing 3 Cass. Civ., 14 March 1900: DP 1900, 1, p. 497; Raymond Sarraute, 'Current theory on the moral right of authors and artists under French law,' 16 *American Journal of Comparative Law* 465, 467 (1968)).

233 Ibid., pp. 93, 127.

234 E.g., *NetChoice v. Moody*, 546 F. Supp. 3d at 1090, *aff'd on other grounds*, 34 F.4th 1196.

235 E.g., Hepp v. Facebook, 14 F.4th 204, 209–14 (3d Cir. 2021) (citing, inter alia, Ford Motor Co. v. Montana Eighth Judicial District Court, 141 S. Ct. 1017, 1029 (2021); Atlantic Recording Corp. v. Project Playlist, Inc., 603 F. Supp. 2d 690,704–05 (S.D.N.Y. 2009)). But see, Perfect 10, Inc. v. CCBill LLC, 488 F.3d 1102, 1118–19 (9th Cir. 2007) (concluding that the exclusion of intellectual property claims from Section 230 immunity requires a nexus with federal copyright, patent, or trademark law).

236 E.g., Internet Archive, Experience DWeb camp, *YouTube* (May 2023), https://www.youtube.com/watch?v=zx7Dduv0Hd4; Mai Ishikawa Sutton, A New Portal for the Decentralized Web and its Guiding Principles, Internet Archive (March 22, 2021), https://blog.archive.org.2021/03/22/a-new-portal-for-the-decentralized-web-and-its-guiding-principles.

237 DWeb Principles (2023), https://getdweb.net/principles/ (numbering omitted). The principles are described as the fruit of many developer events over five years, in which thousands of people participated although there was no explicit agreement to the principles, it seems. Mai Ishikawa Sutton, Behind the scenes of the decentralized web principles, *Internet Archive* (February 18, 2021), https://blog.archive.org/2021/02/18/behind-the-scenes-of-the-decentralized-web-principles/.

238 E.g., Thibault Schrepel, 'The complex relationship between Web2 giants and Web3 projects,' 50 *Computer and Security Law Review*, July 18, 2023, https://www.sciencedirect.com/science/article/pii/S0267364923000559.

239 Ibid., As Professor Schrepel explains, Web2 is centralized but currently more efficient than Web3, and Web2 giants like Apple or Meta could make their services non-interoperable with Web3 services, and even block advertising or app distribution to Web3 companies. Ibid. See also, Janna Anderson and Lee Rainie, The Metaverse in 2040, *Pew Research Center* (June 30, 2022), https://www.pewresearch.org/internet/2022/06/30/what-about-blockchain/ ("Olivier Crépin-Leblond, founding board member of the European Dialogue on Internet Governance and board member for the European At-Large Organisation at ICANN, wrote, 'I would like to think that [blockchain technology] will allow for real decentralised organisations to emerge. I would like to think that traditional top-down firms will be replaced by bottom-up, distributed firms where integrative management is practised as a norm.'"); ibid. ("'It must be demonstrated that a bottom-up, massively distributed firm that uses blockchain to balance its control structure is vastly more efficient and successful than a traditional top-down structure.'").

240 George Gilder, *Life After Google: The Fall of Big Data and the Rise of the Blockchain Economy* (Simon & Schuster, 2018), especially ch. 21.

241 Ibid.; see also, Kevin Werbach, *The Blockchain and the New Architecture of Trust* (The MIT Press, 2018), pp. 142–61.

242 Exceptions might include BitTorrent, Mozilla Firefox, Bitcoin, Ethereum, and NFTs like OpenSea's or Bored Ape Yacht Club's. E.g., Dietrich Ayala, Introducing the DWeb, Mozilla Hacks, July 31, 2018, https://hacks.mozilla.org/2018/07/introducing-the-d-web/. Bitcoin may be the most distributed service in the bunch.

243 Janna Anderson and Lee Rainie, The Metaverse in 2040, *Pew Research Center* (June 30, 2022), https://www.pewresearch.org/internet/2022/06/30/the-metaverse-will-not-fully-emerge-in-the-way-todays-advocates-hope/ (experts on the metaverse have observed that "the public has had the opportunity for many years to participate in a number of fairly immersive virtual spaces but has not broadly embraced them"); ibid., https://www.pewresearch.org/internet/2022/06/30/the-metaverse-in-2040/ (author and journalist Cory Doctorow argues that: "The metaverse as we understand it today is the result of Facebook's desperate bid to stop hemorrhaging users, engineers and reputation."); ibid. (Andre Brock, a professor of literature and communication, suggests that computer-generated metaverses like *Second Life, World of Warcraft*, and *EverQuest* have been "ephemeral" and that Meta's vision of a metaverse which it authenticates assumes that Meta will "convert users from the largely text-driven Facebook platform to a yet-untested platform at scale with demanding hardware and software requirements. History suggests a different outcome.").

244 E.g., Gilder, previous n. 240, ch. 21.

245 Brewster Kahle, Locking the web open, presentation to the Ford Foundation netgain gathering, *Internet Archive* (February 11, 2015), https://blog.archive.org/2015/02/11/locking-the-web-open-a-call-for-a-distributed-web/.

Bibliography

2 U.S.C.A. § 441i(a)(1) (Supp. 2003).
3 Cass. Civ., 14 March 1900: DP 1900, 1, p. 497.
15 U.S.C. § 1 (2006).
15 U.S.C. § 2 (2006).
15 U.S.C. § 45.
17 U.S.C. § 106A.
18 U.S.C. § 201(b).
47 U.S.C. § 157.

47 U.S.C. § 230(c)(1).
47 U.S.C. § 230(c)(2).
47 U.S.C. § 257(a).
47 U.S.C. § 1302(a) (2006).
51 *Congressional Record* 12,146 (1914).
52 U.S.C. §§ 30101(8), 30116, 30121(1)(A), 30125(a)(1).
ACA Connects v. Bonta, 24 F.4th 1233 (9th Cir. 2022).
Ad Hoc Telecomms. Users Committee v. FCC, 572 F.3d 903 (D.C. Cir. 2009).
Administrative Complaint, Buchanan v. CPD, FEC Docket MUR # 4987 (FEC complaint filed Mar. 20, 2000). Administrative Complaint, RNC v. Twitter, FEC Docket MUR #7821 (FEC complaint filed October 16, 2020), https://www.fec.gov/files/legal/murs/7821/7821_01.pdf.
Administrative Complaint, Woodhouse v. Carson, FEC Docket MUR # 6989 (FEC complaint filed November 2015), http://americandemocracy.org/wp-content/uploads/CARSON-FEC-COMPLAINT_001.pdf.
Aidan Macallan on "House of Cards": A Storyline Recap, Heavy, May 29, 2017, https://heavy.com/entertainment/2017/05/aidan-macallan-house-of-cards-refresher-recap/.
Alden-Rochelle, Inc. v. ASCAP, 80 F. Supp. 888 (S.D.N.Y. 1948).
Allred v. Harris, 14 Cal. App. 4th 1386 (Cal. Ct. App., 4th Dist. 1991).
American Council on Educ. v. FCC, 451 F.3d 226 (D.C. Cir. 2006).
American Innovation and Choice Online Act, S. 2992, 117th Cong. (2022).
Appropriate Framework for Broadband Access to the Internet over Wireline Facilities, 17 FCC Rcd. 3019 (2002).
Bobby Allyn, DOJ sues Google, seeking to break up online advertising business, *NPR* (January 24, 2023), https://www.npr.org/2023/01/24/1151055903/doj-files-second-antitrust-suit-against-google-seeks-to-break-up-its-ad-business.
American Professional Testing Service, Inc. v. Hancourt Brace Jovanovich Legal & Professional Publications, Inc., 108 F.3d 1147 (9th Cir. 1997).
Analysis of Proposed Consent Order to Aid Public Comment: In the Matter of Intel Corp., FTC Dkt No. 9341 (2010).
Apple, Inc. v. Psystar Corp., 586 F. Supp. 2d 1190 (N.D. Cal. 2008), *subsequent proceedings at* 673 F. Supp. 2d 931 (N.D. Cal. 2009), *aff'd*, 658 F.3d 1150 (9th Cir. 2011).
Apple Inc. v. Samsung Elecs. Co., No. 11-CV-01846-LHK, 2011 WL 4948567 (N.D. Cal. October 18, 2011).
Application for a Stay of Injunction, Murthy v. Missouri, No. 23A-243 (S. Ct. application filed Sept. 2023).
Apollomedia Corp. v. Reno, 19 F. Supp. 2d 1081 (N.D. Cal. 1998), *aff'd*, 1998 WL 853216, *amended by* 526 U.S. 1071 (1998).
Appropriate Framework for Broadband Access to the Internet over Wireline Facilities, Report and Order and Notice of Proposed Rulemaking, 20 FCC Rcd. 14853, 14855 (2005)).
Phillip E. Areeda and Herbert Hovenkamp, *Antitrust Law: An Analysis of Antitrust Principles and Their Application* (Wolters Kluwer, 4th ed. 2020).
Phillip E. Areeda and Herbert Hovenkamp, *Antitrust Law*, Vol. 3 (Aspen Publishers, 2nd ed. 1996 and Supp. 1999).
Arenson v. Board of Trade of City of Chicago, 372 F. Supp. 1349 (N.D. Ill. 1973).
Arizona Free Enterprise Club v. Bennett, 564 U.S. 721 (2011).
Associated Press v. United States, 326 U.S. 1 (1945).
Aspen Skiing Co. v. Aspen Highlands Skiing Corp., 472 U.S. 585 (1985).
Atlantic Recording Corp. v. Project Playlist, Inc., 603 F. Supp. 2d 690 (S.D.N.Y. 2009).
Janna Anderson and Lee Rainie, The metaverse in 2040, *Pew Research Center* (June 30, 2022), https://www.pewresearch.org/internet/2022/06/30/the-metaverse-will-not-fully-emerge-in-the-way-todays-advocates-hope/ & www.pewresearch.org/internet/2022/06/30/the-metaverse-in-2040/.

Dietrich Ayala, Introducing the DWeb, Mozilla Hacks, July 31, 2018, https://hacks.mozilla.org/2018/07/introducing-the-d-web/.

Backhaut v. Apple, Inc., 74 F. Supp. 3d 1033 (N.D. Cal. 2014).

Bantam Books, Inc. v. Sullivan, 372 U.S. 58 (1963).

Joan Barata et al., *Unravelling the Digital Services Act package*, translated by Julie Mamou et al. (European Audiovisual Observatory, 2022), https://rm.coe.int/iris-special-2021-01en-dsa-package/1680a43e45.

Sara Bazoobandi, 'Populism, jihad, and economic resistance: Studying the political discourse of Iran's supreme leader,' 32 *Digest of Middle East Studies* 321 (2023), https://onlinelibrary.wiley.com/doi/pdf/10.1111/dome.12303.

The BBFC in the 1970s, British Board of Film Classification, https://www.bbfc.co.uk/education/university-students/bbfc-history/the-1970s.

Becker v. FEC, 112 F. Supp. 2d 172 (D. Mass. 2000), *aff'd*, 230 F. 3d 381 (1st Cir. 2000).

Peter Bell, *Creating Commercial Music: Advertising * Library Music * TV Themes * and More* (Berklee Press, 2020).

Katie Benner, Kenneth P. Vogel, and Michael S. Schmidt, Hunter Biden paid tax bill, but federal investigation goes on, *The New York Times* (December 9, 2020), https://web.archive.org/web/20210215004026/www.nytimes.com/2020/12/09/us/politics/hunter-biden-tax-investigation.html (last visited August 2, 2023).

Berne Convention for the Protection of Literary and Artistic Works, revised at Stockholm, July 24, 1971, 25 U.S.T. 1341, 828 U.N.T.S. 221.

Berenson v. Twitter, Inc., No. C 21–09818 WHA, 2022 WL 1289049 (N.D. Cal. April 29, 2022).

Alex Berenson, Lifting the kimono (uh-oh, trigger alert) a little more on *Berenson v. Twitter*, Substack (July 1, 2022), https://alexberenson.substack.com/p/lifting-the-kimono-uh-oh-trigger.

James Bisbee et al., 'Election fraud, YouTube, and public perception of the legitimacy of President Biden,' 1 *Journal of Online Trust and Safety* 3 (2022), https://tsjournal.org/index.php/jots/article/download/60/24.

Blumenthal, Blackburn & Klobuchar Introduce Bipartisan Antitrust Legislation to Promote App Store Competition, Senate.gov, (Aug. 2021), https://www.blackburn.senate.gov/2021/8/blackburn-blumenthal-klobuchar-introduce-bipartisan-antitrust-legislation-to-promote-app-store-competition.

Board of Directors of Rotary International v. Rotary Club of Duarte, 481 U.S. 537 (1987).

Boy Scouts of America v. Dale, 530 U.S. 640 (2000).

Brentwood Academy v. Tennessee Secondary School Athletic Association, 531 U.S. 288 (2001).

Brief for Appellees, HiQ Labs, Inc. v. LinkedIn, Corp., No. 17–16783 (9th Cir. brief filed November 20, 2017).

Brief for Cable-Industry Petitioners, National Cable and Telecomms. Ass'n v. Brand X Internet Servcs., 545 U.S. 967 (2005) (Nos. 04–277 & 04–281).

Brief for the Federal Respondents, Comcast v. FCC, No. 17–498 (D.C. Cir. brief filed April 2018).

Brief of ACLU, Reporters Committee for Freedom of the Press, et al. in Support of Petitioners, NetChoice, LLC v. Moody (U.S. brief filed May 2022) (No. 21–720), https://www.supremecourt.gov/DocketPDF/21/21A720/225626/20220517163128468_RCFP%20Netchoice%20v%20Paxton%20Vacate%20Stay%20for%20Filing%20PDF%20A.pdf.

Brief of Amici Curiae the Electronic Frontier Foundation, Wikimedia, et al. in Support of Petitioners, NetChoice, LLC v. Moody (U.S. brief filed May 2022) (No. 21–720), https://www.eff.org/document/eff-amicus-brief-netchoice-v-florida.

Brief of Amici Curiae State of Ohio et al., NetChoice, LLC v. Moody (U.S. brief filed October, 2022) (No. 22–277), www.supremecourt.gov/DocketPDF/22/22-277/243634/20221021135207159_NetChoice%20Amicus.PDF.

Brief of Amicus Curiae Phillip Hamburger, NetChoice, LLC v. Moody (U.S. brief filed May 2022) (No. 22-277), https://www.supremecourt.gov/DocketPDF/22/22-277/243763/20221024133439836_Moody%20v%20NetChoice%20Petition-Stage%20Amicus%20FINAL.pdf.

Brerit Brogaard, Should hate speech be free speech?, *Psychology Today The Superhuman Mind Blog* (March 29, 2019), https://www.psychologytoday.com/us/blog/the-superhuman-mind/201903/should-hate-speech-be-free-speech.

British Board of Film Classification, Annual Report (1992), https://darkroom.bbfc.co.uk/original/9d1cc41183b62e0e5564c92fd28e57f4:91b2c085b0870d853e37a664ff379a12/bbfc-annual-report-1992.pdf.

George D. Brown, '*McConnell* and the criminalization of politics,' 5 *Virginia Journal of Criminal Law* 1 (2017).

Buchanan v. Federal Election Commission, 112 F. Supp. 2d 58 (D.D.C. 2000).

California Computer Products, Inc. v. International Business Machines Corp., 613 F.2d 727 (9th Cir. 1979).

Campaign Legal Ctr. v. FEC, 31 F.4th 781 (D.C. Cir. 2022).

Austin Carr, FCC pushes for net neutrality and internet regulation: What happens next? [Update], *Fast Company* (May 6, 2010), https://web.archive.org/web/20110719163741/www.fastcompany.com/1639209/fcc-pushes-for-net-neutrality-and-internet-regulation-what-happens-next.

Michael A. Carrier, 'Don't Die! How biosimilar disparagement violates antitrust law,' 115 *Northwestern University Law Review Online* 119 (2020).

Michael A. Carrier and Rebecca Tushnet, 'An antitrust framework for false advertising,' 106 *Iowa Law Review* 1841 (2021).

Cedar Point Nursery v. Hassid, 141 S. Ct. 2063 (2021).

Jen Chaney, "House of cards" Season 4, Episode 7: Rock star candidate, *nytimes.com* (March 8, 2016), www.nytimes.com/2016/03/08/arts/television/house-of-cards-season-4-episode-7.html.

Foo Yun Chee, Amazon May Have to Tweak Proposals for Ending Business Practices Probes, EU's Vestager says, Reuters, September 16, 2022, www.reuters.com.

Chevron U.S.A., Inc. v. Natural Resources Defense Council, Inc., 467 U.S. 837 (1984).

Chicago Gas-Light & Coke Co. v. People's Gas-Light & Coke Co., 121 Ill. 530, 13 N.E. 169 (1887).

Matthew Childs, Cody Buntain, Milo Trujillo, and Benjamin Horne, 'Characterizing YouTube and Bitchute content and mobilizers during us election fraud discussions on Twitter,' in *Proceedings of the 14th ACM Web Science Conference 2022* (2023), pp. 250–59, https://arxiv.org/pdf/2203.16274.

Citizens United v. FEC, 558 U.S. 310 (2010).

Clear Connection Corp. v. Comcast Cable Communications Management, LLC, 149 F. Supp. 3d 1188 (E.D. Cal. 2015).

Scott Cleland, Google's ad blocking exposes the company's hypocrisy on net neutrality, *The Hill* (April 21, 2017), https://thehill.com/blogs/pundits-blog/technology/329920-googles-ad-blocking-exposes-the-companys-hypocrisy-on-net/.

Amal Clooney and Philippa Webb, 'The right to insult in international law,' 48 *Columbia Human Rights Law Review* 1 (2017).

CNN, "Shockingly disappointing": Tapper rebukes Trump's election speech, *YouTube* (November 4, 2020), https://youtu.be/ovLKZFNm-8M.

Code of Federal Regulations, 11 C.F.R. § 109.21 (2023).

Niamh Coghlan et al., Special Rapporteur on the Promotion and Protection of the Right to Freedom of Opinion and Expression: A Report by Students at Leiden Law School (2021), https://www.ohchr.org/sites/default/files/Documents/Issues/Expression/disinformation/3-Academics/Leiden-University-Law-School.pdf.

Raphael Cohen-Almagor, *Confronting the Internet's Dark Side: Moral and Social Responsibility on the Free Highway* (Cambridge University Press, 2015).

CollegeNet, Inc. v. Common Application, Inc., 355 F. Supp. 3d 926 (D. Or. 2018).

Pablo Ibáñez Colomo, 'What is an abuse of a dominant position? Deconstructing the prohibition and categorizing practices,' in *Research Handbook on Abuse of Dominance and Monopolization*, edited by Pınar Akman, Or Brook, and Konstantinos Stylianou (Edward Elgar, 2023), p. 100.

Comcast Corp. v. FCC, 600 F.3d 642 (D.C. Cir. 2010).

Comments of the Radio Music License Committee, Inc. and the Television Music License Committee, LLC, August 6, 2014, www.justice.gov/atr/page/file/1082141/download.

Comments of PandoraMedia, Inc. in Response to the Department of Justice's Review of the ASCAP and BMI Consent Decrees, August 6, 2014, www.justice.gov/sites/default/files/atr/legacy/2014/08/27/307973.pdf.

155 *Congressional Record* S10614–01, S10618–19 (October 21, 2009).

Continental Ore Co. v. Union Carbide & Carbon Corp., 370 U.S. 690 (1962).

Conwood Co. v. United States Tobacco Co., 290 F.3d 768 (6th Cir. 2002).

David L. Aldridge Co. v. Microsoft Corp., 995 F. Supp. 728 (S.D. Tex. 1998).

Denver Area Educational Telecommunications Consortium, Inc. v. FCC, 518 U.S. 727 (1996).

Devin Coldewey, What is Amazon's [redacted] "Project Nessie" algorithm?, *TechCrunch* (September 26, 2023), https://techcrunch.com/2023/09/26/what-is-amazons-redacted-project-nessie-algorithm.

Conseil National Numerique, Platform Neutrality: Building an Open and Sustainable Digital Environment (2014), www.cnnumerique.fr/wp-content/uploads/2014/06/PlatformNeutrality_VA.pdf.

Consent Order, Statement in Support of Consent, In the Matter of Intel Corp., File No. 061–0247 (Dkt. 9341) (July 28, 2010).

Coronavirus Reporter v. Apple, Inc., No. 21-cv-05567-EMC, 2021 WL 5936910 (N.D. Cal. November 30, 2021), *subsequent proceedings at* slip op. (N.D. Cal. February 2, 2022).

Daniel Crane, 'Antitrust's unconventional politics,' 104 *Virginia Law Review Online* 118 (2018), https://virginialawreview.org/articles/antitrusts-unconventional-politics/.

Malena Dailey, Content Moderation by the Numbers, NetChoice (2022), https://netchoice.org/wp-content/uploads/2021/11/Content-Moderation-By-The-Numbers-v5.pdf.

Alan Davidson, 'A Joint Policy Proposal for an Open Internet,' Google Public Policy Blog, August 9, 2010, https://publicpolicy.googleblog.com/2010/08/joint-policy-proposal-for-open-internet.html.

Defendants' Answer, NetChoice, LLC v. Moody, No. 4:21cv220-RH (N.D. Fla. answer filed July 15, 2021) (ECF No. 118).

Defendant's Memorandum of Law in Support of Motion for Judgment on the Pleadings, Hart v. Comcast of Alameda, Inc., No. 07–6350, 2008 WL 2610787 (N.D. Cal. June 25, 2008).

Defendant's Notice of Appeal, NetChoice, LLC v. Moody, No. 4:21cv220-RH-MAF (N.D. Fla. notice of appeal filed July 12, 2021) (ECF No. 115).

Defendant's Reply Brief in Support of Motion for Summary Judgment, Dreamstime.com, LLC v. Google, LLC, No. C 18–01910 WHA (N.D. Cal. brief filed May 28, 2020) (ECF No. 173).

Defendants' Response to Motion for Leave to File Motion for Preliminary Injunction, NetChoice, LLC v. Moody, No. 4:21cs2290RH (N.D. Fla. response filed June 15, 2021) (ECF No. 79).

Deployment of Wireline Servs. Offering Advanced Telecomms. Capability, 13 FCC Rcd. 24012 (1998).

Divino Group, LLC v. Google LLC, No. 19-CV-04749-VKD, 2021 WL 51715 (N.D. Cal. January 6, 2021).

Domen v. Vimeo, Inc., 433 F. Supp. 3d 592 (S.D.N.Y. 2020), *aff'd*, 991 F.3d 66 (2d Cir. 2021).
Dreamstime.com, LLC v. Google, LLC, No. C 18–01910 WHA, 2019 WL 2372280 (N.D. Cal. June 5, 2019), *prior proceedings at* 2019 WL 341579 (N.D. Cal. January 28, 2019), *further proceedings at* 470 F. Supp. 3d 1082 (N.D. Cal. 2020).
Drummond v. Altemus, 60 F. 334 (E.D. Pa. 1894).
Simon Duke, Copy, acquire, kill: How Facebook stays on top, *The Times* (July 31, 2020), www.thetimes.co.uk/article/copy-acquire-kill-how-facebook-stays-on-top-w2f8lxvv6.
E-book MFNs and related matters, 36, Commission Decision of May 4, 2017, Case AT.40153, C (2017) 2876 final, https://ec.europa.eu/competition/antitrust/cases/dec_docs/40153/40153_4392_3.pdf.
e-Ventures Worldwide, LLC v. Google, Inc., 188 F. Supp. 3d 1265 (M.D. Fla. 2016).
Einer Elhauge, 'Defining better monopolization standards,' 56 *Stanford Law Review* 253 (2003).
Energy and Commerce Committee Republican Staff, Big Tech Accountability Platform, April 15, 2021, https://republicans-energycommerce.house.gov/wp-content/uploads/2021/04/2021.04.15-Big-Tech-Memo-Staff-Legislative-Concepts.pdf (last visited August 2, 2022).
Epic Games, Inc. v. Apple, Inc., No. 4:20-cv-05640-YGR, 2020 WL 5073937 (N.D. Cal. mot. for prelim. inj. denied August 24, 2020), *further proceedings at* 493 F. Supp. 3d 817 (N.D. Cal. 2020).
Epic Games, Inc. v. Apple Inc., 493 F. Supp. 3d 817 (N.D. Cal. 2021), *further proceedings at* 559 F. Supp. 3d 898 (N.D. Cal. 2021).
European Court of Human Rights, Gündüz v. Turkey, December 4, 2003, Appl. No. 35071/97.
European Court of Human Rights, Handyside v. United Kingdom, December 7, 1976, Appl. No. 5493/72.
European Union, Consolidated version of the Treaty on the Functioning of the European Union, December 13, 2007, 2008/C 115/01.
European Union, Treaty of Lisbon Amending the Treaty on European Union and the Treaty Establishing the European Community, *Official Journal of the European Union* C 306/1, December 17, 2007, 2007/C 306/01.
Executive Order No. 175: Ensuring Net Neutrality Protections for New Yorkers, N.Y. Comp. Codes R. & Regs. tit. 9 § 8.175 (2018).
Fashion Originators' Guild of America v. FTC, 312 U.S. 457 (1941).
Federal Judicial Center, *Section 1983 Litigation, Third Edition*, edited by Karen Blum and Kathryn Urbonya (Federal Judicial Center, 1998).
FCC v. Allentown Broadcasting Corp., 349 U. S. 358 (1955).
FCC v. Fox Television Stations, Inc., 556 U.S. 502, 129 S. Ct. 1800 (2009).
FCC Chairwoman Jessica Rosenworcel, Remarks at The National Press Club in Washington, DC (September 26, 2023), https://www.fcc.gov/document/fcc-chairwoman-rosenworcels-net-neutrality-remarks.
FEC, Advisory Opinion 2014–20, Make Your Laws PAC.
FEC, Advisory Opinion 2022–12, Ready for Ron.
FEC, MUR # 5928, Kos Media LLC (September 4, 2007), https://www.fec.gov/updates/fec-resolves-two-matters-involving-internet-activity-applies-media-exemption-to-political-blogs/.
FEC, MUR # 7821, Twitter (September 13, 2021), https://www.fec.gov/data/legal/matter-under-review/7821/.
FEC, MURs # 7207, 7268, 7274 & 7623, Donald J. Trump for President (February 15, 2022), https://www.fec.gov/updates/week-of-february-14-18-2022/.
FEC, MURs # 7645, 7663, and 7705, Donald J. Trump (August 31, 2022), https://www.fec.gov/updates/week-of-august-29-september-2-2022/.

Lauren Feiner, Senate committee advances bill targeting Google and Apple's app store profitability, *CNBC* (February 3, 2022), https://www.cnbc.com/2022/02/03/senate-committee-advances-open-app-markets-act.html.

Lauren Feiner, Senate committee votes to advance major tech antitrust bill, *CNBC* (January 20, 2022), https://www.cnbc.com/2022/01/20/senate-committee-votes-to-advance-major-tech-antitrust-bill.html.

Financial Services Roundtable, Statement in Support of Net Neutrality, in H.R. Rep. No. 110–95 (2008).

Klint Finley, States and cities keep the battle for net neutrality alive, *Wired* (January 23, 2018), www.wired.com/story/states-and-cities-keep-the-battle-for-net-neutrality-alive.

Florida Statutes § 106.072(2)

Florida Statutes § 501.2041(2).

Quentin Fontaine, The German NetzDG: A model for future online speech regulation in the European Union?, Master's Degree Thesis, Faculté de droit et de criminologie, Université catholique de Louvain (2020), https://dial.uclouvain.be/downloader/downloader.php?pid=thesis%253A26486&datastream=PDF_01&cover=cover-mem.

Ford Motor Co. v. Montana Eighth Judicial District Court, 141 S. Ct. 1017 (2021).

Eleanor M. Fox, 'An antitrust fable – A tale of predation,' Concurrences No 3–2008, September 2008, www.concurrences.com/en/review/issues/no-3-2008.

Eleanor M. Fox, 'The battle for reform of US antitrust law,' 11 *Journal of Antitrust Enforcement* 179 (2023).

Eleanor M. Fox, 'Monopolization and abuse of dominance: Why Europe is different,' 59 *The Antitrust Bulletin* 129 (2014).

Eleanor M. Fox, 'The efficiency paradox,' in *How the Chicago School Overshot the Mark: The Effect of Conservative Economic Analysis on US Antitrust*, edited by Robert Pitofsky, pp. 77–88 (Oxford University Press, 2008).

Fox News, "Tucker: We heard you. It's hard to trust anything. Here's what we know," *YouTube* (November 2020), https://youtu.be/R5ki6S-WsKU.

Covington & Lexington Turnpike Road Co. v. Sandford, 164 U.S. 578 (1896).

FPC v. Texaco Inc., 417 U.S. 380 (1974).

Rob Friedan, 'Network neutrality or bias? – Handicapping the odds for a tiered and branded Internet,' 29 *Hastings Communications and Entertainment Law Journal* 171 (2006).

Sarah Frier, *No Filter: The Inside Story of Instagram* (Simon & Schuster, 2021).

Brett M. Frischmann and Barbara van Schewick, 'Network neutrality and the economics of an information superhighway: A reply to Professor Yoo,' 47 *Jurimetrics* 383 (2007).

FTC v. Brown Shoe Co., 384 U.S. 316 (1966).

FTC v. Cement Institute, 333 U.S. 683 (1948).

FTC v. Facebook, 560 F. Supp. 3d 1 (D.D.C. 2021).

FTC v. Motion Picture Advertising Service Co., 344 U.S. 392 (1953).

FTC v. Superior Court Trial Lawyers Association, 493 U.S. 411 (1990).

FTC, Policy statement regarding the scope of unfair methods of competition under section 5 of the Federal Trade Commission Act (November 2022), https://www.ftc.gov.

General Comment No. 34, United Nations UN Doc. No. CCPR/C/GC/34 (September 12, 2011).

General Comment No. 34, UN Doc. No. CCPR/C/GC/34 (September 12, 2011).

Gersh v. Anglin, No. 9:2017-cv-0050, slip op. (D. Mont. November, 2018).

George Gilder, *Life After Google: The Fall of Big Data and the Rise of the Blockchain Economy* (Simon & Schuster, 2018).

Global Partners Digital, UN special rapporteur on freedom of opinion and expression: Report on disinformation consultation, *OHCHR* (February 18, 2021), https://www.ohchr.org/sites/default/files/Documents/Issues/Expression/disinformation/2-Civil-society-organisations/Input-for-report-on-disinformation-GPD-Submission.pdf.

Goddard v. Google, Inc., No. C 08–2738 JF (PVT), 2008 WL 5245490 (N.D. Cal. December 17, 2008).

Eric Goldman and Jess Miers, 'Online account terminations/content removals and the benefits of Internet services enforcing their house rules,' 1 *Journal of Free Speech Law* 191 (2021).
Eric Goldman and Jess Miers, Regulating internet services by size, *CPI Antitrust Chronicle*, (May 2021), p. 1, https://www.competitionpolicyinternational.com/wp-content/uploads/2021/05/3-Regulating-Internet-Services-by-Size-By-Eric-Goldman-Jess-Miers.pdf.
Google (2023), https://www.google.com/search?q=hitler+speech+site%3Ainstagram.com & https://www.google.com/search?q=hitler+speech+site%3Afacebook.com#ip=1.
Google and Verizon Joint Submission on the Open Internet, FCC GN Docket No. 09–191, FCC WC Docket No. 07–52 (January 4, 2010), https://docs.fcc.gov/public/attachments/DOC-317413A1.pdf.
Governor's Office, State of Rhode Island, Executive Order 18–02 (2018), https://governor.ri.gov/executive-orders/executive-order-18-02.
Nico Grant, Parler returns to Google Play Store, *The New York Times* (September 2, 2022), https://www.nytimes.com/2022/09/02/technology/parler-google-play.html.
Green v. Miss US of America, LLC, 533 F. Supp. 3d 978 (D. Or. 2021).
Greenberg v. Haggerty, 491 F. Supp. 3d 12 (E.D. Pa. 2020).
Griffith v. United States, 334 U.S. 100 (1948).
H. 381, 117th Cong. (2021), https://www.congress.gov/bill/117th-congress/house-bill/3816/text?r=43&s=1 (last visited August 2, 2022).
H.R. Rep. No. 109–541 (2006).
H.R. Rep. No. 110–95 (2008).
Hall v. Meta, Inc., Civil No. 3: 22-cv-03063-TLB, 2022 WL 18109625 (W.D. Ark. December 14, 2022).
The Handling of Public Issues Under the Fairness Doctrine, 48 F.C.C. 2d 1 (1974).
Richard Hasen, *Cheap Speech: How Disinformation Poisons Our Politics – And How to Cure It* (Yale University Press, 2022).
John Hendel, Twitter CEO: Iran leader's "saber rattling" doesn't violate our policies, *Politico* (October 28, 2020), https://www.politico.com/news/2020/10/28/twitter-ceo-iran-tweets-ok-433259.
Hepp v. Facebook, 14 F.4th 204 (3d Cir. 2021).
HiQ Labs, Inc. v. LinkedIn Corp., 273 F. Supp. 3d 1099 (N.D. Cal. 2017), *aff'd and remanded on other grounds*, 938 F.3d 985 (9th Cir. 2019), *vacated and remanded on other grounds*, 141 S. Ct. 2752 (2021), *reaffirmed on remand*, 31 F.4th 1180 (9th Cir. 2022).
HiQ Labs, Inc. v. LinkedIn Corp., 485 F. Supp. 3d 1137 (N.D. Cal. 2020).
Hosanna-Tabor Evangelical v. EEOC, 565 U.S. 171 (2012).
Huber v. Biden, No. 21-cv-06580-EMC, 2022 WL 927248 (N.D. Cal. March 18, 2022).
Sam Husseini, When government and Big Tech collude against the First Amendment: An interview with Nadine Strossen, *Counterpunch* (July 30, 2021), https://www.counterpunch.org/2021/07/30/when-government-and-big-tech-collude-against-the-first-amendment-an-interview-with-nadine-strossen.
Iancu v. Brunetti, 139 S. Ct. 2294 (2019).
Image Technical v. Eastman Kodak, 125 F.3d 1195 (9th Cir. 1997).
Impeachment Related Publications | GovInfo (2020), https://www.govinfo.gov/collection/impeachment-related-publications (last visited August 2, 2022).
Informed Consent Action Network v. YouTube LLC, 582 F. Supp. 3d 712 (N.D. Cal. 2022).
In re Apple & AT & TM Antitrust Litigation, 596 F. Supp. 2d 1288 (N.D. Cal. 2008).
In re Apple iPod iTunes Antitrust Litig., 796 F. Supp. 2d 1137 (N.D. Cal. 2011).
In re Beltone Electronics Corp., 100 F.T.C. 68 (1982).
In re Coca-Cola Co., 117 F.T.C. 795 (1994).
In re Coleco Industries, 111 F.T.C. 651 (1989).
In re Medical X-Ray Film Antitrust Litigation, 946 F.Supp. 209 (E.D.N.Y.1996).
In re Nasdaq Market-Makers Antitrust Litigation, 894 F.Supp. 703 (S.D.N.Y. 1995).

In the Matter of Restoring Internet Freedom, FCC WC Docket No. 17–108 (FCC report and order Jan. 4, 2018), *further proceedings at* Docket No. 17–108 (FCC report on remand October 27, 2020).

In the Matters of Formal Complaint of Free Press and Public Knowledge against Comcast Corporation for Secretly Degrading Peer-to-Peer Applications, 23 *FCC Rcd. 13028* (2008).

In re Xerox Corp., 86 F.T.C. 364 (1975).

Inform Inc. v. Google LLC, No. 21–13289, slip op. § III.B., 2022 WL 3703958 (11th Cir. Aug. 26, 2022).

Inquiry Concerning High-Speed Access to the Internet Over Cable and Other Facilities, 17 *FCC Rcd.* 4798 (2002).

Pub. L. 104–104, § 706(c)(1), 110 Stat. 56, 153 (1996).

Intellective, Inc. v. Massachusetts Mutual Life Insurance Co., 190 F. Supp. 2d 600 (S.D.N.Y. 2002).

International Boxing Club of N.Y., Inc. v. United States, 358 U.S. 242 (1959).

International Covenant on Civil and Political Rights, 99 U.N.T.S. 171, entered into force 23 March 1976.

Internet Archive, Experience DWeb camp, *YouTube* (May 2023), https://www.youtube.com/watch?v=zx7Dduv0Hd4.

Internet Freedom Preservation Act of 2008: Hearing on H.R. 5353 Before the U.S. House Committee on Energy and Commerce, Subcommittee on Telecomms. and the Internet, 110th Cong. (2008) (statement of Ben Scott, Policy Director, Free Press).

James v. Meow Media, Inc., 90 F. Supp. 2d 798 (W.D. Ky. 2000), *aff'd*, 300 F.3d 683 (6th Cir. 2003).

Joseph v. Scalione, No. 84113459 (Fla. Circuit Civil Ct., 11th Cir. 2019).

JTC Petroleum Co. v. Piasa Motor Fuels, 190 F.3d 775 (7th Cir. 1999).

Prerna Juneja, Md Momen Bhuiyan, and Tanushree Mitra, Assessing enactment of content regulation policies: A post hoc crowd-sourced audit of election misinformation on YouTube, in *Proceedings of the 2023 CHI Conference on Human Factors in Computing Systems* (2023), pp. 1–22.

Brewster Kahle, Locking the web open, presentation to the Ford Foundation netgain gathering (February 11, 2015), https://blog.archive.org/2015/02/11/locking-the-web-open-a-call-for-a-distributed-web/.

Kelley v. Chicago Park Dist., 635 F.3d 290 (7th Cir. 2011).

Daphne Keller, Lawful but awful? Control over legal speech by platforms, governments, and internet users, *University of Chicago Law Review Online* (June 28, 2022), https://lawreviewblog.uchicago.edu/2022/06/28/keller-control-over-speech/.

Daphne Keller, Posting to X, September 17, 2022, https://twitter.com/daphnehk/status/1570952595623268353.

Kennedy v. Bremerton School Dist., 597 U.S. ___, 142 S. Ct. 2407 (2022).

Dara Kerr, FTC Chair Lina Khan's lawsuit isn't about breaking up Amazon, for now, *NPR* (September 28, 2023), https://www.npr.org/2023/09/28/1202205683/amazon-lina-khan-lawsuit-monopoly-prices-sellers-shoppers.

Lina M. Khan, 'Amazon's antitrust paradox,' 126 *Yale Law Journal* 710 (2016).

Lina M. Khan, 'The Separation of Platforms and Commerce,' 119 *Columbia Law Review* 973 (2019).

Lina M. Khan, 'Section 5 in action: Reinvigorating the FTC Act and the rule of law,' 11 *Journal of Antitrust Enforcement* 149 (2023).

Brent Kendall, Justice Department to open broad, new antitrust review of Big Tech companies, *The Wall Street Journal* (July 23, 2019), www.wsj.com/articles/justice-department-to-open-broad-new-antitrust-review-of-big-tech-companies-11563914235.

Thomas G. Krattenmaker and Steven C. Salop, 'Anticompetitive exclusion: Raising rivals' costs to achieve power over price,' 96 *Yale Law Journal* 209 (1986).

Nihal Krishan, Major anti-big tech "self-preferencing" bill headed to senate floor, *The Washington Examiner* (January 20, 2022), https://www.washingtonexaminer.com/policy/technology/major-anti-big-tech-self-preferencing-bill-headed-to-senate-floor#google_vignette.
Katherine Landergan, Murphy order requires New Jersey to establish net neutrality, *Politico* (February 5, 2018), https://www.politico.com/states/new-jersey/story/2018/02/05/murphy-order-requires-new-jersey-to-establish-net-neutrality-protections-236837.
Carlo Lavizzari and Lenz Caemmerer, Moral Rights in the 21st Century – A Perspective from the Standpoint of Publishers or Literary Works, Contribution to ALAI Congress Brussels, Sep 18–19, 2014, http://alai2014.org/IMG/pdf/d2_-_s3_-_1520_-_lavrizzari.pdf.
Axelle Lemaire, 'Which digital strategy for France and Europe in an age of disruption?,' London School of Economics (2015), https://web.archive.org/web/20180309173049/www.lse.ac.uk/newsAndMedia/videoAndAudio/channels/publicLecturesAndEvents/player.aspx?id=2998.
LePage's Inc. v. 3M, 324 F.3d 141 (3d Cir. 2003).
Lawrence Lessig and Ben Scott, Public must fight to maintain net neutrality, *San Francisco Chronicle* (April 17, 2008), https://www.sfgate.com/opinion/article/Public-must-fight-to-maintain-net-neutrality-3219226.php.
George Lipsitz. 'The Hip Hop Hearings,' in *Generations of Youth: Youth Cultures and History in Twentieth-Century America*, edited by Joe Alan Austin and Michael Nevin Willard (New York University Press, 1998), pp. 395–415.
Natasha Lomos, Europe names 19 platforms that must report algorithmic risks under DSA, *TechCrunch* (April 25, 2023), https://techcrunch.com/2023/04/25/europe-names-19-platforms-that-must-report-algorithmic-risks-under-dsa/.
Lorain Journal Co. v. United States, 342 U.S. 143 (1951).
Loretto v. Teleprompter Manhattan CATV Corp., 458 U.S. 419 (1982).
Lugar v. Edmondson Oil Co., 457 U.S. 922 (1982).
Kim Lyons, Prosecutors are investigating Amazon's treatment of third-party sellers, *TheVerge.com* (August 3, 2020), https://www.theverge.com/2020/8/3/21352990/new-york-california-ftc-amazon-investigation-marketplace.
Manhattan Community Access Corp. v. Halleck, 587 U.S. ___, 139 S. Ct. 1921 (2019).
Masters v. Wilhelmina Modeling Agency, No. 02 Civ. 4911, 2004 WL 594396 (S.D.N.Y. Mar. 23, 2004).
Mathis v. Pacific Gas and Elec. Co., 75 F.3d 498 (9th Cir. 1996).
McKell v. Washington Mutual, Inc., 142 Cal. App. 4th 1457 (Cal. Ct. App. 2d Dist. 2006)).
John D. McKinnon, FTC aims new task force at Big Tech, *The Wall Street Journal* (February 26, 2019), https://www.wsj.com/articles/ftc-aims-new-task-force-at-big-tech-11551209556?mod=article_inline.
Memorandum of Points and Authorities in Support of the Alliance for Competition in Telecommunications for Amicus Curiae and Intervenor Status, United States v. Verizon, No. 1:05CV02103 (D.D.C. brief filed May 4, 2006).
Meyer v. Nebraska, 262 U.S. 390 (1923).
Miami Herald Publishing Co. v. Tornillo, 418 U.S. 241 (1974).
Linah Mohammad, Patrick Jarenwattananon, and Ari Shapiro, FTC Chair Lina Khan breaks down the case against Amazon, *WLRN* (September 28, 2023), https://www.npr.org/2023/09/27/1202128274/ftc-chair-lina-khan-breaks-down-the-lawsuit-against-amazon.
Movie 1 & 2 v. United Artists Communications, Inc., 909 F.2d 1245 (9th Cir. 1990).
Mozilla Corp. v. FCC, 940 F.3d 1 (D.C. Cir. 2019).
Multistate Legal Studies, Inc. v. Harcourt Brace Jovanovich Legal and Professional Publications, Inc., 63 F.3d 1540 (10th Cir. 1995).
Erika Morphy, House Committee shoots down net neutrality clause, *E-Commerce Times* (April 27, 2006), https://www.ecommercetimes.com/story/50219.html?wlc=1253664286.

NAACP v. Button, 371 U.S. 415 (1963).
National Association of Pharmaceutical Mfrs. v. Ayerst Laboratories, 850 F.2d 904 (2d Cir. 1988).
National Cable & Telecommunications Association v. Brand X Internet Services, 545 U.S. 967 (2005).
NCAA v. Alston, 594 U.S. ___, 141 S. Ct. 2141 (2021).
NCAA v. Oklahoma, 468 U.S. 85 (1984).
National Numismatic Certification, LLC v. eBay, Inc., No. 6:08-cv-42-Orl-19GJK, 2008 WL 2704404 (M.D. Fla. July 8, 2008).
National Rifle Association of America v. Cuomo, 350 F. Supp. 3d 94 (N.D.N.Y. 2018).
National Rifle Association v. Vullo, 49 F.4th 700 (2d Cir. 2022).
National Society of Professional Engineers v. United States, 435 U.S. 679 (1978).
NCSL, Net Neutrality 2022 Legislation, www.ncsl.org/technology-and-communication/net-neutrality-2022-legislation.
NCTA Board Members Elected; Executive Committee Named, April 11, 2005, http://web.archive.org/web/20060322001325/www.ncta.com/press/press.cfm?PRid=595&showArticles=ok.
Net Neutrality Responses by State, *Ballotpedia* (2019), https://ballotpedia.org/Net_neutrality_responses_by_state.
Net Neutrality: Hearing Before the S. Comm. on Commerce, Sci., & Transp., 109th Cong. 7–9 (2006) (statement of Vinton G. Cerf, Vice President and Chief Internet Evangelist, Google, Inc.), https://web.archive.org/web/20090227173250/http://frwebgate.access.gpo.gov/cgi-bin/getdoc.cgi?dbname=109_senate_hearings&docid=f:30115.pdf.
NetChoice, LLC v. Moody, 34 F.4th 1196 (11th Cir. 2022).
NetChoice, LLC v. Moody, 546 F. Supp. 3d 1082 (N.D. Fla. 2021), *aff'd*, 34 F.4th 1196 (11th Cir. 2022), *cert. denied*, No. 22–393 (U.S. October 2, 2023).
NetChoice, LLC v. Paxton, 49 F.4th 439 (5th Cir. 2022), *cert. granted*, No. 22–555 (U.S. September 29, 2023).
NetChoice, LLC v. Paxton, No. 23–30445, 2023 U.S. Dist. LEXIS 23965 (5th Cir. September 8, 2023), *partially withdrawn on petition for rehearing* (5th Cir. September 26, 2023).
New York v. Facebook, 549 F. Supp. 3d 6 (D.D.C. 2021), *aff'd sub. nom.* New York v. Meta Platforms, Inc., No. 21–7078, – F.4th –, 2023 WL 3102921 (D.C. Cir. April 27, 2023).
New York State Attorney General, Attorney General James Releases Statement on Settlement in Principle with Google (September 6, 2023), https://ag.ny.gov/press-release/2023/attorney-general-james-releases-statement-settlement-principle-google.
Novell, Inc. v. Microsoft Corp., 731 F.3d 1064 (10th Cir. 2013).
Cozen O'Connor, Google reaches settlement with AGs from 50 states, D.C., and PR on Google Play Store antitrust allegations, *JD Supra* (September 8, 2023), www.jdsupra.com/legalnews/google-reaches-settlement-with-ags-from-6180878/.
Jack O'Keefe, Conway has a secret weapon on "house of cards," *Bustle* (March 4, 2016), www.bustle.com/articles/146074-what-is-pollyhop-on-house-of-cards-the-search-engine-poses-a-very-real-threat.
Elijah O'Kelley, 'State constitutions as a check on the New Governors: Using state Free Speech clauses to protect social media users from arbitrary political censorship by social media platforms,' 68 *Emory Law Journal* 111 (2019).
Otter Tail Power Co. v. United States, 410 U.S. 366 (1973).
Office of Public Affairs, U.S. Department of Justice, Justice Department sues Google for monopolizing digital advertising technologies (January 23, 2023), www.justice.gov/opa/pr/justice-department-sues-google-monopolizing-digital-advertising-technologies.
Official Airline Guides, Inc. v. FTC, 630 F.2d 920 (2d Cir. 1980).
Maureen Ohlhausen, U.S. – E.U. convergence: Can we bridge the Atlantic? Remarks at the 2016 Georgetown Global Antitrust Symposium Dinner, The Metropolitan Club (2016), https://www.ftc.gov.

Oltz v. St. Peter's Community Hosp., 861 F.2d 1440 (9th Cir. 1988).
Open App Markets Act, S. 2710, 117th Cong. (2022).
Open Internet Coalition, OIC supports FCC notice of inquiry and third way approach, *Internet Archive* (June 16, 2010), https://web.archive.org/web/20110105132045/www.openinternetcoalition.com/index.cfm?objectid=7587D410-89EB-11DF-A6BC000C296BA163.
Open Internet Coalition, Who we are, *Internet Archive* (2010), https://web.archive.org/web/20110105131040/www.openinternetcoalition.com/index.cfm?objectid=6C43DDC0-5C6A-11DF-9E27000C296BA163 (last visited October 4, 2023).
Order Modifying Judgment, United States v. American Society of Composers, Authors & Publishers, No. 41-cv-1395, slip op. (S.D.N.Y. November 14, 1997).
Organization on Security and Cooperation in Europe, Copenhagen Document (1990).
Organization on Security and Cooperation in Europe, International Election Observation Mission, Türkiye, General Elections, 14 May 2023, www.osce.org/files/f/documents/6/2/543543.pdf.
Ohio v. American Express Co., 138 S. Ct. 2274 (2018).
Osama bin Laden tells the reasons of declaring jihad [etc.], *Facebook* (2022), https://www.facebook.com.
Oversight Board upholds Facebook's decision to suspend Donald Trump's accounts, *Meta* (May 2021), https://about.fb.com/news/2021/05/facebook-oversight-board-decision-trump/.
Pacific Gas & Electric Co. v. Public Utilities Commission of California, 475 U.S. 1 (1986).
Pan American World Airways v. United States, 371 US 296 (1963).
Frank Pasquale, 'Platform neutrality: Enhancing freedom of expression in spheres of private power,' 17 *Theoretical Inquiries in Law* 487 (2016).
Pecover v. Electronic Arts Inc., 633 F. Supp. 2d 976 (N.D. Cal. 2009).
Perfect 10, Inc. v. CCBill LLC, 488 F.3d 1102 (9th Cir. 2007).
Guy Pessach, 'Deconstructing disintermediation: A skeptical copyright perspective,' 31 *Cardozo Arts & Entertainment Law Journal* 833 (2013).
Perot v. FEC, 97 F.3d 553 (D.C. Cir. 1996).
Sundar Pichai, Browsers powered by user choice, *Google Public Policy Blog* (February 24, 2009, https://publicpolicy.googleblog.com/2009/02/browsers-powered-by-user-choice.html.
Plaintiffs' Complaint, FTC v. Amazon, No. 2:23-cv-01495 (W.D. Wash. Complaint filed September 26, 2023).
Plaintiffs' Complaint, FTC v. Facebook, Inc., No. 20–3590 (D.D.C. Complaint filed December 9, 2020).
Plaintiffs' Complaint, In the Matter of Commission on Presidential Debates, FEC Docket MUR # 6869 (FEC complaint filed September 10, 2014), https://www.shapiroarato.com/wp-content/uploads/2015/03/Complaint-against-the-CPD-9.10.14.pdf.
Plaintiff's Complaint, NetChoice, LLC v. Moody, No. 4:21cv220-RH (N.D. Fla. complaint filed May 27, 2021) (ECF No. 1), https://netchoice.org/wp-content/uploads/2021/05/NetChoice-CCIA-Complaint-for-Declaratory-and-Injunctive-Relief-5.27.21.pdf.
Plaintiff's Memorandum in Support of the Application to Modify the Consent Judgment, United States v. ASCAP, No. 42–245 (S.D.N.Y. memorandum filed July 29, 1997).
Press Release, National Cable Telecomms. Association, Comcast's Brian Roberts Elected Chairman of NCTA Board (April 11, 2005), https://www.ncta.com/media/media-room/comcasts-brian-roberts-elected-chairman-of-ncta-board.
Mishaal Rahman, Google clarifies in-app billing requirements, says using third-party app stores will be easier in Android 12, *XDA* (October 5, 2020), https://www.xda-developers.com/google-play-store-in-app-billing-clarity-android-12-third-party-app-stores/.
Prager University v. Google LLC, No. 19CV340667, 2019 Cal. Super. LEXIS 2034 (Cal. Super. Ct. November 19, 2019), *aff'd*, No. H047714, 2022 WL 17414495 (Cal. Ct. App. 6th Dist. December 5, 2022).

Press Release, General Court of the European Union, General Court largely dismisses Google's action against the decision of the Commission finding that Google abused its dominant position by favouring its own comparison shopping service over competing comparison shopping services [Google and Alphabet v. Commission (Google Shopping)] (November 10, 2021), https://content.mlex.com/Attachments/2021-11-10_VU85MP-244SUWSF43/CP210197EN.pdf.

Public Order Act (1936), § 5.

Public Order Act (1986), § 17.

Public Utility Commission of Texas, 13 FCC Rcd. 3460 (1997).

PruneYard Shopping Center v. Robins, 447 U.S. 74 (1980).

Rabat Plan of Action (2013), UN Special Adviser on the Prevention of Genocide, https://www.un.org/en/preventgenocide/adviser/pdf/Rabat_draft_outcome.pdf.

Race Relations Act (1965), https://www.legislation.gov.uk/ukpga/1965/73/contents/enacted.

Race Relations Act (1976), https://www.legislation.gov.uk/uksi/2003/1626/contents/made.

Race Relations (Amendment) Act (2000), https://www.legislation.gov.uk/ukpga/2000/34/contents.

Bernard A. Ramundo, "Counterrevolutionary crimes" under the laws of the Soviet Union, A.M. Thesis, City College of New York (1957).

Reilly v. Apple Inc., No. 21-cv-04601-EMC, Docket No. 41 at 13 n.3 (N.D. Cal. January 7, 2022).

Rumble, LLC v. Google, LLC, No. 21-cv-00229-HSG, 2022 WL 3018062 (N.D. Cal. July 29, 2022).

Red Lion Broadcasting Co. v. FCC, 395 U.S. 367 (1969).

Reader's Digest Association v. FEC, 509 F. Supp. 1210 (S.D.N.Y. 1981).

Ready for Ron v. FEC, No. 22–3282 (RDM), slip op. (D.D.C. May 17, 2023).

Regulation on a Single Market for Digital Services, *Official Journal L* 277 (October 27 2022), pp. 1–102.

Reno v. American Civil Liberties Union, 521 U.S. 844 (1996).

Republican National Committee, RNC sends letter to FEC on Twitter censorship, *GOP.com* (December 20, 2022), https://gop.com/press-release/rnc-sends-letter-to-fec-on-twitter-censorship.

Matt Reynolds, The strange story of section 230, the obscure law that created our flawed, broken internet, *Wired UK* (March 24, 2019), https://web.archive.org/web/20210105000234/www.wired.co.uk/article/section-230-communications-decency-act.

Rice v. Paladin Enterprises, Inc., 128 F.3d 233 (4th Cir. 1997), *cert. denied*, 523 U.S. 1074 (1998).

Roberts v. Elaine Powers Figure Salons, Inc., 708 F.2d 1476 (9th Cir. 1983).

Roberts v. United States Jaycees, 468 U.S. 609 (1984).

Kevin Roose, YouTube cracks down on QAnon conspiracy theory, citing offline violence, *The New York Times* (October 15, 2020), https://www.nytimes.com/2020/10/15/technology/youtube-bans-qanon-violence.html.

Michael Rubin, Why does Big Tech censor conservatives and not terrorists, *American Enterprise Institute* (March 3, 2021), https://tinyurl.com/wx9wm968.

Rumble, Rumble doesn't allow tips in app due to App/Play Store fees (~30%), *X* (December 29, 2022), https://twitter.com/rumblevideo/status/1608510784296087552.

Rumsfeld v. FAIR, 547 U.S. 47 (2006).

Rutenburg v. Twitter, Inc., No. 21–16074, slip op. (9th Cir. May 18, 2022).

S.B. 7072, 2021 Leg. (Fla. 2021).

Sanders v. Acclaim Entertainment, Inc., 188 F. Supp. 1264 (D. Colo. 2002).

Brian Slodysko, How Trump's Ukraine call could violate campaign finance laws, *Associated Press* (September 25, 2019), https://apnews.com/article/560b20b139d943969e17c82eda77ca8d.

Raymond Sarraute, 'Current theory on the moral right of authors and artists under French law,' 16 *American Journal of Comparative Law* 465 (1968).

Satellite Broad. & Communs. Ass'n v. Oman, 17 F.3d 344 (11th Cir. 1994).
Sayre v. Google, Inc. No. No. C 19–02247 WHA, slip op. (N.D. Cal. November 14, 2019).
SC Innovations, Inc. v. Uber Technologies, Inc., No. 18-cv-07440-JCS, slip op. (N.D. Cal. May 1, 2020).
Thibault Schrepel, 'The complex relationship between Web2 giants and Web3 projects,' 50 *Computer & Security Law Review* (2023), https://www.sciencedirect.com/science/article/pii/S0267364923000559.
Danielle Seat, New bill could criminalize recent antisemitic propaganda, WPTV News Channel 5 West Palm (June 26, 2023), https://www.wptv.com/news/state/new-bill-could-criminalize-recentantisemitic-propaganda.
Settlement Agreement, Radio Music License Committee, Inc. v. SESAC Inc., et al., No. 12-cv-05807 (E.D. Pa. filed September 2017), http://dehayf5mhw1h7.cloudfront.net/wp-content/uploads/sites/893/2017/09/22194517/Final-SESAC-RMLC-Settlement-Agreement.pdf.
Silver v. New York Stock Exchange, 373 U.S. 341 (1963).
Skinner v. Railway Labor Executives' Assn., 489 U.S. 602 (1989).
Social Media Content Moderation, C-Span (2020), https://www.c-span.org/video/?476686-1/social-media-content-moderation.
Spencer Soper and Ben Brody, Amazon probed by U.S. antitrust officials over marketplace, *Washington Post* (September 17, 2019), https://www.washingtonpost.com/business/on-small-business/amazon-probed-by-us-antitrustofficials-over-marketplace/2019/09/11/c5cfcb4c-d474–11e9–8924–1db7dac797fb_story.html.
Monica Schreiber, Stanford Cyber Policy Center Panel dissects four SCOTUS cases with major implications for internet platforms (February 22, 2023), https://law.stanford.edu/stanford-lawyer/articles/stanford-cyber-policy-center-panel-dissects-four-scotus-cases-with-major-implications-for-internet-platforms/.
Schwartz-Torrance Investment Corp. v. Bakery & Confectionery Workers' Union, 61 Cal.2d 766, 394 P. 2d 921 (Cal. 1964).
Sears, Roebuck & Co. v. San Diego County Dist. Council, 25 Cal. 3d 317, 599 P. 2d 676 (Cal. 1979).
Arthur Sidney, House Antitrust Nondiscrimination Bill may require covered platforms to host discrimination, *Project Dis-co* (July 27, 2021), https://tinyurl.com/sidneydisco.
Simon-Whelan v. The Andy Warhol Foundation for the Visual Arts, Inc., 2009–1 Trade Cases ¶ 76,657, 2009 WL 1457177 (S.D.N.Y. 2009).
Ilya Somin, Why the Florida and Texas social media laws violate the takings clause, *The Volokh Conspiracy* (September 17, 2022), https://reason.com/volokh/2022/09/17/why-the-florida-and-texas-social-media-laws-violate-the-takings-clause/.
Song fi Inc. v. Google, Inc., 108 F. Supp. 3d 876 (N.D. Cal. 2015).
Spence v. Washington, 418 U.S. 405 (1974).
Standard Oil Co. v. United States, 221 U.S. 1 (1911).
State of Hawaii Office of Enterprise Technology Services, Governor's News Release: Governor Ige Signs Executive Order to Protect Net Neutrality in Hawaii (February 5, 2018), https://ets.hawaii.gov/governors-news-release-governor-ige-signs-executive-order-to-protect-net-neutrality-in-hawaii/.
Marshall Steinbaum and Maurice Stucke, 'The effective competition standard: A new standard for antitrust,' 86 *University of Chicago Law Review* 595 (2019).
Nadine Strossen, *Hate: Why We Should Resist It with Free Speech, Not Censorship* (Oxford University Press, 2018).
Maurice E. Stucke, 'When a monopolist deceives,' 76 *Antitrust Law Journal* 823 (2010).
Tech CEOs descend on Congress to block Antitrust Bill, *Politico* (June 17, 2022), https://login.politicopro.com/?redirect=https%3A%2F%2Fsubscriber.politicopro.com%2Fnewsletter%2F2022%2F06%2Ftech-ceos-descend-on-congress-to-block-antitrust-bill-00040430.

Mai Ishikawa Sutton, Behind the scenes of the decentralized web principles, *Internet Archive* (February 18, 2021), https://blog.archive.org/2021/02/18/behind-the-scenes-of-the-decentralized-web-principles/.

Mai Ishikawa Sutton, A new portal for the decentralized web and its guiding principles, *Internet Archive* (March 22, 2021), https://blog.archive.org.2021/03/22/a-new-portal-for-the-decentralized-web-and-its-guiding-principles.

DWeb Principles (2023), https://getdweb.net/principles/.

Tele Atlas N.V. v. NAVTEQ Corp., 2008 WL 4911230 (N.D. Cal. November 13, 2008).

Telecommunications bill signing, *C-SPAN.org* (February 8, 1996), www.c-span.org/video/?69814-1/telecommunications-bill-signing.

Texas v. Johnson, 491 U.S. 397 (1989).

The White House, Office of the Press Secretary, Statement by the President (June 12, 1996), https://clintonwhitehouse6.archives.gov/1996/06/1996-06-12-president-on-communications-decency-act- decision.html.

Theatre Enterprises, Inc. v. Paramount Film Distribution Corp., 346 U.S. 537 (1954).

Theatres Act (1968) (U.K.), § 5, https://www.google.com/books/edition/The_Public_General_Acts_and_the_Church_A/JnYaAQAAMAAJ.

Time Warner Telecommunications, Inc. v. FCC, 507 F.3d 205 (2d Cir. 2007).

Timken Roller Bearing Co. v. United States, 341 U.S. 593 (1951).

Hannibal Travis, 'Neutralizing the open Internet,' in *Cyberspace Law: Censorship and Regulation of the Internet*, edited by Hannibal Travis (Routledge, 2013), p. 209.

Hannibal Travis, 'Of blogs, ebooks, and broadband: Access to digital media as a First Amendment right,' 35 *Hofstra Law Review* 1519 (2006).

Hannibal Travis, 'The FCC's new theory of the First Amendment,' 51 *Santa Clara Law Review* 417 (2011).

Hannibal Travis, 'The freedom of influencing,' 77 *Miami Law Review* 388 (2023).

Hannibal Travis, 'WIPO and the American Constitution: Thoughts on a new treaty relating to actors and musicians,' 16 *Vanderbilt Journal of Entertainment and Technology Law* 45 (2013).

Pauline Trouillard, 'Social media platforms are not speakers. Why are Facebook and Twitter devoid of First Amendment rights?,' 19 *Ohio State Technology Law Journal* 257 (2022).

Tucker v. Apple Computer, Inc., 493 F. Supp. 2d 1090 (N.D. Cal. 2006).

Twitter, Help Center, April 2022, https://web.archive.org/web/20220415192155/https://help.twitter.com/en/rules-and-policies/hateful-conduct-policy.

U.N. Secretary-General, Say #NoToHate (2023), www.un.org/en/hate-speech.

U.N. Special Rapporteur on the promotion and protection of freedom of opinion and expression, Promotion and protection of the right to freedom of opinion and expression, UN Doc. No. A/73/348 (August 29, 2018).

U.N. Special Rapporteur on the promotion and protection of freedom of opinion and expression, Promotion and protection of the right to freedom of opinion and expression, UN Doc. No. A/74/486 (October 9, 2019).

U.N. Special Rapporteur on the Promotion and Protection of Freedom of Opinion and Expression, Statement at the 47th Session of the Human Rights Council (July 2021), https://www.ohchr.org/en/press-briefing-notes/2021/07/statement-irene-khan-special-rapporteur-promotion-and-protection.

U.N. Special Rapporteur on the promotion and protection of freedom of opinion and expression, Disinformation and freedom of opinion and expression, Report of the Special Rapporteur on the promotion and protection of the right to freedom of opinion and expression, Irene Khan, UN Doc. No. A/HRC/47/25 (April 13, 2021), https://www.undocs.org/Home/Mobile?FinalSymbol=A%2FHRC%2F47%2F25&Language=E&DeviceType=Desktop&LangRequested=False.

U.S. Const., art. I, § 8, cl. 8.

U.S. Copyright Office, Waiver of Moral Rights in Visual Artworks: Executive Summary (1996), https://www.copyright.gov/reports/exsum.html.

U.S. Copyright Office, Annual Report of the Register of Copyrights (1995), https://www.copyright.gov/reports/annual/archive/ar-1995.pdf.

U.S. House of Representatives, Committee on the Judiciary, Subcommittee on Antitrust, Commercial and Administrative Law, Investigation of Competition in Digital Markets: Majority Staff Report and Recommendations (2020), https://bit.ly/32JPE1r.

U.S. House of Representatives, Energy and Commerce Committee Republican Staff, Big Tech Accountability Platform (April 15, 2021), https://republicans-energycommerce.house.gov/wp-content/uploads/2021/04/2021.04.15-Big-Tech-Memo-Staff-Legislative-Concepts.pdf (last visited Aug. 2, 2023).

U.S. Telephone Co. v. Central Union Telephone Co., 171 F. 130 (C.D. N.D. Ohio W.D. 1909).

U.S. v. Landham, 251 F.3d 1072 (6th Cir. 2001).

United States Football League v. National Football League, 634 F. Supp. 1155 (S.D.N.Y. 1986).

United States of America's Unopposed Mot. for Leave to Partic. in Oral Arg., Epic Games, Inc. v. Apple, Inc., No. 21–16506 & 21–16695 (9th Cir. September 16, 2022) (ECF No. 188).

United States v. AT&T, Inc. 524 F. Supp. 1336 (D.D.C. 1981), *further proceedings at* 552 F. Supp. 131 (D.D.C. 1982), *aff'd sub nom.* Maryland v. United States, 460 U.S. 1001 (1983), *vacated sub nom.* United States v. W. Elec. Co., No. 82–5192 (HHG), 1996 WL 255904 (D.D.C. April 11, 1996).

United States v. Columbia Steel Co., 334 U.S. 495 (1948).

United States v. Dentsply Int'l, 2003 U.S. Dist. LEXIS 14139, *191 (D. Del. August 8, 2003).

United States v. Google LLC, Nos. 20-cv-3010 (APM), 20-cv-3715 (APM), slip op. (D.D.C. August 3, 2023).

United States v. Loew's, 371 U.S. 38 (1962).

United States v. Martignon, 346 F. Supp. 2d 413 (S.D.N.Y. 2004), *vacated*, 492 F.3d 140 (2d Cir. 2007).

United States v. Microsoft Corp., 253 F.3d 34 (D.C. Cir. 2001).

United States v. Microsoft Corp., 87 F. Supp. 2d 30 (D.D.C. 2000), *aff'd*, 253 F.3d 34 (D.C. Cir. 2001).

United States v. National Ass'n. of Realtors, 2006–2 Trade Cases ¶ 75,499, 2006 WL 3434263 (N.D. Ill. November 27, 2006).

United States v. Paramount Pictures, Inc., 85 F.Supp. 881 (S.D.N.Y. 1949).

United States v. Philadelphia National Bank, 374 U.S. 321 (1963).

United States v. Terminal Railroad Association, 224 U.S. 383 (1912).

US Telecom Association v. FCC, 227 F.3d 450 (D.C. Cir. 2000).

US Telecom Association v. FCC, 825 F.3d 674 (D.C. Cir. 2016).

US Telecom Association v. FCC, 855 F.3d 381, 418–433 (D.C. Cir. 2017) (Kavanaugh, J., dissenting from denial of petition for rehearing en banc).

User clip: Sydney released the Kraken, *C-SPAN.org* (November 19, 2020), https://www.c-span.org/video/?c4924423/user-clip-sydney-released-kraken.

User clip: Ted Cruz objections to Arizona electors, *C-SPAN.org* (January 6, 2021), https://www.c-span.org/video/?c4933761/user-clip-ted-cruz-objections-arizona-electors.

Sandeep Vaheesan, 'Accommodating capital and policing labor: Antitrust in the two Gilded Ages,' 78 *Maryland Law Review* 766 (2019).

Verizon Communications, Inc. v. Law Offices of Curtis V. Trinko, LLP, 540 U.S. 398 (2004).

Video Recordings Bill, Parliamentary Debates (Hansard). House of Commons (January 6, 2010). col. 183, https://web.archive.org/web/20110604192116/www.parliament.the-stationery-office.co.uk/pa/cm200910/cmhansrd/cm100106/debtext/100106-0005.htm#10010649000001.

Eugene Volokh and Donald M. Falk, 'First Amendment protection for search engine search results,' 8 *Journal of Law, Economics & Policy* 883 (2011).

Walz v. Tax Commission, 397 U.S. 664 (1970).

Ward v. Apple Inc., No. 12-cv-05404-YGR, slip op. (N.D. Cal. class certification denied Feb. 16, 2018), *aff'd*, No. 18–16016, 2019 WL 5957405 (9th Cir. November 13, 2019).

Waremart, Inc. v. Progressive Campaigns, Inc., 102 Cal. Rptr. 2d 392 (Cal. Ct. App., 3d Dist. 2000), *depublished and review granted*, 19 P. 3d 1128 (Cal. 2001), *review dismissed and cause remanded*, 45 P. 3d 1161 (Cal. 2002).

Alexandra Watt, PollyHop has a unique "HoC" connection, *Bustle* (March 22, 2016), https://www.bustle.com/articles/148363-why-is-pollyhop-so-dangerous-on-house-of-cards-frank-underwood-is-not-happy-about-the.

Jackie Wattles, Net neutrality repeal: Facebook, Amazon, Netflix and internet providers react, *CNN Money* (December 14, 2017), https://money.cnn.com/2017/12/14/technology/business/fcc-net-neutrality-reactions/index.html.

Ellen Weintraub, Chair, FEC, The law of a "thing of value," *FEC* (October 2019), https://www.fec.gov/resources/cms-content/documents/2019-10-ELW-the-law-of-a-thing-of-value.pdf.

Kevin Werbach, *The Blockchain and the New Architecture of Trust* (The MIT Press, 2018).

Aoife White and Stephanie Bodoni, The story behind Google's secret offer to settle EU's Android probe, *Bloomberg News* (July 22, 2018), http://bqprime.com/author/28716/aiofe-white.

Richard Whitt, What do we mean by "net neutrality"?, *Google Public Policy Blog* (June 16, 2007), https://publicpolicy.googleblog.com/2007/06/what-do-we-mean-by-net-neutrality.html.

Marc Wiggers and Robin Struijlaart, Commission aims to introduce traffic lights for the digital sector, *Kluwer Competition Law Blog*, http://competitionlawblog.kluwercompetitionlaw.com/2020/12/17/commission-aims-to-introduce-traffic-lights-for-the-digital-sector-detailed-regulation-for-the-digital-sector-instead-of-genuine-ex-ante-enforcement.

Elizabeth Wilkins, Director, FTC Office of Policy and Planning, Keynote remarks: Rethinking antitrust (2023), https://www.ftc.gov.

Tim Wu, Is net neutrality dead?, *Slate* (April 13, 2010), www.slate.com/id/2250700/.

Tim Wu, 'Network neutrality, broadband discrimination,' 2 *Journal on Telecommunications and High Technology Law* 141 (2003).

WUSA9, "Drill rap" playing a role in Maryland murders, prosecutors say, *YouTube* (July 3, 2023), https://www.youtube.com/watch?v=0Wo0cgNFjCw.

Christopher S. Yoo, 'Free speech and the myth of the Internet as an unintermediated experience,' 78 *George Washington Law Review* 697 (2009).

Young v. American Mini Theatres, Inc., 427 U.S. 50 (1976).

Gabriela Zanfir-Fortuna and Vasileios Rovilos, EU's Digital Services Act just became applicable: Outlining ten key areas of interplay with the GDPR, *Future of Privacy Forum* (August 31, 2023), https://fpf.org/blog/eus-digital-services-act-just-became-applicable-outlining-ten-key-areas-of-interplay-with-the-gdpr/.

Deena Zaru, Battle brews over drill rap in NYC after killings of 2 aspiring NYC rappers spark debate about a controversial rap genre, *ABC News* (February 15, 2022), https://abcnews.go.com/US/killings-aspiring-nyc-rappers-spark-debate-controversial-rap/story?id=82798514.

ZF Meritor, LLC v. Eaton Corp., 696 F.3d 254 (3d Cir. 2012).

Conclusion

Authoritarianism and Freedom in Technocracy

Authoritarian governments like the one in Turkey can harness the economic power of digital platforms to further marginalize the political opposition and ethnic minorities like the Kurds and Assyrians.[1] Removal requests to dominant platforms can replicate what media law achieves in terms of newspaper and television broadcast station ownership: the squelching of dissent.[2] The results include unfair elections, destabilization of neighboring countries, and atrocities.[3]

The monetary fines in contemporary Internet law reinforce the problem of algorithmic speech removals, account demonetizations, and flags for users' deplatforming. The CDA threatened websites and other Internet services with fines of $250,000 per incident and two years in prison, potentially per count.[4] The DMCA creates an overwhelming incentive to delete posts quickly in order to avoid millions or billions of dollars in copyright fines.[5] And parts of the DSA conscript the largest platforms as technocrats, tasked with deciding what is illegal or merely "harmful," subject to some user protections such as judicial review.[6]

Parts of the CDA, the DMCA, the DSA, and similar laws provide a constitutional patina for censorship. They mobilize private policy to implement partisan priorities. Persons affected may strive to use the First Amendment and human-rights law to resist conscription into a distorted and inauthentic knowledge environment. Their odds may not look great, but this book has explored seven paths to a free and open Internet on the messy terrain of a contested cyberspace.

Notes

1 Svea Windwehr and Jillian C. York, Turkey's new internet law is the worst version of Germany's NetzDG yet, *Electronic Frontier Foundation Deeplinks Blog* (July 30, 2020), https://www.eff.org/de/deeplinks/2020/07/turkeys-new-internet-lawworst-version-germanys-netzdg-yet; see also, Isabelle Canaan, NetzDG and the German precedent for authoritarian creep and authoritarian learning, ZBW – Leibniz-Informationszentrum Wirtschaft/Leibniz Information Centre for Economics Working Paper (August 10, 2021), p. 34–37, https://www.zbw.eu/econis-archiv/bitstream/11159/483097/1/EBP078475732_0.pdf.

2 As Windwehr and York note: "Local representatives would be tasked with responding to government requests to block or take down content." Windwehr and York, previous n. 1. They add that mainstream news outlets fall victim to the law, because "NetzDG's conferral of policing powers to private companies does seem to lead to takedowns of innocuous posts, thereby undermining the freedom of expression, although to a lesser degree

DOI: 10.4324/9781003496106-7

than originally feared." *Ibid.* (citing Mike Masnick, Germany's speech laws continue to be a raging dumpster fire of censorial stupidity, *Techdirt* (February 21, 2018), https://www.techdirt.com/2018/02/21/germanys-speech-laws-continue-to-be-raging-dumpster-fire-censorial-stupidity/). As Canaan observes, Turkey's leaders obtained control of over 90% of traditional media using laws not tailored to the Internet to seize or close more than 150 outlets, and Facebook was already blocking posts by Turkey's Kurdish minority, but Turkey's 2021 legal reforms would ensure that Facebook along with Twitter and YouTube would perpetually "bow to authoritarians to suppress political dissidents and then claim to be just 'following legal orders.'" Canaan, p. 37 (quoting Justin Elliott, Sheryl Sandberg and top Facebook execs silenced an enemy of Turkey to prevent a hit to the company's business, *Pro Publica* (February 24, 2021), https://www.propublica.org/article/sheryl-sandberg-and-top-facebook-execssilenced-an-enemy-of-turkey-to-prevent-a-hit-to-their-business). See also, Assyrian Policy Institute, API statement on the status of Assyrians in Turkey (August 4, 2019), https://www.assyrianpolicy.org/post/api-statement-on-the-status-of-assyrians-in-turkey. I wrote of this trend back in 2012, in 'YouTube from Afghanistan to Zimbabwe: Tyrannize locally, censor globally,' in *Transnational Culture In The Internet Age*, edited by Sean Pager and Adam Candeub (Edward Elgar, 2012), pp. 76–106.

3 E.g., Organization on Security and Cooperation in Europe, International Election Observation Mission, Türkiye, General Elections, (May 14, 2023), p. 12, https://www.osce.org/files/f/documents/6/2/543543.pdf (intimidation of minority parties precluded fair and free atmosphere for 2023 election); Euronews, OSCE denounce Turkish election campaign as 'unfair,' *YouTube* (2015), https://www.youtube.com/watch?v=k7zNdqB1Kt0 (2015 reelection in Turkey was unfair due to violence, intimidation, and raids on media outlets criticizing incumbent president's party); Associated Press, Turkey's opposition denounces fairness of vote under Erdogan (May 8, 2023), https://apnews.com/article/turkey-elections-opposition-43f8d2c0aba17958c8e7123cf39eeabf ("During April, Erdogan received nearly 33 hours of airtime on the main state-run TV station, according to opposition members of the broadcasting watchdog. His presidential opponent, Kemal Kilicdaroglu, received 32 minutes."). On atrocities, see Antonopoulos, previous n. 34, pp. 4–10; Saman Dawod, Turkish attacks stop displaced Iraqi Yazidis from returning home, *Al Monitor* (February 12, 2022), https://www.al-monitor.com/originals/2022/02/turkish-attacks-stop-displaced-iraqi-yazidis-returning-home; Genocide Watch, Genocide Emergency Alert: Turkey's aggression in northern Syria and Iraq (2022), https://www.genocidewatch.com; Genocide Watch, Turkey's obstruction of aid to Kurds [sic] in Turkey and Syria (March 2023), https://www.genocidewatch.com; Human Rights Watch, Northeast Syria: Turkish strikes exacerbate humanitarian crisis (December 7, 2022), https://www.hrw.org/news/2022/12/07/northeast-syria-turkish-strikes-exacerbate-humanitarian-crisis; Holly Johnston, "We live in constant fear": The exile and occupation of Afrin's Yezidis, *Rudaw* (July 27, 2020), https://www.rudaw.net/english/middleeast/syria/27072020; Alper Keten, 'Human rights violations and medicolegal approach,' in *Human Rights in Turkey: Assaults on Human Dignity*, edited by Hasan Aydin, Winston Langley (Springer, 2020), pp. 293–312; Office of the UN High Commissioner for Human Rights, Report on the impact of the state of emergency on human rights in Turkey, including an update on the South-East: January – December 2017 (2018), pp. 3–4 ("pattern" of rights violations in southeastern Turkey in 2015 and 2016 included allegations of "killings; torture; violence against women; excessive use of force; destruction of housing and cultural heritage; prevention of access to emergency medical care, safe water and livelihoods; and severe restrictions of the right to freedom of expression"); Peace Association of Turkey and Lawyers for Justice, War Crimes Committed Against the People of Syria: Report – December 2013/January 9, 2014 (2014), https://web.archive.org/web20140516192103mp_/http://pwlasowa.blogspot.com/2014/01/war-crimes-committed-against-people-of.html; Tom Stevenson, "Unprecedented destruction," *DW* (May 19, 2016), https://www.dw.com/en/unprecedented-destruction-of-kurdish-city-of-cizre/a-19265927.

4 47 U.S.C. §§ 223(a)(1)(B), 223(a)(2), 223(d)(1)-(2) (1996), *enjoined by* American Civil Liberties Union v. Reno, 929 F. Supp. 824, 883–84 (E.D. Pa. 1996), *aff'd sub nom*. Reno v. American Civil Liberties Union, 521 U.S. 844.

5 E.g., Joe Karaganis and Jennifer Urban, 'The rise of the robo notice,' 58 *Communications of the ACM* 28 (2015) (threshold of one billion DMCA requests to websites and other intermediaries passed in 2015, potentially, due in part to automation); Travis, 'WIPO and the American Constitution,' previous n. 226, p. 85 (Consumer Electronics Association estimated in 2012 that without a certain construction of the DMCA, and continued compliance by Facebook and YouTube with it, damages could be in the billions or even trillions under 17 U.S.C. § 504(c)(1)).

6 Cf., Paola Carbone and Giuseppe Rossi, 'Is bureaucracy the answer of the law to digital technologies?', 17 *Pólemos* 137 (2023) (arguing that enormous fines are used to jolt technocrats into complying with politicians' demands, recalling dystopian narratives from books or films in which authoritarians manipulate anonymous numbered persons as pieces of data enduring governance by machines more powerful and inscrutable than ever).

Bibliography

17 U.S.C. § 504(c)(1).

17 U.S.C. § 512.

47 U.S.C. §§ 223(a)(1)(B), 223(a)(2), 223(d)(1)-(2) (1996).

American Civil Liberties Union v. Reno, 929 F. Supp. 824 (E.D. Pa. 1996), *aff'd sub nom*. Reno v. American Civil Liberties Union, 521 U.S. 844 (1997).

Paul Antonopoulos, Turkey's interests in the Syrian war: From neo-ottomanism to counterinsurgency, *Global Affairs* (March 15, 2018), https://www.academia.edu/38877538/Turkeys_interests_in_the_Syrian_war_from_neo_Ottomanism_to_counterinsurgency.

Associated Press, Turkey's opposition denounces fairness of vote under Erdogan (May 8, 2023), https://apnews.com/article/turkey-elections-opposition-43f8d2c0aba17958c8e7123cf39eeabf.

Assyrian Policy Institute, API statement on the status of Assyrians in Turkey (August 4, 2019), https://www.assyrianpolicy.org/post/api-statement-on-the-status-of-assyrians-in-turkey.

Isabelle Canaan, NetzDG and the German Precedent for Authoritarian Creep and Authoritarian Learning, ZBW – Leibniz-Informationszentrum Wirtschaft/Leibniz Information Centre for Economics Working Paper (August 10, 2021), https://www.zbw.eu/econis-archiv/bitstream/11159/483097/1/EBP078475732_0.pdf.

Paola Carbone and Giuseppe Rossi, 'Is bureaucracy the answer of the law to digital technologies?,' 17 *Pólemos* 137 (2023).

Saman Dawod, Turkish attacks stop displaced Iraqi Yazidis from returning home, *Al-Monitor* (February 12, 2022), https://www.al-monitor.com/originals/2022/02/turkish-attacks-stop-displaced-iraqi-yazidis-returning-home.

Justin Elliott, Sheryl Sandberg and top facebook execs silenced an enemy of Turkey to prevent a hit to the company's business, *Pro Publica* (February 24, 2021), https://www.propublica.org/article/sheryl-sandberg-and-top-facebook-execssilenced-an-enemy-of-turkey-to-prevent-a-hit-to-their-business.

Euro news, OSCE denounce Turkish election campaign as 'unfair,' *YouTube* (2015), https://www.youtube.com/watch?v=k7zNdqB1Kt0.

Genocide Watch, Genocide Emergency Alert: Turkey's Aggression in Northern Syria and Iraq (2022), https://www.genocidewatch.com.

Genocide Watch, Turkey's obstruction of aid to Kurds [sic] in Turkey and Syria (March 2023), https://www.genocidewatch.com.

Human Rights Watch, Northeast Syria: Turkish strikes exacerbate humanitarian crisis (December 7, 2022), https://www.hrw.org/news/2022/12/07/northeast-syria-turkish-strikes-exacerbate-humanitarian-crisis.

Holly Johnston, "We live in constant fear": The exile and occupation of Afrin's Yezidis, *Rudaw* (July 27, 2020), https://www.rudaw.net/english/middleeast/syria/27072020.

Joe Karaganis and Jennifer Urban, 'The rise of the robo notice,' 58 *Communications of the ACM* 28 (2015).

Alper Keten, 'Human rights violations and medicolegal approach,' in *Human Rights in Turkey: Assaults on Human Dignity*, edited by Hasan Aydin and Winston Langley (Springer, 2020), pp. 293–312.

Mike Masnick, Germany's speech laws continue to be a raging dumpster fire of censorial stupidity, *Techdirt* (February 21, 2018), https://www.techdirt.com/2018/02/21/germanys-speech-laws-continue-to-be-raging-dumpster-fire-censorial-stupidity/.

Office of the United Nations High Commissioner for Human Rights, Report on the Impact of the State of Emergency on Human Rights in Turkey, including an update on the South-East: January – December 2017 (2018), https://www.ohchr.org/sites/default/files/Documents/Countries/TR/2018-03-19_Second_OHCHR_Turkey_Report.pdf.

Organization on Security and Cooperation in Europe, International Election Observation Mission, Türkiye, General Elections (May 14, 2023), https://www.osce.org/files/f/documents/6/2/543543.pdf.

Peace Association of Turkey and Lawyers for Justice, War Crimes Committed against the People of Syria: Report, December 2013/January 9, 2014 (2014), https://web.archive.org/web20140516192103mp_/http://pwlasowa.blogspot.com/2014/01/war-crimes-committed-against-people-of.html.

Tom Stevenson, "Unprecedented destruction," *DW* (May 19, 2016), https://www.dw.com/en/unprecedented-destruction-of-kurdish-city-of-cizre/a-19265927.

Hannibal Travis, 'WIPO and the American constitution: Thoughts on a new treaty relating to actors and musicians,' 16 *Vanderbilt Journal of Entertainment and Technology Law* 45 (2013).

Hannibal Travis, 'YouTube from Afghanistan to Zimbabwe: Tyrannize locally, censor globally,' in *Transnational Culture in the Internet Age*, edited by Sean Pager and Adam Candeub (Edward Elgar, 2012), pp. 76–106.

Svea Windwehr and Jillian C. York, Turkey's new internet law is the worst version of Germany's NetzDG yet, *Electronic Frontier Foundation Deeplinks Blog* (July 30, 2020), https://www.eff.org/de/deeplinks/2020/07/turkeys-new-internet-lawworst-version-germanys-netzdg-yet.

Index

Alphabet 3, 75, 106, 136, 160, 175, 181; Android (*see* Android operating system); DoubleClick (*see* Google); Google (*see* Google); Play Store (*see* Google); YouTube (*see* YouTube)
Amazon.com 76, 124, 159–161; District of Columbia v. Amazon.com (D.C. Super. 2022) 76, 104, 159; FTC v. Amazon.com (*see* competition law)
American Innovation and Choice Online Act, S. 2992, 117th Cong. (2022) 175, 204, 213
Android operating system 3, 74–75, 79, 105, 123–127, 158–160, 187, 189
antitrust law *see* competition law
Apple Computer 153–188, 210; App Store 153–176, 210; Epic Games, Inc. v. Apple, Inc. (*see* competition law)

Baidu.com 135, 151
Biden, Joseph 13, 33–34, 37, 56, 65, 68, 88, 92–93, 97–98, 106, 111–112, 136, 162, 166, 170–171, 176, 189, 192, 193, 202, 205, 214, 219
Bush, George W. 65, 98, 163–164

California Constitution 124–126, 172, 201, 205
California law 5, 82, 124–126, 153–154, 157–158, 164, 172, 194–195, 201; ACA Connects v. Bonta 2, 7, 164, 195; California Business and Professions Code, Section 17200 124–126, 134, 153–154, 157–158; California Consumer Privacy Act 5
civil rights law, federal (Section 1983) 161–163, 191–192
Communications Decency Act 4, 9, 15–16, 19, 26, 77–78, 104, 106, 162–163, 170–175, 193, 203, 205, 211; good-faith removals 77, 104, 162–163, 193, 203, 205; publisher status 77–78, 80, 162–163, 205, 211; Section 230 4, 9, 77–78, 104, 162–163, 170–175, 183, 193, 205, 211
competition law 4, 9, 76, 124, 136, 146, 156, 175–177; Clayton Act 185; Commission (European) v. Amazon (Buy Box) 76, 124, 136–137, 146, 156; Commission (European) v. Apple (Apple Pay) 136, 146; Commission (European) v. Apple (App Store Rules for Music Streaming) 75, 103, 136, 146; Commission (European) v. Google (Google Android) 146, 158–160, 186, 189; Commission (European) v. Google (Google Shopping) 146, 186; contract, combination in the form of trust or otherwise, or conspiracy in restraint of trade 23, 32, 121, 123, 127, 129, 133, 141, 156, 161, 180, 191, 209; Court of Justice of the European Union (*see* European Court of Justice); denial of access to essential facilities 121–122; Digital Markets Act 4, 9, 177; Digital Services Act 4, 175–177, 204, 224; Epic Games, Inc. v. Apple, Inc. 122–126, 134, 153–188, 217, 227; European Court of Justice 158; exclusionary conduct 121, 161; exclusive dealing, conditional dealing, refusals to deal 123, 141, 154–157, 161; false statements as 167, 190; Federal Trade Commission (FTC) 167, 177–179, 210; FLorida Digital Bill of Rights 5; Florida law 5, 48, 54, 79, 135, 165, 167, 170–175, 188, 194, 195, 201, 203, 218; Florida Unfair and Deceptive Trade Practices Act

134; French authorities 163, 194; FTC Act 7, 129, 167, 180–181, 185; FTC v. Amazon 76, 159–161, 176, 187; FTC v. Facebook 140, 157, 160, 176–190; FTC v. Meta Platforms 125, 189; General Court of the European Union 186; group boycotts 23, 81, 121, 141, 161, 191, 203; Italian authorities 76; New York v. Facebook 138, 211, 222; New York v. Meta Platforms 138, 160, 185, 222; self-preferencing 76, 123, 134, 145, 156, 176–177, 183–184, 204–205, 221; Sherman Act 120–121, 125, 128–129, 134–135, 141, 156–158, 180, 185, 188, 191; Treaty on the Functioning of the European Union 123–124, 158, 176–177, 186; tying 121, 134, 155, 157, 159; United States v. Apple 138; United States v. Google 74, 102, 123–124, 136, 158, 176–177, 181, 223; United States v. Microsoft 157–161, 181–182, 185–189, 199–200, 209–210
conspiracy to restrain trade *see* competition Law
copyright 16–18, 27–28, 64, 182–183; Berne Convention 182–183; Copyright in the Digital Single Market directive 5, 9–10; Digital Millennium Copyright Act (DMCA) 17, 25, 27–28; fair use in 16–18, 27–28; right of attribution 182–183; right of integrity 182–183

deplatforming 19–22, 30, 62, 72–76, 79–89, 122–124, 162–163, 170–176, 183, 229–231
Digital Markets Act 4, 9, 177
Digital Services Act 4, 175–177, 204, 224
DMCA *see* copyright

elections 6, 24, 67, 152–164, 176–181, 207, 229–231
European Court of Justice 158

Facebook, Meta Platforms 7, 202, 212, 223; Oversight Board of 202, 223
FCC *see* telecommunications Law
Federal Elections Commission (FEC) 2, 178–181; Citizens United v. FEC 2, 178–181; FEC Act 178–181
First Amendment, to the U.S. Constitution 6, 13, 19, 22, 28–30, 42–45, 50–51, 55–56, 77–79, 82–84, 91–92, 106, 122, 152, 161–163, 171, 175–176, 191–193; encouragement 83, 92, 152, 161–163, 171, 175–176, 191–193; entanglement 92, 161–163, 193; state action 83, 92, 161–163, 193
Florida law 169–175; NetChoice, LLC v. Moody 169–176; S.B. 7072 170–175
FTC Act *see* competition law

General Data Protection Regulation 5, 124–125
Google 3, 54, 181, 210, 223; Android operating system (*see* Android operating system); Play Store 3, 74; YouTube (*see* YouTube)

indecency laws 15–22, 33, 83–92, 163, 168, 175, 193, 203–204
Instagram 15–22, 33, 83–92, 181–182, 210
intelligence agencies, U.S. 20, 86–88, 93, 95
International Covenant on Civil and Political Rights 30, 46–47
iOS operating system 75, 126, 134
Iraq 6, 14–15, 65–71, 90, 98–100

Jefferson, Thomas 40–53

Kennedy Jr., Robert F. 192
Klobuchar, Amy 132, 136, 142–143, 175, 204, 213

Lessig, Lawrence 23, 32, 164
LGBTQ persons 15–22, 33, 92
Libya 15, 66, 69–71, 98
LinkedIn 7, 20–21, 75, 88, 103, 134–135, 157, 188

Madison, James 40–53, 140
Massachusetts law 109–110
metaverse 183–184, 212
Microsoft 7, 20–21, 75, 88, 103, 134–135, 157–161, 181–182, 185–189, 199–200, 209–210
monopolization *see* competition law

Nazis 20–21, 30, 46–47, 69, 164–166, 195
NetChoice, LLC 106, 109, 110, 169–176, 200, 203, 205–206
The Network Enforcement Act, Germany (NetzDG) 229–232
New York law 48, 134, 160–161, 187, 189, 190, 194, 202, 217, 221; Executive Order No. 175: Ensuring Net Neutrality Protections for New Yorkers, N.Y. Comp. Codes R. & Regs. tit. 9 § 8.175

(2018) 194, 217; Manhattan Community Access Corp. v. Halleck, 139 S. Ct. 1921 (2019) 202

Obama, Barack 17, 88, 163–164, 167
Open App Markets Act, S. 2710, 117th Cong. (2022) 124–126, 204

Parler 160, 189
Pasquale, Frank 106, 163
Pennsylvania law 77–78, 82–83, 120–121; Pittsburgh Press Co. v. Pittsburgh Comm'n on Human Relations, 413 U.S. 376 (1973) 77–78, 82–83
Presidents of the United States 13, 33–34, 37, 40–53, 56, 65, 68, 72, 88, 92–93, 97–98, 102, 106, 111–112, 123, 136, 140, 162–164, 166–167, 170–173, 176, 189, 192, 193, 202, 205–206, 214, 219
propaganda for war 21, 29–30, 46–47, 65–66, 72, 127
public accommodations laws 77–78, 82–83, 107–110, 137, 143, 201, 206; 303 Creative, LLC v. Elenis, 143 S. Ct. 2298 (2023) 107, 137, 143, 201, 206; Hurley v. Irish-American Gay, Lesbian and Bisexual Group of Boston, Inc., 515 U.S. 557 (1995) 109–110; Masterpiece Cakeshop, Ltd. v. Colorado Human Rights Commission 82–83, 107, 109–110; Pittsburgh Press Co. v. Pittsburgh Comm'n on Human Relations, 413 U.S. 376 (1973) 82–83

right of reply laws 169–172
Rosenworcel, Jessica 166
Rumble 112–113, 155–156, 160–161, 185, 189

Santa Clara Principles on Transparency and Accountability in Content Moderation 1–2, 7
Serbia 66, 68
Sherman Act *see* competition law
Suzor, Nicholas 1, 7, 9, 24, 31, 33, 39
Syria 6, 19, 65–67, 69–71, 73, 93–95, 102, 230–231

telecommunications law 26, 80, 106, 124–126, 168–172, 179–181; Federal Communications Commission (FCC) 80, 91, 152, 162–167, 168–169, 179–182; Telecommunications Act 179–181
Texas law 106, 124–126, 167, 169–170, 177, 194; NetChoice, LLC v. Paxton 106, 169–170, 200
TikTok 3–4, 21, 24, 31, 33, 71, 101, 103, 171, 173, 181
trademarks 3, 23, 123, 161, 195, 211
Trump, Donald 65, 72, 88, 102, 123, 163–164, 170–171, 172–173, 202, 206
Turkey 66–67, 94–95, 197, 207, 217, 229–232
Twitter 65–66, 71–76, 83–87, 106, 109, 111, 112, 113, 123, 160–164, 165, 170–176, 179, 181, 195

Universal Declaration of Human Rights 46–47, 152, 165, 229
U.S. House of Representatives, Committee on the Judiciary 175, 181
U.S. House of Representatives, Committee on the Judiciary, Subcommittee on Antitrust, Commercial and Administrative Law, Investigation of Competition in Digital Markets: Majority Staff Report and Recommendations (2020) 76, 102–104, 136, 138, 160–161, 177, 181, 189–190, 204–205
U.S. Senate, Judiciary Committee 65, 96, 123, 176

video games 124–126, 134, 138, 153–154, 158, 165, 184, 197

X *see* Twitter

Yemen 66, 69–70, 98
YouTube 15–21, 24, 29–30, 65–75, 92, 103–104, 109, 125, 155–156, 173, 181, 182, 189, 230
Yugoslavia 14, 66, 68